SIXTH EDITION

HARBRACE HANDBOOK
FOR
CANADIANS

SIXTH EDITION

HARBRACE HANDBOOK FOR CANADIANS

JOHN C. HODGES
WINIFRED BRYAN HORNER
Texas Christian University

SUZANNE STROBECK WEBB
Texas Woman's University

ROBERT KEITH MILLER
University of St. Thomas

ANDREW STUBBS
University of Regina

THOMSON
NELSON

THOMSON

NELSON

**Harbrace Handbook for Canadians,
Sixth Edition**

by John C. Hodges, Winifred Bryan Horner,
Suzanne Strobeck Webb, Robert Keith
Miller, and Andrew Stubbs

**Editorial Director and
Publisher:**
Evelyn Veitch

Acquisitions Editor:
Anne Williams

Marketing Manager:
Cara Yarzab

Senior Developmental Editor:
Rebecca Rea

Senior Production Editor:
Bob Kohlmeier

Production Coordinator:
Hedy Sellers

Copy-Editor:
Lisa Berland

Proofreaders:
Margaret Crammond and
Lisa Berland

Creative Director:
Angela Cluer

Indexer:
Dennis A. Mills

Cover Design:
Ken Phipps

Compositor:
Computer Composition

Printer:
Transcontinental

**National Library of Canada
Cataloguing in Publication Data**

Harbrace handbook for
Canadians / John C. Hodges ...
[et al.].—6th ed.

Includes index.
First ed. published under title:
Harbrace college handbook.
Canadian ed.
Fourth ed. published under
title: Harbrace college
handbook for Canadian writers.
ISBN 0-17-640431-7

1. English language—Grammar.
2. English language—Rhetoric.
I. Hodges, John C., 1892–1967.

PE1112.H6 2003   808'.042
C2002-905030-8

Preface

A compact yet comprehensive guide, the *Harbrace Handbook for Canadians,* Sixth Edition, offers practical, well-organized, and easily accessible advice for writers. Examples throughout the book demonstrate the principles of writing that apply both to course work and to professional tasks, and the many cross-references show how these principles inform one another. Our aim is to give thorough coverage of research procedure and of all aspects of the writing process—from sentence to paragraph to essay.

This edition is based on the fifth Canadian edition and the fourteenth American edition, by Hodges, Whitten, et al., and it adopts the user-friendly approach to writing and grammar common to both. Revisions have followed several principles:

1. Whenever possible, we explain the reasons or purposes for specific elements of grammar, style, punctuation, and mechanics. Students learn faster and write better when they understand the reasons behind the rules.
2. We have updated the examples, emphasizing contemporary Canadian writers, and included more examples of student work.
3. In sample sentences revised to illustrate the principles being taught, we have, as in the previous Canadian edition, provided handwritten corrections so that the revision is readily apparent.

4. We have extensively revised the exercises by increasing the number that encourage students to write or revise in context, by making many exercises the focus of class discussion, and by providing exercises that give students writing practice.

5. We have significantly expanded and updated our discussion of writing with computers, integrating this discussion with related material throughout the book.

ESL 6. Similarly, we have expanded our discussion of writing issues common to ESL students and speakers of dialect, and have done so in the context of larger discussions rather than group these issues in a separate chapter. This decision was made in response to the increase in the number of students enrolled in universities and colleges whose first language is not English, and for whom this information is essential to their mastering written English. Further, many students whose first language *is* English face these concerns as well, so there seemed to be no benefit in setting them apart for special attention from ESL students.

Readers will find that spelling conventions in the text follow the recommendations of standard Canadian dictionaries. Units of measurement appear in metric. A few quoted excerpts do not conform to these standards, however, as we have respected original spellings, units of measurement, regional usage, and punctuation in the source texts.

Those readers who are familiar with past editions may note some changes in structure. We have added to Chapter 28 a section on personal writing and writing about writing, and we've added to Chapter 32 a section on persuasive writing. Other changes involve content. Our updating of Canadian material draws special attention to the intercultural dimension of writing. We have also included new and freshly annotated student writing, not only to provide examples of effective writing in the context of standard academic practice but also to show non-traditional approaches to writing.

The shift in emphasis involves greater use of student writing samples and on rhetorical considerations of audience and occasion. These changes aim to show students the range of social, political, and cultural contingencies that influence the way we communicate and what we communicate. While spotlighting the need for versatility and for making adjustment to unique circumstances, we have also kept in mind the importance of clear, accessible, student-friendly explanations of key ideas and terms, supported by concise examples at the sentence and paragraph levels. We have maintained the system of cross-references so that students can look up further information about writing points. The cross-references function a set of hyperlinks, as it were, leading students deeper into the text as the need arises.

We have aimed at all times to connect process and product, giving models for standard writing practices, supported by concrete examples, along with procedures for critical thinking, revision, and research. Our goal is to support a wide spectrum of classroom approaches to writing teaching. Students should find the *Harbrace Handbook* a practical introductory guide to successful writing in the first-year classroom as well as a user-friendly resource through their postsecondary careers and, beyond, into their professional careers. We have tried to change existing chapter titles and subtitles as little as possible. And while we have made the book easier to teach and easier to consult, we have not compromised its well-established integrity. On the contrary, we have worked hard to improve it. The new chapter arrangement is based on research of instructor preferences and on our own extensive classroom experience.

A Note from the Publisher

Thank you for selecting the *Harbrace Handbook for Canadians*, Sixth Edition. We have devoted considerable time to the careful development of this book, and we appreciate your recognition of this effort and accomplishment.

The *Harbrace Handbook for Canadians*, Sixth Edition, is accompanied by a separate exercise book: *The Harbrace Workbook for Canadians*, Sixth Edition, by William Connor (ISBN: 0-17-622510-2). For more material and exercises, see also the *Harbrace Handbook for Canadians* website at *www.harbrace6e.nelson.com*.

Contents

EFFECTIVE SENTENCES

PUNCTUATION

MECHANICS

Grammar

Chapter 1

Sentence Sense

Writing a clear, precise sentence is an art, and you can master that art by knowing the different kinds of sentences and the ways they function. You can also revise your sentences more effectively if you recognize the different parts of speech and the ways they work together. Knowing how to revise will help you become a more flexible, effective writer. (For explanations of any unfamiliar terms, see the **Glossary of Terms**.)

The parts of a sentence   An English sentence divides into two parts.

SUBJECT + PREDICATE

Dionne + answered her cellphone in class.

The **movie + is old**.

These parts, the subject and the predicate, are the two essential elements of an English sentence. The **subject** is what the sentence is about and answers the question "Who?" or "What?" The **predicate** says something about the subject (see **1a**) and contains a word that expresses action or state of being. In the sentences above, *answered* expresses the action Dionne took, and *is old* expresses the state of the movie. The pattern is **SUBJECT + PREDICATE**, which is the basic order of English sentences.

1a Verbs form the predicate of sentences.

A verb functions as the predicate of a sentence or as an essential part of the predicate. You can recognize a verb by observing its form as well as its function.

Marco **walks**. [verb by itself]

Marco **walks** very fast. [verb plus modifier]

Verbs can be compound, that is, composed of more than one verb.

Marco **walks** and **arrives** on time.

A verb can consist of more than one word. The **auxiliary** is often called a *helping verb* or *verb marker*. The verbs *have* and *be* are auxiliaries and follow the pattern of **AUXILIARY + VERB**. Modals such as *can/could, may/ might,* and *shall/will* follow the same pattern and express such things as ability or possibility; *shall/will* expresses future tense. (See chapter 7 for a complete discussion of verbs.)

Jason **had painted** their house blue last year.

He **will be painting** it red in April.

He **should decide** on the colour once and for all.

Other words sometimes intervene between the auxiliary and the verb.

Rhoda **will** often **read** her newspaper.

The Internet **will** never completely **replace** books.

Verbs with prepositions When verbs are followed by a preposition (often called a **particle**), they are called

phrasal verbs. A preposition combines with a verb to mean something different from the verb standing alone. For example, the meaning of the verb *turned* is different from the meaning of the combination *turned out*.

> Martha **turned** the car **out of the way.** [prepositional phrase modifying the verb *turned*]

> Nothing **turned out** the way she expected.

Some examples of verbs with prepositions are *look up, burn down, phase out, turn off, watch out, put off, try on.* If a phrasal verb has a direct object, the verb and the preposition can often be separated. The preposition can come before or after the object.

> She **switched on** the computer.

> She **switched** the computer **on.**

If the object is a pronoun, the preposition must follow the object.

> She **switched** it **on.**

ESL   The meanings of phrasal verbs can be found in a good ESL dictionary, together with an explanation of whether or not they are separable. (See chapter 13, page 148 for ESL dictionaries.)

1b   Subjects, objects, and complements can be nouns, pronouns, or word groups serving as nouns.

(1) Subjects of verbs

Except for imperatives, which are commands, or requests, in which the subject *you* may be understood, all grammatically complete sentences contain stated subjects—nouns, pronouns, or word groups serving as nouns. In the following sentences, the subjects are in boldface and the verbs are in italics.

Priah *sings* at the club.

Does **Nelson** also *sing* at the club?

In commands or requests, the subject is often understood.

[You] *Bring* the tickets for the show tonight.

Subjects of verbs may be compound.

Priah and **Nelson** *sing* at the club. [compound subject]

To identify the grammatical subject of a sentence, first find the verb, then use it in a question beginning with *who* or *what*, as shown in the following examples:

The runner leaped the hurdle.	The book covered the subject thoroughly.
Verb: **leaped**	Verb: **covered**
WHO leaped? **The runner** (not the hurdle) **leaped.**	WHAT covered? **The book** (not the subject) **covered.**
Subject: **runner**	Subject: **book**

Subjects usually precede verbs in sentences. Common exceptions occur in questions and after the words *there* and *it,* both of which fill out a sentence without altering the meaning.

Was the *book* interesting? [verb + subject]

There *were* no *refusals.* [there + verb + subject]

It is not easy *to study* on a sunny spring day. [it + linking verb + infinitive subject]

(2) Objects of verbs

Verbs denoting action often require a **direct object** to receive or show the result of the action. Such verbs are called **transitive** verbs. (See chapter 7.) Sometimes a word that shows to whom or for whom the action occurred (**indirect object**) comes between the verb and the direct object. In the following sentence, the objects are in boldface.

> The police officer gave **her** a **speeding ticket**. [indirect object: *her;* direct object: *speeding ticket*]

Like the subjects of verbs, direct and indirect objects are generally nouns or pronouns.

To identify a direct object, find the subject and the verb and then use them in a question ending with *whom* or *what,* as shown in the following example:

> Gina silently took his hand.
>
> Subject and verb: **Gina took**
>
> Gina took WHAT? **hand**
>
> Direct object: **hand**

Direct objects in sentences like the following are directly affected by the action of the verb.

> Mr. Anderson assembled his barbecue. [The subject, *Mr. Anderson,* acts. The object, *barbecue,* receives the action.]

Knowing how to change from *active* to *passive voice* can also help you identify an object. When you make a verb passive, the object of the active verb becomes the subject of the passive verb. The original subject is either omitted or incorporated into a phrase beginning with *by.* (See also examples on pages 78 and 80 of chapter 7 and in **11d(1)**.)

> **Active**   The computer virus **destroyed** his history project. [*Project* is the direct object of *destroyed.*]

Passive　　His **history project was destroyed.** [*Project* is the subject of *was destroyed;* the original subject is omitted.]

His **history project was destroyed** by the computer virus. [The original subject is incorporated into a phrase.]

A form of *be* (such as *is, are, was*) is added when an active verb becomes passive.

Some verbs (such as *give, offer, bring, take, lend, send, buy,* and *sell*) can have both a direct object and an indirect object.

I sent Boris an e-mail. [subject + verb + direct object: **I sent e-mail.**]

I sent an e-mail TO WHOM? **Boris** [indirect object: **Boris**]

Direct and indirect objects of verbs can be compound.

The factory makes **chips** and **salsa.** [compound direct object]

We offered **Alicia** and **Jason** chips and salsa. [compound indirect object]

We offered **Alicia** and **Jason chips** and **salsa.** [compound indirect object and compound direct object]

(3) Subject and object complements

Nouns, pronouns, and adjectives are used as subject and object complements. (See 1c.) A **subject complement** refers to, identifies, or qualifies the subject and helps complete the meaning of the forms of *be* (*am, is, are, was, were, been*), linking verbs (such as *seem, become*), and sensory verbs (such as *feel, look, smell, sound, taste*). These verbs are often called **intransitive verbs.** (See chapter 7.)

Leilani is my **sister.** [*Sister* identifies *Leilani,* the subject.]

Violence became **inevitable.** [*Inevitable* describes or qualifies *violence,* the subject.]

The rose smelled **sweet**. [*Sweet* describes *rose*.]

An **object complement** refers to, identifies, or qualifies the direct object. Object complements help complete the meaning of verbs such as *make, name, elect, call, paint*.

We made Lee **captain**.

He **tinted** it red.

(4) Word order

Becoming thoroughly aware of English word order—usually **SUBJECT + VERB + OBJECT** or **COMPLEMENT**—will help you recognize subjects, objects, and complements. Careful study of the five most common sentence patterns will reveal the importance of word order.

Pattern 1

> SUBJECT + VERB.

    S   V   V
The **students** could not **protest**.

    S   V
The **timer** on the VCR **flashed** constantly.

Pattern 2

> SUBJECT + VERB + OBJECT.

 S   V   O
Mice frighten elephants.

 S   V   O
Elephants frighten mice.

     S   V   O
Kenya's **athletes** often **win** the **marathon**.

Pattern 3

> SUBJECT + VERB + INDIRECT OBJECT
> + DIRECT OBJECT.

```
S    V   IO   DO
```
Manny gave Fido a **snack.**

```
        S              V   IO  DO
```
My **Member of Parliament will send me** a **reply.**

In some sentences (especially questions), the direct object does not always take the position indicated by these basic patterns.

```
       DO  V         S        V
```
What **event do** Kenya's **athletes** often **win?** [direct object + auxiliary + subject + verb]

Pattern 4

> SUBJECT + LINKING VERB
> + SUBJECT COMPLEMENT.

```
     S  V   C
```
My **son's name is Aaron.**

```
     S   V   C
```
The **fence was white.**

Pattern 5

> SUBJECT + VERB + DIRECT OBJECT
> + OBJECT COMPLEMENT.

```
S   V      DO   C
```
I named my **son Aaron.**

```
S    V      DO   C
```
I painted the fence white.

Exercise 1

Label all subjects, verbs (including auxiliaries), and prepositions in the sentences below. Next, label all direct and indirect objects and complements. Be prepared to discuss the basic sentence patterns (and any variations) and the types of verbs used.

1. Jay wanted simple explanations.
2. His problems were quite complicated.
3. Kitchen workers must wash their hands and wear appropriate uniforms.
4. The bartender created a new cocktail.
5. In the journal article, the professor gives us confusing facts and figures.
6. His embarrassed reaction reflected his poor upbringing.
7. Embarrassment, if it is in working order, can produce shock and enlightenment.
8. Jason is a perfect gentleman.
9. He has not always acted hospitably toward his family.
10. Creative writing, particularly poetry, can be full of valuable insights but can be difficult to interpret unless the reader is willing to take the time to understand it.

1c   There are eight classes of words—the parts of speech.

Words are traditionally grouped into eight classes or parts of speech: **verbs, nouns, pronouns, adjectives, adverbs, prepositions, conjunctions,** and **interjections.** Verbs, nouns, adjectives, and adverbs (called **vocabulary** or **lexical words**) make up more than 99 percent of all words listed in the dictionary. But pronouns, prepositions, and conjunctions—although small in number—are important because they are used over and over in speaking and writing. Prepositions and conjunctions (called **function** or **structure words**) connect and relate other parts of speech. Prepositions and conjunctions, as well as interjections, are also the only word classes that do not change their form. (For a summary of the form changes of the other parts of speech, see **inflection** in the Glossary of Terms.)

The function and form of each of the eight parts of speech listed in the chart below are discussed in the following pages. (See also the corresponding entries in the Glossary of Terms.) The chart shows the relationships among parts of speech, form, and function in the following sentences.

Compassionate friends generously offered
her shelter from the Nazis' persecution.

	Form	Function	Part of Speech
Compassionate	-*ate* ending	modifier	adjective
friends	-*s* (plural)	subject	noun
generously	-*ly* ending	modifier	adverb
offered	-*ed* (past)	verb of predicate	verb
her	objective case	indirect object	pronoun
shelter	singular	direct object	noun
from	invariable	connector	preposition
the	invariable	modifier	adjective
Nazis'	*s'* (plural possessive)	modifier	noun
persecution	singular	object of the preposition	noun

Here, one part of speech—the noun (a naming word that forms the plural with -*s* and the possessive with '*s* or *s*')—is used as a subject, a direct object, a modifier, and an object of a preposition.

A dictionary labels words according to their parts of speech. Some words have only one classification—for example, *notify* (verb), *sleepy* (adjective), *practically* (adverb). Others have more than one label because they can function as two or more parts of speech. The label of a word therefore depends on its use in a given sentence. The word *living*, for instance, can be a form of the verb *live* (as in *are living*), an adjective (*a living example*), or a noun (*makes a living*). Another example is the word *up:*

They dragged the sled **up** the hill. [preposition]

She follows the **ups** and downs of the market. [noun]

"They have **upped** the rent again," he complained. [verb]

Kelly ran **up** the bill. [part of a phrasal verb]

The **up** escalator is broken again. [adjective]

Hopkins says to look **up** at the skies! [adverb]

The following chart lists some words showing the common endings that mark different parts of speech.

Noun	Verb	Adjective	Adverb
correlation	correlate	correlated	
motivation	motivate	motivational	motivationally
motivator			
motive			
negotiation	negotiate	negotiated	
negotiator			
progress	progress	progressive	progressively
recognition	recognize	recognizable	recognizably
		recognized	
sensation	sense	sensory	
sense			
validation	validate	valid	validly
validity			

(1) Verbs   *notify, notifies, is notifying, notified*
              write, writes, is writing, wrote, has written

A verb is an essential part of the predicate. (See 1a.)

He **is** no longer **writing** those dreary stories.

Two suffixes frequently used to make verbs are *-ize* and *-ify:*

terror (noun)—*terrorize, terrify* (verbs)

real (adjective)—*realize* (verb)

Verbs often add prepositions to form **phrasal verbs.** (See 1c(6).)

Joseph **turned out** the light.

⚠ **CAUTION** Verbals (infinitives, participles, and gerunds) cannot function as the predicate of a sentence. (See 1d.)

(2) Nouns   *nation, nations, nation's, nations'*
              woman, women, kindness, kindnesses
              Carthage, Canada, William, CRTC
              breakthrough, buddy system, sister-in-law

Nouns function as subjects, objects, complements, appositives, and modifiers, as well as in direct address and in absolute constructions. (See **noun** and **absolute phrase** in the Glossary of Terms.) Nouns name persons, places, things, ideas, animals, and so on. The articles *a, an,* and *the* signal that a noun is to follow (a *chair,* an *activity*).

McKinney drives a **truck** for the **Salvation Army.**

Suffixes frequently used to make nouns are *ance, -ation, -ence, -ism, -ity, -ment, -ness,* and *-ship.*

relax, depend (verbs)—*relaxation, dependence* (nouns)

kind, rigid (adjectives)—*kindness, rigidity* (nouns)

Words such as *father-in-law, Labour Day,* and *swimming pool* are generally classified as *compound nouns.*

ESL　Nouns can also modify other nouns. Noun modifiers are almost always singular even when the noun they modify is plural: *science students, office buildings.* Common exceptions: *men students, women doctors.* A noun modifier used with a number is singular and has a hyphen: a *four-door car, 10-year-old children.*

ESL　*Count/non-count nouns*　(See **16a(1)** for use of articles.)

Count nouns are words that represent individual items that can be counted and cannot be viewed as a mass, such as *book, child,* or *atom.*

Count nouns can be either singular or plural and are preceded by words such as *many, few, a few, a number of,* and *several* with the plural. Use either indefinite (*a, an*) or definite articles (*the*) with count nouns. (See **16a(1)**.)

Non-count nouns, such as *humour* or *furniture,* represent an abstract concept, a mass, or a collection and do not have an individual existence. Modifiers such as *much* or *a little* can be used with non-count nouns but never *a* or *an.* They usually have only a singular form.

(3) Pronouns　　*I, me, my, mine, myself*
　　　　　　　　　you, your, yours, yourself
　　　　　　　　　he, him, his; she, her, hers; it, its
　　　　　　　　　we, us, our; they, them, their
　　　　　　　　　this, these; who, whom, whose; which, that
　　　　　　　　　one, ones; everybody, anyone

A pronoun is a word that can substitute for a noun in sentences. Pronouns change form according to their function. (See chapter **6**.)

They bought **it** for **her**.　　**Everyone** knows **that**.

(4) Adjectives   *shy, sleepy, attractive, famous, historic*
three men, *this* class, *another* one
young, younger, youngest; good, better, best

Adjectives modify or qualify nouns and pronouns—and sometimes gerunds. (See page 21.) Generally, adjectives appear immediately before the words they modify.

These difficult decisions, whether **right** or **wrong**, affect all of us.

In the following example, *strong* is a predicate adjective (subject complement), a word that modifies the subject and helps complete the meaning of the sentence. (See **4b**.)

Competitive gymnasts look **strong**.

Suffixes such as *-al, -able, -ant, -ative, -ic, -ish, -less, -ous,* and *-y* can be added to certain verbs or nouns to form adjectives:

accept, repent (verbs)—*acceptable, repentant* (adjectives)
angel, effort (nouns)—*angelic, effortless* (adjectives)

The articles *a, an,* and *the* are often classified as adjectives. Noun modifiers are also often classified as adjectives. (See **1c(2)**.)

(5) Adverbs   *rarely* saw, call *daily, soon* left, left *sooner*
very short, *too* angry, *never* shy, *not* fearful
practically never loses, *nearly always* cold

As the examples show, adverbs modify verbs, adjectives, and other adverbs. In addition, an adverb can modify a verbal, a phrase, or a clause. (See pages 19 and 24.)

Adverbs that do not modify any verb in the sentence are said to modify the sentence as a whole and are called *sentence modifiers*. They are frequently separated from the rest of the sentence by a comma.

> *Honestly*, Jo wasn't speeding.
>
> *In fact*, I wasn't even there.

(6) Prepositions   *on* a shelf, *between* us, *because of* rain
                        to the door, *by* them, *before* class

A preposition has an object (except when it is part of a phrasal verb such as *look up*), which is usually a noun or a pronoun. The preposition establishes a relationship such as space, time, accompaniment, cause, or manner between its object and another part of the sentence. The preposition with its object (and any modifiers) is called a **prepositional phrase**.

> *With* great feeling, Jean Chrétien expressed his dream *of* a unified country.

The preposition may follow rather than precede its object, and it can be placed at the end of the sentence:

> What was he complaining **about**? [*What* is the object of the preposition. COMPARE "He was complaining about what?"]

Some prepositions, called **phrasal prepositions**, can contain more than one word.

> **According to** Hana, it was a bad experience.

The following list contains the most commonly used phrasal prepositions.

Phrasal Prepositions (two or more words):

according to	by way of	in spite of
along with	due to	instead of
apart from	except for	on account of
as for	in addition to	out of
as regards	in case of	up to
as to	in front of	with reference to
because of	in lieu of	with regard to
by means of	in place of	with respect to
by reason of	in regard to	with the exception of

Prepositions can combine with verbs to form **phrasal verbs.** (See 1a.) They can also combine with other words to form certain idioms.

ESL Some prepositions, such as *by/until* and *except/besides,* pose special problems. *Until* means a continuing situation that will come to an end at a definite time in the future. *By* means an action that will happen at or before a particular time in the future.

I will finish my work **by** six o'clock.

I will be away **until** next Tuesday.

Besides means *with* or *plus* and usually "includes," while *except* means *without* or *minus* and usually "excludes."

Besides a salad, we had soup and crackers.

We had everything we wanted **except** a salad.

(For other preposition problems, consult the Glossary of Usage or one of the ESL resources listed in chapter 13 on page 148.)

(7) Conjunctions

cars *and* trucks, in the boat *or* on the pier will try *but* may lose, *neither* Ana *nor* Chetan
I worked *because* Dad needed money.
The river rises *when* the snow melts.

Conjunctions are connectors. The **co-ordinating conjunctions** (*and, but, or, for, nor, so,* and *yet*), as well as the correlatives (*both . . . and, either . . . or, neither . . . nor, not only . . . but also, whether . . . or*), join sentence elements (words, phrases, or clauses) of equal grammatical rank. (See also chapter 10.) The **subordinating conjunctions** (such as *because, if, since, until, when, where, while*) join subordinate clauses to independent clauses. (See 1e, pages 24–25.)

Words like *consequently, however, nevertheless, then,* and *therefore* (see the list on page 41) serve as conjunctive adverbs (or adverbial conjunctions).

Don seemed bored in class; **however,** he did listen and learn.

(8) Interjections

Interjections are exclamations. They can be followed by an exclamation point or by a comma.

Wow! Oh, that's a surprise.

Exercise 2

Classify each word in the following sentences according to its part of speech. Use your dictionary if you need help.

1. Ahmed frequently walks down the street to the Italian café on the corner.
2. Today, he pulls up his chair and orders an espresso, a strong coffee served in a tiny cup.
3. Newspapers from every major city in North America are sold behind the counter.

4. After he read the *Ottawa Citizen,* Ahmed called his friend Michel and told him to meet him at the music store.

5. Because he was at work and did not want to jeopardize a possible promotion, Michel decided not to meet Ahmed at the music store but left him a message that said he would finish work late and would meet him on the weekend at Club Zodiac.

1d A phrase is a group of words that functions as a single part of speech.

A **phrase** is a word group that lacks a subject and/or a predicate and functions as a single part of speech (noun, verb, adjective, adverb). A short simple sentence can be expanded by adding word groups that function as adjectives or adverbs. (See 1c(4) and 1c(5).)

(1) Kinds of phrases

A phrase is a group of grammatically related words that function as a single part of speech (noun, verb, adjective, or adverb). Phrases are generally classified as follows:

Verb Phrases The flowers **have wilted. Have** you **watered** them? Gerald **has looked up** the word. I **might have been told.**

Noun Phrases **The heavy freeze** killed **fruit trees.** They elected Alexandra **vice president.**

Prepositional Phrases Parking **on campus** is prohibited. We were racing **against time.**

Participial Phrases **Exploring the beach,** we found many treasures. The picnic ground, **covered with trash,** looked pretty bad.

Gerund Phrases   **Swimming across the lake** is fun. They loved **playing in the water.**

Infinitive Phrases   He wanted **to go to the movie.** He asked me **to go with him.**

Absolute Phrases   **The lunch having been packed,** we were ready to go. The star left the gym, **reporters following him eagerly.** (See **absolute phrase** in the Glossary of Terms.)

Appositive Phrases   John, **my brother,** is here today. June 21, **the longest day of the year,** is my birthday.

Noun phrases serve as subjects, objects, and complements, while **verb phrases** serve as predicates. **Prepositional phrases** may modify nouns, pronouns, adjectives, adverbs, or verbs. **Appositive phrases** substitute for and expand the meaning of nouns: Woo, *my oldest sister.*

As you learn to recognize phrases, give special attention to verb forms in word groups that are used as nouns, adjectives, or adverbs. Although such verb forms (called *verbals*) are much like verbs because they have different tenses, can take subjects and objects, and can be modified by adverbs, they cannot function as the predicate of a sentence. These verbal phrases can serve only as adjectives, adverbs, or nouns.

Verbal phrases in sentences

Shoppers **milling around** did not buy much. [participial phrase, *milling around* (see **participle** in the Glossary of Terms), modifying the noun *shoppers*]

Some people win arguments by **just remaining silent.** [gerund phrase *just remaining silent* (see **gerund** in the Glossary of Terms), object of the preposition *by*]

The group arrived in a van **loaded with heavy equipment.** [participial phrase *loaded with heavy equipment* modifying the noun *van*]

Vernon went to Yarmouth **to visit relatives.** [infinitive phrase, *to visit relatives* (see **infinitive** in the Glossary of Terms), modifying the verb *went*]

(2) Phrases used as nouns

Verbal phrases

Verbals may be classified as participles, gerunds, and infinitives. **Verbals** and **verbal phrases** function as adjectives, nouns, or adverbs. **Gerund phrases** are always used as nouns. **Infinitive phrases** are often used as nouns (although they can also function as modifiers), and a **prepositional phrase** occasionally serves as a noun as well ("*After supper is too late!*").

Nouns	Phrases Used as Nouns
The **decision** is important.	**Choosing a major** is important. [gerund phrase—subject]
She likes the **job.**	She likes **to do the work.** [infinitive phrase—direct object]
He uses my garage for **storage.**	He uses my garage for **storing his auto parts.** [gerund phrase—object of a preposition]
He wants two things: **money** and **power.**	He wants two things: **to make money** and **to gain power.** [infinitive phrases in a compound appositive]

Appositive phrases

An **appositive phrase** identifies, explains, or supplements the meaning of the word it adjoins.

The beavertail, **a kind of pastry,** is native to Ottawa.

(3) Phrases used as modifiers

Prepositional phrases nearly always function as adjectives or adverbs, and **infinitive phrases** can also be used as adjectives or adverbs. **Participial phrases**, however, are used as adjectives, and **absolute phrases** are used as adverbs. (See also **sentence modifier** in the Glossary of Terms.)

Adjectives	Phrases Used as Adjectives
It was a **sad** day.	It was a day **for sadness.** [prepositional phrase]
A **destructive** tornado roared through the city.	**Destroying everything in its path,** a tornado roared through the city. [participial phrase containing a prepositional phrase]
My **wet** clothes felt cold.	**Soaked with water,** my clothes felt cold. [participial phrase containing a prepositional phrase]
Adverbs	**Phrases Used as Adverbs**
Drive **carefully.**	Drive **with care on wet streets.** [prepositional phrases]
She sang **joyfully.**	She sang **to express her joy.** [infinitive phrase]
Today I could feel the warm sun on my face.	**My eyes shaded against the glare,** I felt the warm sun on my face. [absolute phrase] (See the Glossary of Terms.)

The preceding examples demonstrate that although phrases function in the same way as single-word modifiers, they are not merely substitutes for single words. Phrases can express more than can be packed into a single word.

Exercise 3

Underline each phrase in the following passage. Then note whether the phrase functions as a noun, an adjective, an adverb, or an appositive.

[1]Within the past few years, many people have become fans of comic books, an art form that was previously considered to be an undignified type of entertainment. [2]This assessment was due to the comic book's reputation, negative but perhaps accurate, which suggested that most readers were withdrawn and unpopular adolescent boys. [3]However, some movies, such as *The X-Men, Spider-Man,* and *The Incredible Hulk,* directly contradict the implications suggested by this reputation, and they show that being the fan of a comic book superhero is "cool." [4]Thus, some people who would never have considered themselves superhero fans are flocking to the cinemas to see the latest special effects technology transform the images, which were previously found on the colourful pages of comic books, into startlingly realistic scenes.

[5]Furthermore, a new wave of writers and illustrators is reviving this art form into illustrated novels, which are being turned into movies, as well. [6]For instance, the movie *Ghost World,* a film that looked at the lives of a disaffected teenage girl and her friends, was actually based on an illustrated novel of the same name. [7]*Ghost World*, a big success in theatres, was nominated for an Academy Award. [8]Indeed, the expansion of the comic book's range of subjects to include portrayals of everyday life may also account for the renewed interest in this art form. Thus, society has been forced to reconsider not only the comic book but also the shy adolescents who made them popular in the first place.

1e Recognizing clauses helps in analyzing sentences.

A clause is a group of related words that contains a subject and a predicate.

(1) Independent clauses

An **independent clause** has the same grammatical structure as a sentence and contains a subject and a predicate. In the example below, the independent clause is in bold.

The boy chased the dog, although he couldn't catch him.

(2) Subordinate clauses

A **subordinate clause** is a group of related words that contains a subject and a predicate but cannot stand alone. Such clauses often begin with words like *because* and *since*. In the example below, the subordinate clause is in bold.

Maria received the gold medal **because her performance was flawless.**

Subordinate clauses provide additional information about the independent clause and establish the relationship of the additional information to the independent clause. Unlike an independent clause, a subordinate clause is grammatically dependent and functions within a sentence as an adverb, an adjective, or a noun.

The last ship carrying passengers had recently arrived in the Beaufort Sea, **which was closed by ice most of the year.** [adjective clause]

I had to leave the meeting early **because I became ill.** [adverb clause]

Geologists know **why earthquakes occur.** [noun clause—
direct object]

The following conjunctions are commonly used to introduce, connect, and relate subordinate clauses to other
words in the sentence.

Words Commonly Used as Subordinating Conjunctions:

after	in case	supposing that
although	in that	than
as (far/soon) as	inasmuch as	though
as if	insofar as	till
as though	lest	unless
because	no matter how	until
before	now that	when, whenever
even if	once	where, wherever
even though	provided (that)	whether
how	since	while
if	so that	why

Relative pronouns also serve as markers of those subordinate clauses called **relative clauses.** (See chapter 6, page
61.)

that	which	who, whoever	whatever
what	whose	whom, whomever	

Subordinate clauses used as nouns

Nouns	**Noun Clauses**
The **news** may be false.	**What the newspapers say** may be false. [subject]
I do not know his **address.**	I do not know **where he lives.** [direct object]
Give the tools to **Rita.**	Give the tools to **whoever can use them best.** [object of a preposition]

Karen's **protest** amazed me.	The fact **that Karen protested** amazed me. [appositive]

The conjunction *that* before a noun clause can often be omitted.

I know she will come.

Subordinate clauses used as modifiers

Two types of subordinate clauses—adjective clauses and adverb clauses—serve as modifiers.

Adjective Clauses   Any clause that modifies a noun or a pronoun is an adjective clause. Such clauses, which nearly always follow the words they modify, usually begin with relative pronouns but may sometimes begin with words such as *when, where,* or *why.*

Adjectives	Adjective Clauses
Everyone needs **loyal** friends.	Everyone needs friends **who are loyal.**
The **golden** window reflects the sun.	The window, **which shines like gold**, reflects the sun.
My sister lives in a **peaceful** town.	The town **where my sister lives** is peaceful.

If not used as a subject, the relative pronoun (*who, whom, that, which,* and so on) in an adjective clause can sometimes be omitted:

He is a man **I admire.** [COMPARE "He is a man *whom I admire.*"]

Adverb Clauses   An adverb clause usually modifies a verb, but it also may modify an adjective, an adverb, or even the rest of the sentence in which it appears. Adverb clauses are ordinarily introduced by subordinating conjunctions.

Adverbs	Adverb Clauses
Next, the disk controller failed.	**After I backed up my files,** the disk controller failed.
His popularity dropped **locally**.	His popularity dropped in areas **where people knew him.**

Some adverb clauses may be elliptical. (See also 5b(3).)

If I can save enough money, I'll go to St. John's next summer. **If not**, I'll take a trip to Montreal. [Clearly implied words are omitted.]

Exercise 4

Underline the independent clauses in the following paragraph. Then find the subordinate clauses, place brackets around them, and label each as a noun clause, an adjective clause, or an adverb clause.

¹The eighties had been a decidedly dry period for Canadian pop, a time of forgettable industry-tailored bands and requisite easy-listening Cancon. ²Then, in the early nineties, much of the Canadian music industry was taken aback when a healthy independent music scene suddenly clamoured for attention from the East Coast. ³Really, there was no reason to be surprised. ⁴In a region besieged by Celtic music and isolated from the North American touring circuit, an alternative sound had to be created locally. ⁵If no one were willing to stretch beyond Celtic reels, naught but Celtic reels would be heard.

⁶After the unexpected success of grunge, the American music industry came calling and found, in Canada's heart of Celtic sounds, a blistering scene of jangly, slightly dissonant pop, not so angry as the disaffected supergroup

Nirvana, but close enough for an industry desperate to cash in on some developed, salable talent. [7]Some of these bands inked deals with major American labels, while others stuck closer to home, signing with or creating their own smaller Canadian labels.

[8]The early nineties added credibility to the East Coast's, and by association Canada's, alternative music scene. [9]Today, with over 200 Canadian labels, Canada's music scene is healthier than it's been since the seventies and is finally revelling in its own independent diversity.

1f   Sentences may be analyzed by form and function.

The form of a sentence is identified by the number and kinds of clauses it contains. The function of a sentence refers to its purpose.

(1) Examining sentence forms

a. A **simple sentence** consists of a single independent clause:

I [subject] **had lost my passport.** [predicate containing a verb and a direct object]

b. A **compound sentence** consists of at least two independent clauses and no subordinate clauses:

I had lost my passport, but **I did not worry about it.** [A comma and a co-ordinating conjunction (*but*) link the two independent clauses.]

c. A **complex sentence** has one independent clause and at least one subordinate clause:

Although I had lost my passport, I did not worry about it. [A subordinate clause—indicated here by *although* and followed by a comma (see **17b**)—precedes the independent clause.]

d. A **compound-complex sentence** consists of at least two independent clauses and at least one subordinate clause:

When I lost my passport, **I ordered** a new one, but **I did not worry** about it. [*When* signals the subordinate clause; *but* connects the two independent clauses.]

(2) Examining the purpose or function of sentences

English sentences make statements (**declarative**), give commands or make requests (**imperative**), ask questions (**interrogative**), and make exclamations (**exclamatory**).

Declarative	She refused the offer. [statement]
Imperative	Refuse the offer now. [request or command]
Interrogative	Did she refuse the offer? She refused, didn't she? She refused it? [questions]
Exclamatory	What an offer! And she refused it! [exclamations]

Be aware of the forms and functions of the sentences you read and note how writers use them to achieve particular effects. (See also chapter **12.**) In your own writing, think about what you want your readers to understand from each sentence and make sure you have used the forms and functions that will most effectively express your thoughts.

Exercise 5

Analyze the passage below: (1) Identify the form (simple, compound, complex, or compound-complex) and the function (declarative, imperative, interrogative, or exclamatory) of each sentence. (2) Underline the independent clauses. (3) Bracket subordinate clauses and note whether they are noun, adjective, or adverb clauses.

¹Certainly something had to be done. ²Just think: Matthew and Nathan had told me four times in as many minutes just how bored they were and how much they really didn't appreciate it. ³I have to think of something for them to do, I mused, looking at the pile of books on the table in front of me, since whether they were bored, or I was bored, or we were all bored, I was sure of one inescapable fact: I had to finish reading six chapters for an exam the following day.

⁴As I saw it, the best way to handle their boredom was to get them to go outside and play; I suggested this because I had reached my wits' end, and I was relieved when they hurried outside.

⁵In fact, they were ecstatic! ⁶Had they been, perhaps, waiting until I gave them my seal of approval? ⁷Were they behaving like frustrated, lazy couch potatoes merely because they were afraid they'd anger me by asking to go outside? ⁸At that point, I decided it was time for a break, so I, too, went outside and joined in their fun.

Exercise 6

Write ten sentences of your own. Make sure you write at least one simple sentence, two compound, three complex, and one compound-complex. Make at least one of the sentences declarative, one imperative, one interrogative, and one exclamatory. Identify the main and subordinate clauses in your sentences, and label the subordinate clauses as noun, adjective, or adverb.

Chapter 2 | Sentence Fragments

A **fragment**, an incomplete sentence starting with a capital and ending with a period, is ordinarily avoided in formal writing. Fragments can be difficult to recognize within a context.

> He has a cellphone and a pager. **Which he uses to keep in touch with his friends.**
>
> She got her face painted. **First her nose and then her cheeks.**

Fragments are often phrases or subordinate clauses. In the above examples, the fragments (in bold) can be corrected by making them independent sentences or by connecting them to an adjoining sentence.

> He has a cellphone and a pager. **He uses them to keep in touch with his friends.**
>
> She got her face painted, **first her nose and then her cheeks.**

Testing for fragments   You can ask three questions to help identify fragments:

1. Is there a verb? If not, supply one or attach the fragment to a related sentence (**2a**). Remember, a verbal is not a verb.
2. Is there a subject? If not, supply one or attach the fragment to a related sentence (**2a**).
3. Is there a subordinating conjunction? If so, remove it or attach the subordinate clause to a related sentence (**2b**).

Occasionally, writers deliberately use fragments for emphasis. For example, writing that mirrors speech often contains grammatically incomplete sentences or expressions. Similarly, exclamations and answers to questions are often single words, phrases, or subordinate clauses written as sentences.

> **Understand?** [question with an implied subject (*you*), informal use]

> **Unbelievable! No pain, no gain.** [exclamation and phrases, informal use]

> Why does Camilla's radio always play classic rock? **Because that is her favourite kind of music.** [subordinate clause, answer to a question, informal use]

> I don't remember a world without language. From the time of my earliest childhood, there was language. **Always language, and imagination, speculation, utters of sound. Words, beginnings of words.** —SIMON J. ORTIZ [phrases, literary use. Repetition links the first fragment to the preceding sentence and telegraphs Ortiz's emphasis in the second fragment.]

 CAUTION   Have a good reason for any sentence fragment you allow to stand.

2a   Phrases are sometimes mistakenly punctuated as sentences.

Verbal phrases, prepositional phrases, parts of compound predicates, and appositives are sometimes written as fragments. They can be revised in one of the ways listed below.

1. *Make the phrase into a sentence by supplying the missing subject and/or verb.*

He reached the top. *He was* ‸Panting and puffing all the way.

I'm getting an ice cream cone. *I want* ‸One scoop of chocolate swirl and one of butter pecan.

2. *Attach the fragment to a related sentence.*

He reached the ~~top.~~ *top,* Panting and puffing all the way.

I'm getting an ice cream cone*. with* ‸One scoop of chocolate swirl and one of butter pecan.

2b Subordinate clauses are sometimes mistakenly punctuated as sentences.

Fragments can be revised in one of the ways listed below.

1. *Remove the subordinating conjunction and supply the missing elements.*

They tried to understand André's objections. *They* ~~Which~~ were unfounded.

2. *Attach the fragment to a related sentence.*

They tried to understand André's ~~objections. Which~~ *objections, which* were unfounded.

3. *Reduce the fragment to a single-word modifier and include it in the related sentence.*

They tried to understand André's *unfounded* ‸objections. ~~Which were unfounded.~~

Exercise 1

Revise each item below to eliminate the sentence fragment. In each case, explain why you chose to revise as you did. If any fragment does not require revision, explain your reason for allowing it to stand.

1. After watching Kevin put jam and syrup on his scrambled eggs and bacon. Denise thought he might as well have asked for cake for breakfast.
2. He insisted on answering his cellphone. While they were in the middle of a conversation.
3. She began to wonder about her new boyfriend. Who was turning out to be more odd than interesting.
4. She criticized Kevin for talking incessantly on his cellphone. Very harshly.
5. After finishing breakfast. Kevin was too busy reading the paper to notice that Denise had left.

Exercise 2

The paragraph below contains several fragments. Follow the guidelines in **2a** and **2b** to revise the paragraph so it contains no fragments. Give your reasons for revising each fragment as you did.

[1]Most of the kids in her neighbourhood—Marcy, Jake, and Bernadette—owe their sense of security to the Barnwells, the older couple living at the end of the block. [2]Not just because Mrs. Barnwell takes the time to help them with their homework whenever their parents are at work. [3]The Saturdays at the park, the snacks Mr. Barnwell makes once in a while in the late afternoon, and the woodworking projects they encourage kids to begin and that sometimes are visible in their front yard. [4]These are just as valuable. [5]Their official roles as neighbourhood baby sitters are more complex than one might think. [6]Though it's easy to see that if you take the time to think about it. [7]You're not likely to forget it. [8]Some people report hearing that they

never had children because they decided not to have any. [9]But that's not really what happened. [10]Unfortunately, they were unable to have them. [11]Making them both rather sad and leaving them with a lot of extra love to give. [12]In fact, the kinds of disappointments we all have to face in some form. [13]They can alter the way we deal with other people, many times for the better. [14]People changing positively in the way they interact with the world. [15]People may become kinder to each other. [16]Because the most important things people have in this world are their relationships with others.

Chapter 3

Comma Splices and Fused Sentences

A **comma splice** consists of two (or more) independent clauses joined simply by a comma. It is an error that occurs only in compound or compound-complex sentences. A **fused sentence** (also called a *comma fault* or *run-on sentence*) occurs when neither a conjunction nor appropriate punctuation joins two independent clauses.

Comma Splice   She was late, she called home.

Fused Sentence   She was late she called home.

Both comma splices and fused sentences can be corrected by separating the clauses with a semicolon or period or by joining them with a conjunction.

To separate:

1. Independent clauses may be separated by placing a period after each clause.

   She was late. She called home.

2. Independent clauses may be separated by a semicolon (see 18a).

   She was late; she called home.

The semicolon relates but keeps separate two grammatically equal units of thought: **SUBJECT + PREDICATE**;

SUBJECT + PREDICATE. Writers generally do not use the semicolon between parts of unequal grammatical rank.

A comma, a semicolon, or a period can be used between independent clauses not linked by a co-ordinating conjunction when the clauses are short, parallel in form, and unified in thought.

They sat, they ate, they drank.

The comma emphasizes similarity in idea and grammatical structure, the semicolon emphasizes difference, and the period denotes separation.

To link and relate:

1. A comma can be inserted before the appropriate co-ordinating conjunction (*and, but, or, nor, for, so, yet*—see 17a).

   The wind was cold, **so** they decided not to walk.
   They decided not to walk, **for** the wind was cold.

2. One clause can be subordinated to the other (see 17b).

   The wind was so cold **that** they decided not to walk.
   Because the wind was cold, they decided not to walk.

3. One of the clauses can become an introductory phrase (see 17b).

   Because of the cold wind, they decided not to walk.

Ways to recognize independent clauses and distinguish them from phrases and subordinate clauses are fully explained in chapter 1, especially 1d and 1e.

3a **Commas are used between independent clauses only when they are linked by a co-ordinating conjunction (*and, but, or, for, nor, so, yet*). (See also 18a.)**

Comma Splice   Women's roles have changed radically in recent decades, women now make up a larger percentage of the work force.

Revised   Women's roles have changed radically in recent decades**,** **for** women now make up a larger percentage of the work force. [co-ordinating conjunction *for* added after the comma]

OR   Women's roles have changed radically in recent decades**;** women now make up a larger percentage of the work force. [A semicolon separates the independent clauses.]

Comma Splice   He was not an outstanding success at his first job, he was not a complete failure either.

Revised   He was not an outstanding success at his first job**,** **nor** was he a complete failure. [Note the shift in the word order of subject and verb after the co-ordinating conjunction *nor*.]

OR   He was **neither** an outstanding success at his first job **nor** a complete failure. [a simple sentence with a compound complement]

Comma Splice   I ran over some broken glass in the parking lot, it did not puncture my tires.

Revised   I ran over some broken glass in the parking lot**,** **but** it did not puncture my tires. [the co-ordinating conjunction *but* added after the comma]

OR   **Although** I ran over some broken glass in the parking lot**,** it did not puncture my tires. [Addition of *although* makes the first clause subordinate: see **17b**.]

To avoid a fused sentence, use a period or a semicolon between independent clauses not linked by a co-ordinating conjunction.

Fused   She wrote him a love letter he answered it in person.

Revised   She wrote him a love letter. **He** answered it in person. [each independent clause written as a sentence]

OR   She wrote him a love letter; he answered it in person. [independent clauses separated by a semicolon: see 18a]

The comma is also used to separate a statement from a tag question.

You can come, can't you? He rides a bike, doesn't he?

They couldn't be wrong, could they—not all those millions!
—WILLIAM GOLDING

Exercise 1

Connect each pair of sentences in two of the following ways: separate them with a semicolon, join them with a co-ordinating conjunction, reduce one to an introductory phrase, make one subordinate with a subordinating conjunction. (See the list of subordinating conjunctions in 1e(2).)

1. Marvia read about a new karaoke club downtown. She went there with James after work on Friday.
2. The club was very crowded. It took a long time for their requests to get played.
3. Marvia requested to sing a Glen Campbell song. James hates country and western music and prefers music from the sixties and seventies.
4. James's request finally got played. It was the Nancy Sinatra song "These Boots Are Made for Walkin'."
5. Other patrons of the club admired James's and Marvia's dedication to karaoke. They advised them not to give up their day jobs.

Exercise 2

Revise any sentence that needs it. Put a check mark after correctly punctuated sentences.

1. It was evening and that meant it was time for Morris to call his mother before she went to sleep she lived by herself in a condominium by the riverfront he and his sister bought it for her to live in when their father died.

2. Student writing often suffers from faulty punctuation another problem is faulty diction.

3. Francine got married when she was very young her husband had been her high-school sweetheart who turned out to be a high-school dropout and eventually a deadbeat dad.

4. The students and the teacher did not get along very well, therefore, I can remember a riot breaking out each day in class.

5. Most students do not find the subject matter of the course too difficult, they will not pass if they do not study, no matter how easy the material.

6. Most of my family returned to Ottawa after spending a weekend in the Thousand Islands. The only members who did not return with us were my Aunt Zelda and Uncle Butch, who decided to do some shopping in Cornwall.

7. Every day on his way home from work he would have a banquet burger and fries followed by a chocolate sundae, it's no wonder he gained nine kilos in two months.

8. Through careful negotiation and a mutual desire to achieve a compromise, both union and management agreed to a new contract, they managed to put aside their squabbles for another five years.

9. To be successful, a birthday party requires snacks, pop, and cake. It also requires somebody to have a birthday.

10. The salsa dancing competition was delayed for half an hour, Daryl showed up with a huge bag of nachos demanding to sample the winning salsa dip.

3b Semicolons are used before conjunctive adverbs or transitional phrases that are placed between independent clauses. (See also 18a.)

Comma Splice Sexual harassment is not just a women's issue, after all, men can be sexually harassed too.

Revised Sexual harassment is not just a women's issue; after all, men can be sexually harassed too. [independent clause; *transitional phrase*, independent clause]

Fused Sentence The nineteenth-century European imperialists left arbitrarily drawn boundaries in Africa therefore, each country is composed of a mix of languages and cultures.

Revised The nineteenth-century European imperialists left arbitrarily drawn boundaries in Africa; therefore, each country is composed of a mix of languages and cultures. [independent clause; *conjunctive adverb*, independent clause]

Below is a list of frequently used conjunctive adverbs and transitional phrases.

Conjunctive adverbs:

also	however	next
anyhow	incidentally	nonetheless
anyway	indeed	otherwise
besides	instead	similarly
consequently	likewise	still
finally	meanwhile	then
furthermore	moreover	therefore
hence	nevertheless	thus

Transitional phrases:

after all	even so	in the second place
as a result	for example	on the contrary
at any rate	in addition	on the other hand
at the same time	in fact	
by the way	in other words	

Unlike a co-ordinating conjunction, which has a fixed position between the independent clauses it links, many conjunctive adverbs and transitional phrases either begin the second independent clause or take another position in it.

She believed daily exercise has many benefits; **however,** she couldn't fit it into her schedule. [The conjunctive adverb begins the second independent clause. See also 18a, page 207.]

She believed daily exercise has many benefits; she couldn't, however, fit it into her schedule. [The conjunctive adverb (set off by commas) appears later in the clause.]

COMPARE

She believed daily exercise has many benefits, **but** she couldn't fit it into her schedule. [The co-ordinating conjunction has a fixed position.]

Exercise 3

Write five correctly punctuated compound sentences using various conjunctive adverbs and transitional phrases to connect and relate independent clauses.

3c   Divided quotations can trick you into making a comma splice. (See also chapter 20.)

Comma Splice   "Who won the lottery?" he asked, "how much money was in the pot?"

Revised "Who won the lottery?" he asked. "How much money was in the pot?"

Comma Splice "Injustice is relatively easy to bear," says Mencken, "it is justice that hurts."

Revised "Injustice is relatively easy to bear," says Mencken; "it is justice that hurts."

Exercise 4

Comma splices and fused sentences have been incorporated into the following paragraphs. Indicate how the comma splices and fused sentences could be revised, and mark sentences that need no revision with a check mark.

¹"I really like magazines and newspapers," he said "I read the sections discussing world news and business because they use my mind. ²I read the sections discussing entertainment and gossip," he continued, "because the stories are either informative or so unusual that I can't put them down. ³When I was in the hospital, I read the sections of the newspaper that discussed medical issues many articles in this section often focus on what can go wrong, this one, however, discussed some of the success stories as well as reports of excellent emergency-room care in Canadian hospitals."

⁴"I also read a lot of books, particularly in the evening it's a good way to relax and exercise my imagination. ⁵There's not one genre or type I read religiously. ⁶Someday, I'd like to read more science fiction books I always see them at the bookstore, but I haven't bought any yet."

Exercise 5

First, review chapter 2 and study chapter 3. Then identify and mark the sentence fragments (SF), comma splices (CS), and fused sentences (FS) in the following passage. Next, write down why you classified them as you did, indicating how they could be revised. Put a check mark after each sentence that needs no revision.

[1]He looks frail, thin. [2]Almost vulnerable. [3]The baggy grey sweater I gave him for his birthday is loosely pulled around him like a cape his shoulders are stooped. [4]And he holds a book. [5]There is a sound, however, in my father's voice it is a tone of tired strength.

[6]We sit alone at the kitchen table only a few hours after the funeral. [7]"From day to day, we all must wear our painful experiences as a sign to others," he says with the vigour of pride and past victories, reading from the journal he's kept for the past 50 years, his constant companion. [8]"Here then is a glimpse of the sign I send to you," he says, however he still smiles and speaks of healing, happiness, and the future. [9]He tells me stories about my mother. [10]The idea being that the stories we tell are important parts of the real lives we live. [11]After a few moments, he looks at me directly and leans in closer. [12]"In our stories, we can live with complete abandon" he says this in a respectful cadence. [13]"In life, we must proceed slowly, gradually. [14]Primarily with balance and stealth. [15]Never with insensitivity."

Chapter 4
Adjectives and Adverbs

Adjectives and adverbs are modifiers that qualify, restrict, or intensify the meaning of other words. They also describe degrees of comparison. **Adjectives** modify nouns and pronouns; **adverbs** modify verbs, adjectives, and other adverbs.

Adjectives	Adverbs
a **quick** lunch	eat **quickly**
armed squads	**heavily** armed squads
She looked **angry**.	She looked **angrily** at me.
the **most brilliant**	shone **more brilliantly**

The articles *a, an,* and *the* are often classified as adjectives.

ESL See **16a(1)** for the use of articles.

Adverbs that modify verbs commonly describe how (manner), when (time), or where (place) the action occurred.

Manner We partied **endlessly**.

Time We recovered **today**.

Place We stayed **home**.

Adverbs can also modify verbals (gerunds, infinitives, participles—see **1d**, page 20) and whole clauses as well. Whole clauses may even function as adverbs. (See **1e**, pages 26–27.)

Walking rapidly is good for you. [adverb *rapidly* modifying gerund *walking*, which serves as the subject]

After they had eaten, Big Tom pushed the cracked and dirty supper things to the back of the table and took the baby from its high chair carefully, so as not to spill the flotsam of bread crumbs and boiled potatoes from the chair to the floor.

—HUGH GARNER

[an adverbial clause of time modifying the verb *pushed*]

The *-ly* ending is usually associated with adverbs formed from adjectives (*lightly*), but certain adjectives formed from nouns also have the *-ly* ending (*cost, costly*). A number of words can function as either adjectives or adverbs (*fast, well*), and a few adverbs have two acceptable forms (*quick, quickly; slow, slowly*). When in doubt, consult the dictionary for the labels *adj.* and *adv.* and any usage notes.

Nouns used as adjectives are almost always singular: *science students, executive women.* Common exceptions are **man** and **woman**, which change to the plural when they modify a plural noun: *men doctors, women doctors.*

4a   Adverbs modify verbs, adjectives, and other adverbs.

Leela played her part ~~perfect~~. [The adverb *perfectly* modifies

the verb *played*.]

The plane departs at a ~~reasonable~~ early hour. [The adverb

reasonably modifies the adjective *early*.]

Most dictionaries still label the following as informal usage: *sure* for *surely, real* for *really,* and *good* for *well.*

Informal   The Raptors played **real good** during the first quarter.

Formal   The Raptors played **very well** during the first quarter. [appropriate in both formal and informal usage—see also 13b]

Exercise 1

In the following sentences, convert any informal or unacceptable modifier into an adverb acceptable in academic writing. Put a check mark after each sentence that needs no revision.

1. Since he got new glasses, Winston does not go out as regular as he used to.
2. He needed new glasses because he could not see good anymore.
3. He used to be a local known celebrity.
4. People would crowd close about him at the Legion and in pubs to hear his wild stories.
5. He had no acting lessons, but he sure told his stories dramatic.
6. People would listen to him intent as he told about his days in the Royal Canadian Navy during the Second World War.
7. He was awarded a medal for acting brave when a ship he was on was torpedoed in the Gulf of St. Lawrence.
8. With his new glasses, however, Winston's eyesight has improved remarkable.
9. A friend then gave him a real good idea.
10. Winston is now working diligent at writing down his amazing tales with the hopes of reaching an even wider audience.

4b There is a distinction between adverbs used to modify verbs and adjectives used as subject or object complements.

A common error is to use an adjective as an adverb or an adverb as an adjective.

The couple was *frantic*. [subject complement]

The couple danced *frantically*. [adverb]

Object complements (usually adjectives or nouns) modify the direct object as they help complete the meaning of such verbs as *make, name, elect, call, find, consider*. (See also 1b(3).)

They found Collette **trustworthy**. [The adjective *trustworthy* refers to the direct object *Collette* and completes the meaning of the verb *found*.]

! **CAUTION** Do not omit the *-d* or *-ed* of a past participle used as an adjective. (See also 7b, page 94.)

The dog was too frighten*ed* to go to him.

Exercise 2

Using adjectives as complements, write two sentences that illustrate each of the following patterns.

Subject + linking verb + subject complement.
Subject + verb + direct object + object complement.

4c   Many adjectives and adverbs change form to indicate the degree of comparison.

Generally, shorter adjectives (and a few adverbs) form the comparative by adding *-er* and the superlative by adding *-est*.

large, larger, largest

quick, quicker, quickest

Most two-syllable adjectives with stress on the first syllable also form their comparative or superlative by adding -*er* or -*est*. For words whose base form ends in -*y*, change the -*y* to -*i* when adding the comparative or superlative ending. (See **22d(3)**.)

> lucky, luckier, luckiest

Longer adjectives and most adverbs form the comparative by using *more* (or *less*) and the superlative by using *most* (or *least*).

> fortunate, more/less fortunate, most/least fortunate
>
> rapidly, more/less rapidly, most/least rapidly

A few common modifiers have irregular forms.

> little, less, least
>
> good/well, better, best
>
> bad/badly, worse, worst
>
> far, further/farther, furthest/farthest [See the Glossary of Usage.]

When in doubt, consult your dictionary.

(1) **The comparative denotes a greater degree or refers to two in a comparison.**

Make sure to complete the comparison, and always make clear what the subject is being compared with. In the examples, the conjunction *than* signals the second element being compared.

> The Canadian team won **more** medals in Salt Lake City **than** they did in Nagano.
>
> Home-cooked food can be **more** unhealthy **than** fast food. [a comparison of two groups]
>
> **More** exhausted **than** hungry, he sat in the busy restaurant content with a glass of water.

Note that the comparison may be implied by the context.

> She wrote **two** papers, and the instructor gave her a **better** grade on the second.

The comparative form when used with *other* sometimes refers to more than two.

> Bert can run **faster** than the *other* players.

(2) The superlative denotes the greatest degree or refers to three or more in a comparison.

> The interests of the family are **best** served by open communication.
>
> Bert is the **fastest** of the three runners.
>
> **OR**
>
> Bert is the **fastest** runner of all.

The superlative occasionally refers to two, as in "Put your *best* foot forward!"

Adjectives and adverbs that have absolute meanings, such as "perfect," "dead," "completely," and "unique," cannot be compared. In informal speech and writing, however, comparisons such as "a *more perfect* society," "the *deadest* campus," "*less completely* exhausted," and "*rather unique* clothing" are becoming more common.

(3) A double comparative or superlative is incorrect.

> Our swimming hole is much ~~more~~ shallower than Conestogo Lake.

> That was the ~~most~~ funniest movie.

Exercise 3

Provide the appropriate comparative or superlative form of the modifier given in parentheses.

[1]"This fish weighs (little) than the one I caught yesterday," Uncle Verne said as he reeled in his line. [2]But this isn't the (bad) day for fishing. [3]Uncle Verne, a veteran fisherman, finds the silver shad the (useful) lure available for catching bass. [4]A (lively) bait has never before been produced. [5]Its movement attracts even the (tiny) of bass. [6]Of course, Uncle Verne hopes to haul in the (big) fish of all; however, at times one must be prepared to deal with the (small) fish. [7]When a big bass strikes at the bait, only the (strong) fisherman will be able to fight the battle. [8]Although, physically, Uncle Verne appears to be the (weak) fisherman in the boat, when the catch is weighed at the end of the day, there is no doubt he is good.

4d Use of a word group or a noun as an adjective can be awkward or ambiguous.

Many word groups or nouns effectively modify other nouns (as in *reference* manual, *Groundhog* Day, *goods and services* tax), especially when appropriate adjectives are not available. Avoid such forms, however, when they are awkward or confusing.

Awkward	Many candidates entered the mayor race.
Better	Many candidates entered the mayoral race.
Confusing	The Mr. Brown dinnertime tantrum was embarrassing.
Better	Mr. Brown's tantrum at dinnertime was embarrassing.

4e   A single rather than a double negative is correct.

The term **double negative** refers to the use of two negatives within a sentence or clause to express a single negation. Like the double comparison, the double negative is considered incorrect.

He did **not** keep ~~no~~ records.

I can~~not~~ do **no**thing about it.

Because **hardly**, **barely**, and **scarcely** already denote severely limited or negative conditions, use of **not**, **nothing**, or **without** with these modifiers creates a double negative.

I could~~n't~~ **hardly** quit in the middle of the job.

The motion passed with ~~not~~ **scarcely** a protest.

E S L   Cumulative adjectives follow a specific order. Writers often use up to three adjectives to modify a noun. English requires that the adjectives occur in the following order: determiners, subjective opinion (beautiful, happy, angry), physical description (size, shape, age, and colour), origin, material, purpose.

that ugly brick building   their large English watercolour

Dad's old threshing machine   a round Italian pizza dish

Using more than three adjectives before a noun is awkward and is usually avoided.

Exercise 4

After you have reread rules **4a** through **4e** and have studied the examples, correct all errors in the use of adjectives or adverbs in the sentences below. Also eliminate any awkward use of nouns as adjectives, and correct double negatives. Put a check mark after any sentence that needs no revision.

1. I have more work to do now than I used to.
2. The job advertisement asked for young willing intelligent native Greek speakers to apply.
3. The restaurant was so packed I couldn't hardly move.
4. Although I didn't change the recipe much, the soup seemed much more tastier than usual.
5. He said it was easy the biggest turnout they had ever seen.
6. They never went nowhere new.
7. The professor says that it is very difficult to judge the poetry writing contest.
8. The coffee tastes real well when he adds some raw sugar to it.
9. The young man believed he led a much fuller life than his friends.
10. The bookstore information person told me they had run out of that novel.

Chapter 5

Coherence: Misplaced Parts and Dangling Modifiers

Keeping related parts of the sentence together and avoiding dangling modifiers makes meaning clearer to your reader.

5a Placing modifiers near the words they modify clarifies meaning.

The meaning of the following sentences changes according to the position of the modifiers.

Martin ate **only** one of the green mangoes.
Martin ate one of the **only** green mangoes.
Only Martin ate one of the green mangoes.

The firefighter **who was burned** tried to help the old lady.
The firefighter tried to help the old lady **who was burned**.

(1) In formal English, place modifiers such as *almost,
only, just, even, hardly, nearly,* and *merely*
immediately before the words they modify for
emphasis and clarification of meaning.

We were| only| notified about the rent increase.

I | hardly ever| think that they| go out.

(2) **Place a modifying prepositional phrase to indicate clearly what the phrase modifies.**

Arne says *in the first paragraph* that he means to leave the country ~~in the first paragraph.~~

(3) **Place adjective clauses near the words they modify.**

I put the chair *that I had recently purchased* in the middle of the room ~~that I had recently purchased.~~

(4) **Revise "squinting" constructions—modifiers that may refer to either a preceding or a following word.**

The student who ⌊sits in the front row⌋ currently⌋ needs a haircut.

(5) **Revise awkward constructions that split an infinitive.**

Jim failed to ⌐early enough⌐ study⌐ for the exam.

However, splitting an infinitive is sometimes not only natural but desirable.

He forgot to **completely** close the gate. [COMPARE: He forgot **completely** to close the gate.]

Exercise 1

Revise the following sentences, placing the modifiers in correct relation to the words they modify.

1. Louis returned yesterday from his trip to the West Coast by plane.
2. Some of his classmates went west to find work; he went just to Vancouver to visit friends.
3. Louis did not want to, because he was not adventurous, see more of the West Coast.

4. At a local Japanese restaurant, Louis saw staff serve trays of sushi to customers on ceramic trays.
5. Trevor talked Louis into going with him to his hometown on Vancouver Island, which was Port Hardy.
6. It took almost two hours from North Vancouver to Nanaimo to cross by ferry.
7. Logging companies had cut down much of the forest along the highway to Port Hardy.
8. They visited a small town on one of the neighbouring islands called Sointula.
9. The residents of the town of Sointula only spoke Finnish.
10. Louis will never forget the scenery on the drive along the Sunshine Coast, which was of incredible beauty, back to Vancouver.

5b   There are several ways to revise dangling modifiers.

Dangling modifiers   Dangling modifiers are primarily verbal phrases that do not clearly refer to other words or phrases in the sentence, although any misplaced word, phrase, or clause can be said to dangle. The words in the sentence can be rearranged, or words can be added, to make the meaning clear.

(1) Revise dangling participial phrases. (See 1d.)

Dangling   *Taking our seats,* the game started. [no clear word for the phrase to refer to]

Revised   *Taking our seats,* **we** started the game. [word supplied—participants]

OR

Taking our seats, **we waited** for the game to start. [words supplied—observers]

Placed after the basic sentence, the participial phrase in the revision below refers to the subject.

Dangling	The evening passed very pleasantly, *munching* popcorn and *watching* a late movie. [no clear reference]
Revised	We passed the evening very pleasantly, *munching* popcorn and *watching* a late movie. [reference supplied]

(2) Revise dangling phrases containing gerunds or infinitives. (See 1d(1).)

Dangling	On *entering* the stadium, the size of the crowd surprised Theo. [no clear subject]
Revised	On *entering* the stadium, **Theo** was surprised at the size of the crowd. [subject supplied]
Dangling	*To write* well, good books must be read. [no clear subject]
Revised	*To write* well, **I** must read good books. [subject supplied]

(3) Revise dangling elliptical adverb clauses. (See 1e(2).)

Elliptical clauses imply some words that are not stated.

Dangling	*When only a small boy,* my father took me with him to Toronto.
Revised	*When* **I was** *only a small boy,* my father took me with him to Toronto.

Sentence modifiers (see the Glossary of Terms) are considered standard usage, not danglers. (See also 1c(5).)

First, I will learn to dance.

I just don't care, **frankly.**

Exercise 2

Revise the following sentences to eliminate dangling modifiers. Put a check mark after any sentence that needs no revision.

1. Dusk having fallen, the kids went inside.
2. Our conversation ended by exchanging phone numbers and promising a visit in the near future.
3. Leaving the house, the front door was locked.
4. To paint memorable pictures, the colours should be vivid.
5. Having repeated their vows, the minister married the couple.
6. By following the rules of the road, accidents are less likely to happen.
7. In determining an appropriate university, considering the degrees offered is important.
8. After working on assignments for three hours, the rain began.
9. Knowing how to drive is necessary before getting a driver's licence.
10. Even though expecting a large reward, the money wasn't the main motive.

Chapter 6

Pronouns

Whereas nouns have different endings only for the possessive and the plural, pronouns have a number of forms (cases) that show their relation to other parts of the sentence.

> I [the subject] want **my** [modifier showing possession] cousin to help **me** [direct object].

I, the subject, is in the *subjective* (or nominative) case; *my,* showing possession, is in the *possessive* (or genitive) case; and *me,* the object, is in the *objective* case.

ESL   Unlike many other languages, which include the subject pronoun in the verb, English requires that it be stated, except in certain imperatives. (See **1b(1)**.)

Pronouns also have singular and plural forms.

> **We** [plural subject] want **our** [plural modifier] cousins to help **us** [plural direct object].

The personal pronouns   Personal pronouns identify the speaker (first person: *I, we*), the person spoken to (second person: *you*), and the person or thing spoken about (third person: *he, she, it, they*). The pronouns *I, we, he, she,* and *they* have distinctive forms for all three cases and for both singular and plural. *You* is the same in both singular and plural, and *you* and *it* change case form only in the possessive.

Modifiers that indicate ownership or a comparable relationship are in the **possessive case**. A few possessive pronouns (such as *mine* and *theirs*) sometimes function as nouns.

That book is **mine**.

	Singular	Plural
Subjective	I	we
	you	you
	he, she, it	they
Possessive	my, mine	our, ours
	your, yours	your, yours
	his, her, its	their, theirs
Objective	me	us
	you	you
	him, her, it	them

! CAUTION Although *their* and *they* can be confused in spoken English, *their* is the possessive pronoun, while *they* is subjective. These must be distinguished in written English.

their
~~they~~ book   *their*
~~they~~ house

See Glossary of Usage for confusion of *their, there, they're,* and *there're.*

The pronouns *my, our, your, him, her, it,* and *them* combine with *self* or *selves* to become **intensive/reflexive pronouns**, which are used primarily for emphasis.

Luba, **herself**, showed up for dinner.

Intensive/reflexive pronouns also often refer to a noun or pronoun already mentioned in the sentence. They always follow the person or thing to which they refer.

Luba had a high opinion of **herself**.

! **CAUTION** Do not use *myself* or *me* in place of *I* in a compound subject.

Luba and ~~myself~~ *I* exchanged insults.

Luba and I
~~Me and Luba~~ exchanged insults.

Hisself and *theirselves*, although the logical forms for the reflexive pronouns (possessive plus *-self* as in *myself, yourself, herself*), are not accepted in formal English; instead, use *himself, themselves*.

Luke and Laura drove to Ottawa by ~~theirselves.~~ *themselves*

Relative pronouns Relative pronouns (*what, who, whom, which, whose,* and *that*) introduce clauses that refer to a noun in the main clause.

Julieta, **who** is my sister, lives in Moose Jaw.

Who, whose, and *whom* ordinarily refer to people; *which* to things; and *that* to either. The possessive pronoun *whose* (in place of an awkward *of which*) sometimes refers to things:

The poem, **whose** author is unknown, has recently been set to music.

	Singular or Plural
Subjective	who, which, that
Possessive	whose
Objective	what, whom, which, that

(See also 1e.)

! **CAUTION** Do not confuse *who's* and *whose*. (See Glossary of Usage to distinguish between them.)

6a Pronouns agree with their antecedents.

The subject of a verb and the subject complement are in the **subjective case.**

Subjective   **He** left early. **Who** noticed? [subjects of verbs]

It was **I** on the phone. [subject complement—COMPARE "*I* was on the phone."]

The object of a verb, verbal, or preposition is in the **objective case.**

Objective   Marcella blamed **me.** [direct object]

Telephoning **them** is a nuisance. [object of verbal]

I gave **him** the book. [indirect object]

To **whom** was it addressed? [object of preposition]

Pronouns should agree in number and gender with the noun or phrase (antecedent) to which they refer.

The cousins gave us **their** [plural modifier referring to cousins] help.

George gave us **his** [masculine pronoun referring to George] help willingly. Lucinda, on the other hand, gave us **her** [feminine pronoun referring to Lucinda] help grudgingly.

When referring to a noun that can include both men and women, you can avoid the pronoun *he* by dropping the pronoun.

A student should hand ~~his~~ papers in promptly.

You can also avoid the problem by recasting in the plural, in the passive, or in the imperative.

Students should hand their papers in promptly. [plural]

Papers are to be handed in promptly. [passive]

Hand your papers in promptly. [imperative]

6b Pronouns refer to the nouns immediately preceding them.

Each boldfaced pronoun below clearly refers to its italicized antecedent, which can be a single word or a word group:

> Denying *women* the right to vote clearly denied **them** a voice in choosing who would govern **them** and, equally importantly, denied **them** direct input into the formulation of laws that affected **them**, bestowing that right on men instead.
>
> —MONICA BOYD

> *Perception-checking* is an important communication skill because it helps people arrive at mutual understandings of each other and their relationships.
>
> —JULIA WOOD AND ANGELA HENRY

Without any loss of clarity, a pronoun can often refer to a noun that follows it:

> Unlike **their** predecessors, today's *university and college students* can expect to carry the debt of student loans far into the future.

The meaning of each pronoun should be immediately obvious. To avoid any confusion, repeat the antecedent, use a synonym for it, or recast your sentence.

(1) Clear antecedents

When a pronoun could refer to either of two possible antecedents, the reader is confused. Recasting the sentence or replacing the pronoun with a noun makes the antecedent clear.

In talking with

~~Jean told~~ Pierre, *Jean admitted* that he had made a mistake. [Whom does *he*

refer to?]

The books ˄*that* were standing on the shelf ~~that~~ needed sorting.

[Did the books or the shelf need sorting?]

A pronoun may sometimes clearly refer to two or more antecedents.

Jack and Jill met **their** Waterloo.

(2) Clear references

If a pronoun is too far away from its antecedent, the reader may have to backtrack to get the meaning. A pronoun that refers to a modifier can also obscure meaning. Recasting the sentence to bring a pronoun and its antecedent closer together or substituting a noun for the obscure pronoun will clarify the meaning.

Remote	The *student* found herself the unanimously elected president of a group of animal lovers, *who* was not a joiner of organizations. [*Who* is too far removed from the antecedent *student*. (See also 5a(3).)]
Better	The **student, who** was not a joiner of organizations, found herself the unanimously elected president of a group of animal lovers.
Obscure	Before Ellen could get to the jewellery store, *it* was all sold. [reference to a modifier]
Better	Before Ellen could get to the jewellery store, all the **jewellery** was sold.

(3) Broad or implied references

Pronouns such as *it, this, that, which,* and *such* may refer to a specific word or phrase or to the sense of a whole clause, sentence, or paragraph.

Specific Reference	Irene bent and kissed her on the mouth, on the forehead, then tugged at Jill's collar, adjusting *it* so. —LINDA SVENDSEN [*It* refers to *collar.*]
Broad Reference	Deep inside, whites know that Blacks have a hard time, but will not acknowledge *it*. —HENRY MARTEY CODJOE [*It* refers to the sense of the whole clause.]

When used carelessly, broad references can make writing unclear.

Avoid broad references to an expressed idea.

When class attendance is compulsory, some students feel that education is being forced on them. This is not true. [*This* has no antecedent.]

Make the antecedent explicit rather than implicit.

Lois said that she would stay in Moncton for at least a year. This *remark* suggests that she is happy there. [*This* has no expressed antecedent.]

My father is a music teacher. *Teaching music* It is a profession that requires much patience. [*It* has no expressed antecedent.]

(4) Awkward use of *it* or *you*

Awkward	It was no use trying.
Revised	**There was** no use trying.
	OR
	Trying was useless.

In an informal context, the use of the impersonal, or indefinite, *you* is both natural and acceptable. It is also becoming more acceptable in academic writing. In the following example, *you* is equivalent in meaning to "people in general" or "the reader."

> The study of dreams has become a significant and respectable scientific exploration, one that can directly benefit **you**.
> —PATRICIA GARFIELD

You in this sense is generally still not appropriate in very formal writing.

Avoid the awkward placement of *it* near another *it* with a different meaning.

Awkward	It would be unwise to buy the new model now, but it is a superior machine. [The first *it* is an expletive (see **Glossary of Terms**). The second *it* refers to *model*.]
Revised	Buying the new model now would be unwise, but it is a superior machine.

Exercise 1

Revise the following sentences as necessary to make all references clear. Put a check mark after any sentence that needs no revision.

1. Sandra did not buy a season ticket, which turned out to be a mistake.
2. If you are taken to the courthouse, they will fine you.
3. When the termite eggs are hatched, they grow wings and fly around the country in swarms.
4. In the book it says that the author dislikes anteaters.
5. Sherry decided not to go to the movie, which she came to regret.
6. Everyone has trouble writing, but this is not true when you are excited about your subject.
7. Collette told Li that she was a good friend.

8. Marilyn decided not to attend the reunion, which was a disappointment for our grandparents.
9. When building railroads, the engineers planned embankments for fear that flooding would cover them and make them useless.
10. The increase in tuition discouraged students, which seemed unreasonably high.

6c Pronoun form in compound constructions varies.

Multiple *subjects or subject complements* are in the subjective case.

> **She and her father** buy groceries on Saturday morning.
>
> I thought **he or Dad** would come to my rescue.
>
> It was **Maria and I** who solved the problem. [See 6g.]

The first person pronoun *I* occurs last in a compound construction.

> ~~Me and~~ Omar‸ are good friends.
> *and I*

Multiple objects of prepositions are in the objective case.

> between Merrill and I̶ *me*   with Amanda and I̶ *me*

You can test the case of a pronoun after a preposition by eliminating the accompanying noun or pronoun.

> Gabriel gave it to (Edwyn and) me.

Multiple objects of verbs or verbals and *subjects of infinitives* are in the objective case.

> Clara may appoint **you or me**. [direct object]
>
> They lent **Tom and her** ten dollars. [indirect object]

He gets nowhere by scolding **Bea or him**. [object of gerund]

Dad wanted **Sheila and me** to keep the old car. [subject of the infinitive]

If an appositive follows a pronoun, normal case rules still apply.

We
~~Us~~ students need this.

us
Dylan told ~~we~~ girls to go home.

Exercise 2

Choose the correct pronoun in the parentheses in each of the following sentences. Explain your choice.

1. Two of our friends, Gilroy and (she, her), went on a camping trip last summer.
2. After one day of camping, Gilroy and (she, her) called Juanita and (me, I) to pick them up from the bus terminal.
3. After stopping to visit Juanita and (him, he) in Mississauga, we went to the bus terminal on Elizabeth Street to pick up Gilroy and (she, her).
4. People like Gilroy and (her, she) should never leave the safe confines of the city.
5. The first campsite assigned to (they, them) by the camp warden was overrun with poison ivy.
6. They were assigned a new site by (he, him), but before they had a chance to settle in, a heavy hailstorm began pelting (them, they) with baseball-sized blocks of ice.
7. (Her, She) and (him, he) ran for cover in a nearby forest, leaving their belongings behind.
8. Both (he, him) and (she, her) were lucky to escape as a powerful wind picked up their camping gear and blew it all into the lake.
9. There is a great deal of competition between Gilroy and (I, me, myself), but this time I felt a lot of sympathy for (he, him) and his girlfriend.

10. Since they lost everything, we lent them some money to pay for their bus tickets, knowing they would do the same for (us, ourselves).

6d The use of a pronoun in its own clause determines its case.

(1) *Who* or *whoever* as the subject of a clause

The subject of a verb in a subordinate clause takes the subjective case, even when the whole clause is used as an object:

> I forgot **who** won the game. [*Who* is the subject of the clause *who won the game*. The clause is the object of the verb *forgot*.]

> He has consideration for **whoever** needs his help. [*Whoever* is the subject of the clause *whoever needs his help*. The clause is the object of the preposition *for*.]

(2) *Whom* for all pronouns used as objects in formal written English

Pronouns take their form according to their use in a subordinate clause. *Whom*, the form used for the object of a verb or a preposition in a subordinate clause, is often misused.

> They helped the people ~~who~~ *whom* they liked.

> Gabriel liked all the people ~~who~~ *whom* he met that day.

> This is a friend ~~who~~ *whom* I write to once a year.

> I don't know ~~who~~ *whom* he voted for.

In spoken English, the pronoun *who* is commonly used when it occurs as the first word in the sentence, even when it is the object of a verb or preposition. Dictionaries increasingly accept this usage, although in formal writing it is better to use the traditional *whom* as the object even when it is the first word in a sentence.

Informal	**Who** do you want to speak to?
Formal	**Whom** will they elect premier?

Whom is omitted (or *that* substituted) in sentences where no misunderstanding would result.

The friend he relied on moved away.

The friend that he relied on moved away.

(3) Confusing constructions with *who* or *whom*

Such expressions as *I think, he says, she believes,* and *we know* can follow either *who* or *whom.* The choice depends on the position of *who* or *whom* in its own clause.

Walter picked Jan **who** he knows speaks well. [*Who* is the subject of the verb *speaks.*]

Walter picked Jan **whom** he knows we all respect. [*Whom* is the object of the verb *respect.*]

(4) Pronouns after *than* or *as*

In sentences with implied (rather than stated) elements, the choice of the pronoun form is important to meaning:

She likes Clarice more than **I**. [subjective case, meaning "more than I like Clarice"]

She likes Dana more than **me**. [objective case, meaning "more than she likes me"]

He talks with Jerry as much as **her**. [objective case, meaning "as much as he talks with her"]

Exercise 3

Using the case form in parentheses, convert each pair of sentences in the following paragraph into a single sentence.

¹ᵃFor Maurice Genereux, treating people with AIDS in the country's largest gay community had been a ticket to fame and fortune. ¹ᵇBut last December he became the first Canadian doctor to be convicted of assisting suicide. (who) ²ᵃGenereux, a loner, separated himself from the medical community. ²ᵇOften, he spoke of having served as doctor to the Inuit in a remote Canadian Arctic settlement and of having spent 10 years in Africa. (who) ³ᵃStill, he had a few supporters like Edward Kaminski. ³ᵇThe physician continues to publicly defend Genereux. (who) ⁴ᵃAnd there are the countless patients he treated. ⁴ᵇMany of these people have suffered indescribable pain. (whom) ⁵ᵃThe majority of medical professionals, however, agree with the assessment of a Toronto doctor: "Genereux is not respected in the HIV medical community—or the medical community at large." ⁵ᵇThis physician practises in the gay community and asked not to be identified. (who)

Exercise 4

In the sentences below, insert *I think* after each *who*.

1. It was Margaret Atwood who won the Booker Prize in 2000 for her novel *The Blind Assassin*.
2. Michael Ondaatje, who is the author of *The English Patient*, is the only other Canadian author to win the Booker Prize.
3. Mordecai Richler, who lived in Montreal before he died in 2001, wrote about life in Montreal in such works as *The Apprenticeship of Duddy Kravitz* and *Solomon Gursky Was Here*.

In the following sentences, complete each comparison by using first *I* and then *me*. Explain the difference in meaning.

4. She loves her dog more than _____.
5. Beatrice likes you as much as _____.

6e   A pronoun before a gerund uses the possessive form.

Like nouns, pronouns take the possessive form before a gerund (a verb form ending in *-ing* and used as a noun).

> I appreciated Tom's helping Denise.
> I appreciated ~~him~~ *his* helping Denise.

The *'s* to show possession is often not heard in rapid speech, but it must be included in writing.

> ~~Susan~~ *Susan's* stopwatch

! **CAUTION** The *-ing* ending marks both gerunds and participles. A participle is a verbal used as an adjective; a gerund is a verbal used as a noun. The possessive case precedes gerunds, but not participles. The sentences below have different meanings. In the first sentence *sitting* is a participle modifying *the man* who annoys us; in the second sentence his *sitting* is what annoys us.

> The man sitting (participle modifying *man*) at the desk annoyed us.

> The man's sitting (gerund acting as subject) at the desk annoyed us.

6f   Pronouns use the objective form for the subject or the object of an infinitive.

> They wanted Dave and **me** to help **him**.

6g Pronouns use the subjective form for a subject complement.

That certainly could be **she** sitting near the front. [COMPARE "She could be sitting . . ."]

It was **I** who first noticed the difference. [COMPARE "I first noticed . . ."]

Informal English accepts *It's me* (*him, her, us,* and *them*).

Exercise 5

Following the guidelines for formal written English, choose the appropriate form of the pronouns in parentheses. Remember: choose *whom* when the pronoun functions as an object and *who* when it functions as the subject of a verb or as a subject complement.

1. Josephine thinks she knows (who/whom) in her class is her secret admirer.
2. Maurice cannot possibly be the one (who/whom) is sending her the flowers.
3. When she needs to get picked up from school at night, she knows (who/whom) to call on her cellphone.
4. Do you know (who/whom) I ran into at Martin's the other night?
5. You cannot ask (whoever/whomever) you meet on the street out for dinner and drinks.
6. You always have to be careful with (who/whom) you associate.
7. Is she the English instructor with (who/whom) you talked about publishing your essay?
8. The fundamental question in politics is (who/whom) does what to (who/whom).
9. In Canada, there are people (who/whom) speak several languages fluently.
10. (Whoever/Whomever) I asked for help at the information desk tried to sell me some lottery tickets.

Exercise 6

Find and revise all pronoun forms in the following paragraph that would be inappropriate in formal English. Put a check mark after each sentence that needs no revision.

¹Marcie and Chris wanted Elizabeth and I to go to the movies with them. ²In fact, they wanted us—Elizabeth and I—to choose the movie we would all see. ³As for Elizabeth and I, we both like movies, but Chris and Marcie like them more than we. ⁴Marcie didn't know this, however, and she strongly urged us to come with them. ⁵Moreover, Elizabeth and I, stammering a response, did not suggest to Chris and her that we really didn't want to go with them. ⁶Eventually, I whispered to Elizabeth, "It looks like those two are going to force you and me to go to the movies even though they could go by themselves." ⁷She replied, "Although we really don't have to go, they would probably be mad if we didn't." ⁸Obviously, we two had wanted to do something other than go to the movies, but neither of us actually spoke up. ⁹Unfortunately, the movie was really awful, and Chris and Marcie enjoyed the movie no more than we did, although they generally enjoy movies more than us. ¹⁰When all was said and done, though, it was Elizabeth and I who I blamed for us having a bad time.

Chapter 7 | Verbs

Verbs express the action in a sentence. They show what someone (or something) does (see **1a**), whether the subject is singular or plural and what its relationship to the audience (first, second, or third person) is (see **1b, 7a**), when an action occurred, who did it, and whether it is hypothetical or conditional. They are the heart of a sentence.

Tense   Verbs change form to show whether an action happened in the present, the past, or the future. This change of form is called **tense,** and through tense a verb can show, for example, that one action began yesterday and is still going on, but that another action began yesterday and ended yesterday. English traditionally recognizes six tenses: three simple tenses and three perfect tenses.

Simple Tenses

Present: We often eat nachos.
Past: After the game, we ate nachos.
Future: We will eat nachos after the game.

Perfect Tenses

Present: We have eaten many nachos since the end of the game.
Past: We had eaten many nachos after the game.
Future: We will have eaten many nachos before the game.

A **perfect tense** refers not only to the time in which the action began but also to the time in which the action is completed.

Tenses are based on primary forms called principal parts (*ask, asked, asked, asking*). (See 7b.)

ESL The tenses described above actually refer to time relationships rather than to tense forms (of which English has only two—present and past). To express the idea that an action happened at some unspecified time, English uses the simple tenses, either present or past. To specify how the complex time relationships of completed actions are to be understood, English speakers combine the auxiliary verb *have* with one of the principal parts of the verb to form the perfect tense: *have asked. Will* combines with a different principal part to show future time: *will ask.*

Regular and irregular verbs   The way the past tense of a verb is formed determines its classification as regular or irregular. A **regular verb** takes the *-d* or *-ed* ending to denote the past tense.

Regular   *laugh (laughs), laughed*
           believe (believes), believed

Irregular verbs do not take the *-d* or *-ed* ending. Their past tense is formed in other ways (see pages 90–93).

Irregular   *eat (eats), ate*
             run (runs), ran
             cut (cuts), cut

Auxiliary verbs   **Auxiliary verbs** (or helping verbs) combine with other verbs to indicate tense, voice, or mood. **Modal auxiliary verbs** join the present form of the verb to make requests, give instructions, and express doubt, certainty, necessity, obligation, possibility, or probability.

Checklist of Auxiliary Verbs ✓

Auxiliary Verbs		Modal Auxiliary Verbs	
be	have	shall	may
am	has	should	might
is	had		must
are		will	
was	do	would	can
were	does		could
been	did		
being			

The present form of a verb combines with *shall* or *will* to show the future tense. (See the **Glossary of Usage** for the limited use of *shall*.) *Have* combines with the past participle of a verb to show the perfect tense, and forms of *be* combine with the past participle of a verb to form the passive voice (see page 80). *Be* also combines with the present participle (the *-ing* form of a verb) to show the progressive (an action in progress). *Do* joins the present form of the verb to express emphasis or form questions.

E S L   In English, the present progressive expresses action that is occurring now, whereas the simple present expresses activities that occur at an unspecified time (timeless or habitual present):

I am boiling eggs.	The act of boiling eggs is occurring now.
I boil eggs.	The act of boiling eggs is habitual.

She **will** skate next. [future tense]

She **has** skated already. [perfect tense]

She **is** skating. [present progressive]

She **was** skating. [past progressive]

She **will be** skating. [future progressive]

The song **is** sung often. [passive voice—present tense]

The song **has been** sung often. [passive voice—present perfect tense]

I **do** like my economics class. [emphasis—present tense]

Did he go to economics class? [question—past tense]

I **should** study tonight. [obligation]

I **might** study tonight. [possibility]

In formal writing, *can* refers to ability; *may* refers to permission. (See the **Glossary of Usage**.)

I **can** save the file. [ability]

May I use your phone? [permission]

Although the auxiliary always precedes the basic verb, other words may intervene.

Has the movie **ended**?

Newspapers **will** never completely **replace** gossip.

E S L   In English, when more than one auxiliary precedes a basic verb, the modal comes first, followed by the auxiliary showing perfect tense (*have*), then the progressive form (*been* + *-ing*) or passive voice (*been* + *-ed*).

We should have been basting the turkey more often. [The modal *should* is followed by the perfect tense marker *have* and the progressive *been basting*.]

The turkey should have been basted more often. [The modal *should* is followed by the perfect tense marker *have* and the passive *been basted*.]

Forms of be   The most irregular verb in the English language is *be*. It has eight forms: *am, are, is, was, were, be, been, being*.

That may **be** true.   He **was being** difficult.

Following is a list of forms of *be* used with various subjects in the present and past tenses.

	First	Second	Third	
Present	I am	you are	he/she/it is	[singular]
	we are	you are	they are	[plural]
Past	I was	you were	he/she/it was	[singular]
	we were	you were	they were	[plural]

Some dialects use *be* in place of *am, is,* or *are,* the present forms of *be*. Some dialects also use *be* with the present participle to indicate habitual action. In formal written English, use the conventional forms of *be,* as shown in the list above.

She ~~be~~ *is* a fine hockey player.

He ~~be~~ *is* walking to class.

Be can serve as a linking verb between a subject and its complement. (See **1b**.)

Gabriel **is** a very good student.

E S L   English recognizes two kinds of verbs, those that express states of being (sometimes called **stative** verbs) and those that express action (**dynamic** verbs). Some verbs have two meanings, one stative, the other dynamic:

stative   I have [possess] time to waste.

dynamic   I was having [experiencing] trouble understanding him.

Voice   Voice indicates the relationship between the action of the verb and the subject. Two kinds of relationships are possible: active and passive. **Active voice** emphasizes the subject as the **doer** of the action. **Passive voice** de-emphasizes the doer of the action and makes the subject the **receiver**. (See also **6a, 11d(1)**, and the **Glossary of Terms**.) To make an active verb passive, use the appropriate tense form of *be* with the base verb.

Active   The dog **chases** the cat. [The subject *dog* acts on the object *cat*.]

Passive   The cat **is chased** by the dog. [The subject *cat* is acted upon. The prepositional phrase identifying the doer of the action could be omitted.]

Most writers choose the active voice because it is clearer, more precise, more concise, and more vigorous than the passive. Use passive voice only when you have good reason. (See **11d(1)**.)

Transitive and intransitive verbs   In the examples above, the subject and the object of an active verb (the actor and the receiver of the action) switch places when a verb becomes passive. The subject of a passive verb receives the action. This transformation to passive voice is possible only with verbs that accept a direct object—**transitive verbs**. Although an **intransitive verb** can take a subject complement, it does not accept a direct object and cannot be made passive. (See the **Glossary of Terms**.)

Transitive   The hammer **bent** the nail. [*Nail*, the direct object, receives the action of *hammer*.]

Intransitive   The bell **looks** fragile. [The subject complement, *fragile*, identifies *bell*.]
The bell **feels** smooth. [The predicate adjective *smooth* completes the verb *feels* and modifies the subject *bell*.]

Some verbs can be transitive or intransitive, depending on the sentence.

Transitive   Claudia **studies** the book.

Intransitive Claudia **studies** all night.

A dictionary will indicate if a verb is transitive, intransitive, or both.

Mood   Mood indicates speakers' or writers' attitudes about what they are saying. The **indicative mood** makes statements—a definite attitude; the **imperative mood** issues commands or requests—an insistent attitude; and the **subjunctive mood** expresses situations that are hypothetical or conditional—a tentative attitude. (See also 7d.)

The following conjugation of the verb *see* shows the relationships among tense, person, voice, and mood. It also shows how auxiliary verbs help make a verb passive and also form the perfect tenses.

THE CONJUGATION OF A VERB

Indicative Mood

Active Voice   *Passive Voice*

Present Tense

Singular	*Plural*	*Singular*	*Plural*
1. I see	we see	I am seen	we are seen
2. you see	you see	you are seen	you are seen
3. one (he/she/it) sees	they see	one (he/she/it) is seen	they are seen

Past Tense

1. I saw	we saw	I was seen	we were seen
2. you saw	you saw	you were seen	you were seen
3. one saw	they saw	one was seen	they were seen

Future Tense

1. I shall (will) see | we shall (will) see | I shall (will) be seen | we shall (will) be seen
2. you will see | you will see | you will be seen | you will be seen
3. one will see | they will see | one will be seen | they will be seen

Present Perfect Tense

1. I have seen | we have seen | I have been seen | we have been seen
2. you have seen | you have seen | you have been seen | you have been seen
3. one has seen | they have seen | one has been seen | they have been seen

Past Perfect Tense

1. I had seen | we had seen | I had been seen | we had been seen
2. you had seen | you had seen | you had been seen | you had been seen
3. one had seen | they had seen | one had been seen | they had been seen

Future Perfect Tense
(seldom used)

1. I shall (will) have seen | we shall (will) have seen | I shall (will) have been seen | we shall (will) have been seen
2. you will have seen | you will have seen | you will have been seen | you will have been seen
3. one will have seen | they will have seen | one will have been seen | they will have been seen

Imperative Mood

Present Tense

See.   Be seen.

Subjunctive Mood

Active Voice   **Passive Voice**

Present Tense

Singular if I, you, one see   if I, you, one be seen
Plural   if we, you, they see   if we, you, they are seen

Past Tense

Singular if I, you, one saw   if I, you, one were seen
Plural   if we, you, they saw   if we, you, they were seen

Present Perfect Tense

Singular if I, you, one have   if I, you, one have been
            seen   seen
Plural   if we, you, they have   if we, you, they have been
            seen   seen

Past Perfect Tense (same as the Indicative)

7a Verbs must agree with their subjects.

Agree means that the subject and verb must match. That is, if a subject is plural, the verb must have a plural form, and if the subject is singular, the verb must have a singular form. (If you cannot easily recognize verbs and their subjects, study 1a and 1b.)

Singular   The **monkey** in the cage **is** sleeping. [*monkey is*]
Plural   The **monkeys** in the cage **are** sleeping. [*monkeys are*]

Because only present-tense verbs change form to indicate the number and person of their subjects, most problems with subject-verb agreement occur when present tense is used. It is easy to confuse the endings of *verbs* (where -s indicates **singular**) with those of *nouns* (where it indicates **plural**).

subject + *s*	verb + *s*
The puppies need hugs.	The puppy needs hugs.
Zinnias bloom best in the sun.	A zinnia blooms best in the sun.

If the subject of your sentence is singular but is not *I* or *you*, the verb needs the -s ending:

That talk-show host asks silly questions. [The sound of the -*s* may be masked in speech if the word that follows begins with an *s*.]

E S L Although some languages do not permit clusters of more than one consonant at the end of a word (such as the *sks* in *asks*), English requires the addition of an -*s* to make most nouns plural and to form third-person singular verbs.

 Since grammar checkers cannot catch agreement errors, it pays to be alert for situations that cause them.

(1) Other words between the subject and the verb

The **rhythm** of the pounding waves **is** calming. [*Waves* is the object of a prepositional phrase, not the subject.]

All of the dogs in the neighbourhood **were barking**. [*Dogs* and *neighbourhood* are both objects of prepositional phrases. *All* is the subject.]

Phrases such as *accompanied by, along with, as well as, in addition to, including, no less than, not to mention,* and *together with* generally introduce a prepositional phrase and do not affect the number of the subject.

David as well as my friends **wins** frequently at bingo.

My **friends** as well as David **win** frequently at bingo.

(2) Endings of subjects and verbs not clearly sounded in rapid speech

Economists seem concerned. [might sound like **Economist seem** concerned, but the former is correct]

asks
She ~~ask~~ Sybil first.

(3) Subjects joined by *and*

My two best **friends** and my **fiancé hate** each other.

The **coach** and the **umpire were** at home plate.

Writing on a legal pad and **writing with a computer are** not the same at all. [gerund phrases—COMPARE "Two actions are not the same."]

A compound subject that refers to a single person or unit takes a singular verb.

The **founder and president** of the art association **was** elected to the board of the museum.

The **co-creator and first artist** of *Superman* **was** Joe Shuster.

(4) Subjects joined by *either . . . or*

Fido or Rex **barks** a lot when we are not home.

Neither Bret nor Candice **has** volunteered to unclog the toilet.

Either Jo or Shola **is** working in the ICU tonight.

If one subject is singular and one is plural, the verb agrees with the subject nearer to the verb.

Neither the doctor nor the **nurses were** on duty.

Neither the nurses nor the **doctor was** on duty.

The verb also agrees in person with the nearer subject.

Either Oswald or **you are** going to apologize.

Either you or **Oswald is** going to apologize.

(5) Inverted word order or *there* + *verb* constructions

VERB + SUBJECT

Hardest hit by the snows and sub-zero temperatures **were** the large **cities** of the Maritimes.

There + **VERB + SUBJECT**

There **are** several **ways** to protect yourself from a tornado.

(6) Relative pronouns (*who, which, that*) used as subjects

Meighen Centre, which is the computer science building, is always open.

It is the **doctor who** often **suggests** a diet.

It is among the **books that are** out of print.

This is the only **store that gives** triple coupons. [COMPARE "Only one store gives triple coupons."]

It is not bigger discounts but **better service that makes** the store successful. [COMPARE "Better service (not bigger discounts) makes the store successful."]

He is one of **those who agree** with my decision. [*Who* refers to *those*, a plural pronoun. The plural form of the verb is necessary for agreement.]

(7) *Either, one, everybody, all, any, some, none,* and other such indefinite pronouns

Each, either, one, everybody, and *anyone* are considered singular and so require singular verbs.

Either of them **is willing** to shovel the driveway.

Each has bought a first-class ticket.

Everybody in our apartment building **has** a parking place.

Depending on the sentence, *all, any, some, none, half,* and *most* can be either singular or plural.

Wendy collects comic books; **some are** very valuable. [COMPARE "Some comic books are very valuable."]

The bank would not take the money because **some was** foreign. [COMPARE "Some money was foreign."]

Use a singular verb with singular subjects preceded by *every* or *each* and joined by *and:*

Every cat and dog in the county **has** to be vaccinated.

Each fork and spoon **has** to be dried carefully.

Placing *each* after a plural subject does not affect the verb form:

The cat and the dog **each have** their good points.

(8) Collective nouns and phrases

Collective nouns and phrases refer to a group of individual things as a unit. (See 1c.) Whether they require a singular or a plural verb depends on whether the sentence refers to the group as a whole or to the individual items in the collection.

Singular (regarded as a unit):

> The **committee is** meeting today.
>
> **Four million litres is** a lot of oil.
>
> The **jury convenes** today.
>
> The **number is** very small.

Plural (regarded as individuals or parts):

> The **majority** of us **are** in favour.
>
> **Four million litres** of oil **were spilled.**
>
> A **number were** absent.

Although the use of *data* and *media* as singular nouns (instead of *datum* and *medium*) has gained currency in informal English, most writers still use *data* and *media* as plural nouns in formal written English.

Formal	The media **have** shaped public opinion.
Informal	The media **has** shaped public opinion.
Formal	The data **are** in the appendix.
Informal	The data **is** in the appendix.

(9) Linking verbs

Linking verbs include the forms of *be* (*am, is, are, was, were, being, been*), the verbs referring to the senses (*look, feel, smell, sound, taste*), and some others such as *appear, become, grow, make, prove, remain,* and *seem*.

> The **bread machine is** louder than a truck.

That **student looks** confused.

Pizza and **apples seem** inappropriate for breakfast.

Because the pronoun *what* is singular or plural depending on whether the word (or word group) it refers to is singular or plural, the verb agrees with its complement in sentences like these:

What I think **is** my own **business.**

What our parents gave us **were memories** to be cherished.

(10) **Titles of single works, words spoken of as words, nouns plural in form but singular in meaning**

Romeo and Juliet **sticks** in the memory. [The play itself, not the characters in it, sticks in the memory.]

Kids **is** informal for *children.*

Nouns that look plural but are treated as singular include *economics, electronics, mathematics, measles, mumps, news,* and *physics.*

Measles **is** a serious disease.

Economics **is** important for a business major.

Some nouns (such as *athletics, politics, series, deer,* and *sheep*) can be either singular or plural, depending on the meaning:

Statistics is an interesting subject. **Statistics are** often misleading.

A **series** of natural disasters **has** occurred recently. Two **series** of natural disasters **have** occurred recently.

The **sheep strays** when the gate is left open. **Sheep stray** when the gate is left open.

Exercise 1

Use each of the following to make a complete sentence. Be sure that subjects and verbs agree.

1. My cellphone and pager . . .
2. It is my English professor who . . .
3. Neither the (plural subject) nor (singular subject) . . .
4. Anybody . . .
5. The congregation of Hutterites . . .

7b Verbs have at least three principal parts.

The three principal parts of verbs are the simple present form (*see*), which is also part of the infinitive (*to see*); the past form (*saw*); and the past participle (*seen*). (See **principal parts** in the **Glossary of Terms**.) The present participle (*seeing*) is often considered a fourth principal part.

The **present form** can be a single-word verb (*demand*) or a combination of a single-word verb and a helping verb (*is demanding, can demand*). In the case of regular verbs, the **past form** can also be a single-word verb with -*d* or -*ed* (*demanded*). (See page 76.) It can be combined with helping verbs (*might have demanded*).

This checklist of principal parts includes regular and irregular verbs that are sometimes misused.

Checklist of Principal Parts of Verbs		✓
Present	**Past**	**Past Participle**
arise	arose	arisen
ask	asked	asked

continued

continued from previous page

		✓
attack	attacked	attacked
awake	awoke OR awaked	awaked
bear	bore	borne/born
begin	began	begun
blow	blew	blown
break	broke	broken
bring	brought	brought
burst	burst	burst
choose	chose	chosen
cling	clung	clung
come	came	come
dive	dived OR dove	dived
do	did	done
drag	dragged	dragged
draw	drew	drawn
drink	drank	drunk
drive	drove	driven
drown	drowned	drowned
eat	ate	eaten
fall	fell	fallen
fly	flew	flown
forgive	forgave	forgiven
freeze	froze	frozen
get	got	got OR gotten
give	gave	given
go	went	gone
grow	grew	grown
hang (things)	hung	hung
hang (people)	hanged	hanged
happen	happened	happened
know	knew	known
ride	rode	ridden
ring	rang	rung
rise	rose	risen

continued

continued from previous page

run	ran	run	✓
see	saw	seen	
shake	shook	shaken	
shrink	shrank OR shrunk	shrunk OR shrunken	
sing	sang OR sung	sung	
sink	sank OR sunk	sunk	
speak	spoke	spoken	
spin	spun	spun	
spit	spat	spat	
spring	sprang OR sprung	sprung	
steal	stole	stolen	
sting	stung	stung	
stink	stank OR stunk	stunk	
strive	strove OR strived	striven OR strived	
swear	swore	sworn	
swim	swam	swum	
swing	swung	swung	
take	took	taken	
tear	tore	torn	
throw	threw	thrown	
wake	woke OR waked	woken OR waked	
wear	wore	worn	
weave	wove	woven	
wring	wrung	wrung	
write	wrote	written	

Some troublesome verbs, especially the following, are easy to confuse and tricky to spell:

PRINCIPAL PARTS OF TROUBLESOME VERBS

Present	Past	Past Participle	Present Participle
lay	laid	laid	laying
lead	led	led	leading
lie	lay	lain	lying

loosen	loosened	loosened	loosening
lose	lost	lost	losing
pay	paid	paid	paying
set	set	set	setting
sit	sat	sat	sitting
study	studied	studied	studying

Exercise 2

Respond to the questions written in the past tense with a past tense verb; respond to the questions in the future tense with a present perfect verb (*have* or *has* + past participle). Follow the pattern of the examples.

EXAMPLES
Did it really happen? Yes, it really happened.
Will the bubble burst? The bubble has burst.

1. Will they call about the job?
2. Did they call you?
3. Did you phone the travel agent?
4. Will this band ever stop playing?
5. Did she buy a new mirror for her bathroom?
6. Will they bring the car keys?
7. Did Team Canada win the gold medal?
8. Will the women's hockey team win?
9. Did you remember to bring a towel?
10. Has September 11 changed our lives?

Participles in predicates

Participles are never used alone as the predicate of a sentence. When an -*ing* form is part of the predicate, it always has at least one helping verb. Both the past and present participles can work as modifiers and they can also form part of the predicate:

pastries *baked* last week
[past participle]

We *baked* pastries last
week. [sentence]

heat waves *rising* from
the road [present
participle]

Heat waves *rise* from the
road. [sentence]

Be especially careful not to confuse nouns modified by participles with actual sentences. (See 2a.)

When the subject causes the action, combine the helping verb with the *-ing* form (**present participle**); when the subject is affected by the action, use the *-ed* form (**past participle**). These forms are sometimes referred to as *present progressive* and *past progressive* tenses.

She **was filing** the briefs. [subject acts]

The briefs **were being filed**. [subject acted upon]

He **has asked** them. I **was asked**. I **will be asking** questions.

They **have begun**. **Had** he **begun**? It **is beginning** to snow.

⚠ CAUTION   Although it is easy to remember a clearly pronounced *-d* or *-ed* (*added, repeated*), it is sometimes harder to remember a needed *-d* or *-ed* in such expressions as *supposed to* or *used to* when the sound is not emphasized in speech. (See 4b.)

Yesterday, I ~~ask~~ *asked* myself, Is the judge prejudice*d*?

He ~~use~~ *used* to smoke.

I am not ~~suppose~~ *supposed* to be the boss.

She ~~talk~~ *talked* to Ellen yesterday.

7c   Tense forms express differences in time.

(1) The meaning of tense forms

Although **tenses** refer to time (see page 75), the actual tense forms often do not point to specific divisions of actual time. For instance, as the following examples show, the present tense form is certainly not restricted to present time. It can refer to past and future occurrences as well. Furthermore, auxiliaries and other words in the sentence can also indicate time.

Present tense (timeless or habitual present, now)

> I **see** what you meant by that remark.
>
> Dana **uses** common sense. [habitual action]
>
> Mistakes **are** often **made.** [passive verb, habitual action]
>
> Blind innocence **sees** no evil. [universal or timeless truth]
>
> In 1939 Hitler **attacks** Poland. [historic present]
>
> Joseph Conrad **writes** about what he **sees** in the human heart. [literary present]
>
> The store **opens** next week. [present form, used with the adverbial *next week* to denote future time]
>
> I **am trying** to form an opinion. [present progressive form indicating action occurring now]

Past tense (past time, not extending to the present)

> I **ate** the cake.
>
> They **played** a good game.
>
> We **were continuing** our work. [continuing action in the past]
>
> The paper **was reviewed** by two people. [passive]

Kareem **used to be** happy. [COMPARE "Kareem was happy then."]

Future tense (at a future time, sometime after now)

We **will see** the movie.

Shall we **try** a different road?

He **will be having** his dinner. [progressive]

A different colour **will be used**. [passive]

Present perfect tense (sometime before now, up to now)

I **have taken** the prize.

She **has** consistently **broken** her previous records.

Has Michelle **been using** her talents? [progressive]

Deer **have been seen** in those woods. [passive]

Past perfect tense (before a specific time in the past)

Terese **had planned** to meet with me before school.

After Shawn **had left** for work, he realized it was a holiday.

Had they **been sailing** along the coast? [progressive]

He **had been interviewed** by the police before the arrest. [passive]

When they married, they **had known** each other for ten years.

Sometimes the simple past can replace the past perfect.

Daphne **had talked** [or **talked**] to me before class started.

Future perfect tense (before a specific time in the future)

Our bumpers **will have rusted** by the time he changes his mind.

The future perfect is almost always replaced by the simple future.

After graduation, I **will have seen** [or **will see**] my dreams come true.

Exercise 3

For each sentence, explain the differences in the meaning of the tense forms separated by slashes.

1. It has rained/had rained for days.
2. Jean cut/did cut/was cutting her hair.
3. My mother-in-law had bought/will have bought the car by then.
4. Time flies/does fly/has flown/had been flying by rapidly.
5. Margaret Laurence writes/wrote of a woman's relationship with her family in *The Stone Angel*.

(2) Logical sequence of tense forms

Combinations of tense forms can make very fine distinctions in relation to actual time.

> When the speaker **finished,** everyone **applauded.** [Both actions took place at the same definite time in the past.]

> Collette **has stopped walking** at night because she **had heard** that several women were mugged. [Both forms indicate action at some time before now, but *had heard* indicates a time before the action indicated by *has stopped.*]

> I **had been** here for two weeks when I **learned** that my application for financial aid **had been denied.** [The *had* before *been* indicates a time before the action described by *learned* and *denied.*]

Infinitives The present infinitive expresses action occurring at the same time as, or later than, that of the main verb; the present perfect infinitive shows action that occurred before the time shown by the main verb:

> I want **to show** you my new trick. [present infinitive—for the same time as the main verb, *want*]

> He preferred **to go** home. [present infinitive—for time later than *preferred*]

I would like **to have won** first place. [present perfect infinitive—for time before the main verb *would like*. COMPARE "I wish I *had won*."]

ESL   *Infinitive and gerund phrases after verbs*   Although there is no set rule for the correct usage, certain verbs are followed by infinitives, and others by gerunds.

I offered **to help** her.

I avoided **calling** her.

Some of the most common verbs followed by a gerund are *appreciate, avoid, consider, delay, discuss, enjoy, finish, keep (on), mention, mind, postpone,* and *suggest.*

I **mind missing** the party.

Some of the most common verbs followed by an infinitive are *agree, appear, ask, decide, expect, intend, need, plan, pretend, promise, refuse,* and *want.*

I **decided to go** home.

Some verbs that are followed by a noun or a pronoun plus an infinitive are *advise, allow, ask, encourage, expect, force, invite, remind, require,* and *want.*

I **encouraged** Pavi **to study** with her.

The verb *go* is followed by the gerund in certain expressions that for the most part concern recreational activities.

Let's **go swimming**.

Participles   The present form of participles expresses action occurring at the same time as that of the main verb; the present perfect form indicates action that took place before that of the main verb:

Planning for the election, he decided what he should advocate. [The planning and deciding were simultaneous.]

Having built the house themselves, they felt a real sense of pride. [The building took place first; then came their sense of pride.]

Exercise 4

In the following paragraph, insert the appropriate form of the word in parentheses so that the events in the paragraph form a logical sequence.

[1]Last night I (going) (seeing) the school's spring revue. [2]When I (arriving) at the auditorium, everyone (standing) in line (waiting) (getting) in. [3]As soon as the doors (opening) everyone (rushing) (finding) their seats. [4]I (finding) mine right away and (sitting) down, but I (standing) up often for all the other people who (sitting) in my row. [5]After the lights (dimming), the music (beginning), and the curtains (opening), the cast (beginning) (singing) and (dancing) and I (losing) all track of time until the curtain (coming) down for the intermission. [6]After the intermission, an entirely different cast (performing) from the one that (beginning). [7]I (being) (startling) until I (remembering) the article in the campus paper that (reporting) how a dispute between the producer and the director (is settling).

 7d   Although rare, the subjunctive mood is still used for specific purposes.

The subjunctive mood, though rare, still occurs in fixed expressions such as *so be it, be that as it may, as it were,* and *God bless you* and is also used to express certain other meanings.

Forms for the subjunctive

For the verb *be:*

> PRESENT, singular or plural: **be**
>
> PAST, singular or plural: **were**

For all other verbs with third-person singular subjects, the subjunctive omits the characteristic -*s* ending:

> PRESENT, singular only: **see** [The -*s* ending is dropped.]

Examples
It is important that Nancy **see** me first.
Suppose we **were** to leave before she does.
The Crown prosecutor insisted that the witness not **avoid** the question.

Alternatives
Nancy **has to see** me first.
Suppose we **leave** before she does.
The Crown prosecutor urged the witness not **to avoid** the question.

Should and *would* (past forms of *shall* and *will*) are also used for the subjunctive.

Subjunctives are used under the following conditions:

1. **After *that* with such verbs as *demand, recommend, urge, insist, request, suggest, move***

   I demand that the parking ticket **be** voided.

   I suggested that she **move** to a new apartment.

   The committee requested that we **adjourn.** [COMPARE "The committee wanted to adjourn."]

2. **To express wishes or (in *if* or *as if* clauses) a hypothetical, highly improbable, or contrary-to-fact condition**

   I wish I **were** in Trois Rivières.

If I **were** you, I'd accept the offer.

Eat as if every meal **were** your last.

Although formal English still calls for *should* in conditional clauses, informal English accepts *would,* just as it accepts *will* instead of *shall*—except in questions such as "Shall we go?"

I would think she felt rich enough.

3. As *had* rather than *would have* in *if* clauses expressing an imagined condition

If he ~~would have~~ *had* arrived earlier, he wouldn't have lost the sale.

OR

Had ~~If~~ he ~~would have~~ arrived earlier, he wouldn't have lost the sale.

Exercise 5

Explain the use of the subjunctive in the following sentences in each of these situations: (a) a formal letter of application and (b) an informal letter to a friend.

1. Had Linda been here, she would have explained everything.
2. She insisted that Victor be heard.
3. I wish that Laurette were here.
4. If there should be a change in policy, we would have to make major adjustments.

Exercise 6

Compose five sentences illustrating various uses of the subjunctive.

7e   **Unnecessary shifts in tense or mood can confuse readers. (See also 8e.)**

He *came* to the meeting and ~~tries~~ *tried* to take over. [shift in tense from past to present]

It is necessary to restrain an occasional foolhardy park visitor. If a female bear *were* to mistake his friendly intentions and *supposes* him a menace to her cubs, he would be in trouble. [shift in mood from subjunctive to indicative] But females with cubs ~~were~~ *are* only one of the dangers. [a correct sentence if standing alone, but inconsistent here with the present tense in the preceding sentence and therefore misleading] All bears are wild animals and not domesticated pets. It is therefore an important part of the park ranger's duty to watch the tourists and above all ~~don't~~ *not to* let anyone try to feed the bears. [shift in mood from indicative to imperative]

Exercise 7

Look carefully at the following passage to note any errors or inconsistencies in tense and mood or other problems with verb usage and revise as needed.

¹It is hard for me to realize that it were only three years ago that I first begin to send e-mail to my friends. ²Today I got most of my mail online, and I also did much of my other business online, too. ³For instance, I can paying my bills electronically since I had an account at an electronic

bank, and I can also ordering almost any thing I wanted from a catalogue that I could have looked at on the World Wide Web. [4]I even buys my last car online. [5]Of course, I go to a dealer and drove a model that I like first, but then I order the car on the Web. [6]It was less expensive, and I didn't have the hassle of dealing with a pushy salesperson.

[7]One of the best things about the electronic revolution, though, is the way it was changing the academic world. [8]My World Civilizations class meets online in a special chat room calls a MOO (for Multiple-user dungeon Object Oriented), and we also will look at the various sites on the World Wide Web that showed pictures of archaeological digs (like the one on the Mayans), architecture, and so on. [9]Taking a history class this way makes it lived for me. [10]It also makes my Shakespeare class more interesting. [11]I will look at the William Shakespeare pages on the World Wide Web and can find comments that famous scholars will make and citations to books and articles that helped me understanding the plays better. [12]I don't think I will have taken the time to go to the library for the same material— and it wouldn't have been as much fun to look at, either.

Effective Sentences

Chapter 8

Sentence Unity: Consistency

Good writing is unified and sticks to its purpose. It does not contain unrelated ideas, mixed constructions, or faulty predication. It is consistent throughout, with no shifts in grammatical structure, tone, style, or viewpoint.

8a   Making the relationship of ideas in a sentence immediately clear helps the reader.

Unrelated   My cousin graduated recently, but must repay her library fines. [unity thwarted by a gap in thought]

Related   My cousin graduated recently, but **to receive her diploma** she must repay her library fines.

8b   Arranging details in a clear sequence makes your point clear.

The first sentence below has excessive detail. Although detail usually makes writing more interesting, too much can be distracting. Do not include details that are not necessary to develop the point that you are making.

Excessive	When I was only 17, I left home to attend a university that was nearby and that my uncle had graduated from 20 years earlier.
Clear	I left home when I was only 17 to attend a nearby university. [If the detail about the uncle is important, include it in another sentence. If not, delete it.]

When getting rid of excessive details, remember that length alone does not make a sentence ineffective. Sometimes you may need a long sentence in which every detail contributes to the central thought. Parallel structure (see chapter 10), balance, rhythm, effectively repeated connectives, and careful punctuation can make even a paragraph-length sentence coherent.

> They went up the street at a walk, the slow, sombre pace of a funeral procession, past the shuttered house Fort Benton's merchant prince, I.G. Baker, had built so his wife would not have to give birth to their first baby in the fort, past the ox wagons and trailers parked by the warehouses, past the sporting and gaming houses at this hour black as the heart of sin, past the old adobe fort which had stood godfather to the town, its four massive blockhouses featureless and blank but for the rifle slits in the walls.
>
> —GUY VANDERHAEGHE, *The Englishman's Boy*

Exercise 1

All the sentences below contain apparently unrelated ideas. Adding words when necessary, rewrite each sentence to indicate a logical relationship between the ideas. If you cannot establish a close relationship, put the ideas in separate sentences.

1. We moved into an apartment in Chinatown that was convenient because it was centrally located and because we became tired of ordering pizza all the time.

2. I read Ann-Marie MacDonald's book *Fall on Your Knees* for an English class that focussed on eastern Canadian writers, but her writing was different in a lot of ways from the work of Alistair MacLeod.

3. In the summertime, he worked as a tree planter in northern Ontario near a town to where his sister would eventually move three years later.

4. The mountain climbers set off to conquer Mt. Logan, and had dinner with their parents before they departed.

5. The hamburgers at the Gristle Pit were among the worst they had ever had, and most of the customers could not get enough of them.

Exercise 2

Revise each sentence in the following passage to eliminate excessive detail.

[1]I have never seen a place that was as filled with history that had been passed along by various family members who cherished every moment of it. [2]Finally I returned to the place where I had lived for years, which had been built decades before my birth.

[3]The old farm, considered a model of technological advances only 30 years before, but then in need of paint and repairs, as is so often the case with places long inhabited, had to be renovated for future use. [4]Because of this, when I was eight years old, sleeping in the bedroom at the far north corner of the main house, because the larger bedrooms were occupied by my older brothers and sisters, my parents decided that they wanted to move us to a more modern home located in the suburbs of the city. [5]The renovation of the old farm lasted only a few years, which really seemed much longer than that but made us appreciate our history, as many fail to do until it is too late.

8c Mixed metaphors and mixed constructions are illogical.

(1) Mixed metaphors

A **mixed metaphor** combines different images, creating an illogical comparison.

Mixed	Her climb up the ladder of success was nipped in the bud.
Revised	She slipped on her climb up the ladder of success.
	OR
	Before her career could blossom, it was nipped in the bud.

(2) Mixed constructions

A sentence that begins with one kind of construction and shifts to another is a **mixed construction**. (See also **8d** and **8e**.) Mixed constructions often omit the subject or the predicate.

Mixed	When Ajanta plays the accordion attracts the audience's attention. [adverb clause + predicate; no subject]
Revised	When Ajanta plays the accordion, she attracts the audience's attention. [adverb clause + main clause]
	OR
	Ajanta's playing of the accordion attracts the audience's attention. [subject + predicate]
Mixed	It was an old ramshackle house but that was quite livable.
Revised	It was an old ramshackle house, but it was quite livable. [main clause + independent clause]

OR

It was an old ramshackle house that was quite
livable. [noun + adjective clause]

8d   Faulty predication can lead to problems.

Faulty predication occurs when the subject and predicate
do not fit together logically.

Faulty   One book I read believes in eliminating subsidies.
            [A person, not a thing, believes.]

Revised   The author of one book I read believes in elimi-
            nating subsidies.

Faulty   An example of discrimination is an apartment
            owner, especially after he has refused to rent to
            people with children. [The refusal, not the owner,
            is an example of discrimination.]

Revised   An example of discrimination is an apartment
            owner's refusal to rent to people with children.

8e   Unnecessary shifts are disconcerting.

Avoid abrupt, unnecessary shifts—for example, from past
to present, from singular to plural, from formal diction to
slang, or from one perspective to another. Such inconsistencies make reading difficult and obscure the meaning.

(1) **Faulty** *is . . . when, is . . . where,* or *is . . . because*
    constructions

Constructions combining *is* with *when, where,* or *because*
are often illogical since forms of *to be* signify identity or
equality between the subject and what follows.

Faulty   The reason the package arrived so late is because he didn't mail it soon enough.

Revised   The package arrived so late because he didn't mail it soon enough.

(2) Consistent tense, mood, and person

Marcus **believed** in hydraulic power while Mary ~~believes~~ *believed* in solar power. [both verbs in the past tense]

If I **were** not so stupid and he ~~was~~ *were* not so naïve, we would have known better. [both verbs in the subjunctive mood]

I had to exercise daily and ∧*I especially despised* the rowing **machine** ~~was especially despised.~~ [persons made consistent]

When using the literary or historical present, avoid slipping from the present into the past tense. (See the Glossary of Terms.)

Romeo and Juliet **fall** in love at first sight, **marry** secretly, and ~~died~~ *die* together in the tomb within the same hour. [verbs in present tense]

(3) Consistent person and number (See also 6a **and** 6b.)

If ~~a person is~~ *you are* going to improve, you should work harder. [Both subjects are in the second person.]

The team is counting on winning ~~their~~ *its* game. [The subject, verb, and possessive pronoun are all singular.]

(4) Shifts between direct and indirect discourse (See also 10a.)

Janet wondered how the thief got the computer out and why
he didn't
~~didn't he~~ steal the TV.

Her assistant said, "She's out," and "would *you* I please wait?"

(5) Consistent tone and style

It seemed to Romeo, as he gazed up at the balcony, that
a lily
Juliet's face was as white as ~~the underbelly of a fish~~.

(6) Consistent perspective and viewpoint

Standing on the shore, I could see the speedboats hurrying
later, standing　　*I could see*
past and ‸ on the small island, ‸ the gulls bouncing on the waves.

Exercise 3

Correct all unnecessary shifts. Put a check mark after any sentence that needs no revision.

1. I could hardly move at the party, so I said to Celina, "Wow, it's really crowded" and "we should leave soon."
2. There was not enough to finish painting the hallway, so Jason decides not to do it.
3. We spent our days travelling around the countryside around Prince Edward Island, and the nights were spent experiencing the local pubs.
4. From the pier, we could see the ferry carrying people to Toronto Island and from the CN Tower the lights of Rochester, New York.
5. Whenever Barbara's cat walked into the room, Frank's eyes begin itching and his skin turns red.
6. The reason we did not get the package on Thursday is because we had to leave for work early and come home late.

7. After retiring from his job as a teacher, our bellicose neighbour began to devote himself to cultivating peonies and entering his prized blooms in flower and gardening shows.

8. Dennis felt that the movie's dialogue was weak while Mehri feels the special effects dominated the good acting.

9. I have seen many colours of peonies, but red is a colour I've hardly saw.

10. We packed up our belongings, moved to our new house, and unpack all in one weekend.

Exercise 4

Revise the following paragraph to eliminate all unnecessary shifts.

¹She was an honest young woman, it always seemed to me. ²She has an astonishingly open manner, and her face suggests a wisdom beyond her years. ³She said that I always try to speak my mind but tried to be diplomatic. ⁴Nevertheless, she will let it be seen that she is not voicing her entire opinion. ⁵Take these observations and use them wisely; it may help one in interpreting this woman's true thoughts.

Chapter 9

Subordination and Co-ordination

Subordination and **co-ordination** establish clear structural relationships between ideas. Subordinate structures— phrases, appositives, or subordinate clauses—make the ideas they express appear less important than ideas expressed in main independent clauses. In the following sentence, the subordinate clause is italicized; the main clause containing the main idea is boldfaced.

> *Since it was pouring rain,* **the game was cancelled.**

When two ideas in a sentence are equal, they are expressed in co-ordinate structures (**SUBJECT + PREDICATE**, and **SUBJECT + PREDICATE**). In the following example, ideas of equal importance are expressed in co-ordinate structures—two main clauses.

> They did their best, and they ran the course.

Co-ordination in words and phrases also gives equal structural emphasis to equal ideas.

> a **stunning** and **unexpected** conclusion [co-ordinating adjectives]
>
> **in the attic** or **in the basement** [compound prepositional phrases]

(See **1d** and **1e** for an explanation of the difference between phrases and clauses and between subordinate and main clauses.)

9a Careful subordination can combine a series of related short sentences into longer, more effective units.

Choppy I was exhausted from work. I put my feet up on the sofa. I wanted to take a nap. The budgies were making too much noise. I covered up their cage. They still made too much noise. I put them outside on the veranda. I fell asleep. A strong wind blew. It tipped over the cage. The cage crashed on the cement. I woke up. The budgies had escaped. We heard them squawking. They were in the nearby trees for weeks after.

Better I was exhausted from work, so I put my feet up on the sofa to take a nap. The budgies, however, were making too much noise. I covered up their cage, but they still made too much noise. Then I decided to put them out on the veranda. Just as I fell asleep, a strong wind blew, tipping over the cage. It crashed on the cement, and the noise woke me up. The budgies had escaped, but we heard them squawking in the nearby trees for weeks after.

When combining a series of related sentences, select the main idea, express it in the structure of a base sentence (**SUBJECT + PREDICATE**) and use some of the following subordinate structures to relate less important ideas to the main one.

(1) Adjectives and adjective phrases

Choppy The limbs were covered with ice. They sparkled in the sunlight. They made a breathtaking sight.

Better **Sparkling in the sunlight**, the **ice-covered** limbs made a breathtaking sight. [participial phrase and hyphenated adjective]

(2) Adverbs and adverb phrases

Choppy   Sand the surface you want to paint. Use fine-grade sandpaper. Clean the surface. Use a damp cloth.

Better   After sanding with fine-grade sandpaper the surface you want to paint, use a damp cloth to clean the surface.

OR

Use fine-grade sandpaper to sand the surface you want to paint, then clean the surface with a damp cloth.

Choppy   The car was covered in scratches. And with dents. It looked like a wreck.

Better   Covered in scratches and dents, the car looked like a wreck. [The first two sentences are combined in an absolute phrase.] (See **absolute phrase** in the **Glossary of Terms.**)

(3) Appositives and contrasting elements

Choppy   His behaviour at the party was rude and obnoxious. He was drunk. Everybody felt embarrassed.

Better   Everybody felt embarrassed by his rude, obnoxious, and drunken behaviour at the party.

(4) Subordinate clauses

Subordinate clauses are linked and related to main clauses by markers (subordinating conjunctions and relative pronouns) that signal whether a clause is related to the base sentence by **time** (*after, before, since, until, when, while*), **place** (*where, wherever*), **reason** (*as, because, how, so that, since*), **condition** (*although, if, unless, whether*), or **additional information** (*that, which, who, whose*). (See page 25 for a list of these markers.)

Choppy	The blizzard ended. Then helicopters headed for the mountaintop. It looked dark and forbidding.
Better	**As soon as the blizzard ended,** helicopters headed for the mountaintop, **which looked dark and forbidding.** [adverb clause and adjective clause]

9b Using subordination and co-ordination is preferable to stringing several main clauses together.

Do not overuse co-ordinating connectives like *and, but, or, so, then, however,* and *therefore.* For ways to revise stringy or loose compound sentences, see **12c.** Methods of subordination that apply to combining two or more sentences (**9a**) also apply to revising faulty or excessive co-ordination in a single sentence.

(1) Subordinate structures for ideas that are less important than main ideas

In the following example, the main idea, expressed in the main clause, is boldfaced; the less important idea, expressed in the subordinate clause, is italicized.

Since he already had a job, **Jim didn't really mind losing the election.**

(2) Co-ordinate structures for ideas of equal importance

The dam broke, and the town was destroyed.

(3) Logical connection of ideas by subordinate and co-ordinate structures

The gasoline tank sprang a leak, ~~when~~ *so* all hope of winning the race was lost.

On your way
~~You can walk~~ to school~~, and~~ you can mail the letter.

⚠ **CAUTION** Do not use *but* or *and* before *which*, *who*, or *whom* when introducing a single adjective clause.

Leela is a musician ~~and~~ who can play several instruments.

9c   Faulty or excessive subordination can confuse the reader.

Faulty   Chen was only a substitute pitcher, winning half of his games.

Better   Although Chen was only a substitute pitcher, he won half of his games. [*Although* establishes the relationship between the ideas.]

Excessive   Some people who are not busy and who are insecure when they are involved in personal relationships worry all the time about whether their friends truly love them.

Better   Some insecure, idle people worry about whether their friends truly love them. [two subordinate clauses reduced to adjectives]

Exercise 1

Observing differences in emphasis, convert each pair of sentences below to (a) a simple sentence, (b) a compound sentence consisting of two main clauses, and (c) a complex sentence with one main clause and one subordinate clause. Be prepared to discuss the most effective revision.

1. In the morning, a cool breeze floated in off the blue ocean. Felix opened the windows of the bedroom to let in the fresh air.

2. Before sitting down to the elegant dinner, the father and daughter argued over who would get the turkey drumstick. The mother reminded them that they would be having ham.

3. Ben and Flora live in an unusual house at the end of Crawford Street. It is painted sky blue and has two white lions on columns near the gate.

4. Liao stopped in Brandon after leaving Winnipeg on a bus. He stayed there for the night.

5. Danielle likes to have a cup of coffee in the morning following her statistics class. She finds that it revives her after the boring lecture.

Exercise 2

Revise the following passage using effective subordination and co-ordination.

[1]Euler House is a residence unit at our university and it is an old building. [2]It is nearer to my classes than the other dorm rooms would be since it is only a five-minute walk to the centre of campus. [3]It has large, spacious bedrooms. [4]It is a good distance away from the stadium and it offers a great deal of privacy to its residents. [5]There's little noise. [6]My room is on the far side of the building. [7]It faces east. [8]It has a balcony overlooking the yard below. [9]There are dark green shrubs that are covered with small white flowers. [10]The place is comfortable and I enjoy living there.

Chapter 10 | Parallelism

Ideas in parallel grammatical form express ideas parallel in meaning. Parallelism contributes to ease in reading by making ideas that are parallel in meaning parallel in structure. It also provides clarity and rhythm. Parallel elements regularly appear in lists or series, in compound structures, in comparisons, in comparisons using *than* or *as,* and in contrasting elements.

I like to swim, to dance, and ~~having~~ *to have* fun.

OR

I like swimming, dancing, and ~~to have~~ *having* fun.

Many parallel elements are linked by a co-ordinating conjunction (such as *and, or, but*) or by correlatives (such as *neither . . . nor, whether . . . or*). Others are not. In the following examples, verbals used as subjects and complements are parallel in form.

To define flora is **to define** climate.   —NATIONAL GEOGRAPHIC

Seeing is **believing.**

Parallel structures are also used in outlines to indicate elements of equal importance. (See **27b(3),** page 309.)

We are not so much what we eat as ~~the thoughts~~ *what* we think.

OR

We are not so much ~~what~~ *the food* we eat as the thoughts we think.

If elements are not parallel in thought, rather than trying to make them parallel in grammatical structure, rethink the sentence.

We can choose ~~ham, tuna salad,~~ or ˄television.

to eat ham or tuna salad *we can watch*

10a Similar grammatical elements need to be balanced.

For parallel structure, balance nouns with nouns, prepositional phrases with prepositional phrases, and clauses with clauses. In the examples that follow, repetition emphasizes the balanced structures.

(1) Parallel words and phrases

They initiate and sustain many community programs and services and are prepared to deal with societal problems such as

|| family violence,
|| child abuse,
|| unemployment,
and || alcohol abuse.   —CORA J. VOYAGEUR

|| To die,
|| to sleep,
|| to sleep,
perchance || to dream.   —WILLIAM SHAKESPEARE

(2) Parallel clauses

Some were wonderful at times, but uneven;
|| others read the same poems at every event;
|| others were insufferably mannerist;
|| others were clearly there mostly to pick up women, or men.
                    —MARGARET ATWOOD

(3) Parallel sentences

|| When I breathed in, I squeaked.
|| When I breathed out, I rattled. —JOHN CARENEN

Exercise 1

Write three sentences: one containing parallel words, one containing parallel phrases, and one containing parallel clauses. Use the examples in **10a** as models.

10b Parallels should be clear to the reader.

Repeating a preposition, an article, the *to* of the infinitive, or the introductory word of a phrase or clause can make parallel structure clear.

To be Canadian is
|| **to live** in the space between certainties,
|| **to dwell** in the gap that separates conviction from
speculation. —GEOFF PEVERE and GREIG DYMOND

Emma's hands are pudgy now, but
|| **once they** flailed like tiny stars;
|| **once they** drifted through air like soft fronds under water.
—MARY SWAN

I was happy in the thought
|| **that** our influence was helpful
and || **that** I was doing the work I loved
and || **that** I could make a living out of it. —IDA B. WELLS

10c Correlatives can be used with parallel structures.

With the correlatives (*both . . . and, either . . . or, neither . . . nor, not only . . . but also, whether . . . or*), parallel structures are required.

Whether at home or at work, he was always busy.

The team not ~~practises~~
~~Not~~ only ~~practising~~ at 6 a.m. during the week, but ~~the team~~

also scrimmages on Sunday afternoons.

OR

does the team practise *it*
Not only ~~practising~~ at 6 a.m. during the week, but ~~the team~~

also scrimmages on Sunday afternoons.

Exercise 2

Make the structure of each sentence parallel.

1. To lose weight after her pregnancy, Sheila began walking, cycling, and to swim.
2. Ali uses the Internet to invest in the stock market and communicating with his brother in Germany.
3. Farah's first steps in setting up her own business were to open a bank account and purchasing her own Internet domain.
4. Denise was praised by her superiors but her colleagues loathed her.
5. A friendly game of pickup hockey can often result in bruised shins and to have your teeth knocked out.
6. Buying a new car, taking a vacation, or to pay off her student loan were some of the things Frances considered doing with her share of the lottery winnings.
7. Determination, skill, and the ability to skate quickly are what gave Canada's men's and women's hockey teams gold medals at the Olympics.
8. She dislikes movies and going to concerts because she hates crowds.
9. His true love is philosophy rather than to read literature.
10. Lin is not only hardworking but also enjoys having a good time.

Chapter 11 | Emphasis

You can emphasize ideas by using subordination and co-ordination (**9**), parallelism (**10**), and exact word choice (**14**) and also by writing concisely (**15**). This chapter presents additional ways to emphasize material.

11a   Words at the beginning or end of a sentence receive emphasis.

Because words at the beginning or end of a sentence—especially the end—receive emphasis, place important words in these positions whenever possible.

~~In today's society, most~~ ᴳgood jobs *today* require a university education ~~as part of the background you are supposed to have.~~

~~I could hear the roar of~~ ᵀtraffic *roared* outside my hotel room in Montreal ~~when I was there.~~

As these examples show, you can often make your sentences more concise (chapter **15**) by revising them so that important words occur at the beginning or end. Sometimes, however, you may need to add a few words to make a sentence emphatic.

Because the semicolon (chapter **18**) is a strong punctuation mark when used between main clauses, the words placed immediately before and after a semicolon tend to be emphasized.

The colon and the dash often precede an emphatic ending. (See also **21d** and **21e**.)

The strategic plan is the workaholic manager's hypodermic needle. Its main function is to inject enough chaos and inefficiency into the system to ensure that there will be an inexhaustible supply of work in its pure form: that is, work that is devoid of all meaning and lacking any goal beyond itself.

—ALAN RUTKOWSKI

Being able to make small tasks out of one large one is an important component of effective time management. A mature student, who had a lot of home commitments in addition to his studying, had this down to a fine art! He was in the Honours English programme and had numerous essays each term. He allowed himself four weeks per essay. In week one he would gather his source materials together. In week two he read and researched his topic. In week three he wrote his essay, and in week four he revised his draft and produced the final copy. In any one week he might be working concurrently on several essays, all at different stages. He had the start dates for the different stages mapped out as soon as he received the assignment and knew the due dates—what a great idea!

—JOANNE FLEET and DENISE REAUME

Exercise 1

Placing important words carefully, revise the following sentences to improve emphasis.

1. The Internet has become an important tool to research with.
2. Over the past two years, Santos's English writing and speaking skills have improved.
3. In my opinion, reading poetry is the best way to learn any language; as well as this, singing songs and reading children's stories are also good ways to learn a language.
4. There was a sign on the professor's office door saying that he would return from his lecture in two hours, more or less.

5. They say that the area between Edmonton and Calgary has experienced the fastest growth in population, even faster growth than taking place in Toronto and Montreal, according to some experts.

 When surrounded by cumulative sentences, a periodic sentence receives emphasis.

In a **cumulative sentence,** the main idea (the independent clause or sentence base) comes first; less important ideas or details follow. In a **periodic sentence,** however, the main idea comes last, just before the period.

Cumulative	History has amply proved that large forces can be defeated by smaller forces superior in arms, organization, morale, and spirit.
Periodic	That large forces can be defeated by smaller forces superior in arms, organization, morale, and spirit has been amply proved by history.
Cumulative	Memory operates by way of the senses, by way of detail, which is the stuff of fiction, the fabric of good stories. —DAVID HUDDLE
Periodic	In a profession that tutored its practitioners in the baseness of human nature, that revealed the corroded metal of civilization, Quoyle constructed a personal illusion of orderly progress. —E. ANNIE PROULX

Both types of sentences can be effective. Because cumulative sentences are more common, however, the infrequently used periodic sentence is often the more emphatic.

11c When ideas are arranged from least important to most important, the most important idea receives the most emphasis.

In the following examples, the ideas are arranged in an order that places the writer's most dramatic or important idea last.

> He heard ringing in his ears and felt his arm stiffen and a sharp pain in his chest.

> He decided that his son did not need the expense of equipment, the pressure of the coaches, and the bruises and broken teeth associated with junior hockey.

> When David Usher's limo appeared, the MuchMusic fans pressed closer, screamed, and fainted.

The violation of this principle can achieve a humorous effect when a writer shifts suddenly from the dignified to the trivial or from the serious to the comic. This effect is appropriate only when a writer intends to be humorous.

> Contemporary man, of course, has no such peace of mind. He finds himself in the midst of a crisis of faith. He is what we fashionably call "alienated." He has seen the ravages of war, he has known natural catastrophes, he has been to singles bars. —WOODY ALLEN

Exercise 2

Arrange the ideas in the following sentences in order of what you consider the least important to the most important.

1. Brad was known for his wisdom, humour, and efficiency.
2. She majored in communications because she wanted to understand people, inspire them, and influence them.

3. Unless we rebuild downtown, the city will become dangerous, unattractive, and unlivable.
4. I bought my share of supplies for the picnic: ribs, mustard, paper plates, and pickles.
5. Alcoholism destroys families, ruins health, and leads to erratic behaviour.

11d Forceful verbs can make sentences emphatic.

(1) The active is more emphatic than the passive voice.

Active voice emphasizes the *doer* of the action by making the doer the subject of the sentence. **Passive voice** emphasizes the *receiver* of the action, minimizes the role of the doer, and results in wordier sentences. One sign of passive construction is that a form of the verb *to be* is added to the action conveyed by another verb in the sentence.

Active	Sylvia won the race.
Passive	The race was won by Sylvia.
Active	All citizens should insist on retaining universal medical care.
Passive	Retaining universal medical care should be insisted on by all citizens.

Because whoever or whatever is responsible for the action in the sentence is no longer the subject, sentences in the passive voice are often less precise. It is grammatically correct but stylistically undesirable to write "The race was won." Such a sentence leaves unanswered the question of who did the winning. Politicians sometimes favour the passive voice because it allows them to avoid assigning responsibility—hence constructions like "a meeting has been called" or "your taxes have been raised."

The passive voice is appropriate, however, when the doer of an action is unknown or unimportant.

Passive The television set was stolen. [The thief is unknown.]

Passive We couldn't watch the Olympics because our television had been stolen. [The identity of the thief is unimportant, given the emphasis of the sentence.]

When reporting research or scientific experiments, writers often choose to use the passive voice to preserve their objectivity and to emphasize the work being done on a project rather than who is doing it.

Passive The experiment was conducted under carefully controlled conditions over several months.

Unless they have a strong reason to use the passive voice, good writers prefer the active voice because it is clearer and more emphatic.

(2) **Action verbs and forceful linking verbs are more emphatic than forms of *have* or *be*.**

Forms of *have* or *be*, when used without an action verb, rob your writing of energy and forcefulness. The real action often lies in a verbal phrase or in the object or complement.

Our college ~~is~~ always ^{*wins*} ~~the winner of~~ the debate. [The subject complement—*winner*—contains the real action that the verb *win* conveys more forcefully.]

The meat ~~has a~~ *smells* rotten ~~smell~~. [Action is in the direct object—
smell. Used as a verb, *smell* conveys the action.]

You can ~~be more effective at solving~~ *solve* a problem ~~by~~ understanding *more effectively if you* the problem first. [The objects of the prepositions (*solving*,
understanding) contain the action more forcefully conveyed by
verbs.]

Exercise 3

Make each sentence more emphatic by substituting active voice
for passive or by substituting a more forceful verb for a form of
have or *be*.

1. Over 1000 workers were laid off at the Ford plant in Oakville,
   Ontario.
2. The sculpture was made by the Toronto artist Michael Snow.
3. A fantastic dinner was put on by the Macedonian delegation
   at the annual multicultural festival in Brampton.
4. The MP3 files were downloaded by somebody who works on
   the night shift.
5. Many Americans were unwittingly interviewed by Rick
   Mercer about their knowledge of Canada.

11e   Repeating important words gives them emphasis.

Although good writers avoid unnecessary repetition (chapter 15), they also understand that deliberate repetition
emphasizes key terms.

> We forget all too soon the things we thought we could never
> forget. We forget the loves and the betrayals alike, forget what
> we whispered and what we screamed, forget who we are.
>
> —JOAN DIDION

When you decide to repeat a word for emphasis, make sure that it is a word worth emphasizing, that it conveys an idea central to your purpose.

 ## Inverting the standard word order of a sentence gives it emphasis.

The herbal mixtures and tonics he could prescribe automatically, so well did he know the signs of disease.
—DIANA HARTOG
[COMPARE "He could prescribe the herbal mixtures and tonics automatically, so well he knew the signs of disease."]

Basic to all the Greek achievement was freedom.
—EDITH HAMILTON
[COMPARE "Freedom was basic to all the Greek achievement."]

When you invert standard word order for emphasis, you should make sure your sentence has not become so awkward or artificial that it is difficult to read.

 ## Balanced sentence construction provides emphasis.

A sentence is balanced when grammatically equal structures—usually main clauses with parallel elements—express contrasting (or similar) ideas. (See chapter 10.) A balanced sentence emphasizes the contrast (or similarity) between parts of equal length and movement.

Love is positive; tolerance negative. Love involves passion; tolerance is humdrum and dull. —E. M. FORSTER

11h A short sentence following one or more long ones is emphasized.

One winter, when I was flat on my back with fever, indisposed through health, in a small attic room on College Street near where the main Public Library used to be, I took out and read *Crime and Punishment* in two days of delirium and high temperature. I got worse.   —AUSTIN CLARKE

Exercise 4

Revise each sentence for emphasis. Be prepared to explain why your revision provides appropriate emphasis in the context you have in mind.

1. I gave him the letter, two weeks ago, when he asked me.
2. Scouting develops a person morally, mentally, and physically.
3. The monsoon devastated Buru on a hot and humid day.
4. As the station is reached, the train is seen coming around the bend.
5. In university she devoted herself to studying hard, making new friends, going to parties, and working part-time.
6. He thought about the children, he considered the budget, he reflected on past experience, and a decision was reached by him.
7. Lots of angry protesters were all around us for a while.
8. It is often required by a school that students show a portfolio before being considered for a scholarship.
9. We will give our hearts, we will donate our money, and we will share our time.
10. The paintings in the exhibit were unoriginal, but the use of colour was appealing in them.

Chapter 12

Variety

Varying the kinds of sentences you use can make your writing lively and distinctive. Many writers tend to rely too heavily on a few familiar structures, and the result often seems predictable. If you experiment with sentence structure, you increase the chance of readers' paying attention to what you write.

Compare the two paragraphs below. Both express the same ideas in virtually the same words, both use acceptable sentence patterns, and both are grammatically correct. Variety in sentence structure and length, however, gives one paragraph a stronger rhythm than the other.

Not Varied

I am sure there are university undergraduates today looking forward to careers as dentists or public relations officers. They're still fresh with the dew of youth. But are there any who yearn to be literary critics? They would have to be blessed with the love of language. I doubt that these people exist. You usually have to discover that you can't write a novel to save your life before you think of turning your hand to literary criticism. That's what the American critic Sven Birkerts confesses in *The Gutenberg Elegies.* Literary criticism is also basically a middle-aged profession. You have to know your mind. You have to have discarded or modified early enthusiasms for certain writers and modes of writing. That could take decades. [eleven sentences: three complex, eight simple; one question; two starting with *I*, three starting with *You*]

Varied

There are, I am sure, university undergraduates today, still fresh with the dew of youth, who are looking forward to careers as dentists or public relations officers. But are there any, blessed with the love of language, who yearn to become literary critics? I doubt it. You usually have to discover, as the American critic Sven Birkerts confesses in *The Gutenberg Elegies,* that you can't write a novel to save your life before you think of turning your hand to literary criticism. Besides, it's also basically a middle-aged profession. You have to know your mind, and you have to have discarded or modified early enthusiasms for certain writers and modes of writing—it takes decades. [six sentences: one compound-complex, three complex, two simple; one question]

—PHILIP MARCHAND

If you have difficulty distinguishing various types of structures, review the fundamentals treated in chapter **1**, especially **1b**.

12a   A series of short, simple sentences sounds choppy. (See also 11h.)

To avoid the choppiness produced by a series of short, simple sentences, you can lengthen some sentences by showing how the ideas are subordinate or co-ordinate. (See chapter **9**.)

Choppy	Our old and new homes are similar in some ways. Our old house is smaller. It was built during the Depression. It was built to accommodate the simpler needs of poorer families.
Better	Although our old and new homes are similar, our old house is smaller because it was built during the Depression and accommodated the simpler needs of poorer families. [use of subordination to combine sentences]

Choppy	Frank asked a lot of questions during the class. Next he adopted a very thoughtful look. He also took lots of notes. Finally he laughed at the professor's corny jokes. He did this in order to look like he had read the required material for class.
Effective	To look like he had read the required material for class, Frank asked a lot of questions, adopted a very thoughtful look, took lots of notes, and laughed at the professor's corny jokes. [use of co-ordination to combine sentences]

Occasionally, as the example below illustrates, a series of brief, subject-first sentences can be used for special effect:

> Although it had been an easy enough day, much like any other, something seemed wrong just before dinner. I felt hot. My chest hurt. The room began to tilt. [The feeling of a heart attack is conveyed by a series of abrupt sentences.]

Exercise 1

Convert the following series of short, simple sentences into single sentences. Use no more than one co-ordinating conjunction in each.

1. It looked like the Americans were going to win the game. Team USA had a strong start. The crowd in Salt Lake City was behind them. They scored the first goal in the Olympic gold-medal game.
2. Team Canada played hard. The Canadians tied the game. They took the lead on a goal by Jarome Iginla.
3. The chants and cheers of the crowd were not enough to help the home team. The American defenders began to buckle. The Canadian forward lines pressured them unrelentingly.
4. Team Canada's Joe Sakic skated past the American defence. Sakic cut in close to the American goaltender. He scored the goal that sealed the gold medal for Canada.
5. Canadians have always felt they had the best hockey players. The last time Canada won the Olympic gold medal in men's hockey was in 1952. The victory was a sweet one for Canada.

12b Writing sounds monotonous when too many sentences begin the same way.

Most writers begin more than half their sentences with the subject—far more than any other construction. Although this pattern is normal for English sentences, relying too heavily on it can make your writing monotonous. Experiment with the following alternatives for beginning sentences.

(1) Begin with an adverb or an adverbial clause.

When I was a little boy, we called the Blackfish.
—JOHN DIXON [adverbial clause]

Individually, it is the difference between acquaintanceship and friendship. —AUSTIN CLARKE [adverb]

Shortly after the turn of the century, M. O. Hammond was elected spokesman for a group of reporters demanding higher pay. —PETER DESBARATS [adverbial clause]

(2) Begin with a prepositional phrase or a verbal phrase.

Out of necessity they stitched all of their secret fears and lingering childhood nightmares into this existence.
—GLORIA NAYLOR [prepositional phrase]

To bring his plan to fruition, he needed money and the birth certificate of a Canadian-born Chinese about the same age as his imported concubine. —DENISE CHONG [infinitive phrase]

Spitting into the dirt to ward off ill-intentioned hexes, he would tip his hat and continue home for his midday meal.
—JUDITH KALMAN [participial phrase]

(3) Begin with a sentence connective—a co-ordinating conjunction, a conjunctive adverb, or a transitional expression.

In the following examples, each sentence connective shows the relationship between the ideas in each set of sentences. (See also 27b(4).)

Many restaurants close within a few years of opening. **But** others, which offer good food at reasonable prices, become well established. [co-ordinating conjunction]

Difficulty in finding a place to park is one of the factors keeping people from shopping downtown. **Moreover,** public transportation has become too expensive. [conjunctive adverb]

This legislation will hurt the economy. **In the first place,** it will cost thousands of jobs. [transitional expression]

(4) Begin with an appositive, an absolute phrase, or an introductory series. (See 9a.)

A beautifully scenic city, Vancouver has become a popular filming location. [appositive]

His fur bristling, the cat attacked. [absolute phrase]

Light, water, temperature, minerals—these affect the health of plants. [introductory series—see 21e(3)]

Exercise 2

Rewrite each sentence so that it begins with an appositive, an absolute phrase, or an introductory series.

1. Home-decorating and renovation magazines have grown in popularity because more people are choosing to fix up older houses rather than buy new ones.
2. A department store full of bargains stood before them.
3. Jason liked to wear his Edmonton Eskimos cap in Paris in order to identify himself as a Canadian more easily.

4. He began to write about his childhood in the Prairies after he finished university.
5. Marcia is storing all the crocheted doilies and knitted tea cozies her grandmother gave her over the years because she believes that one day they will come back in fashion.

<h2>12c   Stringing simple sentences together to make compound sentences is less effective than experimenting with sentence structure.</h2>

Although compound sentences are often useful, some are ineffective. If you normally write short, simple sentences, and then revise your sentence structure by just linking simple sentences with *and* or *but,* your writing will still lack variety. Remember that subordination is as important as co-ordination. (See chapter 9.) To revise an ineffective compound sentence, you can use one of the following methods.

(1) Make a compound sentence complex.

Compound	Seafood is nutritious, and it is low in fat, and it has become available in a greater variety.
Complex	Seafood, which is nutritious and low in fat, has become available in a greater variety.

(2) Use a compound predicate in a simple sentence.

Compound	She caught the bird expertly, and next she held it so its feet were still, and then she slipped a numbered yellow band around its left leg.
Simple	She caught the bird expertly, held it so its feet were still, and slipped a numbered yellow band around its left leg.

(3) Use an appositive in a simple sentence.

Compound	William Vickrey was a noted Canadian economist, and he passed away within a week of learning he had won the Nobel Prize in 1996.
Simple	William Vickrey, a noted Canadian economist, passed away within a week of learning he had won the Nobel Prize in 1996.

(4) Use a prepositional or verbal phrase added to a simple sentence.

Compound	The rain was torrential, and we could not see where we were going.
Simple	Because of the torrential rain, we could not see where we were going.
Compound	I checked into the hotel at about 4:30, and then I called the office about my return flight.
Simple	After checking into the hotel at about 4:30, I called the office about my return flight.
Compound	The town is near the expressway, and it attracted commuters, and its population grew rapidly.
Simple	The town, located near the expressway, attracted commuters and grew rapidly in population.

(5) Use additional conjunctions to increase the compounds in a sentence.

Experienced writers sometimes achieve interesting effects by exaggerating what could be considered a flaw. By using a number of conjunctions in close succession, you can slow the pace and dignify material that might otherwise seem unremarkable.

The door shuts and her mind retreats and she is relieved at her lack of morbidity and she is aghast at her cowardice and it goes around and around.   —GABRIELLA GOLIGER

Exercise 3

Using the methods illustrated in **12c**, revise these compound sentences.

1. My sister became frustrated in her job, so she quit after a few months, and now she is collecting unemployment and feeling that she made a mistake.
2. Annuals can add colour to your garden, and many of them are inexpensive, but you have to do a lot of replanting.
3. First term was difficult, and I almost dropped out of school, but I learned how to plan my time, and then my grades improved.
4. Greg is always talking about taking a vacation, but he never does it, and he is overworking himself.
5. Coffee shops are popular meeting places, and they have improved the standard of coffee served in town, but there are too many of them, and I wonder how they can all stay in business.

12d   Occasionally using words or phrases to separate subject and verb can vary the conventional subject-verb sequence.

Although it is usually best to keep the subject next to the verb so that the relationship between the two is clear, breaking this pattern on occasion can lead to variety. In the following examples, subjects and verbs are in boldface.

Subject-Verb   **Armenia was** once part of the USSR, but **it has become** a separate nation.

Varied	Armenia, once part of the USSR, **has become** a separate nation.
Subject-Verb	The **crowd applauded** every goal and **cheered** the team to victory.
Varied	The **crowd**, applauding every goal, **cheered** the team to victory.

An occasional declarative sentence with inverted word order can also contribute to sentence variety. (See **11f**.)

Exercise 4

Using the methods illustrated in **12d**, vary the conventional subject-verb sequence in these sentences.

1. The video store is across from the high school, and it attracts many students.
2. His ability to listen is an acquired skill that makes him a good counsellor.
3. Sidharth was hurrying to get home before the storm broke, but he flooded the engine of his car.
4. The manager identified with the employees, so she supported their decision to ask for shorter hours.
5. The customers were frustrated by the lack of service and walked out of the restaurant.

12e When surrounded by declarative sentences, a question, an exclamation, or a command adds variety.

What was Shakespeare's state of mind, for instance, when he wrote *Lear* and *Antony and Cleopatra*? It was certainly the state of mind most favourable to poetry that there has ever existed. —VIRGINIA WOOLF [Woolf's answer follows the initial question.]

Now I stare and stare at people, shamelessly. Stare. It's the way to educate your eye. —WALKER EVANS [A one-word imperative sentence provides variety.]

Exercise 5

Prepare for a class discussion on the sentence variety in the following paragraph.

¹It is too much that with all those pedestrian centuries behind us we should, in a few decades, have learned to fly; it is too heady a thought, too proud a boast. ²Only the dirt on a mechanic's hands, the straining vise, the splintered bolt of steel underfoot on the hangar floor—only these and such anxiety as the face of a Jock Cameron can hold for a pilot and his plane before a flight, serve to remind us that, not unlike the heather, we too are earthbound. ³We fly, but we have not "conquered" the air. ⁴Nature presides in all her dignity, permitting us the study and the use of such of her forces as we may understand. ⁵It is when we presume to intimacy, having been granted only tolerance, that the harsh stick falls across our impudent knuckles and we rub the pain, staring upward, startled by our ignorance. —BERYL MARKHAM

Diction

Chapter 13

Good Usage

Traditionally, a distinction was made between "good" and "bad" ("improper," "inappropriate") usage—that is, between formal language (normally required for university, college, or business writing) and informal language (usually associated with ordinary, everyday conversation and often involving colloquialisms, slang, or dialect words). As we have become more aware of and sensitive to varieties of English, this division has come to seem overly rigid. It is no longer possible to assert categorically that there is a single, standard English that everyone writes or speaks (or ought to write or speak). This is not to say that there are no rules regarding usage, only that such rules may be influenced by particulars of audience and occasion. In other words, they may be subject to change from one writing situation—or task—to another.

For example, it is possible that your instructor might give an assignment that allows you, even asks you, to adopt a more "informal" language in order to produce certain effects. Meanwhile, thanks in part to electronic modes of communication, there has been a trend in business writing (certainly in North America) toward more informal (direct, open-ended, reader-friendly) styles. In short, the differences between formal and informal writing have been blurred both in the academic and professional worlds.

When deciding on a style of writing and types of word choice, keep in mind the audience you are addressing. Audiences may be academic or non-academic, small or large, close or far away in space or time, and so on. They may have specific gender, age, ethnic, and other character istics. And they may vary with respect to the kind and level of interest they bring to your subject. Finally, they may be reading your work to be informed, instructed, to be persuaded, to see a problem solved, or for countless other reasons. It's true that at university or college you are generally writing for an audience of one: your instructor. But writers also have an imaginary reader in mind when they write. This reader is a projection, a slightly ideal construction, whom writers picture as tuned to their thought, providing feedback, posing questions. It is helpful to have such a reader in mind, since it makes writing seem less lonely.

The problem with so-called informal writing was that it could be used to express private or secret meanings unavailable to an uninitiated reader. Such writing possibly could mean more to the author, or a tightly knit "in-group" of readers, than to a wider audience. As well, informal language sometimes involves a more metaphorical kind of writing, which means it may lend itself to pure expression rather than exposition.

Broadly speaking, instructors prefer a non-metaphorical to a metaphorical writing style, even when the subject you are discussing is literature. Although many philosophers of language would say that all language is metaphorical anyway, still the illusion of a non-metaphorical (a language that refers directly to reality) is widely maintained.

Again, the trick is to decide what type or range of audience you are appealing to and keep in mind their motives for reading your work. Choose a style and vocabulary that they would be familiar with and feel empowered by. Your language should reflect the relationship you seek to create with your reader.

The following information will be helpful for making decisions about effective usage.

A thesaurus, which alerts you to possible synonyms, is an important aid to writing. A dictionary, however, is indispensable to alert you to subtle differences in meaning. In addition to furnishing the meaning of a word, a dictionary also provides its pronunciation, its part of speech, and the forms of plurals and verb tenses. Although a dictionary includes words appropriate for both speech and formal writing, it also includes usage labels and short usage paragraphs to distinguish between the two. Note words labelled **dialect, slang,** or **non-standard,** as well as words no longer in common use labelled **archaic** or **obsolete.** Again, decide what effect the use of such words might have on your audience. (See the Glossary of Usage.)

Dictionaries

It helps to have ready access to a good, recent desk dictionary such as one of those listed below. The date is important because language is constantly changing. Many desk dictionaries are available either in paperback or on CD-ROM, both of which usually include the same information. The pocket version, which is useful for spelling and a quick definition, omits important information on usage and derivation.

The Canadian Oxford Dictionary

Funk & Wagnalls Canadian College Dictionary

Gage Canadian Dictionary

Merriam-Webster's Collegiate Dictionary

Nelson Canadian Dictionary of the English Language

Occasionally you may need to refer to an unabridged or a special dictionary. Also, check with your college or university library to see if your institution subscribes to any online dictionaries, such as *The Oxford English Dictionary*.

Unabridged dictionaries

The Oxford English Dictionary. 2nd ed. 20 vols. 1989–.

Random House Webster's Unabridged Dictionary. 3rd ed. 2001.

Webster's Third New International Dictionary of the English Language. 2000.

Special dictionaries

Ammer, Christine. *The American Heritage Dictionary of Idioms*. 1997.

Avis, Walter S., et al., eds. *A Dictionary of Canadianisms on Historical Principles*. 1991.

Chapman, Robert L., ed. *Roget's International Thesaurus*. 6th ed. 2001.

Fee, Margery, and Janice McAlpine. *Guide to Canadian English Usage*. 2001.

Follett, Wilson. *Modern American Usage: A Guide*. 1966.

Hoad, T. F., ed. *The Concise Oxford Dictionary of English Etymology*. 1993.

Lighter, J. E., ed. *Historical Dictionary of American Slang*. 1997.

Miller, Casey, and Kate Swift, eds. *The Handbook of Non-Sexist Writing for Writers, Editors and Speakers*. 3rd British edition. 1995.

Pratt, T. K., ed. *Dictionary of Prince Edward Island English*. 1997.

Story, G. M., W. J. Kirwin, and J. D. A. Widdowson, eds. *Dictionary of Newfoundland English*. 2nd ed. 1990.

Merriam-Webster's Collegiate Thesaurus. 1993.

Webster's Dictionary of English Usage. 1993.

E S L   The following dictionaries are recommended for people who speak English as a second language.

Collins COBUILD English Dictionary, 1995.

Longman Dictionary of Contemporary English. 4th ed. 1999.

Longman Dictionary of English Language and Culture. 2nd ed. 1993.

Oxford Advanced Learner's Encyclopedic Dictionary. 1992.

Two excellent resources for ESL students are the following:

Longman Language Activator. 1995. (This book supplies definitions, usage, and sample sentences: a cross between a dictionary and a thesaurus.)

Swan, Michael. *Practical English Usage.* 1995. (This is a practical reference guide to problems encountered by users of English as a second language.)

Inexpensive collections that include a dictionary, thesaurus, usage guide, and certain other reference works are beginning to be available on a single CD-ROM.

 !   **CAUTION** Most word processing programs also include a thesaurus. When using a computer thesaurus, do not merely substitute one word for another without understanding subtle differences in meaning. In listing synonyms, dictionaries often point out such distinctions.

13a Dictionaries provide information beyond the definition of a word.

Reading the introductory material and noting the meaning of any special abbreviations will help you understand the information your dictionary provides. The following sample entry from the *Gage Canadian Dictionary* provides important information. Almost all desk dictionaries provide the same information, although possibly in a different order.

Syllabication Pronunciation   Vb forms

          Part of speech

Spelling —— ¹ad·mit [æd′mit] *v* -mit·ted, mit·ting. **1** say that (an undesirable or damaging fact, etc.) is true or valid; acknowledge, often unwillingly or hesitantly: *He admitted that he had lied. She admitted her mistake.* **2** accept as true or valid: *to admit a hypothesis.* **3** allow to enter a place or use something; let in: *The head waiter refused to admit him without a tie.* **4** give the right to enter to: *This ticket admits one person.* **5** allow; leave room for; permit (*usually used with* **of**): *Her argument* —— Illustrative sentence *admits of no reply.* **6** give access or entry to: *the new window admits more light. The harbour admits three ships at one time.* **7** allow to attain (*to* a position, privilege, etc.): *She was admitted to the bar last year.* ⟨ME ⟨ L *admittere* ⟨ *ad-* to —— Origin + *mittere* let go⟩

☛ *Syn.* **1. Admit,** ACKNOWLEDGE, CONFESS = disclose or own that something is true. **Admit** = own or grant the existence or truth of something, usually after giving in to outside forces or the dictates of one's own conscience or judgment: *I admit that she is right.* **Acknowledge** = bring out into the open one's knowledge of the existence or truth of something, sometimes reluctantly: *They have now acknowledged defeat.* **Confess** = admit something unfavourable or embarrassing about oneself: *I confess I am a coward.*

Synonyms and distinctions with usage examples

☛ *Usage.* **Admit** is followed by *to* or *into* when it means 'give the right to enter or allow to enter': *Fifty cents will admit you to the game. The butler would not admit him into the house.* **Admit** is followed by *of* when it means 'leave room for': *Her conduct admits of no complaint.*

Usage notes

NEL

Spelling, syllabication, and pronunciation

The dictionary describes both written and spoken language. You can check spelling and word division (syllabication) as well as pronunciation of unfamiliar words. A key to sound symbols appears in the introduction and/or at the bottom of the entry pages. Alternative pronunciations usually represent regional differences. When alternative spellings are given, the first spelling is the more common one.

Parts of speech and inflected forms

The dictionary also labels the possible uses of words in sentences—for instance, *tr. v., adj*. It identifies the various ways that nouns, verbs, and modifiers change form to indicate number, tense, and comparison.

Word origin/etymology

The origin of a word—also called its derivation or etymology—can be useful in understanding its meaning and in realizing the many cultures that have influenced, and continue to influence, the English language.

Definitions

Definitions are listed in different order in different dictionaries. Often they are ordered according to how common they are.

Synonyms

Dictionaries always list synonyms, sometimes with detailed explanations of subtle differences in meaning. When discussions such as the one in the above sample are used in conjunction with a thesaurus, they are extremely helpful. The entry for the word *admit* lists two one-word synonyms. The entry for each one-word synonym has a cross-reference to the entry for *admit*.

Usage

Most dictionaries give guidance on usage through discussion and quotations showing how the word has been used in context.

Exercise 1

Study the pronunciations of the following common words in your dictionary and determine how you might pronounce them in your own region. Be prepared to discuss your pronunciations with your classmates, whose pronunciations may differ.

1. news   2. which   3. either   4. wash   5. orange

Exercise 2

Study the definitions for the following pairs of words, and write a sentence for each pair to illustrate the subtle differences in meaning.

1. clemency-mercy
2. provoke-excite
3. vampire-necrophile
4. ingenuous-innocent
5. putrefy-rot
6. courageous-fearless
7. charm-charisma
8. practicable-viable
9. liberate-free
10. sensuous-sensual

 Most dictionaries label words according to dialectical, regional, or stylistic usage.

Dictionaries provide important guidelines for the appropriate use of words. For example, *Nelson Canadian Dictionary of the English Language* furnishes examples of words in context and also quotations that include the word. In addition, **usage notes** give further information on points of grammar, diction, pronunciation, and level of language.

Many words carry labels that act as guides for appropriate use. Again, however, it is essential to keep in mind the occasion, purpose, and audience for which you are writing. The following labels are commonly used in dictionaries.

(1) Colloquial or informal

Words labelled **colloquial** or **informal** are common to speech and used by writers in dialogue and informal writing.

Informal   nerdy   belly button
Formal   socially inept   navel

Although contractions, such as *it's* and *aren't,* are common in English, they are sometimes considered inappropriate in more academic writing.

E S L   If you are in doubt about the correct form of contractions, it is acceptable not to use them.

(2) Slang

Slang is usually defined as words belonging to a particular age group, locality, or profession. Slang, in fact, covers a wide range of words that are variously considered breezy, racy, excessively informal, facetious, or taboo. Sometimes they are newly coined or highly technical. Slang can easily become dated, and it may be meaningless to your readers.

(3) Regionalisms

Regional or dialectal usages are markers of the region where they are current. Speakers and writers can safely use regional words known to the audience they are addressing, but such words may not be understood by outsiders.

(4) Non-standard and substandard

Words and expressions labelled non-standard or substandard should generally be avoided in formal writing, except possibly in direct quotations. For example, *I ain't* can be replaced with *I am not* and "He done ate" with "He has already eaten."

(5) Archaic and obsolete

All dictionaries list words (and meanings for words) that have long since passed out of general use. Such words as *rathe* (early) and *yestreen* (last evening) are still found in dictionaries because they occur in our older literature and so must be defined for the modern reader.

A number of obsolete or archaic words—such as *worser* (for *worse*) or *holp* (for *helped*)—are still in use but are now non-standard.

13c Writers consider their audience when selecting words to convey meaning and appropriate tone.

(1) Technical words

It is important to keep in mind the interests, needs, and overall level of expertise of your audience. Not all audiences are the same. Indeed, excessive reliance on the imprecise notion of a general reader may cause you to overlook certain unique audience characteristics. One way of responding to audience needs is through appropriate word choice. Decide, then, whether to use highly technical or relatively non-technical language. If you are addressing a group of communications specialists, it is probably acceptable to refer to an organized way of finding something as a *heuristic*. If you are speaking at a medical convention, you could refer to a need for bifocals as *presbyopia*. The advantage of technical language is that it is exact, but readers need to be comfortable with it. Thus, if you are addressing a comparatively non-specialized readership, decide how much, if any, technical language to use. Cutting down on the sheer number of technical terms is a good idea. But if you must use some technical terms, provide brief definitions in your text. Do not be afraid to teach new terms to readers as a way of initiating them into the subject area.

Jargon is technical language tailored specifically for a particular occupation. Again, such language can be an efficient shortcut for conveying abstract concepts. The appearance of jargon in a text helps define the knowledge field or community that writer and reader belong to. However, its overuse can be demeaning by implying that the writer is sophisticated in a way the reader is not. Write to empower your reader.

Keep in mind, too, that thanks to the increase in the amount and technical means of developing, presenting, and distributing information, the style of communication—even in academic circles—has moved in the direction of greater flexibility, accessibility, and in some cases informality. The emphasis is now more than ever on finding ways of providing readers with efficient—quick and relatively easy—access to the meanings we want to convey.

(2) Inclusive language

In the interest of building community between writer and reader, it is obviously important to use language that does not discriminate between persons on the basis of race, religion, age, sex, or other attributes.

Making language inclusive (that is, avoiding sexist language) means treating men and woman equally. There are several types of error writers can fall into. One is the unthinking use of derogatory terms, such as the use of *babes* to refer to women. Another is the use of combinations that imply that men and women are unequal, such as *men and girls*. Note too that certain words may imply exclusiveness, such as using *man* to denote all of humanity.

Man's achievements in the twentieth century are impressive.

Along similar lines, it is important to avoid the habit, ingrained in the language, of distinguishing arbitrarily between men and women in terms of vocation or aptitude. Do not assume, for example, that all nurses are women and all doctors men. (See list below.)

A problem can arise with respect to nouns and pronouns. For example, it is incorrect to write, "A student typically brings a wide range of interests and previous knowledge to his academic career" (because it implies that all students are male). However, though correct, it sounds stylistically awkward to replace *his* alone with *his or her,* as in "A student typically brings a wide range of interests and previous knowledge to his or her academic career." It is acceptable in such cases to make the noun plural, so that the pronoun can also be plural: "**Students** typically bring a wide range of interests and previous knowledge to **their** academic **careers**." This avoids sexist language, while assuring that noun and pronoun are in agreement.

Inappropriate	Appropriate
authoress	author
the common man	the average person, ordinary people
actress	actor
male nurse	nurse
mankind	humanity, human beings, people
policeman	police officer
weatherman	meteorologist, weather forecaster
Have your *mother* send a snack.	Have your **parent** send a snack.
The law should prohibit someone with a drinking problem from driving *his* car.	The law should prohibit someone with a drinking problem from driving **a** car.
My *girl* will call the members.	My **assistant** will call the members.
The professors and their *wives* attended.	The professors and their **spouses** attended.

Exercise 3

Make the following sentences inclusive by eliminating all sexist language.

1. Ann-Marie MacDonald is a well-known authoress as well as an actress.
2. Everyone has to be at his best in order to win the university debating team championships.
3. The student had to sell her used books.
4. We haven't received the letter yet, but that may only be because the mailman hasn't shown up.
5. Two policemen were seriously injured when their cruiser was involved in a traffic accident at Broadview and Danforth.
6. The fishermen protested the quotas set by the Ministry of Fisheries, saying that they were too restrictive.

7. Mankind may always be asking the fundamental questions concerning his existence.
8. The repairman didn't have the right parts to fix the dishwasher, so we'll have to go another day without clean dishes.
9. The story's outcome makes the reader question his assumptions.
10. Adam is studying to become a male nurse.

(3) Confusion of *sit/set* and *lie/lay* and *rise/raise*

You will pick the correct form most of the time if you remember that you can *set, lay,* or *raise* something, but you yourself *sit, lie* or *rise.* Thinking of these verbs in pairs and learning their principal parts can help you remember which form to use.

Present	Past	Past Participle	Present Participle
sit	sat	sat	sitting
lie	lay	lain	lying
risc	rose	risen	rising
set	set	set	setting
lay	laid	laid	laying
raise	raised	raised	raising

Set, lay, and *raise* mean "to place or put something somewhere." For example, to *set* the table means to *lay* the silverware next to the plates. *Sit, lie,* and *rise,* the intransitive verbs of the pairs, mean "be seated" or "get into a horizontal position" or "get up." For example, *you sit down* or *lie down* or *rise up.*

Sit	Sit down. Sitting down, I thought it over. He sat up.
Set	I set the clock. It had been set there.
Lie	Lie down. Lying down, I fell asleep. He lay there for hours.

Lay	We **laid** these aside. These **had been laid** aside.
Rise	I **rise** before daylight. I **rose** even earlier yesterday. I am **rising** earlier each day.
Raise	I **raise** the window each night. I **raised** the window last night. I am **raising** the window to clear the smoke.

Exercise 4

Without changing the tense, substitute the appropriate form of *sit/set, lie/lay,* or *rise/raise* for the italicized verbs in the following sentences.

1. Last week they *established* their plans for the trip.
2. I often *rest* on the old stone wall and watch the sunset.
3. I *lifted* the window shade.
4. I try to *get up* in time to work out each morning.
5. After he weeded the garden, Chen decided to *nap* on the front porch.
6. I *am putting* your book on the front porch.
7. I have *slept* here for at least three hours.
8. Hugh was *sprawling* on the couch when I arrived.
9. Marcella *got up* in time to see me off.
10. Kalynda was *adjusting* her watch.

Exercise 5

Make a list of 10 words or phrases that you would ordinarily consider informal and prepare for a class discussion on whether you would use them (a) in a job interview, (b) in a conversation with a friend, (c) in a conversation with one of the deans, (d) in a letter of application, or (e) in an essay. Check your dictionary to see how each word is labelled.

Exercise 6

Rewrite the following paragraph in standard English appropriate for a paper in an English composition class. Consult the **Glossary of Usage** or a dictionary to determine appropriate usages.

[1]I've been blessed by having a large amount of friends throughout my life, but as far as friends go, Claudette is one of the best. [2]We've had alot of fun together through the years. [3]Several years ago, however, I found a job where I could move up the ladder of success, so I moved away, knowing that Claudette and myself would keep in touch. [4]Even though my leaving saddened us both, it didn't affect our basic friendship at all. [5]We write to each other most every week, and not long ago, I made a surprise visit to her, and I stayed for a week. [6]If she had known I was arriving that afternoon, she would have taken off of work to meet me at the airport. [7]Even though we stay in touch, I still miss her; hopefully we'll be able to see each other again soon.

Chapter 14 | Exactness

Good writing often consists of short, familiar words precisely used. When drafting (chapter 28), choose words that express your ideas and feelings. When revising (chapter 29), make those words exact, idiomatic, and fresh. Use the words you already know effectively, but add to your vocabulary to increase your options for choosing the exact word that suits your purpose, audience, and occasion. Make new words your own by mastering their denotations and connotations and by writing clear definitions.

14a Accurate and precise word choice conveys meaning efficiently.

(1) Accuracy is essential.

The **denotation** of a word indicates what it names, not what it suggests. For example, the noun *beach* denotes a sandy or pebbly shore, not suggestions of summer fun. Inaccurate usage misstates your point, inexact usage diminishes it, and ambiguous usage confuses your reader. Select words that state your point exactly.

The letter from the University of Western Ontario ~~advised~~ *informed* me

that I had been accepted for the upcoming academic year.

[*Advise* means "to provide advice." For example: My father

advised me to take the offer of acceptance from the University

of Western Ontario. *Inform* means "to tell, to impart

in formation," so *inform* is the exact word for the sentence drafted.]

underprivileged

The inner-city high school had many ~~poor~~ students who went on to university. [*Poor* can mean "not wealthy" or it can mean "academically weak." In this case, the use of *underprivileged* makes the meaning clear.]

assertive

Harold realized that he had to become more ~~aggressive~~ toward his boss if he were to be promoted. [*Aggressive* means "openly hostile"; *assertive* means "forthright" and is therefore the more precise word in this case.]

Exercise 1

The italicized words in the following sentences are inaccurate, inexact, or ambiguous. Replace these words with exact ones.

1. Louise worked hard to *obtain* a higher position in the company.
2. Have you decided to *except* his proposal?
3. That movie was very *unique*.
4. She has based her campaign on four basic *principals*.
5. Tom likes good food, *but* he frequently tries new restaurants.
6. I cried at the end of the movie because it was so *sentimental*.
7. We need to consider how this change will *effect* our budget.
8. Let's hire a consultant so that we can get an *uninterested* opinion.
9. There were *little* people in the store.
10. After I write my first draft, I always like to *proofread* it.

(2) Definitions clarify the precise meaning of words.

A short dictionary definition may be adequate when you need to define a term or a special meaning of a word that may be unfamiliar to the reader.

Here *galvanic* means "produced as if by electric shock." [See also **20d**.]

Giving a synonym or two may clarify the meaning of a term. Such synonyms are often used as appositives.

A *dolt* is a dullard, a blockhead.

Young Blackfoot-speaking children in present-day southern Alberta, for example, learn many stories about Napi or "Old Man," the creator of the world.   —R. DOUGLAS FRANCIS et al.

Writers frequently show—rather than tell—what a word means by giving examples.

Many homophones (*be* and *bee, in* and *inn, see* and *sea*) are not spelling problems.

Words often have a number of meanings. It must be clear to the reader which meaning you are using.

In this paper, I use the word *communism* in the Marxist sense of social organization based on the holding of all property in common.

By stipulating your meaning in this way, you set the terms of the discussion.

You can also formulate your own definitions of the concepts you wish to clarify.

To be embarrassed is to be disclosed, in public.
—MARGARET VISSER

All identities are a construction of the mind.   —GUY BEDARD

A formal definition first states the term to be defined and puts it into a class, then differentiates the term from other members of its class.

A phosphene [term] is a luminous visual image [class] that results from applying pressure to the eyeball [differentiation].

Exercise 2

Define any two of the following terms in full sentences using first (a) a short dictionary definition, then (b) a synonym, and finally (c) an example.

1. neurotic	4. integrity	7. racism
2. humanism	5. uncanny	8. liberal
3. novel	6. wetlands	9. peer

(3) Connotations enrich meaning.

The **connotation** of a word is what the word suggests or implies. *Beach*, for instance, may connote natural beauty, warmth, surf, water sports, fun, sunburn, crowds, or even gritty sandwiches. Context has much to do with the connotations a word evokes; in a treatise on shoreline management, *beach* has scientific, geographic connotations, whereas in a fashion magazine it evokes images of bathing suits. In addition to being influenced by context, most readers carry with them a wealth of personal associations that can influence how they respond to the words on the page. The challenge for writers is to choose the words that are most likely to evoke the appropriate connotations.

One of the reasons I am recommending Mr. Krueger for this job is that he is so ~~relentless~~ *persistent*. [*Relentless* has negative connotations that are inappropriate for a recommendation.]

I love the ~~odour~~ *aroma* of freshly baked bread. [Many odours are unpleasant; *aroma* sounds more positive, especially in association with food.]

He gets into trouble sometimes because he is so ~~innocent~~ *naïve*. [*Innocent* suggests virtue; *naïve* suggests a lack of judgment.]

E S L   Familiarity with the connotations of words will increase as your vocabulary grows. As you learn new words that seem to mean exactly the same thing, use them in conversation with persons for whom English is their first language; they will help you decide whether these words have different connotations.

(4) Specific and concrete words are usually stronger than general and abstract ones.

A **general** word is all-inclusive, indefinite, and sweeping in scope. A **specific** word is precise, definite, and limited in scope.

General	Specific	More Specific/Concrete
food	fast food	cheeseburger
prose	fiction	short stories
place	city	Edmonton

An **abstract** word deals with concepts, with ideas, with what cannot be touched, heard, or seen. A **concrete** word signifies particular objects, the practical, what can be touched, heard, or seen.

Abstract	democracy, loyal, evil, hate, charity
Concrete	mosquito, spotted, crunch, grab

Some writers use too many abstract or general words, leaving their writing vague and lifeless. As you select words to fit your context, you should be as specific and concrete as you can. For example, instead of the word *bad,* consider using a more precise adjective.

bad planks:	rotten, warped, scorched, knotty, termite-eaten
bad children:	rowdy, rude, ungrateful, perverse, spoiled
bad meat:	tough, tainted, overcooked, contaminated

To test whether or not a word is specific, you can ask one or more of these questions about what you want to say: Exactly who? Exactly what? Exactly when? Exactly where? Exactly how? As you study the following examples, notice what a difference specific, concrete words can make in expressing an idea and how specific details can expand or develop ideas.

Vague	She has kept no reminders of performing in her youth.
Specific	She has kept no sequined costume, no photographs, no fliers or posters from that part of her youth. —LOUISE ERDRICH
Vague	Before she died, my mother visited Quebec to see her home.
Specific	Toward the end of her life, sick and very old but still full of the great wish of her life to see the sites and beauties of the world, she was anxious to make a farewell visit to Quebec to see some distant cousins again, she said, to call on this one or that one; but I suspect that the real purpose of her trip, perhaps unknown to herself, may have been to climb to the top of a Laurentian hill to listen to the wind in a tall pine, just to see if it sang as it had when she was a child. —GABRIELLE ROY
Vague	When I hear and see the rains begin, I know that I'm home.
Specific	When the Chacalaca bird screams coarse as stones in a tin bucket, signalling rain across this valley, when lightning strafes a blue-black sky, when rain as thick as shale beats the xora to arrowed red tears, when squat Julie trees kneel to the ground with the wind and I am not afraid but laugh and laugh and laugh I know that I am travelling back. —DIONNE BRAND

As these examples show, sentences with specific details are often longer than sentences without them. But the need to be specific does not necessarily conflict with the need to be concise. (See chapter 15.) Simply substituting one word for another can often make it far easier to see, hear, taste, or smell what you are hoping to convey.

I ~~had an accident~~ *fell out of the canoe* while trying to ~~catch a fish~~ *land a muskie*.

Occasionally, a skilful writer can achieve a dramatic effect by mixing concrete and abstract terms, as in the following example:

> We inhaled those nice big fluffy fumes of human sweat, urine, effluvia, and sebaceous secretions. —TOM WOLFE

And all writers use abstract words and generalizations when these are vital to communicating their ideas, as in the following sentence:

> The romantic principles of Existentialism in its broadest, most vernacular sense have much to do with one's volition and one's will in creating oneself as an ethical being by way of a chosen action. —JOYCE CAROL OATES

Abstract words are exact when they are used to express abstractions—words like "immortal," "inexhaustible," "soul," "spirit," "compassion," "sacrifice," and "endurance." When you use abstract words and generalizations, make sure you do so deliberately and with good reason.

Exercise 3

Replace the general words and phrases in italics with specific ones.

1. You can't believe what you read in the *media*.
2. *Everyone in today's society* seems concerned about staying fit.

3. Cities have *a lot of problems* today.
4. When my family gets together, we fall into *old routines*.
5. I thought about *the numerous advantages* of my major.
6. The police searched *the whole area* thoroughly.
7. No matter how often she gets hurt, she keeps going out with *the same kind of guy*.
8. I've got to have the freedom *to do what I need to do*.
9. That girl needs *a complete make-over*.
10. You'll love this program because it offers such *a spiritual experience*.

(5) Figurative language can contribute to exactness.

Commonly found in non-fiction prose as well as in fiction, poetry, and drama, figurative language uses words in an imaginative rather than a literal sense. Simile and metaphor are the chief **figures of speech**. A **simile** is the comparison of dissimilar things using *like* or *as*. A **metaphor** is an implied comparison of dissimilar things not using *like* or *as*. Of the two, metaphor is the more radical in that it departs more from nature. It not only states a *likeness* but creates an imaginative *identity* between dissimilar things.

Similes

The marbles moved and rolled and plashed, like glassy, magical, colourful water. —ROHINTON MISTRY

The thick blood welled out of him like red velvet, but still he did not die. —GEORGE ORWELL

She sat like a great icon in the back of the classroom, tranquil, guarded, sealed up, watchful. —REGINALD McKNIGHT

She considers how much their feelings for each other have grown over the years, silently, underground, like the roots of a plant, by this time all entangled and intertwined.
—JAMES RISEBOROUGH

Metaphors

His money was a sharp pair of scissors that snipped rapidly through tangles of red tape. —HISAYE YAMAMOTO

Nevertheless, Moira was our fantasy . . . She was lava beneath the crust of everyday life. —MARGARET ATWOOD

My flesh is boundless. An Everest of lipoids. —SAUL BELLOW

Single words are often used metaphorically:

These roses must be **planted** in good soil. [literal]

Keep your life **planted** wherever you can put down the most roots. [metaphorical]

We always **sweep** the leaves off the sidewalk. [literal]

He seems likely to **sweep** her right off her feet. [metaphorical]

Similes and metaphors are especially valuable when they are concrete and point up essential relationships that cannot otherwise be communicated. (For faulty metaphors, see 8c.) Similes and metaphors can also be extended throughout a comparison paragraph. (See 27d(5).)

Other common figures of speech include **personification** (attributing to non-humans characteristics possessed only by humans), **paradox** (a seemingly contradictory statement that actually makes sense when you think about it), and **irony** (a deliberate incongruity between what is stated and what is meant). In addition, experienced writers often enjoy using **overstatement, understatement, images,** and **allusions.** Figures of speech such as these can contribute to lively, memorable writing even if they do not always contribute to exactness. (For a discussion of these figures of speech, see 35a(4).)

14b Exact word choice requires an understanding of idioms.

An **idiom** is an expression whose meaning is peculiar to the language or differs from the individual meanings of its elements. Be careful to use idiomatic English, not unidiomatic approximations. *She talked down to him* is idiomatic. *She talked under to him* is not. Occasionally, the idiomatic use of prepositions proves difficult. If you do not know which preposition to use with a given word, check the dictionary. For instance, *agree* may be followed by *about, on, to,* or *with*. The choice depends on the context. Writers sometimes have trouble with expressions such as these:

accuse **of** perjury
bored **by** it
comply **with** rules
conform **to/with** standards
in accordance **with** policy
independent **of** his family
inferior **to** ours
happened **by** accident
jealous **of** others

Many idioms—such as *all the same, to mean well, eating crow, raining cats and dogs*—cannot be understood from the individual meanings of their elements. Some, such as *turning something over in one's mind,* are metaphorical. Such expressions cannot be meaningfully translated word for word into another language. Used every day, they are at the very heart of the English language. As you encounter idioms that are new to you, master their meanings just as you would when learning new words.

ESL When learning how to use idioms, study how writers use them. The context in which idioms appear will often clarify their meaning. For example, if you read "I never eat broccoli because I can't stand it," you would probably understand that *to not be able to stand something* means *to dislike something*. As you learn new idioms from your reading, try using them in your own writing. If you are not sure about the meaning of an idiom, check an idiom dictionary.

Exercise 4

Write sentences using each of the following idioms correctly. Use your dictionary when necessary.

1. hang up, hang out
2. differ from, differ with
3. wait on, wait for
4. get even with, get out of hand
5. on the go, on the spot

14c Fresh expressions are more distinctive than worn-out ones.

Such expressions as *bite the dust, breath of fresh air,* or *smooth as silk* were once striking and effective. Excessive use, however, has drained them of their original force and made them **clichés.** Some **euphemisms** (pleasant-sounding substitutions for more explicit but possibly offensive words) are not only trite but wordy or awkward—for example, *correctional facility* for *jail* or *pre-owned* for *used.* Many political slogans and the catchy phraseology of advertisements soon become hackneyed. Faddish or trendy expressions such as *whatever, impacted, paradigm, input,* or *be into* (as in "I am into dieting") were so overused that they quickly became clichés.

Nearly every writer uses clichés from time to time because they are so much a part of the language, especially the spoken language. But experienced writers often give a fresh twist to an old saying.

> "The way to a man's heart," she used to like to quip for her friends, "is an unmarked minefield."
> —DIANE SCHOEMPERLEN
> [COMPARE with the expression "The way to a man's heart is through his stomach."]

Variations on familiar expressions from literature or the Bible, many of which have become part of everyday language, can often be used effectively in your own writing.

> Now is the summer of my great content.
> —KATHERINE LANPHER
> [COMPARE Shakespeare's "Now is the winter of our discontent. . . . "]

Good writers, however, do not rely too heavily on the words of others; they choose their own words to communicate their own ideas.

Exercise 5

From the following list of trite expressions, select 10 that you often use or hear and replace them with carefully chosen words or phrases. Use 5 of them in sentences.

EXAMPLES
beyond the shadow of a doubt: *undoubtedly*
slept like a log: *slept deeply*

1. don't judge a book by its cover
2. it takes one to know one
3. it's six of one, half a dozen of the other
4. don't look a gift horse in the mouth
5. in today's society
6. when it rains, it pours
7. every cloud has a silver lining
8. for all intents and purposes
9. in this day and age
10. clear as mud
11. as strong as an ox
12. as a matter of fact
13. last but not least
14. few and far between
15. by leaps and bounds
16. sight for sore eyes
17. nipped in the bud
18. safe to say
19. each and every
20. new and unique

Exercise 6

Choose 5 of the 10 items below as the basis for 5 original sentences containing figurative language, exact denotations, and appropriate connotations.

1. the look of her hair
2. a hot summer day
3. studying for an exam
4. your favourite food
5. buying a car
6. an empty street
7. amateur athletes
8. a heavy rain
9. a traffic jam
10. the way he talks

Exercise 7

Study the following paragraphs and prepare to discuss in class your response to the authors' choice of words—their use of exact, specific language to communicate their ideas.

[1]The first Monday in October, and the fall weather has arrived. [2]Arctic light, white light. [3]Pale blue skies, gray clouds tinged with red. [4]I love the cooler wind. [5]It makes the sound of the city sharper and finer, a sound that can enter and carry everywhere, penetrating me. [6]Listen to the air, to what it stirs inside us and outside us, the incoherent fears and hopes, the waves of unspoken longing, the current that pulses toward a blowout in time.   —B. W. POWE

[1]At the back of the festival tent, called the mandap, Alfred Corbin stood beside the mukhi, in casual shirt and trousers and somewhat dazzled by the celebrations. [2]The air was laden, a heady mix of strong perfumes and sweat, incense and condensed milk, and dust stamped through the mats after a long day. [3]Boys raced about, babies wailed, old folk sat quietly in their corners, sherbet servers beseeched people to drink. [4]And in all this chaos, the uninterrupted drumbeat in the background, the sharp, regular clicking of the dancers' sticks, which made him flinch, the dancers' dizzying motion, the weaving and unweaving of the checkered sheaths.   —M. G. VASSANJI

Chapter 15

Conciseness: Avoiding Wordiness and Needless Repetition

Using words economically is fundamental to writing clearly because unnecessary words or phrases distract readers and blur meaning. Good writers know how to make their points concisely.

Wordy	During the latter part of the War of 1812, the British moved offensively against their American foes.
Concise	Near the end of the War of 1812, the British attacked the Americans.
Wordy	My sudden angry outburst was due to the fact that I was fatigued.
Concise	My angry outburst was due to fatigue.

In some situations, repetition of a word or phrase can be useful. (See **10b**, **11e**, and **27b(3)**.) But in most cases, repetition is a sign of inefficiency.

 15a Every word should count; words or phrases that add nothing to the meaning should be omitted.

(1) Redundancy

Restating a key point in different words can help readers understand it. (See **33h(4)**.) But there is no need to explain the meaning of readily understood terms by using different words that say the same thing. If you use additional words to convey meaning already conveyed by the words you've written, your work will suffer from redundancy: being repetitious for no good reason.

> Ballerinas auditioned ~~in the tryouts~~ for *The Nutcracker*.
>
> Each actor has a unique talent, ~~and ability that he or she uses in his or her acting.~~

In the common phrases listed below, useless words appear in brackets.

yellow [in colour]	circular [in shape]
at 9:45 a.m. [in the morning]	return [back]
[basic] essentials	rich [and wealthy] nations
bitter[-tasting] salad	small[-size] potatoes
but [though]	to apply [or utilize] rules
connect [up together]	[true] facts
because [of the fact that]	was [more or less] hinting
[really and truly] fearless	by [virtue of] his authority
fans [who were] watching TV	the oil [that exists] in shale

Avoid grammatical redundancy, such as double subjects (*my sister [she] is*), double comparisons ([*more*] *easier than*), and double negatives (*could[n't] hardly*).

(2) Unnecessary words

~~In the event that~~ *If* taxes are raised, expect complaints ~~on the part of the~~ *from* voters.

One or two words can replace expressions such as these:

at all times	**always**
at this point in time	**now**
by means of	**by**

for the purpose of	**for**
in an employment situation	**at work**
in spite of the fact that	**although**
on account of the fact that	**because**
somewhere in the neighbourhood of $2500	**about $2500**

One exact word can say as much as many inexact ones. (See also **14a**.)

spoke in a low and hard-to-hear voice	**mumbled**
persons who really know their particular field	**experts**

(3) Expletives

There followed by a form of *to be* is an *expletive*—a word that signals that the subject will follow the verb. (See also **11f**.) Because expletives shift emphasis away from the subject, they can result in the use of unnecessary words.

~~There were~~ ᴛhree children play~~ing~~ *ed* in the yard.

It is also an expletive when it lacks an antecedent and is followed by a form of *to be*.

Learning to ski
~~It~~ is easy ~~to learn to ski.~~

The *it* construction is necessary only when there is no logical subject. For example: It is going to snow.

Exercise 1

Substitute one or two words for each of the following phrases.

1. in this day and age
2. has the ability to sing
3. was of the opinion that
4. in a serious manner
5. prior to the time that
6. did put in an appearance
7. located in the vicinity of
8. has a tendency to break
9. during the same time that
10. involving too much expense

Exercise 2

Revise each of the following sentences to make them more concise.

1. When going on a cycling tour, I have two good tires on my bike, but in addition I always carry a spare tire besides.
2. I reflectively contemplated the fact that the machine was manually controlled and had to be operated by hand and not by another machine.
3. Muneer is an only child as he has no brothers or sisters.
4. It was clear to all of us at first glance that the houses were well built in their construction, but the interior furnishings within the houses left much to be desired.
5. Seldom in the annals of human history has there been an invention by mankind like the computer, which has managed to change irrevocably and completely the way we do business in our day-to-day affairs.

15b Combining sentences or simplifying phrases and clauses can eliminate needless words.

Note the differences in emphasis as you study the following examples.

~~The grass was like a carpet. It~~ *A carpet of blue-green grass* covered the whole playing field.

~~The colour of the grass was blue-green.~~

Some ~~phony~~ unscrupulous brokers are ~~taking money and sav-~~ *cheating*

~~ings from elderly~~ old people ~~who need that money because~~

~~they planned to use it as a retirement~~ *out of their* pension*s*

15c Repetition is useful only when it improves emphasis, clarity, or coherence. (See also 10b, 11e, and 27b(3).)

~~Your teacher is unlike my teacher.~~ Your teacher likes teaching better than mine ~~does.~~

She hoped he understood that ~~the complaint she made was~~ *her comment* ~~not the way that she really felt about things.~~ *did not reflect her real feelings*

We will not rest until we have pursued every lead, inspected every piece of evidence, and interviewed every suspect. [In this case, the repetition of *every* is useful because it emphasizes the writer's determination.]

15d Pronouns and elliptical constructions can eliminate needless repetition. (See chapter 6.)

Instead of needlessly repeating a noun or substituting a clumsy synonym, use a pronoun. If the reference is clear (6b), several pronouns can refer to the same antecedent.

The hall outside these offices was empty. ~~The hall~~ *It* had dirty floors, and ~~the~~ walls ~~of this corridor~~ *its* were covered with graffiti.

An **elliptical construction** (the omission of words that will be understood by the reader without being repeated) helps the writer of the following sentence be concise.

Speed is the goal for some swimmers, endurance [is the goal] for others, and relaxation [is the goal] for still others.

Sometimes, as an aid to clarity, commas mark omissions that avoid repetition.

My family functioned like a baseball team; my mom was the coach; my brother, the pitcher; and my sister, the shortstop.

As these examples show, parallelism facilitates elliptical constructions. (See chapter 10.)

Exercise 3

Revise the following sentences to eliminate wordiness and needless repetition.

1. People of all sorts used to flock to Niagara Falls to experience on a first-hand basis the loudly thundering falls, but now people throng to Niagara Falls because it has become a well-known resort for gambling.
2. Then, from the general direction of the back staircase, I detected a smell that resembled the odour of gasoline.
3. Mankind has used two basic and fundamental forms of communication. These two forms of communication are writing and speaking.
4. Ms. Legros, an instructor in the Department of Political Science, presented a lecture on feminization of poverty in Canada.
5. From the bluffs that run through the northern part of the city of Calgary, we could see the peaks of the Rocky Mountains, which were covered in snow.

15e A clear, straightforward style is preferable to an ornate one.

An ornate or flowery style makes reading slow and calls attention to your words rather than your ideas. Although different styles are appropriate for different situations—depending, for example, on purpose, audience, and occasion (28a)—you should usually keep your writing simple and straightforward.

Ornate   The majority believes that the approbation of society derives primarily from diligent pursuit of allocated tasks.

Simple   Most people believe that success results from hard work.

ESL North American rhetoric derives many of its principles from the work of philosophers in classical Greece and Rome who advocated a plain, straightforward style. Other cultures, shaped by different traditions, may tend to favour a more indirect style. If you initially feel uncomfortable writing the straightforward North American form of English, consider your word choice (chapter 13) and your tone (29a). By making careful choices, it is possible to be both straightforward and polite.

Exercise 4

Rewrite the following passages for a friendly audience that likes a simple, straightforward style.

1. Expert delineation of the characters in a work of fiction is a task that is difficult to facilitate.
2. In an employment situation, social pleasantries may contribute to the successful functioning of job tasks, but such interactions should not distract attention from the need to complete all assignments in a timely manner.
3. Commitment to an ongoing and carefully programmed schedule of physical self-management can be a significant resource for stress reduction.
4. The Centre for Automotive Maintenance recommends regular monitoring of fluids necessary for internal combustion vehicles and increasing the allocation level of such fluids when necessary.
5. Students troubled by dysfunctions in interpersonal relationships can receive support from information specialists in the counselling division of health services.

Chapter 16

Clarity and Completeness

In rapid speech we often seem to omit words because our listeners simply do not hear them. These words are necessary in writing, however, to make the meaning clear. For example, instead of "We had better study hard" a listener might hear "We better study hard." Although *had* is often not heard in speech, it must be included in writing.

16a   **Articles, pronouns, conjunctions, or prepositions are sometimes necessary for clarity and completeness.**

(1) Use of articles

Review material on count and non-count nouns. (See 1c(2).)

 E S L   Indefinite articles

The indefinite articles *a* and *an* are used with singular countable nouns in the following situations:

with descriptive or general nouns

     a house   **an** orange

with something mentioned for the first time

     Our history professor assigned **a** test for next Monday.

with the meaning of *one,* not *more*

> I chose **a** piece of fruit from the basket.

with reference to a member of a group

> **a** novel

Use *a* before a consonant sound: **a** yard, **a** university. Use *an* before a vowel sound: **an** apple, **an** hour.

Plural count nouns use words such as *some* or *any*. (See 7a(7).)

> **some** magazines   **any** books

Definite articles

The definite article *the* is used with singular or plural non-count nouns to indicate a specific person, place, or thing in the following situations:

when the noun has been previously introduced or when you and the reader know what you are referring to

> I will replace **the** hard drive.

> I need to record a program tonight. **The** program is on global warming.

when the noun is unique

> **the** Confederation Bridge

when an ordinal number (fourth, sixth) or superlative (least, best) comes before the noun

> **the** eighth day of the month

> **the** least expensive

Omission of the article

The article is omitted entirely in a number of cases and is optional in others. Some general directions for omitting the article follow:

with another determiner

> Sign up for this new course.

before a non-count noun

> Let's have ice cream and cake.

before a plural countable noun that does not refer to a specific item

> Buy oranges and apples.

before a plural noun that has a general meaning

> Everyone wants benefits.

in certain common expressions

> go to school, go to class, go to college, go to bed

Confusion with omitted articles

The sentence in the following example is ambiguous. Unless edited, the person "standing nearby" could be either one person or two.

> A friend and *a* helper stood nearby.

(2) Omitted conjunctions or prepositions

In the following example, the *of* is often omitted in speech but is added in writing.

> We had never tried that type *of* film before.

Although often omitted in speech, two prepositions may be required after different verbs to make the meaning clear.

> I neither believe *in* nor approve of those attitudes.

In the following sentences, use a comma when the conjunction *and* is omitted.

> Habitat for Humanity built the house, (**and**) then later painted it.

16b **Verbs and auxiliaries that are sometimes omitted in speech are necessary in writing to avoid awkwardness or to complete meaning.**

The revision eliminates the awkwardness in the following sentence.

Voter turnout has never *been* and will never be 100 percent.

Although *is* may not be heard in speech, it is included in writing.

Lamont *is* strong and very tall.

In sentences such as the following, omitting or including the second verb is optional.

The storm was fierce and the thunder (**was**) deafening.

16c **Complete comparisons are needed in writing to complete the meaning if it is not suggested by the context.**

He is taller *than his brother.*

Most people think television is more violent *than it used to be.*

Comparisons can be completed by other words or phrases in the sentence, by other sentences in the paragraph, or by the context.

In the next century, people will need more education.

16d The intensifiers *so, such,* and *too* need a completing phrase or clause.

In informal writing, a completing phrase is often omitted after intensifiers such as *so, such,* and *too* when they are used for emphasis.

The smell is **so** strong.

We had **such** a good time.

He is **too** broke.

In formal writing, intensifiers are followed by a completing phrase or clause.

The smell is **so** strong **that we had to open a window.**

We had **such** a good time **that we decided to go to Calgary for the Stampede next year.**

He is **too** broke **to go out clubbing tonight.**

Exercise 1

Supply the words needed for formal writing in the following verb phrases and comparisons.

1. They always have and always will go to the coast for vacation.
2. Cars with standard transmissions are better.
3. Arman likes his hardcover books better.
4. The airline passengers better pay attention to the safety guidelines.
5. Siobhan been trying to make her research paper more persuasive.

Exercise 2

Insert words where needed.

1. In the winter, the rain in Toronto is often as heavy as Vancouver.
2. Stephen and Donna had an unusual party their last anniversary.
3. She is one of my favourite and definitely most skilful hockey players.
4. The union members were angered and protested against the British Columbia government's cutbacks in the public service.
5. The meeting was full of delegates and still coming.

Punctuation

Chapter 17

The Comma

Punctuation lends to written language a flexibility that facial expressions, pauses, and variations in voice pitch give to spoken language. For instance, a pause after *called* in the first example below makes it clear that the spoken sentence refers to only two people—the *sister* and a person named *Mary Ellen*. In the second example, a pause after *Mary* lets us know that the sentence refers to three people—the *sister, Mary,* and *Ellen*. In written language, a comma creates this pause.

When my sister called, Mary Ellen answered.

When my sister called Mary, Ellen answered.

If you understand the following four principles, you will see through most of the mystery surrounding commas and find them easier to use consistently.

Commas

- come before co-ordinating conjunctions when they link independent clauses.
- follow introductory adverb clauses and, usually, introductory phrases.
- separate items in a series (including co-ordinate adjectives).
- set off nonrestrictive and other parenthetical elements.

17a A comma comes before a co-ordinating conjunction that links independent clauses.

CONJUNCTION

INDEPENDENT
CLAUSE,

Subject + predicate,

{ and
but
or
for
nor
so
yet }

INDEPENDENT
CLAUSE.

subject + predicate.

There was no cheating, and we played until one of us won everything the other players had. —ALOOTOOK IPELLIE

Canadian society must also accept responsibility, yet many Canadians remain unaware of Aboriginal history.
—JAN HARE and JEAN BARMAN

The first Europeans borrowed many words from the natives during their first century or so of occupation, but only a few of these "wigwam" words survive today in their original form. —VICTOR STEVENSON

There wasn't much on the ground, so it took her a while to get a good load. —DAVID MICHAEL KAPLAN

I am not complaining, nor am I protesting either.
—RALPH ELLISON

Very early in the morning, it was still almost night, Gregor had the chance to test the strength of his new resolutions, for his sister, nearly fully dressed, opened the door from the hall and peered in. —FRANZ KAFKA

He saw something, or he did something. —ALLEN ABEL

When a sentence contains multiple clauses, a comma comes before each co-ordinating conjunction.

> I chose to follow in the footsteps of my unconventional Aunt Esther, and I have never regretted my choice, but I think my mother was jealous of Aunt Esther, and I fear she never approved of me.

When the clauses are short, the comma can be omitted before *and, but,* or *or,* but not usually before *for, nor, so,* or *yet.* (See also page 37.)

> The windshield was a planetarium of open space and in the midday light the full moon hovered like a destination.
> —STEVEN HEIGHTON

Sometimes a semicolon separates independent clauses, especially when the second one contains commas or when it reveals a contrast. (See also **18a.**)

> Most people, according to my mother, skip cleaning in the corners; on the other hand, she used to say, they don't skip payday.

Not all co-ordinating conjunctions, however, are preceded by commas. A common slip is to place one before the *and* linking the parts of a compound predicate.

> I find myself **tapping** my toes to the prancing rhythms of the bongos and **following** the flights of invention and dexterity on guitar and cello and sax. —PETER GZOWSKI [compound predicate—no comma before *and*]

Especially when a sentence is long, writers occasionally use a comma to emphasize a distinction between the parts of the predicate, as in E. M. Forster's "Artists always seek a new technique, and will continue to do so as long as their work excites them."

Exercise 1

Follow **17a** as you insert commas before conjunctions to link the independent clauses in these sentences. (Remember that not all co-ordinating conjunctions link independent clauses and that *but*, *for*, *so*, and *yet* do not always function as co-ordinating conjunctions.)

1. My wife and I have trouble with our eyes. We both wear eyeglasses.
2. We should have reached the cottage an hour ago. We had a flat tire and got lost around Peterborough.
3. Millions of people from all over the world immigrated to Canada through Pier 21 in Halifax, Nova Scotia. The federal government will make it a historic site.
4. The instructor told the students to form research groups at the beginning of the semester. Only two groups were formed by mid-semester.
5. He had never gone fly-fishing before going to the Grand River. He had never caught a trout, either.

17b A comma usually follows introductory words, phrases, and clauses.

(1) Adverb clauses before independent clauses

ADVERB CLAUSE, INDEPENDENT CLAUSE.

When you write, you make a sound in the reader's head.
—RUSSELL BAKER

The safest automobile on the road is expensive, but if I consider the protection it offers, I cannot find the cost unreasonable. [adverb clause preceding the second independent clause]

If the omission does not make reading difficult, writers may omit the comma after an introductory adverb clause, especially when the clause is short.

> If I were the president of a bank I would have a fine statue of the Goddess of Fortune standing in the middle of every branch, and I would have Cicero's great dictum "Man's life is ruled by Fortune, not by wisdom" embossed on all the bank's stationery.   —ROBERTSON DAVIES

A comma is usually unnecessary when the adverb clause follows the independent clause.

> Max was an expert at changing tires because he had watched his dad do it hundreds of times. [*Because,* a subordinating conjunction, introduces an adverbial clause.]

If an adverb clause does not affect the meaning of the independent clause, a comma can precede it.

> Women must be able to take their birth names from their mothers and keep them after marriage, if they wish to be truly equal.

(2) Introductory phrases before independent clauses

> INTRODUCTORY PHRASE, ⎫
> INTRODUCTORY WORD, ⎬ subject + predicate.

Prepositional phrases

> Through the poplars, the forks of light plunge into the flanks of the mountains, and for an instant the ribbed gullies stand out like skeletons under a sheet.   —MICHAEL IGNATIEFF

If the comma after an introductory prepositional phrase is not necessary to prevent misreading, it can be omitted:

For safety the university installed call boxes linked directly to campus security.

Other types of phrases

Having travelled nowhere, she believed the rest of the world was like her own small town; having read little, she had no sense of how other people think. [participial phrases before both independent clauses—see also 1d and 1e]

The language difference aside, life in Germany doesn't seem much different from life in Canada. [absolute phrase—see also 17d(7)]

Introductory words

Furthermore, the person responsible for breaking or damaging university equipment will be fined. [transitional expression—see the lists on pages 41–42]

Well, move the ball or move the body.
—ALLEN JACKSON [interjection]

Yes, I bought my tickets yesterday. No, I didn't pay cash. [introductory *yes* or *no*]

Commas are not used after phrases that begin inverted sentences. (See also 11f.)

With the doughnuts came free coffee. [COMPARE "Free coffee came with the doughnuts."]

Of far greater concern than censorship of bad words is censorship of ideas. —DONNA WOOLFOLK CROSS

Exercise 2

Insert a comma where needed in the following sentences. Explain why each comma is necessary. Put a check mark before any sentence in which a comma is not needed.

1. In order to do well on an exam it's usually a good idea to study a little bit after every class.

2. Since you retain less information when you cram cramming is not an effective way of studying for a test.
3. In addition to excellent notes mnemonic devices can also help you remember important information for a test.
4. In order to work properly a mnemonic device has to be memorable and personalized.
5. During a lecture it's important to listen for cues from your professor that can help you determine what might be included on a test.
6. Summarizing your readings and your lecture notes is an important step in synthesizing course material.
7. Although tests can determine students' knowledge of a subject at a particular time they cannot be considered adequate measures of intelligence or creativity.
8. By sitting front and centre in the classroom during history class Janet was able to get more out of her classroom time.
9. To control feelings of anxiety and panic that come with taking a test try breathing deeply and relaxing your muscles from head to toe.
10. With plenty of time left in the test Fatima was able to check her answers and catch a couple of mistakes she had made.

17c Commas separate items in a series (including co-ordinate adjectives).

A series contains three or more parallel elements. (See chapter 10.) The punctuation of a series depends on its form:

The melon was *pink*, *sweet*, and *juicy*. [a, b, and c—a preferred comma before *and*]

The melon was *pink*, *sweet* and *juicy*. [a, b and c—an acceptable omission of the comma before *and* when there is no danger of misreading; compare "Leila was my mother's sister, my aunt and my friend," a compound appositive indicating two elements: a, a and b]

The melon was *pink*, *sweet*, *juicy*. [a, b, c]

(1) Words, phrases, and clauses in a series

A pet should be affectionate, trusting, obedient, and intelligent. [words in a series]

We had to climb over several hills, walk for miles through a dark forest, and fight off a bear to get to the cottage. [phrases in a series]

My idea of a great vacation spot is one where no telephone rings, someone else fixes me great food, and I sit on the porch in the cool shade all day and read mystery novels. [clauses in a series]

If items in a series contain internal commas, you can make the meaning clear by separating the items with semicolons. (See **18b**.)

For special emphasis, writers sometimes use commas to slow the pace when co-ordinating conjunctions link all the items in a series.

We cannot put it off for a month, or a week, or even a day.

The melon was *pink* and *sweet* and *juicy*. [a and b and c]

(2) Co-ordinate adjectives

Co-ordinate adjectives are two or more adjectives that modify the same noun or pronoun. One test for co-ordinate adjectives is to switch them; another is to put *and* between them. If the meaning does not change, the adjectives are co-ordinate. Commas separate co-ordinate adjectives not linked by a co-ordinating conjunction.

It is a waiting, silent, limp room. —EUDORA WELTY [*Waiting, silent,* and *limp* all modify *room*. COMPARE "It is a silent, limp waiting room."]

Walking along the rushing, shallow creek, I slipped on a rock and sank above my boot tops into a small, still pool. [*Rushing* and *shallow* modify *creek*, and *small* and *still* modify *pool*.]

Exercise 3

Using commas as needed, write sentences supplying co-ordinate adjectives to modify any 5 of the following 10 word groups.

EXAMPLE
metric system   *Most countries use the familiar, sensible metric system to measure distances.*

1. onion bagel
2. classical music
3. cheddar cheese
4. metal sculpture
5. computer software

6. community college
7. baseball parks
8. office buildings
9. sports car
10. regional road

17d   Commas set off nonrestrictive and other parenthetical elements, as well as contrasted elements, items in dates, and so on.

Nonrestrictive clauses or phrases give nonessential information about a noun or pronoun. They can be omitted without changing the meaning.

To set off a nonrestrictive word or word group, use two commas, unless the element is placed at the beginning or the end of the sentence. (Expressions that come at the beginning of a sentence are also treated in **17b**.) Of course, not all words preceded and followed by commas are nonrestrictive.

Most single people in their twenties, according to my brother, prefer to live at home where Mom and Dad pay the big bills. [COMPARE "According to my brother, most single people . . ." and ". . . Mom and Dad pay the big bills, according to my brother."]

Restrictive clauses or phrases follow and limit the words they modify. They are essential to the clear identification of the word or words they refer to.

(1) Adjective clauses or phrases

Adjective clauses that describe the noun they modify are nonrestrictive, but those that limit the noun are restrictive. In the first example below, the proper name "Marilyn Greer" identifies which woman at the bank the sentence is describing. As a result, the sentence requires no additional information unless there are two Marilyn Greers. "The woman," however, could be any woman, not just the bank manager, and so needs a modifier that limits it to someone in particular.

Nonrestrictive	Restrictive or Essential
Clauses	
I spoke with Marilyn Greer, who manages the bank.	I spoke to the woman who manages the bank.
We climbed Mt. Logan, which is over 5000 metres high.	We climbed a mountain that is over 5000 metres high.
Phrase	
The new Saturn, covered in mud, looks worn out.	The new car covered in mud looks worn out.

Sometimes only the omission or use of commas indicates whether a modifier is restrictive or nonrestrictive and thus signals the writer's exact meaning. Although many writers prefer to use *that* at the beginning of restrictive clauses, *which* has become acceptable if it does not cause confusion.

I like to drive a car that [or which] has fast acceleration and nimble handling.

(2) Appositives

Appositives can supply additional but nonessential details about a noun or pronoun (nonrestrictive), or else they limit the meaning of a noun or pronoun by indicating which one—or ones—is meant (restrictive).

Nonrestrictive	Restrictive or Essential
Even Rifka Cole**, my friend,** let me down.	Even my friend **Rifka Cole** let me down.
Voyager photographed Saturn**, the ringed planet.**	Voyager photographed the planet **Saturn**.

Abbreviations after names are treated as nonrestrictive appositives: "Was the letter from Frances Evans**, Ph.D.,** or from F. H. Evans**, M.D.**?"

Exercise 4

Set off nonrestrictive adjective clauses or phrases and nonrestrictive appositives with commas. Put a check mark after any sentence that needs no commas.

1. The woman who heads the food-drive committee at work broke her leg on a skiing trip to Kananaskis.
2. Doreen Grey who heads the food-drive committee at work broke her leg on a skiing trip to Kananaskis.
3. Few people in Canada know that there is a town in Australia called Toronto which is about 200 kilometres north of Sydney.
4. The Toronto in Australia was named after the hometown of Ned Hanlan the world champion rower in 1880.
5. The Edmonton Fringe Festival which is held annually draws thousands of visitors to the city each year.

(3) Contrasted elements

Human beings**, unlike oysters,** frequently reveal their emotions.   —GEORGE F. WILL

Some writers put a comma before *but* and *not* in such sentences as the following, while others do not.

Other citizens who disagree with me base their disagreement**,** not on facts different from the ones I know**,** but on a different set of values.   —RENÉ DUBOS

Family members relate to one another not through biological programming but rather through negotiating and renegotiating their idiosyncratic version of received cultural blueprints.

—MARLENE MACKIE

(4) Geographical names, items in dates, and addresses

Drumheller, Alberta, is home to the Royal Tyrrell Museum of Paleontology.

I had to write to Ms. Melanie Hobson, 2873 Central Avenue, Parrsboro, NS B0M 1S1. [no comma between the province abbreviation and the postal code]

Hunter applied for the job on Wednesday, June 12, 1996, but turned it down on June 14 because it paid only minimum wage.

OR

Hunter applied for the job on Wednesday 12 June and turned it down on Friday 14 June because it paid only minimum wage. [Commas are omitted when the day of the month precedes rather than follows the month.]

(5) Parenthetical expressions

Language, then, sets the tone of our society.

—EDWIN NEWMAN

Much of the court and, thus, a good deal of the action are often invisible to a basketball player, so he needs more than good eyesight. —JOHN McPHEE

When they cause little or no pause in reading, expressions such as *also, too, of course, nonetheless, perhaps, at least, therefore,* and *likewise* need not be set off by commas.

Everyone nonetheless appeared from the woods and converged on the fishing spot within minutes of one another.

—HUGH BRODY

I'm trying to keep my spending to a minimum **at least** until I finish my degree.

(6) Mild interjections and words used in direct address

Ah, that's my idea of a good meal. [interjection]

Now is the time, **animal lovers,** to protest. [direct address]

(7) Absolute phrases

His temper being what it is, I don't want a confrontation.

Glaciers would move in and clobber the range, **gouging out its current profile.** —JAMIE FINDLAY

17e Commas are occasionally needed for ease in reading.

Some commas are necessary to prevent misreading. Without them the following sentences would confuse the reader, if only temporarily.

Still, water must be transported to dry areas. [COMPARE "Still water. . . . "]

The day before, I had talked with her on the phone. [COMPARE "I had talked with her the day before."]

Someone predicted that by the year 2025, 50 million people will live in Canada. [COMPARE "Someone predicted that by the year 2025 50 million people will live in Canada."]

The earth breathes, in a certain sense. —LEWIS THOMAS [COMPARE "The earth breathes in moisture."]

Sometimes a comma replaces a clearly understood word or group of words.

Politicians sometimes make controversial remarks; bureaucrats, never. —MARGARET McCARTHY

Exercise 5

Explain the reason for each comma used, and point out which commas are optional and which are a matter of stylistic preference.

1. The wet, chill first of the spring, its blackness made tender by the lilac wash of the afterglow, lay upon the high, open stretches of the stump lots. —SIR CHARLES G. D. ROBERTS
2. My guess is that as the family breaks down, friendships will grow in importance. —SUSAN LEE
3. The road in the mountains was slick and black, and when the bus slowed for hairpins, I looked down into the damp Northwest, at tops of trees so green they were grey.
   —LINDA SVENDSEN
4. But alas, I do not rule the world and that, I am afraid, is the story of my life—always a godmother, never a god.
   —FRAN LEBOWITZ
5. We have grown powerfully accustomed to change, whether it is real change, or whether it is the change we experience as a result of what we find out as we grow older. —JOEY SLINGER

Exercise 6

For humorous effect the writer of the following paragraph deliberately omits commas that can be justified by the rules in this chapter. Identify where commas might be inserted to contribute to ease in reading. Compare your version with someone else's and comment on any differences you find.

[1]The commas are the most useful and usable of all the stops. [2]It is highly important to put them in place as you go along. [3]If you try to come back after doing a paragraph and stick them in the various spots that tempt you you will discover that they tend to swarm like minnows into all sorts of crevices whose existence you hadn't realized and before you know it the whole long sentence becomes immobilized and lashed up squirming in commas. [4]Better to use them sparingly, and with affection precisely when the need for one arises, nicely, by itself.

—LEWIS THOMAS, *The Medusa and the Snail*

17f   Unnecessary (or misplaced) commas send false signals that can confuse a reader.

Although a comma ordinarily signals a pause, not every pause calls for a comma. As you read the following sentence aloud, you may pause naturally at several places, but no commas are necessary.

> The wedding ceremony was scheduled for the early afternoon and it came off without a hitch except for the fact that my wife wore a silky dress and she kept slipping off the satin cushion when we knelt in front of the minister.
>
> —GARY LAUTENS

To avoid using unnecessary commas, observe the following guidelines.

(1) Commas do not separate the subject from its verb or the verb from its object.

Remove the circled commas.

> Most older, married students⊙ must hold a job in addition to going to school. [separation of subject (*students*) and verb (*must hold*)]
>
> The lawyer said⊙ that I could appeal the speeding ticket. [separation of verb (*said*) and direct object (a noun clause: *that I could . . .*)]

(2) Commas do not follow co-ordinating conjunctions, and they immediately precede them only when they link independent clauses. (See chapter 3 and 17a.)

Remove the circled commas.

> I fed the dog⊙ and put it out for the night. [separation of compound verbs (*fed . . .* and *put out*)]

> For three decades the government has warned us about the dangers of smoking, but⊙ millions of people still smoke. [separation of the conjunction (*but*) and the subject of the clause (*millions of people*)]

(3) Commas set off only those words and short phrases that are clearly parenthetical.

Remove the circled commas.

> Martha was born⊙ in Windsor⊙ in 1976.

> Perhaps⊙ the valve is not correctly calibrated.

(4) Commas do not set off restrictive (necessary) clauses, phrases, or appositives. (See 17d.)

Remove the circled commas.

> Everyone⊙ who owns an automobile⊙ needs to have collision insurance.

> With strains of bagpipes in the background, crowds watched two men⊙ carrying lances as they charged each other on horseback.

(5) Commas do not precede the first or follow the last item of a series (including a series of co-ordinate adjectives).

Remove the circled commas.

> Field trips were required in a few courses, such as⊙ botany, geology, and sociology.

> I've always wanted a low-slung, fast, elegant⊙ convertible.

Exercise 7

Study the structure of the following sentences, then answer the question that follows by giving a specific reason for each item. Be prepared to explain your answers in class.

[1]At the age of eighty my mother had her last bad fall, and after that her mind wandered free through time. [2]Some days she went to weddings and funerals that had taken place half a century earlier. [3]On others she presided over family dinners cooked on Sunday afternoons for children who were now gray with age. [4]Through all this she lay in bed but moved across time, traveling among the dead decades with a speed and ease beyond the gift of physical science.

—RUSSELL BAKER

Explain why there is no comma after the following words: (1) *eighty,* (2) *and* (sent. 1), (3) *that* (sent. 1), (4) *weddings,* (5) *and* (sent. 2), (6) *others,* (7) *dinners,* (8) *this* (sent. 4), (9) *bed,* and (10) *and* (sent. 4).

Exercise 8

Change the structure and punctuation of the following sentences according to the pattern of the examples.

EXAMPLE

A fishing boat saw their distress signal, and it stopped to offer aid. [an appropriate comma: see 17a]

A fishing boat saw their distress signal and stopped to offer aid. [The second main clause is reduced to a part of the compound predicate, so the comma is no longer needed.]

1. Our employers gave us very good annual evaluations, and they also recommended us for raises.
2. Much modern fiction draws on current psychological knowledge, and it presents very believable characters.
3. Kim has several jobs to put herself through college, and she works hard at all of them.

EXAMPLE
If a person suffers physical abuse, he or she should notify the police. [an appropriate comma: see 17b(1)]
Any person who suffers physical abuse should notify the police. [The introductory adverb clause is converted to a restrictive clause, so the comma is no longer needed.]

4. When people make requests rather than give orders, they generally get cooperation.
5. If older folks want younger folks to take advice, they would do well to listen to what the young people say.

Exercise 9

Explain each comma in the following paragraph (from *Time* magazine).

[1]Yet punctuation is something more than a culture's birthmark; it scores the music in our minds, gets our thoughts moving to the rhythm of our hearts. [2]Punctuation is the notation in the sheet music of our words, telling us when to rest, or when to raise our voices; it acknowledges that the meaning of our discourse, as of any symphonic composition, lies not in the units, but in the pauses, the pacing and the phrasing. [3]Punctuation adjusts the tone and color and volume till the feeling comes into perfect focus. . . . [4]A world which has only periods is a world without inflections. It is a world without shade. [5]It has a music without sharps and flats. [6]It has a jack-boot rhythm. [7]Words cannot bend and curve. . . . [8]A comma, by comparison, catches the gentle drift of the mind in thought, turning in on itself and back on itself, reversing, redoubling and returning along the course of its own sweet river music; while the semicolon brings clauses and thoughts together with all the silent discretion of a hostess arranging guests around her dinner table. . . . [9]Punctuation, then, is a matter of care. [10]Care for words, yes, but also, and more important, for what the words imply. —PICO IYER

Chapter 18

The Semicolon

The semicolon has two uses: First, it links closely related independent clauses.

> Veronica watched *Fashion TV*; Elias wanted to watch the hockey game.

Second, by acting as a stronger mark of punctuation than the comma, it separates sentence elements that contain internal commas.

> Watching stupid, sentimental, dull soap operas; eating junk food like french fries, cheeseburgers, and milkshakes; and just doing nothing are my favourite vices.

Semicolons connect independent clauses not linked by a co-ordinating conjunction.

Two or more related independent clauses can be linked by a semicolon, connected by co-ordinating conjunctions (*and, but, for, or, nor, so, yet*), or punctuated as separate sentences.

> Some french fries are greasy; others are not; I like them all.
>
> Some french fries are greasy, **and** others are not, **but** I like them all.
>
> Some french fries are greasy. Others are not. I like them all.

The semicolons indicate a close connection between the ideas, the conjunctions indicate a less close connection, and the periods separate the ideas. Note the different intonation patterns when you read the above sentences aloud.

This principle also applies in compound-complex sentences. (See also 18b.)

> When you discover yourself lying on the ground, limp and unresisting, head in the dirt, and helpless, the earth seems to shift forward as a presence; hard, emphatic, not mere surface but a genuine force—there is no other word for it but *presence*.   —JOYCE CAROL OATES

Sometimes a semicolon (instead of the usual comma) precedes a co-ordinating conjunction when a sharp division between the two independent clauses is desired. (See also 17a, page 190.)

> Politicians may refrain from negative campaigning for a time; but when the race gets close, they can't seem to resist trying to dredge up personal dirt to use on their opponents.

Occasionally, a comma separates short, very closely related main clauses.

> We are strengthened by equality, we are weakened by it; we celebrate it, we repudiate it.   —THOMAS GRIFFITH   [A semicolon is used between pairs of independent clauses joined by commas.]

A semicolon precedes conjunctive adverbs only when they come between independent clauses. (See 3b and the list on page 41.)

> Some french fries are greasy; **however**, others are not. I like them any way you fix them.

After a conjunctive adverb or transitional expression, the comma is often omitted when the adverb is not considered parenthetical or when the comma is not needed to prevent misreading.

Quebec is unique among North American cities; indeed it has a more European feel.

When the second main clause explains or amplifies the first, a colon is sometimes used between main clauses. (See 21d(1), page 227.)

Amit's history essay touches on several important points: these include class differences, industrialization, and government motivation.

The semicolon is characteristic of very formal or literary writing. It is often better to revise compound sentences using a subordinate construction or sentence punctuation. (See chapter 9.)

 18b Semicolons separate elements that themselves contain commas.

I subscribe to several computer magazines that include reviews of new, better-designed hardware; descriptions of inexpensive commercial software programs; advice from experts; and actual utility programs that make keeping track of my files easier.

Exercise 1

Substitute a semicolon for any comma that could result in misreading.

1. A large number of today's popular authors include politicians and their advisers, experts in the social sciences, such as psychologists and sociologists, and physicists and geologists.
2. In her research paper, Brigitte cited Noam Chomsky, the father of transformational linguistics, Bertrand Russell, the famous logician, philosopher, and pacifist, and Carl Rogers, a clinical psychologist interested in counselling.

18c Semicolons do not connect parts of unequal grammatical rank.

Semicolons do not connect clauses and phrases. (See 1d and 1e.)

I admired Mr. Nguyen, the repair wizard.

We drove two cars to Cape Breton, it being perhaps the most scenic island in the country.

Semicolons do not connect a main clause and a subordinate clause.

I learned that she had lost her job, which really surprised me.

This suit is really too tight, although I can still wear it.

Exercise 2

Find the semicolons used between parts of unequal rank and punctuate appropriately. Do not change properly used semicolons.

1. While walking near Osoyoos, B.C., I found myself eye to eye with a dangerous animal; a rattlesnake to be exact.
2. Maureen had convinced herself that she needed a make-over; no more brush cuts and Doc Martens; it was time for a shoulder-length bob and sensible pumps.
3. Swimming in the surf; having a barbeque on the beach; watching the eerie mist blow in from the Pacific Ocean; were what we did on Long Beach on Vancouver Island.
4. Despite the fact that she walked from the centre of Penticton to Naramata; her feet weren't sore at all.
5. On the east coast of Prince Edward Island, a sundial stands in the middle of a forest; it is one of the unique local curiosities.

Chapter 19

The Apostrophe

Apostrophes show possession (except for personal pronouns), mark omissions in contractions, and form certain plurals.

19a The apostrophe shows possession for nouns and indefinite pronouns (*everyone, everybody*).

The possessive case shows ownership: Tonya's car. The possessive case of nouns and of indefinite pronouns is indicated by the use of *'s*—see **19a(1)**—or by the apostrophe alone—see **19a(2)**.

Guy's pie   someone's car

Occasionally, the possessive is indicated by both an *of* phrase and *'s* (often called a **double possessive**):

that book of Emil's [Emil owns or wrote the book.]

that book of Emil [The book describes Emil.]

A possessive can follow the word it modifies:

Is that new computer Ana's or Kim's? [COMPARE Ana's or Kim's computer.]

(1) Singular nouns, indefinite pronouns, and acronyms add the apostrophe and -*s*.

Nona's house   anyone's computer   CAF's goal

When the '*s* results in the awkward repetition of an *s*, *x*, or *z* sound, the -*s* is omitted: *Ramses' tomb.*

(2) Plural nouns ending in -*s* add only the apostrophe.

the boys' game   the babies' toys

Plurals not ending in -*s* add the apostrophe and -*s*.

men's lives   women's cars

(3) Compounds and expressions that show joint ownership add the apostrophe and -*s* to the last word only.

Olga and Nadia's house [COMPARE Olga and Nadia's houses—they jointly own more than one house.]

her mother-in-law's telephone

Walter Bryan, Jr.'s edited version [To avoid confusion, no comma follows *Jr.'s* although *Jr.* is often set off by commas.]

(4) Individual ownership is indicated by adding the apostrophe and -*s* to each name.

Tamiko's and Sam's apartments

(5) Sometimes a relationship comparable to ownership adds the apostrophe, especially in time relationships, in academic titles, or before gerunds. (See 1d(2).)

an hour's delay   in a week's time
Bachelor's degree   Asa's dancing
Asif's having to be there seemed unnecessary.

Proper names (organizations, geographical locations, and so on) sometimes do not use the apostrophe or the apostrophe and -*s*. Follow local usage.

Devil's Island   Devils Tower   Devil Mountain

Exercise 1

Change the modifier after the noun to a possessive form before the noun, following the pattern of the examples.

EXAMPLES

proposals made by the committee	the committee's proposals
poems written by Keats	Keats's poems
	OR Keats' poems

1. the mansion of Conrad Black
2. a hat belonging to somebody else
3. shoes for children
4. the glossary of that book
5. an error made by the math professor
6. the desires of the employer
7. the coat belonging to Maurice Champaign, Jr.
8. the sounds of the video game and dishwasher
9. the apartment inhabited by Govind
10. the aspirations of my brother
11. worth 50 cents
12. paintings by Picasso
13. a paper written by David and Jennifer
14. the description of the child
15. the friends of Mary and Ashevak

19b   **The apostrophe marks omissions in contractions and numbers.**

don't   they'll   class of '98

E S L   Since contractions are seldom used in academic writing, you can safely write out the two words in question and omit contractions altogether: *do not, they will*.

19c   The apostrophe and -*s* form certain plurals.

The apostrophe and -*s* are used for the plural forms of lowercase letters and of abbreviations followed by periods.

his *p*'s and *q*'s.

When needed to prevent confusion, '*s* shows the plural of capital letters and of words referred to as words.

too many A's   three minus's

When no confusion would result, either '*s* or -*s* forms such plurals as the following:

the 1990's OR the 1990s   his 7's OR his 7s
her and's OR her ands   the UFO's OR the UFOs
the &'s OR the &s

Who's is the contraction of *who is*. *Whose* is the possessive form of the relative pronoun *who*.

Who's [Who is] responsible?   **Whose** responsibility is it?

! **CAUTION** An '*s* is not used to indicate plurals of words: The Smiths are home.

19d   Personal pronouns and plural nouns that are not possessive do not take an apostrophe.

A personal pronoun (*I, we, you, he, she, it, they*) has its own form to show possession (*my, mine, our, ours, your, yours, his, her, hers, its, their, theirs*).

A friend of **theirs** knows a cousin of **yours**.

! **CAUTION** Do not confuse *it's* with *its*. *It's* is a contraction for *it is*. *Its* is the possessive form of *it*. Used with a personal pronoun, *'s* always indicates a contraction.

Its glass is cracked.	**It's** [it is] cracked.
The bear has **its** cave.	**It's** [it is] the bear's cave.
The board made **its** plan.	**It's** [it is] the board's plan.

Exercise 2

Insert apostrophes where needed. Indicate sentences that need no revision by a check mark.

1. There are three *es* in the word *receive.*
2. My wife loves the CBCs program *This Hour Has 22 Minutes.*
3. The mens coats will have to go on sale before hell buy one.
4. Malcolm has two weeks holidays at the end of this month.
5. The Smiths wont be coming to our party tonight; they have decided to go to the Johnsons party instead.
6. Plumbers assistants are no use to electricians.
7. It cant be one oclock so soon.
8. The fashions today are strongly influenced by those of the 1970s.
9. Theres a growing gap between the rich and the poor in Canadian society.
10. Filbert often wonders why his mother named him after a nut when there were so many other nice names she could have chosen.

Chapter 20

Quotation Marks

Quotation marks are always used in pairs. They enclose direct quotations (except those in indented blocks), some titles, and words used in a special sense. The first mark indicates the beginning of the quotation, and the second indicates the end. Any other marks associated with the quotation follow the rules explained below.

20a Quotation marks set off direct quotations and dialogue.

Double quotation marks set off direct quotations, but not indirect ones. Single quotation marks enclose a quotation within a quotation.

(1) Direct quotations

Looking away in horror, Moira said, "I'm afraid of going on the roller coaster." [Quotation marks enclose only the quotation, not expressions like *she said* or *he replied*. Place the period within the quotation marks—see 20f.]

(2) Indirect quotations

Looking away in horror, Moira said that she was afraid of going on the roller coaster. [Quotation marks are not used for indirect quotations.]

(3) Quotations within quotations

"Jennifer keeps telling me to 'get a life,'" Mark complained. [The comma appears in the quotation within a quotation; the period goes at the end of the sentence. See page 218 for how to punctuate a quotation within a quotation presented as an indented block.]

ESL   British English and some other languages reverse the use of single (') and double (") quotation marks. It is important to learn the correct system to use in North American writing. (See also **20f**.)

Other usage: The police officer said, 'When I saw the thief running away, I shouted, "Stop! You are under arrest."'

North American English: The police officer said, "When I saw the thief running away, I shouted, 'Stop! You are under arrest.'"

In direct quotations, reproduce all quoted material exactly as it appears in the original, including capitalization and punctuation. If the quoted material contains an error, insert "sic" within brackets immediately after the error. (See **21g**.) If the quoted material contains a reference that would be unclear once the material is taken out of context, explain the reference in one or two words immediately after the reference. (See **33f(2)**.) Indicate an omission within a quotation by the use of ellipsis points. (See **21i**.)

(4) Dialogue

Dialogue is directly quoted conversation. When quoting conversation, write what each person says, no matter how short, as if it were a separate paragraph. It helps to include expressions such as *he said,* as well as closely related bits of narrative, in the same paragraph as the direct quotation.

Through an interpreter, I spoke with a Bedouin man tending nearby olive trees.

"Do you own this land?" I asked him.

He shook his head. "The land belongs to Allah," he said.

"What about the trees?" I asked. He had just harvested a basket of green olives, and I assumed that at least the trees were his.

"The trees, too, are Allah's," he replied.

I marveled at this man who seemed unencumbered by material considerations . . . or so I was thinking when, as if in afterthought, he said, "Of course, I own the *olives*."

—HARVEY ARDEN

When quoting more than one paragraph by a single speaker, put quotation marks at the beginning of each new paragraph. There is only one set of closing quotation marks, at the end of the last paragraph.

(5) Thoughts

Double quotation marks set off thoughts, as if they were stated.

"I won't make that mistake again," I thought.

20b   Long quotations are indented.

Indention sets off long quotations of prose and poetry, but short quotations are run in to the text.

(1) Prose

When using the Modern Language Association (MLA) style of documentation (34a), set off any quotation consisting of more than 4 lines by indenting all lines 2.5 cm (or 10 typewritten spaces). When using the American Psychological Association (APA) style (34d), set off quotations of more than 40 words by indenting all lines 1.25 cm (or 5 typewritten spaces). When using either MLA or APA style, double-space the lines in the block.

If you quote one or more complete paragraphs, indicate the beginning of each paragraph by indenting its first line an additional 0.75 cm (or three typewritten spaces) in MLA style and an additional 1.25 cm (or five typewritten spaces) in APA style. If you quote only part of a paragraph, do *not* indent its first line the additional spaces.

A colon usually introduces a long quotation. Use internal quotation marks only if they appear in the original.

> Metal coins replaced bartering. Then paper money became more convenient to use than metal coins not only because it is easy to handle but also because, as Cetron and O'Toole say in *Encounters with the Future,* it has other advantages:
>> Printing more zeros is all it takes on a bill to increase its value. Careful engraving makes it easy to recognize and difficult to counterfeit. The fact that private individuals cannot create it at will keeps it scarce. Karl Marx once said that paper money was valued "only insofar as it represents gold" but that may never have been true. (188)
> Today, cheques and credit cards are even more convenient than paper money.

(2) Poetry

Except for very special emphasis, enclose a quotation of three (or fewer) lines of poetry in quotation marks and run it in to the text as you would a short prose quotation. Indicate the divisions between lines by a slash with a space on each side. (See **21h.**) Passages of more than 3 lines should be set off—double-spaced and indented 2.5 cm (or 10 typewritten spaces) unless unusual spacing is part of the poem. Use quotation marks only if they appear in the original. Numbers in parentheses placed two spaces after the close of the quotation can be used to indicate line numbers of the poem.

> In "London" William Blake expresses his horror of institutional callousness:
> How the Chimney-sweeper's cry
> Every black'ning Church appalls;
> And the hapless Soldier's sigh
> Runs in blood down Palace walls.   (9–12)

20c Quotation marks enclose the titles of short works such as stories, essays, poems, songs, episodes of a radio or television series, articles in periodicals, and subdivisions of books.

> *The Whistling Thorn* contains such wonderful stories as "Lend Me Your Light" and "The Cage." [short stories]

> "And I Remember" is my favourite of the poems by Afua Cooper that we studied this term. [poem]

> I always want to laugh when I hear "Ironic." [song]

> Coral Browne starred in "An Englishman Abroad," part of the *Great Performances* series. [episode in a television series]

> Did you read David Menzies's "Waste Blues" when it appeared in the *Financial Post Magazine*? [article in a periodical]

Use double quotation marks to enclose a secondary title appearing in a longer italicized (underlined) title. Use single marks for a title within a longer title enclosed in double quotation marks.

> *Interpretations of "The Secret Sharer"*

> "Cynicism in Hardy's 'Ah, Are You Digging on My Grave?'"

20d   Used sparingly, quotation marks may enclose words intended in a special or ironic sense.

His "gourmet dinner" tasted as if it had come out of a grocer's freezer. [COMPARE His so-called gourmet dinner tasted as if it had come out of a grocer's freezer. The use of *so-called* eliminates the need for quotation marks.]

And I do mean good and evil, not "adjustment and deviance," the gutless language that so often characterizes modern discussions of psychological topics.   —CAROL TAVRIS

Either quotation marks or italics can be used in definitions. (See also 24e.)

Ploy means "a strategy used to gain an advantage."

Ploy means *a strategy used to gain an advantage.*

20e   Overusing quotation marks detracts from readability.

Quotation marks are not needed in the following cases:

(1) To call attention to a cliché (See 14c.)

Highlighting a cliché in this way emphasizes an unwillingness to think of a fresh expression.

A poor person does not look a gift horse in the mouth.

(2) To enclose *yes* or *no* in indirect discourse

He's said yes to too many excesses.

(3) To indicate questionable diction

> A wimp can't say no to anyone. [Neither *wimp*, a slang term,
> nor *no* is set off with quotation marks.]

20f Follow North American printing
conventions for using various marks of
punctuation with quoted material.

(1) Comma and period

Generally speaking, commas go inside the closing quotation marks; so do periods if the quotation ends the
sentence.

> "Hey," he said, "what's that glowing light there?"
> She replied, "You've been watching too many movies."

The period goes at the end of the sentence if other words
follow the end of the quotation.

> "I can't explain the intricacies of Fermat's Last Theorem,"
> Mortimer said.

The period goes after a parenthetical citation when it follows a quotation that ends a sentence. For example, in
MLA-style documentation, a page number in parentheses
follows a quotation. (See 34a(1).)

> In his book on modern society, *The Unconscious Civilization*,
> John Ralston Saul describes "a society addicted to ideo-
> logies—a civilization tightly held . . . in the embrace of a dom-
> inant ideology: corporatism" (2). [The ellipsis marks show
> that only a part of the original sentence is quoted. The final
> period comes after the parenthetical citation.]

For block quotations, see pages 217–18.

(2) Semicolon and colon

Semicolons and colons always go outside the quotation marks.

> She spoke of "the gothic tale"; I immediately thought of "The Dunwich Horror": H. P. Lovecraft's masterpiece is the epitome of "gothic."

(3) Question mark, exclamation point, and dash

When a question mark, an exclamation point, or a dash applies only to the quoted matter, it goes inside the quotation marks. When it does not, it goes outside.

Inside the quotation marks:

> Pilate asked, "What is truth?"
>
> Gordon replied, "No way!"
>
> "Achievement—success!——" states Heather Evans, "has become a national obsession."
>
> Why do children keep asking "Why?" [a question within a question—one question mark inside the quotation marks]

Outside the quotation marks:

> What is the meaning of the term "half-truth"?
>
> Stop whistling "All I Do Is Dream of You"!
>
> The boss exclaimed, "No one should work for the profit motive!"——no exceptions, I suppose.

Exercise 1

Write a page of dialogue between two friends who are disagreeing about songs or stories. Punctuate the quotations carefully.

Exercise 2

Insert quotation marks where they are needed and change any direct quotations to indirect, any indirect quotations to direct.

1. Who said conscription if necessary, but not necessarily conscription?
2. We now have more than 20 bunnies in the pen, dear, she said. Don't you think we have enough?
3. Have you read Mordecai Richler's essay London Then and Now?
4. To rip and burn means to copy a song in computer file format onto a compact disk.
5. Can you please help your mother pick some strawberries this year, Martin? his father said. Every year I get stuck going with her, and my back aches for weeks after.
6. Benoit said that the article My Favourite Place by David Adams Richards brings to mind the year that he spent living and travelling in Australia.
7. Don't you want to sit down, Jane? David asked his pregnant wife. Thanks, she said, I was beginning to wonder how long it would take before you noticed I needed a seat.
8. David Rakoff's latest book *Fraud* has many memorable essays; Lush Life is one of them.
9. Wendel said that he'd be starting his diet on Monday.
10. Zoi said that everything would turn out all right if we just forgot about the money she lost at the casino.

Chapter 21

The Period and Other Marks

Periods, question marks, exclamation points, colons, dashes, parentheses, brackets, slashes, and ellipsis points are important in writing and in transferring meaning from spoken to written language. (For use of the hyphen, see 22f.) In the sentences below, the marks in colour signal meaning and intonation.

> The days are dark. Why worry? The sun never stops shining!
>
> In *Lady Windermere's Fan* (1892) is this famous line: "I [Lord Darlington] can resist everything except temptation."
>
> According to *Consumer Reports,* "The electronic radio/clock . . . is extremely complicated——enough so as to require five pages of instruction in the owner's manual."

Current practice, as dictated in contemporary style manuals (MLA, APA) allows for only one space following all punctuation marks: the period, the question mark, the exclamation point, the colon, the ending parenthesis and bracket, and each of the dots in ellipsis points. No spaces precede or follow the hyphen or dash.

21a Periods punctuate certain sentences and abbreviations.

(1) Use the period to mark the end of a declarative or a mildly imperative sentence.

Canadians know the pain of being confused with Americans. [declarative]

Drive slowly and watch out for animals. [mild imperative]

"Open this pickle jar," she commanded. [declarative sentence containing an imperative]

She says she can't explain why some students never want to assume responsibility for their actions. [declarative sentence containing an indirect question]

"How can people belittle the ethnic heritage of others?" she asked. [declarative sentence containing a direct quotation]

"I'm as good as you are!" he shouted. [declarative sentence containing an exclamation]

(2) Use periods after some abbreviations.

Dr., Jr.   a.m., p.m.   vs., etc., et al.

Periods are not used with all abbreviations (for example, *MVP, kPa, FM*—see chapter 25). When in doubt about whether to punctuate an abbreviation, consult a desk dictionary. Dictionaries often list options, such as *QC* or *Q.C., CAF* or *C.A.F.*

Use only one period after an abbreviation that ends a sentence:

The study was performed by Ben Werthman et al.

21b The question mark occurs after direct (but not indirect) questions.

What in the world is Tulee doing? [direct question]

They want to know what Tulee is doing. [indirect question]

Did you hear them ask, "What is Tulee doing?" [A direct question within a direct question is followed by one question mark inside the closing quotation mark: see chapter 20.]

What is Tulee doing? dancing? playing? [A series of questions having the same subject and verb can be treated as elliptical; that is, only the first item need include both the subject and verb.]

Declarative sentences sometimes contain direct questions:

He asked, "Did E. Annie Proulx write *The Shipping News*?" [Put a question mark inside quotation marks when it concludes a direct question—see 20f(3).]

When we ask ourselves, Why does evil happen? we seek a logical explanation for the irrational. [A question mark follows the interpolated question not enclosed in quotation marks. Capitalize the word beginning a formal question.]

A question mark within parentheses expresses the writer's uncertainty about the correctness of the preceding word, figure, or date.

Chaucer was born in 1340 (?) and died in 1400.

! **CAUTION** Do not write an indirect question as a direct question.

She asked him ~~would~~ he go.
       if   *would*

21c **The exclamation point occurs after an emphatic interjection and after other expressions to show strong emotion, such as surprise or disbelief.**

Wow!   That was so cool!   Amazing!

The comma or period that normally follows a direct quotation is omitted when the quotation has an exclamation point.

"Get off the road!" he yelled.

He yelled, "Get off the road!"

Use the exclamation point sparingly; overuse diminishes its value. A comma is better after mild interjections, and a period is better after mildly exclamatory expressions and mild imperatives.

Oh, look at that cracked windshield.

How quiet the lake was.

Exercise 1

Illustrate the chief uses of the period, the question mark, and the exclamation point by composing and punctuating brief sentences of the types specified.

1. a declarative sentence containing a quoted exclamation (**21a**, **21c**)
2. a mild imperative (**21a**)
3. a direct question (**21b**)
4. a declarative sentence containing an indirect question (**21b**)
5. a declarative sentence containing a direct question (**21b**)

21d The colon calls attention to what follows and separates time and scriptural references and titles and subtitles.

(1) A colon directs attention to what follows: an explanation or summary, a series, or a quotation.

To say that is not to diminish the past or our culture, but to acknowledge a simple truth: Indigenous peoples must not turn inward and cling to nostalgia for sustenance.

—KEN WIWA

The colon can introduce a second independent clause that explains or amplifies the first independent one.

Canadians are noticeably inclined to turn a statement into a question by means of a rising intonation: this expresses hope

that there are no objections, and simultaneously requests a sign
from the listener that the statement has been understood.
—MARGARET VISSER

Similarly, a colon occasionally follows one sentence to
introduce the next.

The sorrow was laced with violence: In the first week of dem-
olition, vandals struck every night. —*SMITHSONIAN*

Style manuals vary in their instructions on whether to capitalize a complete sentence after a colon. MLA permits the
use of a lowercase letter, but APA does not. All style manuals, however, use a capital letter to begin a quoted sentence that follows a colon.

Claire Safran points out two of the things that cannot be
explained: "One of them is poltergeists. Another is teenagers."

Be especially careful not to use an unnecessary colon
between a verb and its complement or object, between a
preposition and its object, or after *such as*.

Unnecessary Colon   The winners were: Asa, Vanna, and
   Jack.

Use Instead   There were three winners: Asa, Vanna, and
   Jack.

   OR

   The winners were as follows: Asa, Vanna, and Jack.

   OR

   The winners were Asa, Vanna, and Jack.

Unnecessary Colon   Many vegetarians do not eat dairy
   products, such as: butter and cheese.

Use Instead   Many vegetarians do not eat dairy products,
   such as butter and cheese.

(2) Use the colon between figures in time references and between titles and subtitles.

We are to be there by 11:30 a.m.

I just read *Shadow Maker: The Life of Gwendolyn MacEwen.*

Many writers prefer to use a colon in scriptural references: He quoted from Psalms 3:5. MLA recommends periods (Psalms 3.5), and recent biblical scholarship follows this practice.

(3) Use a colon after the salutation of a business letter.

Dear Dr. D'Angelo: Dear Faustine:

The colon also appears in bibliographic data. (See chapter 34.)

Exercise 2

Punctuate the following sentences by adding colons or semicolons. Put a check mark after those sentences that require no revision.

1. At 530 in the morning what everyone had been expecting occurred a meteor shower.
2. Uncle Harold hates to shave he also hates beards.
3. At his new job, Bennet remembered some of the factors that led to his dismissal from his old job drunkenness, lateness, and rudeness to his coworkers.
4. My brother tries to live a bohemian lifestyle in Toronto however, he spends a lot of his time working to pay his rent instead of working on his art.
5. Denise suggested we go for Thai food 15 minutes later we were stuffing ourselves with pad Thai.
6. The only magazines she ever reads are *Canadian House and Home, Canadian Home and Garden,* and *Cottage Life.*
7. For Tuesday's assignment, we are supposed to read the short stories by the following writers André Alexis, Timothy Findley, and Barbara Gowdy.

8. Upon being invited to what was sure to be a dull party, Oscar Wilde said "I must decline your invitation due to a subsequent engagement."

9. Five North American cities chosen for their high standard of living are these Vancouver, Victoria, Calgary, Toronto, and Kelowna.

10. The medication Chailaya took had an unwelcome side effect headaches.

21e   **The dash marks a break in thought, sets off a parenthetical element for emphasis or clarity, and sets off an introductory series.**

On a keyboard, use an em-dash with no spaces; in handwriting, an unbroken line the length of an em-dash.

⚠ CAUTION Use dashes sparingly, not as easy or automatic substitutes for commas, semicolons, or end marks.

(1) A dash marks a sudden break in thought, an abrupt change in tone, or faltering speech.

Once they shone, a rich dark brown lateral glint of——no.
—GEORGE BOWERING

When I was six I made my mother a little hat——out of her new blouse.   —LILY DACHÉ

But perhaps Miss——Miss——oh, I can't remember her name——she taught English, I think——Miss Milross? She was one of them.   —GARRISON KEILLOR

(2) A dash sets off a parenthetical element for emphasis or (if it contains commas) for clarity.

Lying on Minna's bed, more or less beneath the duvet——one foot and both hands sticking out——there was a tiny figure.
—TIMOTHY FINDLEY

Sentiments that human shyness will not always allow one to convey in conversation——sentiments of gratitude, of apology, of love——can often be more easily conveyed in a letter.

—ARISTIDES

(3) A dash occurs after an introductory list or series.

In the main part of the following sentence, *all* points to or sums up the meaning of the list.

Keen, calculating, perspicacious, acute and astute——I was all of these. —MAX SHULMAN

21f Parentheses set off nonessential matter and enclose characters used for enumeration.

Use parentheses to set off parenthetical, supplementary, or illustrative matter and to enclose figures or letters used for enumeration within a sentence.

Through the use of the Thematic Apperception Test (TAT) they were able to isolate the psychological characteristic of a *need to achieve.* —MATINA HORNER [first-time use of an acronym in an article: see 25e and the **Glossary of Terms**]

The night (dusk was drawing brightness from torches all along the street) added its own impetus.

—STEVEN HEIGHTON

[an explanatory parenthetical expression]

When analyzing the service economy, it is helpful to divide the work that people do into three major economic sectors: (1) the primary sector, which includes natural resources, agriculture, mining, forestry, fisheries, and other resource extraction industries; (2) the secondary sector, which includes manufacturing and construction, where processed goods are produced; and (3) the service sector, in which information is the main product.   —GRAHAM S. LOWE   [In long sentences especially, enumeration highlights the points.]

In the next example both sentences are parenthetical. (See also 23e.)

As we start down the steep hillside, we watch a woman planting seedlings in a rice paddy near the village of Banga-an itself. (We guess the bent figure is a woman and as we draw nearer we see we are right. In this village, as in so many others in the region, men are working to make money elsewhere, and only the women, children, and elderly are left.)

—ISABEL HUGGAN

Use parentheses sparingly; the elements they enclose should still read smoothly in the sentence as a whole.

Dashes, parentheses, and commas are all used to set off parenthetical matter, but they express varying degrees of emphasis. Dashes set off parenthetical elements sharply and usually emphasize them:

It occurred to Ruthie even then that the Stinks spend about as much time going backward as they do forward, and that marriage into the Stink clan probably would be——and *was*——like a three-ring circus, complete with the animal acts and the clowns.   —TERRY GRIGGS

Parentheses usually de-emphasize the elements they enclose:

It occurred to Ruthie even then that the Stinks spend about as much time going backward as they do forward, and that marriage into the Stink clan probably would be (and *was*) like a three-ring circus, complete with the animal acts and the clowns.

Commas separate elements, usually without emphasizing them:

It occurred to Ruthie even then that the Stinks spend about as much time going backward as they do forward, and that marriage into the Stink clan probably would be, and *was*, like a three-ring circus, complete with the animal acts and the clowns.

21g Brackets set off interpolations in quoted matter and replace parentheses within parentheses. (See also 20a(4).)

The *Gazette* printed the beginning of the mayor's speech "My dear fiends [sic] and fellow citizens." [A bracketed *sic*—meaning "thus"—tells the reader that the error appears in the original.]

Donn Downey has written, "Although he was not the first to write about the Canadian prairie, [W. O.] Mitchell certainly did it the best." [An unclear reference is explained by the bracketed material.]

The gap between the advantaged . . . and the disadvantaged . . . is slowly increasing. (See, for example, Harvey Krahn and Graham S. Lowe's *Work, Industry, and Canadian Society* [Toronto: Nelson, 1993].)

21h The slash occurs between terms to indicate that either term is applicable and also marks line divisions in quoted poetry.

A slash is used unspaced between terms, but with a space before and after it between lines of poetry.

Equally rare is a first-rate adventure story designed for those who enjoy a smartly told tale that isn't steeped in blood and/or sex. —JUDITH CRIST

[Homer's *Odyssey*] begins with an invocation of the Muse, which is both a request for information—"Tell me, Muse, of

the man of many ways, who was driven / far journeys, after
he sacked Troy's sacred citadel"—and an indication of where,
more or less, in the story Homer would like the Muse's narration to begin: "From some point / here, goddess, daughter
of Zeus, speak, and begin our story." —MICHAEL KEEFER

Extensive use of the slash to indicate that either of two
terms is applicable (as in *and/or*, *he/she*) can make writing
choppy.

Exercise 3

Punctuate each of the following sentences by supplying commas,
dashes, parentheses, brackets, or slashes. Prepare to explain the
reason for all marks you add, especially those you choose for
setting off parenthetical matter.

1. There is only one other possibility Jack ate the last burrito.
2. There is only one thing Denise needs for her complete happiness love.
3. The directions for getting to Victor's cottage I am sure they
   are accurate should be thoroughly studied before we leave
   the city.
4. As a result of his lack of interest in graduate school not to
   mention his lack of funds Martin decided to withdraw from
   the doctoral program at McGill University.
5. Taking a vacation which many people think is a relaxing
   experience can be an especially stressful event.
6. Determination, dedication, and the unflagging desire to win
   these are hardly the qualities one would associate with someone who grows championship roses.
7. In March of that year 1953 Mavis Gallant wrote her short
   story "The Other Paris."
8. The high-school principal's letter to his staff began as follows: "All teachers should bear in mind that skills in reading
   and writting sic generally accompany successful social
   development."

9. I'd have the vet take a look at your dog if I were you before it's too late.
10. She found the lead singer of the band to be egocentric, selfish, and extremely attractive.

21i Ellipsis points (three equally spaced periods) mark an omission from a quoted passage or a reflective pause or hesitation.

(1) Ellipsis points mark an omission within a quoted passage.

Original   The newcomers and the growing number of deaths due to foreign diseases, especially smallpox, set in motion a major demographic shift in favour of the immigrant society. The smallpox epidemic of 1862, which began in Victoria and swept rapidly up the coast and into the interior, was the worst calamity to strike the coastal people since the epidemics of early contact. When it ended three years later, as many as twenty thousand Native people had died, reducing their total population to about forty thousand. The populations of some groups, such as the Haida, declined more than 80 per cent.   —ARTHUR J. RAY

Omission within a quoted sentence

Arthur J. Ray explains that as a result of the smallpox epidemic, which began in 1862, "as many as twenty thousand Native people had died . . . [and] the populations of some groups, such as the Haida, declined more than 80 per cent."

Omission at the beginning or end of a quoted sentence

Neither ellipsis points (nor capitals) are used at the beginning of a quotation, whether it is run in to the text or set off in a block.

An omission at the end of the quoted sentence that coincides with the end of your sentence requires a period in addition to the three ellipsis points, with no space immediately after the last word in the sentence. In a parenthetical reference, the period comes after the second parenthesis instead.

> Arthur J. Ray explains that by the time the smallpox epidemic of the 1860s ended, "as many as twenty thousand Native people had died. . . ." [OR died . . ."] (191).

Omission of a sentence or more

A period before ellipsis points (that is, four dots) marks omissions within a quoted passage if a complete sentence stands on either side of the ellipsis. Also, a period before ellipsis points marks the omission of a sentence or more (even a paragraph or more) within a quoted passage. If the quoted material ends with a question mark or exclamation point, three ellipsis points are added and the mark is retained.

Original   There's an uncertainty in our minds about the engineering principle of an elevator. We've all had little glimpses into the dirty, dark elevator shaft and seen the greasy cables passing each other. They never look totally safe. The idea of being trapped in a small box going up and down on strings induces a kind of phobia in all of us.

—ANDREW A. ROONEY

Of the common fear of riding in an elevator, Andrew A. Rooney writes, "We've all had little glimpses into the dirty, dark elevator shaft. . . . The idea of being trapped in a small box going up and down on strings induces a kind of phobia in all of us." [Thirteen words have been omitted from the original, but a sentence comes before and after the period and ellipsis points.]

Andrew A. Rooney writes about the fear of riding in an elevator: "We've all had little glimpses into the dirty, dark elevator shaft and seen the greasy cables passing each other. . . . The idea of being trapped in a small box going up and down on strings induces a kind of phobia in all of us." [Five words have been omitted from the original, all in a single sentence.]

To indicate the omission of a full line or more in quoted poetry, use spaced periods covering the length either of the line above it or of the omitted line.

Down from the purple mist of trees on the mountain, lurching
through forests of white spruce and cedar,
. . . .
came the bull moose
to be stopped at last by a pole-fenced pasture.
—ALDEN NOWLAN

(2) **Although ellipsis points can mark a reflective pause or hesitation, they should not be overused.**

Love, like other emotions, has causes . . . and consequences. —LAWRENCE CASTER

Ellipsis points to show a pause can also come after the period at the end of a sentence:

He knew the country, but he had been away. And then he had returned alone to this place, where for so long every year the winter buried you, snow blinded you, the wind screamed up the hill at night, and the water thundered. . . .

—JOYCE MARSHALL

Exercise 4

Punctuate the following sentences by supplying appropriate end marks, commas, colons, dashes, and parentheses. Do not use unnecessary punctuation. Be prepared to explain the reason for each mark you add, especially when you have a choice of correct marks (for example, commas, dashes, or parentheses).

1. I keep remembering what my father used to say jokingly "Some day you'll grow up and have kids who will treat you the way you treat me"

2. For his birthday Matthew requested the following gifts a Spider-Man action figure a squirt gun some new running shoes

3. "Good and" can mean "very" "I am good and mad" and "a hot cup of coffee" means that the coffee not the cup is hot

4. Many small country towns are very similar a truck stop a gas station a crowded diner

5. Gretchen, Jordan's best friend, sat at the back of the church where she wouldn't be seen and cried quietly and softly through the entire wedding

6. As my grandmother used to say "Love trust and considerate behaviour are all necessary for a good marriage"

7. I imagine that the tickets will seem expensive to all my friends employed or unemployed who want to go to the Lollapalooza concert

8. "Is he is he okay" I stammered

9. She believed the best way to age gracefully was to look at the world through a child's eyes not to act like a child

10. "Mark" I yelled "Mark how could you have done such a thing" I tried to hurry out the door before he could respond but he caught up with me

Mechanics

Chapter 22

Spelling, the Spell Checker, and Hyphenation

Spelling problems are highly visible, and misspellings may make a reader doubt whether the writer can present information clearly and correctly. Therefore, always proofread to detect misspellings or typographic errors. (See **29d.**)

People often feel that they no longer need to worry about spelling since computers have spell checkers to correct errors. While a spell checker can be helpful, it does not solve all spelling problems. For example, the computer cannot tell when you confuse such words as *principal* and *principle* because it cannot know which meaning is called for. As well, a spell checker may be based on an American dictionary and will not recognize British spellings used in Canada.

ESL   British spelling is traditional in Canada, although more and more people are adopting American spellings. Examples of differences include:

British	theatre	catalogue	colour	travelled
American	theater	catalog	color	traveled

Popular usage combines British and American spellings, as is evidenced in good Canadian dictionaries. (See chapter **13.**) However, depending on the purpose of your writing and your audience, you may choose to use all British or all

American spellings. Once you decide which spelling to use, it's important to be consistent.

In addition, there are times when you will be writing in-class papers or essay exams. Spelling errors in such situations can give your reader a poor initial impression and cause your work to be taken less seriously, or your grade to be lowered. So a basic knowledge of spelling is always important.

One way to improve spelling is to record the words you have misspelled and study them. Another way is to develop your own tricks to help you remember. For example, you might remember the spelling of "separate" by reminding yourself that it has "a rat" in it or the spelling of "attendance" by remembering that it includes "dance."

If you have doubts about spelling, consult your dictionary. Watch for restrictive labels such as *U.S.* or *chiefly British*.

In ordinary writing, do not use spellings labelled *obsolete* or *archaic, dialectal* or *regional, non-standard* or *slang*.

| **Not** | afeard | heighth | chaw | boughten |
| **But** | afraid | height | chew | bought |

If your dictionary lists two unlabelled alternatives, either form is correct—for example, *fulfil* or *fulfill, jewellery* or *jewelry*. The first option listed is usually the more common form.

22a   Spelling often does not reflect pronunciation.

Many words in English are not spelled as they are pronounced, so we often cannot rely on pronunciation for correct spelling. One trick you might use is to be aware of how the word would sound if it were pronounced as it is spelled. Following is a list of such words with the trouble spots boldfaced.

acciden**tal**ly	congra**tu**lations	govern**ment**	**per**spire
ath**le**te	February	mo**dern**	real**tor**
candi**date**	gene**ral**ly	nuc**le**ar	stren**gth**

Many unaccented syllables have acquired a neutral vowel sound, usually an indistinct *uh* sound in spoken English, although the spelling can use any one of the vowels (*a, e, i, o, u*). In your dictionary, this neutral vowel sound is represented by a special symbol /ə/ called a *schwa,* as in *confidence,* /'kän-fə-dən(t)s/.

It is sometimes helpful to think of the spelling of the root word as a guide to correct spelling.

confidence, confide	exultation, exult
different, differ	indomitable, dominate

A word that is difficult to spell, such as *often,* sometimes has alternate pronunciations (ôf'ən, ôf'tən). Of these, one might be a better guide to spelling. Here are examples of other such words.

everybody	literature	veteran
interest	gorilla	which

⚠ CAUTION Words like *and, than,* and *have* are often not stressed in speech and are thus misspelled. A spell checker will not catch these misspellings.

I would ~~of~~ *have* preferred fish rather ~~then~~ *than* soup ~~an~~ *and* salad.

22b When words sound alike but have different meanings, the spelling determines the meaning.

Words such as *forth* and *fourth* or *sole* and *soul* are homophones: They sound alike but have vastly different meanings and spellings. Be careful to choose the right word for your context. A spell checker will not catch such errors.

Many frequently confused spellings can be studied in groups.

(1) Contractions and possessive pronouns

It's my turn next.   Each group waits **its** turn.

You're next.   **Your** turn is next.

There's no difference.   **Theirs** is no different.

(See 19b and 19d.)

(2) Single words and two-word phrases

A number of words function both as single words and as two-word phrases with different meanings. The following are examples of such words.

He wore **everyday** clothes.   He wears them **every day**.

Maybe we will go.   We **may be** going.

You ran **into** my car.   We can run **in to** check it.

Nobody was there.   The police found **no body**.

Other examples are *anymore, any more; awhile, a while; everybody, every body; everyone, every one.*

! **CAUTION** *A lot* and *all right* are still spelled as two words; *alot* and *alright* are considered incorrect, although *alright* is often used in journalistic and business writing. (See the Glossary of Usage.)

(3) Singular nouns ending in *-nce* and plural nouns ending in *-nts*

Assistance is available.   I have two **assistants**.

For **instance**, Jack can go.   They arrived **instants** ago.

My **patience** is frayed.   Some **patients** waited for hours.

The following list contains words that sound exactly alike (*break/brake*), ones that sound alike in certain dialects (*horse/hoarse*), and ones that are similar in sound, especially in rapid speech (*believe/belief*), but are different in meaning. The spell checker cannot identify words that are correctly spelled but wrongly used. In general, the words listed here present common spelling rather than usage problems. You probably understand the distinction in meaning between the terms in most of the following pairs but sometimes confuse the spelling because they sound so much alike. If you are unsure about the difference in meaning between any pair of words, consult the Glossary of Usage, the Index, or your dictionary.

WORDS WHOSE SPELLINGS ARE
FREQUENTLY CONFUSED

accept, except	allude, elude
access, excess	already, all ready
adapt, adopt	altar, alter
advice, advise	altogether, all together
affect, effect	always, all ways
aisles, isles	amoral, immoral
alley, ally	angel, angle

ante-, anti-
ascent, assent
ask, axe
assistance, assistants
baring, barring, bearing
began, begin
believe, belief
board, bored
break, brake
breath, breathe
buy, by, bye
canvas, canvass
capital, capitol
censor, censure, sensor
choose, chose
cite, site, sight
clothes, cloths
coarse, course
complement, compliment
conscience, conscious
council, counsel
cursor, curser
dairy, diary
decent, descent, dissent
desert, dessert
device, devise
discreet, discrete
dominant, dominate
dyeing, dying
elicit, illicit
emigrate, immigrate

envelop, envelope
fair, fare
faze, phase
fine, find
formerly, formally
forth, fourth
forward, foreword
gorilla, guerrilla
have, of
hear, here
heard, herd
heroin, heroine
hole, whole
holy, wholly
horse, hoarse
human, humane
idea, ideal
instance, instants
its, it's
knew, new
later, latter
lay, lie (see 13c(3))
lead, led
lessen, lesson
lightning, lightening
lose, loose
marital, martial
maybe, may be
midst, mist
minor, miner
moral, morale

of, off	road, rode
passed, past	sat, set (see 13c(3))
patience, patients	sense, since
peace, piece	shown, shone
persecute, prosecute	stationary, stationery
personal, personnel	straight, strait
perspective, prospective	than, then
plain, plane	their, there, they're, there're
pray, prey	threw, through, thorough
precede, proceed	throne, thrown
predominant, predominate	to, too, two
presence, presents	tract, track
principle, principal	waist, waste
prophecy, prophesy	weak, week
purpose, propose	weather, whether
quiet, quit, quite	were, wear, where, we're
raise, rise (see 13c(3))	which, witch
respectfully, respectively	who's, whose
right, rite, write	your, you're

22c   Adding a prefix to a base word changes the meaning.

Prefixes are added to the beginning of the base word, called the root.

necessary, unnecessary   moral, immoral

 No letter is added or dropped when a prefix is added. These misspellings are usually detected by a spell checker.

22d Adding a suffix may require changing the spelling of the base word.

Suffixes are added to the end of the base word.

> resist, resistant   beauty, beautiful

Spelling, however, is irregular and follows certain conventions. These misspellings are usually detected by a spell checker.

(1) Dropping or retaining a final unpronounced *e*

A word ending in an unpronounced *e* drops the final *e* before a suffix beginning with a vowel.

> bride, bridal   combine, combination
> come, coming   prime, primary

A word ending in an unpronounced *e* retains the final *e* before a suffix beginning with a consonant.

> rude, rudeness   entire, entirely
> sure, surely   place, placement

Some exceptions are *ninth, truly, duly, awful, wholly.*

To keep the /s/ sound in *ce* or the /j/ sound in *ge*, do not drop the final *e* before *-able* or *-ous*:

> noticeable   manageable   courageous

(2) Doubling a final consonant before a suffix

Double the final consonant before a suffix beginning with a vowel if (a) the consonant ends a one-syllable word or a stressed syllable and (b) the consonant is preceded by a single vowel.

drop, dropping   BUT   droop, drooping

admit, admitted   BUT   figure, figured

In Canadian usage, a final *l* is doubled regardless of accent (but an exception is *unparalleled*). A final *s* is often doubled *(focussed),* though usage varies. When in doubt, consult a Canadian dictionary.

(3) Changing or retaining a final *y* before a suffix

Change the *y* to *i* before suffixes—except *-ing.*

defy: defies, defied, defiance   BUT   defying

modify: modifies, modifier, modified   BUT   modifying

Most verbs ending in *y* preceded by a vowel do not change the *y* before *-s* or *-ed*: *stay, stays, stayed.* Similarly, nouns like *joys* or *days* retain the *y* before *-s.* The following irregularities in spelling are especially troublesome: *lays, laid; pays, paid; says, said.*

(4) Retaining a final *l* before *-ly*

usual, usually   real, really   cool, coolly

formal, formally

Exercise 1

Add the designated suffixes to the following words.

EXAMPLES

-er, -ness, -ly: late   *later, lateness, lately*
-ing, -ed: rebel   *rebelling, rebelled*
-ing: lose, guide, rise   *losing, guiding, rising*

1. -ous: courage, continue
2. -ly: like, sure, safe
3. -ing, -ed, -ance: admit
4. -ment, -ed, -ing: manage
5. -able: notice, manage, desire

6. -ed, -ing, -ment: conceal
7. -ing, -ed, -ful: care, use, hope
8. -ing, -ed, -er: play, jog
9. -ed, -ing, -ly: complete
10. -ed, -ing: pay, plan

(5) Adding -s or -es to form the plural of nouns

Form the plural of most nouns by adding -s to the singular.

toys   scientists   tables

the Smiths [proper names], sisters-in-law [chief word pluralized]

For nouns ending in an *f* or *fe,* change the ending to *ve* before adding -s when the plural changes from an *f* sound to a *v* sound: *thief, thieves; life, lives;* BUT *proof, proofs.*

For nouns ending in *s, z, ch, sh,* or *x,* add -es when the plural adds another syllable.

box, boxes   peach, peaches   crash, crashes

the Kurtzes

For nouns ending in *y* preceded by a consonant, add -es after changing the *y* to *i*:

company, companies   ninety, nineties

Although usage varies, for most nouns ending in *o* preceded by a consonant, add -es. Consult a dictionary if you have a question.

echoes   heroes   potatoes   vetoes [-es only]
autos   memos   pimentos   pros   [-s only]

Some words, like *mottoes/mottos* and *zeroes/zeros,* can add -es or -s.

Certain irregular nouns, including retained foreign spellings, do not add -s or -es to form the plural. Again, the dictionary will answer your questions.

NEL

Singular	woman	goose	analysis	datum	species
Plural	women	geese	analyses	data	species
Singular	criterion	alumnus	alumna		
Plural	criteria	alumni	alumnae		

Exercise 2

Supply plural forms (including any optional spellings) for the following words. If a word is not covered by the rules, use your dictionary.

1. half
2. speech
3. phenomenon
4. woman
5. potato
6. theory
7. radius
8. bath
9. story
10. genius
11. passerby
12. halo
13. tomato
14. leaf
15. scarf
16. bush
17. hero
18. Kelly
19. church
20. life

22e *Ei* and *ie* are often confused.

When the sound is /ē/ (as in *me*), write *ie* except after *c*, in which case write *ei*.

chief   yield   priest

[BUT after *c*] receive   perceive   conceit

When the sound is other than /ē/, you should usually write *ei*:

eight   heir   rein   their   weight   foreign

Some exceptions include *either, neither, seize, friend, sieve,* and *species*.

22f Hyphens both link and divide words.

Hyphens link, or make a compound of, two or more words that function as a single word and divide words at the end of a line.

(1) Linking two or more words to form a compound that functions as a single word

Nouns We planted forget-me-nots and Johnny-jump-ups.

Verbs He soft-soaped his boss. My broker double-
She two-timed her boyfriend. crossed me.

Some compounds are conventionally connected with hyphens (*eye-catcher, cross-examine*), others are written separately (*eye chart, cross street*), and still others are written as one word (*eyewitness, crossbreed*). When in doubt, consult your dictionary.

! CAUTION Do not confuse the hyphen with the dash, which is input differently. (See 21e.)

Hyphenate two or more words serving as a single adjective before a noun.

a well-built house [COMPARE a house that is well built]

He has that get-it-done, make-it-happen attitude.

In a series, hyphens can carry over from one item to the next.

eighteenth- and nineteenth-century houses

Omit the hyphen in the following cases.

(a) after an adverb ending in *-ly* (*quickly frozen foods*),
(b) in chemical terms (*sodium chloride solution*), and
(c) in a modifier using a letter or numeral as the second element (*group C homes, type IV virus*).

Hyphenate spelled-out fractions and compound numbers from twenty-one to ninety-nine (or twenty-first to ninety-ninth).

one-eighth eighty-four twenty-third

Also hyphenate combinations of figures and letters (*mid-1990s*).

Hyphenate to avoid ambiguity or an awkward combination of letters or syllables between a prefix and root or a suffix and root.

re-sign the petition [COMPARE "resign the position"]

Hyphenate the prefixes *ex-* ("former"), *self-*, and *all-*; the suffix *-elect*; and a prefix with a capitalized word.

mayor-elect   ex-husband   all-important   self-made

non-British   anti-Semitism   mid-August

In Canadian usage, the prefix *non-* is sometimes hyphenated.

non-standard   non-selective

non-treaty   non-biodegradable

Exceptions include *nonflammable* and *nonsmoker*, though the trend is to drop the hyphen and spell the two parts closed up. When in doubt, consult a Canadian dictionary.

Exercise 3

Refer to **22f(1)** and to your dictionary as you convert each phrase (or words in each phrase) to a compound or to a word with a prefix. Use hyphens when needed.

EXAMPLES

a movie lasting two hours   a two-hour movie

glasses used for water   water glasses

1. people who sacrifice themselves
2. politicians who make decisions
3. a lamp costing 20 dollars
4. a vacation lasting two weeks
5. a paint that is the blue colour of the sky
6. in the shape of a U
7. hair that was blown by the wind
8. a man who speaks softly
9. a poet born in Jamaica
10. a musician based in Winnipeg

(2) Breaking a word at the end of a line with a hyphen

If you must divide a word at the end of a line, use a hyphen to separate syllables. In dictionaries, dots usually divide words into syllables: **re • al • ly, pre • fer, pref • er • ence, sell • ing, set • ting**. But not every division between syllables is an appropriate place for dividing a word. The following principles are useful guidelines.

Do not divide abbreviations, initials, capitalized acronyms, or one-syllable words.

p.m. [NOT p.-m.]   CNIB [NOT CN-IB]

UNESCO [NOT UNES-CO]   through [NOT thr-ough]

Do not create one-letter syllables by putting the first or last letter of a word at the end or beginning of a line.

omit   *able*   *boa*
~~o-mit~~   ~~a-ble~~   ~~bo-a~~

Do not put the last two letters of a word at the beginning of a line.

dated   *doesn't*   *safely*   *gravel*   *taxis*
~~dat-ed~~   ~~does-n't~~   ~~safe-ly~~   ~~grav-el~~   ~~tax-is~~

Divide hyphenated words only at the hyphen.

mass-| produce

father-| in-law   OR   father-in-| law

Divide words between two consonants that come between vowels—except when the division does not reflect pronunciation.

pic-| nic   dis-| cuss   thun-| der   BUT   co-| bra

Divide words between those consonants that you double when adding *-ing*.

set-| ting   jam-| ming   plan-| ning

[COMPARE "sell-| ing"]

Exercise 4

Write a list of five cues that help you remember certain difficult spellings. Share your devices with other members of the class.

Exercise 5

Edit the following paragraph for misspellings and correct usage of the hyphen.

[1]Non-verbal communication is similir to verbal communication in expressing cultural values. [2]Like verbal communication, non-verbal patterns reflec values, perspectives, and heritige of specific cultures. [3]In addition to diversity among groups within our country, non-verbal behaviours vary from one country to another. [4]As you might expect, dissimilarities reflect cultural values. [5]For example, have you ever seen the bumper sticker "If you can read this, your to close"? [6]That slogan proclaims North Americans' feirce territoriality. [7]We prise private space, and we resent, and sometimes fight, anyone who trespasses on what we consider our turf. [8]German culture is also private space oriented. [9]Germans routinely build walls and hedges to insulate themselves from neighbours. [10]In cultures where individuality is not such a pronounced value, people are less territorial. [11]For instance, Brazilians tend to stand close in shops, busses, and elevators, and when they bump into one another they don't apologize or draw back. [12]In many Middle Eastern countries, men often walk arm in arm, but in Canada touch between male friends is less comon. [13]Indeed, norms for touching also reflect cultureal values. [14]In one study, North Americans, who are relatively reserved, were observed engaging in an average of only four touches in a two hour period. [15]However, Parisians, who are well known for their emotional expressiveness, touched 110 times per hour.

Chapter 23

Capitals

Capital letters denote such things as proper names, peoples and their languages, geographical names, and certain organizations. Different conventions for capitalization have prevailed in different eras, and some conventions continue to vary. The following guidelines will help in specific cases, however. When special problems arise, consult a good, recent dictionary (13a). Dictionaries list not only words and abbreviations that begin with capitals but also acronyms (25e) that use full capitals.

Jim Carrey, Italians, Manitoba, Federal Express, Rev., NATO

A recent dictionary is also useful when the capitalization of a word depends on a given meaning: "*mosaic* pictures" but "*Mosaic* Laws," "damp *earth*" but "the planet *Earth*."

A style manual for the discipline in which you are writing is another useful guide for capitalization. (For a list of such manuals, see pages 539–40.)

When capitalizing something is optional, be consistent in your use of the option you choose:

golden triangle OR Golden Triangle, a.m. OR A.M.

23a Proper names are capitalized and so usually are their abbreviations and acronyms.

As you study the following examples, observe that common nouns like *college, company, park,* and *street* are capitalized when they are essential parts of proper names.

(1) Names and nicknames of persons or things and trademarks

Austin Clarke, John Paul II, Rocket Richard, Canadarm, Flight 224, Canada Dry, Pablum, Juno Award, Volkswagen Golf, Polaroid picture, Scotch tape

(2) Peoples and their languages

French Canadians, Asians, Inuit, Somalis, Poles, Scots, English, Korean, Spanish, Swahili, Urdu

(3) Geographical names

Arctic Circle, Macedonia, Baffin Island, Niagara Escarpment, Havana, Saskatchewan, Mecca, Prairies, Rideau Canal, Nova Scotia, Nigeria, Crawford St., Banff National Park

(4) Organizations, government agencies, institutions, and companies

B'nai B'rith, Federation of Students, International Red Cross, Statistics Canada, Glenbow Museum, Dalhousie University, Museum of Civilization, Ottawa Senators, The Second Cup Ltd.

(5) Days of the week, months, and holidays

Wednesday, August, Tet, Thanksgiving, Canada Day, Remembrance Day

The names of the seasons—spring, summer, fall, winter—are not capitalized.

(6) **Historical documents, periods, events, and movements**

Charter of Rights and Freedoms, Stone Age, the Renaissance, Boer War, Impressionism

(7) **Religions and their adherents, holy books, holy days, and words denoting the Supreme Being**

Christianity, Hinduism, Islam, Judaism
Buddhist, Hindu, Muslim, Jew, Sikh
Book of Mormon, Bible, Koran, Talmud
Easter, Ramadan, Yom Kippur
Allah, Buddha, God, Vishnu, Yahweh

Some writers always capitalize pronouns referring to a deity (except *who, whom, whose*). Others capitalize such pronouns only when the capital is needed to prevent ambiguity, as in "The Lord commanded the prophet to warn *His* people."

(8) **Personifications**

Then into the room walked Death. [COMPARE His death shocked everyone.]

Her heart belonged to Envy. [COMPARE She frequently experienced envy.]

(See also page 659.)

(9) **Words derived from proper names**

Canadianize [verb]; Marxism [noun]; Orwellian [adjective]

When a proper name and its derivatives become the name of a general class of objects or ideas, it is no longer capitalized.

zipper [originally a capitalized trademark]

blarney [derived from the Blarney stone, said to impart skill in flattery to those who kiss it]

When in doubt about whether a proper name or derivative has become a general class, consult a dictionary. Many such words can be treated with or without capitalization.

French fries OR french fries, Venetian blinds OR venetian blinds

When you have the option to capitalize or not, it is important to follow one option consistently.

(10) Abbreviations and acronyms or shortened forms of capitalized words

AMEX, CBC, B.A., CNR, CST, NHL, OPEC, P.E.I., UNESCO, Y.M.C.A. [words derived from the initial letters of capitalized word groups]

(See also chapter 25 and 21a(2).)

23b   Titles of persons that precede the name are capitalized but not those that follow it or stand alone.

Governor General Adrienne Clarkson, Captain Smith, Uncle Verne

Adrienne Clarkson, the governor general; Smith, our captain; Verne, my uncle

Prime Minister Chrétien, the prime minister of Canada

Words denoting family relationships are usually capitalized when serving as substitutes for proper names:

Tell Mother I'll write soon. [COMPARE "My mother wants me to write."]

23c In titles and subtitles of books, plays, essays, and other titled works, the first and last words are capitalized, as well as most other words.

All words in titles and subtitles are capitalized, except articles, co-ordinating conjunctions, prepositions, and the *to* in infinitives (unless they are the first or last word). The articles are *a, an, the;* the co-ordinating conjunctions are *and, but, or, nor, for, so, yet.* (Formerly, longer prepositions like *before, between,* or *through* in titles were capitalized; MLA style, however, favours not capitalizing prepositions, whatever the length.) (See **34a**.)

> *Nights below Station Street*
> "Why Women Are Paid Less Than Men"
> "What It Takes to Be a Leader"
> *A Discovery of a Stranger*
> *The Thinking Heart*
> *Thirty-Two Short Films about Glenn Gould*

In a title, capitalize the first word of a hyphenated compound. As a rule, capitalize the word following the hyphen if it is a noun or a proper adjective or if it is equal in importance to the first word.

> *The Building of the H-Bomb* [noun]
> *The Arab-Israeli Dilemma* [proper adjective]
> *Stop-and-Go Signals* [words of equal importance]

Usage varies with respect to the capitalization of words following such prefixes as *anti-, ex-, re-,* and *self-:*

> *Overcoming Self-Destructive Behaviour* OR *Overcoming Self-destructive Behaviour*

In all cases, use the style appropriate to your discipline, or ask your instructor. (See **20c**, **24a**, and **34a** and **b**.)

23d The pronoun *I* and the interjection *O* are capitalized.

If I forget thee, O Jerusalem, let my right hand forget her cunning. —PSALMS

The interjection *oh* is not capitalized except when it begins a sentence.

23e The first word of every sentence (or of any other unit written as a sentence) and of directly quoted speech is capitalized.

Procrastination is the thief of time.

Oh, really! Do you want to become more efficient? Not right now.

Experienced cooks are usually ready to try something new. (You can learn from them.) [a parenthetical sentence]

Beth got out of the car and shouted, "Home at last!"

He says, "Stop dieting and start exercising."
OR   "Stop dieting," he says, "and start exercising."
OR   "Stop dieting," he says. "And start exercising."

One thing is certain: We are still free. [an optional capital after the colon—see also **21d**]

For the treatment of directly quoted written material, see chapter 20.

23f Capitals sometimes indicate emphasis.

Occasionally, a common noun is capitalized for emphasis or clarity.

The inspiration of many business people is Greed.

If you overuse this strategy, it will not achieve its purpose. There are alternative methods for achieving emphasis. (See chapter 11.)

23g Unnecessary capitals are distracting.

Do not capitalize common nouns preceded by the indefinite articles *a* and *an* or by such modifiers as *every* or *several*.

a speech course in theatre and television [COMPARE Speech 324: Theatre and Television]

a university, **several** high schools [COMPARE University of British Columbia, MacKenzie High School]

However, always capitalize proper nouns, even when preceded by *a* or *an* or by modifiers like *every* or *several*. In such cases, capitalized nouns name one or many of the members of a class: *a* St. Bernard, *every* Nova Scotian, *several* Canadians.

STYLE SHEET FOR CAPITALIZATION

Capitals	No Capitals
Seven Years' War	an eighteenth-century war
a Chihuahua, a Ford tractor	a poodle, a farm tractor
University of New Brunswick	a university
Charter of Rights and Freedoms	a charter
May, Victoria Day	spring, holiday
the East, Easterners	to drive east, the eastern regions
German, Italian, Japanese	the language requirement
the NHL	a hockey league
Parkinson's disease	flu, asthma, leukemia

the Canadian Forces	the armed forces
two Liberal candidates	liberal policies
Dr. Leo Shack	every doctor, my doctor

Exercise 1

Write brief sentences using each of the following words correctly.

1. prime minister	6. West
2. Prime Minister	7. avenue
3. company	8. Avenue
4. Company	9. conservative
5. west	10. Conservative

Exercise 2

Supply capitals wherever needed.

¹my eccentric uncle theodore can certainly tell some great tales in the maritime tradition. ²for hours on end, uncle theodore would keep us riveted to our seats with tales of micmac warriors who camped in the woods near the annapolis valley in nova scotia; french-speaking acadians who built a nearby church; and the mayor's wife, hortense, who fell in love with a local teacher named ferguson and ran off with him to new york city. ³perhaps his most memorable tale is that of a covered bridge near bridgeport that is supposedly haunted. ⁴uncle theodore says he has not only seen the ghost but claims to have known the phantom when she was alive. ⁵"maude blackett," he said, "used to teach english and mathematics in a small town nearby until, broken-hearted over her lost love, she threw herself off the bridge in despair." ⁶walking home from town, theodore can often be seen tipping his hat before crossing the covered bridge and saying, "well, hello, maude. ⁷you're looking as splendid as usual." ⁸many of his stories were compiled in a book called *tall tales and seven bells: stories of the east coast.* ⁹once he was even featured on the cbc show *ideas.*

Chapter 24

Italics

When using a word processing program, you can follow the conventions of professional typesetters who use italics to indicate certain titles—and also, occasionally, for other purposes. In handwritten or typewritten papers, you can indicate italics by underlining. In most situations, either italicizing or underlining is acceptable. If in doubt, follow your audience's preference. (See 28a(2).)

It was on *The National*.   It was on <u>The National</u>.

24a Italics identify the titles of separate publications.

A separate publication is a work published as a whole rather than as part of a larger published work. A newspaper, for example, is a separate publication but an editorial in that newspaper is not. So different conventions are used for indicating the title of the newspaper and the title of the editorial. (See 20c.) Following these conventions helps readers gauge the size of a work and the relation between one work and another.

Did you see Richard Nadeau's "What We Think of Trudeau" in *The Globe and Mail* today?

I especially enjoyed "None for Us, Thanks, There's Butter on It" in Peter Gzowski's *Canadian Living*.

In addition to newspapers, the titles of books, magazines, pamphlets, plays, and films are usually italicized. Italics also indicate the titles of television and radio programs, entire recordings, works of art, long poems, comic strips, genera, species, and software programs.

Books	*The Englishman's Boy*	*Fall on Your Knees*
Magazines	*Chatelaine*	*Canadian Geographic*
Newspapers	*The Vancouver Sun*	*The Globe and Mail*
Plays, Films	*Unidentified Human Remains and the True Nature of Love*	*Atanarjuat (The Fast Runner)*
Recordings	*Clumsy*	*Great Verdi Overtures*
Works of Art	*Blue Sky*	*The Last Supper*
Long Poems	*Paradise Lost*	*The Rime of the Ancient Mariner*
Comic Strips	*Peanuts*	*For Better or For Worse*
Genera, Species	*Homo sapiens*	*Rosa setigera*
Software	*VirusScan*	*Microsoft Word*

Neither italics nor quotation marks are used in references to major historical documents or religious texts.

The Magna Carta marked a turning point in English history.

Exodus is the second book of the Old Testament.

A title is not italicized when it stands at the beginning of a book or article. Accordingly, the title at the top of a paper or report (unless it is also the title of a book or includes the title of a book) should not be italicized. (See also 23c.)

24b Italics identify foreign words and phrases in the context of an English sentence.

> I tell her I know Chinese. "*Beyeh fa-foon*," I say. "*Shee-veh, Ji nu*," meaning "Stop acting crazy. Rice gruel, Soy sauce."
> —GISH JEN

> When the visit with my grandmother was over the old people would unfailingly sit in the kitchen with my mother for another hour, watching her make *lokshen*, slurping lemon tea out of a saucer. —MORDECAI RICHLER

Countless words borrowed from other languages are a part of the English vocabulary and are therefore not italicized. The more familiar the word becomes, the less likely it is to be italicized.

cliché (French)	pizza (Italian)	versus (Latin)
chutzpah (Yiddish)	patio (Spanish)	karate (Japanese)

24c Italics identify the names of legal cases.

> *Lovelace v. Canada*
>
> *Barcan v. Zorkin*

Italics also indicate the shortened name of a case.

> The rights of male and female Native Canadians are equal because of *Lovelace*.

Italics are not used when referring to a case by other than its official name.

> I think the media did not give enough attention to the Randal Doolcy case.

24d   Italics identify the names of specific ships, satellites, and spacecraft.

Bluenose   the space shuttle *Discovery*

The names of trains and the names of a general class or a trademark are not italicized: Orient Express, Kleenex, Boeing 747, Anik.

24e   Italics indicate words, letters, or figures spoken of as such or used as illustrations, statistical symbols, or the variables in algebraic expressions.

Finally he told my mother to put an *H* in that blank. "For *human* race," he said.   —ELIZABETH GORDON

$c = r^2$

In APA style, volume numbers in reference lists are italicized. (See 34d.)

Memory & Cognition, 3, 635–647.

24f   When used sparingly, italics indicate emphasis.

If they take offence, then that's *their* problem.

These *are* the right files.

Overuse of italics for emphasis (like overuse of the exclamation point) defeats its own purpose. If you tend to rely on italics to stress ideas, study chapter 11 and try substituting more specific or forceful words for those you are tempted to underline.

Exercise 1

Underline all words that should be italicized in the following sentences.

1. NotaBene is a word processing program designed especially for use in colleges and universities.
2. I borrowed a copy of Found Treasures: Stories by Yiddish Women Writers in order to read The Road of No Return, a story by Rachel Korn.
3. Carlos enjoys watching classic films like Casablanca.
4. I like to find appropriate quotations in The New Quotable Woman.
5. The New York Times reported that another attempt has been made to explore the ruins of the Britannic, sister ship of the Titanic.

Chapter 25

Abbreviations, Acronyms, and Numbers

Abbreviations and numbers are used in tables, notes, and bibliographies and in some kinds of special or technical writing. In formal writing, follow the principles outlined in this section. The first time abbreviations or acronyms are used in a paper, they should be spelled out.

> Behaviours that rate high on the Sensation Seeking Scale (SSS) include engaging in risky sports, occupations, or hobbies; seeking variety in sexual and drug experiences; behaving fearlessly in common phobic situations; and preferring exotic foods.

Traditionally abbreviations are marked with periods; acronyms are not.

25a Designations such as *Ms., Mr., Mrs., Dr.,* and *St.* appear before a proper name, and those such as *Jr., Sr.,* and *II* appear after.

Mrs. Adrienne Marcus	Mr. William Ng
Dr. Sonya Allen	Ms. Lena Nobré
P. T. Lawrence III	Mark Ngo, Sr.
St. Paul	Erika C. Scheurer, Ph.D.

Avoid redundant titles.

> Dr. Carol Ballou OR Carol Ballou, M.D. [NOT Dr. Carol
> Ballou, M.D.]

Most abbreviations form plurals by adding *-s* alone,
without an apostrophe: *PCBs, CODs*.

Use abbreviations such as *Prof., Sen., Capt.,* or *Rev.* only
before initials or full names. In formal writing, *Reverend*
or *Rev.* and *Honourable* are adjectives and are preceded by
the and followed by title, full name, or initials.

> the Reverend Dr. Campbell   OR
> the Reverend George Tyler Campbell   OR
> the Honourable G. T. Campbell

E S L Other cultures sometimes use *the* before
titles. North American English omits *the* except when using
Reverend or *Honourable*.

> ~~the~~ Dr. Sonya Allen   ~~the~~ Professor Rodriguez

25b The names of provinces, countries,
continents, months, days of the week,
and units of measurement are not
abbreviated when they appear in a
sentence.

> Last Friday, we drove all the way to Montreal, Quebec; the
> following Monday, we drove on to Bathurst, New Brunswick.

For addresses in correspondence, however, use appropriate
postal abbreviations. (No period follows the abbreviation.)

POSTAL ABBREVIATIONS

AB	Alberta
BC	British Columbia
MB	Manitoba
NB	New Brunswick
NL	Newfoundland and Labrador
NT	Northwest Territories
NS	Nova Scotia
NU	Nunavut
ON	Ontario
PE	Prince Edward Island
QC	Quebec
SK	Saskatchewan
YT	Yukon Territory

25c   **Words such as *Street, Avenue, Road, Park,* and *Company* are abbreviated only when they appear in addresses.**

Crawford Street is west of Elm Avenue.

When used as part of an address in correspondence, such words can be either written out or abbreviated: **Elm Ave.**

25d   **The words *volume, chapter,* and *page* are written out when they appear in sentences but abbreviated when they appear in bibliographies and reference lists.**

I read pages 82–89 of chapter 10 in volume 3 for my sociology course.

Following is a list of abbreviations commonly used in documenting research papers.

abr.	abridged, abridgment
Acad.	Academy
anon.	anonymous
app.	appendix
Apr.	April
Assn.	Association
Aug.	August
biog.	biography, biographer, biographical
bk., bks.	book, books
bull.	bulletin
c.	circa, "about" (for example, "c. 1960")
cf.	compare
ch., chs.	chapter, chapters
col., cols.	column, columns
Coll.	College
comp.	compiled by, compiler
cont.	contents OR continued
DCB	*Dictionary of Canadian Biography*
Dec.	December
dept.	department
dir.	directed by, director
diss.	dissertation
div.	division
ed., eds.	edition(s) OR editor(s)
enl.	enlarged (as in "rev. and enl. ed.")
et al.	et alia, ("and others")
Feb.	February
fig.	figure
fwd.	foreword, foreword by
gen. ed.	general editor
govt.	government
illus.	illustrated by, illustrator, illustration
inc.	incorporated OR including
Inst.	Institute, Institution
intl.	international

introd.	[author of] introduction, introduced by
Jan.	January
jour.	journal
l., ll.	line, lines (omitted before line numbers unless the reference would be unclear)
mag.	magazine
Mar.	March
ms., mss.	manuscript, manuscripts
n, nn	note, notes (used immediately after page number: 6n3)
natl.	national
n.d.	no date [of publication]
no., nos.	number [of issue], numbers
Nov.	November
n.p.	no place [of publication] OR no publisher
n. pag.	no pagination
Oct.	October
P	Press (used in documentation; see "UP")
p., pp.	page, pages (omitted before page numbers unless the reference would be unclear)
pref.	preface, preface by
pseud.	pseudonym
pt., pts.	part, parts
rept.	reported by, report
rev.	revision, revised, revised by OR review, reviewed by
rpt.	reprinted, reprint
sec., secs.	section, sections
Sept.	September
ser.	series
sic	thus, so; reproduced exactly as written
Soc.	Society
supp.	supplement
trans.	translated by, translator, translation
U	University (used in documentation; see "UP")
UP	University Press (used in documentation; Oxford UP)
vol., vols.	volume, volumes (omitted before volume numbers unless the reference would be unclear)

The following kinds of abbreviations and acronyms are commonly used in writing. (See also 25a.)

(1) Clipped forms of some words

A clipped form is an abbreviation that can be pronounced as a word; it is not marked with a period.

Some clipped forms—such as rep, exec, or info—are avoided in formal writing. Others—such as exam, lab, U Vic, and math—are so common that they are becoming acceptable.

(2) Certain words used with dates or figures

82 B.C. [or B.C.E.]	A.D. 95 [or 95 C.E.]
7:40 a.m. [or A.M.]	4:52 EST [or E.S.T.]
No. 19	85 BTU [or Btu]

(3) The abbreviation for British Columbia (B.C.) when used as an adjective

Kamloops, B.C.; the B.C. scenery [COMPARE "British Columbia has many different geographic features, including mountains, forests, and plains."]

(4) The names of some organizations, agencies, countries, persons, or things commonly referred to by their capitalized initials

CSA	VCR	CFL	PC	CBC
IQ	TV	NDP	UW	CTV

(5) Certain common Latin expressions (with the English equivalent spelled out in brackets here)

cf.	[compare]	etc.	[and so forth]
e.g.	[for example]	i.e.	[that is]
et al.	[and others]	vs. OR v.	[versus]

 When unfamiliar with an acronym, readers benefit from seeing it spelled out the first time it is used.

Acronyms are words formed from the initial letters of other words or from the combination of syllables of other words: *AIDS* (**a**cquired **i**mmuno**d**eficiency **s**yndrome), *sonar* (**so**und **na**vigation and **r**anging).

> The NWMP (North-West Mounted Police) existed for 47 years before changing its name to the RCMP (Royal Canadian Mounted Police).
>
> **OR**
>
> The North-West Mounted Police (NWMP) existed for . . .

Your reader will probably be familiar with such terms as NATO, NASA, radar, and laser but perhaps not with CAD or ROM.

Exercise 1

Strike out any form that is inappropriate in formal writing.

1. after 8 P.M.; after eight in the P.M.
2. on November 15; on Nov. 15
3. in Sask. and Ont.; on TV; 85 km/h
4. for Jason Ross, Jr.; for Jr.
5. Mr. Robert Lyons; a prof.
6. on Eastwood Ave.; on Eastwood Avenue

25f Numbers are written in different ways depending on the size of the numbers and the frequency with which they appear.

When you use numbers infrequently in a piece of writing, you can spell out those that can be expressed in one or two words and use figures for the others. When you use numbers frequently, spell out those from one to nine and use figures for all others. Very large numbers can be expressed by a combination of words and figures.

Always   over three centimetres

But   one-half of a metre

Always   after 124 days

But   after thirty-three days   OR   after 33 days

Always   758 students

But   seven hundred students   OR   700 students

Eleven million customers, 11 000 000 customers, or 11 million customers

In a discussion of related items containing both single- and double- or triple-digit numbers, use figures for all numbers.

Lana ate 7 cookies but Allaban ate 12.

If a sentence begins with a number, spell out the number.

Two hundred twenty-five contestants competed in the talent show.

Some numbers follow special usages.

Specific time of day

> 4 p.m.   OR   4:00 p.m.   OR   four o'clock in the afternoon
> 9:30 a.m.   OR   half past nine in the morning

Dates

> November 8, 1962   OR   8 November 1962 (NOT November 8th, 1962)
>
> December fourth   OR   the fourth of December   OR December 4
>
> the fifties   OR   the 1950s
>
> the fourteenth century
>
> in 1362   in 1320–21   OR   the winter of 1320–21
>
> from 1330 to 1335

E S L   Many languages invert the numbers for the month and the day. For *September 18, 1997,* they would use the numbers **18/9/97**. In American practice, the numbers would read **9/18/97**. Both forms are used in Canadian practice.

Addresses

> 25 Arrow Drive, Apartment 1, Calgary, Alberta T2P 2L7
>
> OR 25 Arrow Dr., Apt. 1, Calgary, AB T2P 2L7
>
> 21 Second Street
>
> 459 East 35 Street   OR   459 East 35th Street

Identification numbers

> Channel 10   Highway 27   Edward III   Room 222

Pages and divisions of books and plays

page 15   chapter 8   part 2

in act 2, scene 1   OR   in Act II, Scene I

Decimals and percentages

a 2.5 average   12½ percent   0.853 tonnes

Large round numbers

forty million dollars   OR $40 million   OR $40 000 000

[Figures are often used for emphasis.]

Repeated numbers (in legal or commercial writing)

The lawyer's fee will exceed two million (2 000 000) dollars.   OR   The lawyer's fee will exceed two million dollars ($2 000 000).

ESL   In Canada, there are different ways to present numbers. The SI Metric system, found in mathematics and science writing and increasingly in general usage, uses a decimal point (period) to mark any amount smaller than one. For numbers with five digits or more on either side of the decimal point, a space is used to separate every group of three digits.

10 000	(ten thousand)
7.65	(seven point six five OR seven and sixty-five one hundredths)
7000.65	(seven thousand and sixty-five one hundredths)
70 000.000 65	(seventy thousand and sixty-five hundred thousandths)

Other forms of writing use a comma between every third and fourth number to the left of the decimal point to separate thousands.

10,000	(ten thousand)
7,000.65	(seven thousand and sixty-five one hundredths)
70,000.00065	(seventy thousand and sixty-five hundred thousandths)

French-speaking people use a comma instead of a decimal point to indicate any amount smaller than one.

7,65	(seven point six five OR seven and sixty-five one hundredths)

Exercise 2

Using accepted abbreviations and figures, change each item to a shortened form.

1. in the second scene of the first act
2. five o'clock in the morning
3. on the ninth of March
4. Doctor Michael Polanyi
5. fifty two thousand four hundred twenty-five students

Chapter 26

Document Design

The preceding chapters contain advice for presenting your writing as clearly and correctly as possible. This chapter, however, contains information on presenting your writing so that it is as readable as possible. As the volume of information grows, so does the importance of its delivery—the visual design that gives readers the cues that lead them to the information they require and enable them to read it efficiently.

Visual design sends messages to readers. A dense, tightly packed page with narrow margins signals difficult material. Ample white space signals openness and availability. White space frames the material on the page, preventing it from seeming oppressive and burdensome, and so contributes to ease in reading regardless of the difficulty of the content. But too much white space can send a negative message: for instance, a triple-spaced term paper with huge margins announces that the writer has little to say.

Because the way you design your documents tells a reader much about you, a well-designed letter of application and résumé can mean the difference between being hired and not being hired. Similarly, a well-designed term paper can make a difference in how favourably a professor regards the quality of your work.

26a Using the proper materials enhances readability.

(1) Paper and binding

Use good 20-pound (9.1 kg) white 8½-by-11-inch (21.6 cm by 27.9 cm) paper (neither onionskin nor erasable bond); this kind of paper is suitable for use with typewriters, word processors, and most printers linked to a computer. If your printer requires continuous sheets, choose paper that allows clean removal of pin-feed strips and separation of sheets. If you write your papers by hand, use regular 8½-by-11-inch (21.6 cm by 27.9 cm) lined white notebook paper and follow your instructor's recommendations.

Use a paper clip or a staple to fasten pages; do not fasten them by folding down one corner. Unless your instructor tells you differently, do not use folders of any kind.

(2) Electronic documents

If you submit your work electronically (by e-mail, on a bulletin board, in a Web document, or on disk), follow your instructor's directions exactly. Label disks clearly. If you submit your work using e-mail or a bulletin board, use the subject line correctly and ensure that your work is error free before you send it. Whatever the requirements, the computing facilities to meet them are likely to be available on campus at no cost.

(3) Type, fonts, and justification

Although laser and ink-jet printers can print different type-sizes and -styles (fonts) on a single page, most academic papers should be printed using a font that looks like typewriter type, such as Courier 10 or 12, or a simple proportional font such as 10- or 12-point Times Roman. Using a variety of fonts detracts from the content. Resist the impulse to justify (make straight) your right margins. Unless your printer has proportional spacing, it will justify the right margin by inserting spaces between words so that every line is the same length; this irregular spacing within the line can be distracting and at times misleading to readers. Because university and college classes often simulate professional writing situations and since publishers and editors of learned journals generally request that manuscripts not be justified, it is usually inappropriate to justify the right margin of academic documents even if the printer has proportional spacing. Justification may be appropriate if a document will not be re-formatted before being printed, as is the case with some business documents or documents intended for desktop publishing.

Pages from a good ink-jet or laser printer are always acceptable. Before you start, make sure that the printer cartridge has enough ink or toner to complete your document. If your instructor accepts handwritten papers, write in blue or black ink on one side of the paper only.

26b Clear and orderly arrangement contributes to ease in reading.

The advice here follows the guidelines in the *MLA Handbook for Writers of Research Papers,* sixth edition (New York: MLA, 2003). If you are using another style manual, check the most recent edition. (See the list of style manuals, pages 539–40.)

(1) Layout

Follow your instructor's directions about margins and other formatting. Word processing software can be set to lay out pages exactly to your specifications: it can number your pages, print a certain number of lines per page, and incorporate appropriate word divisions. Software also allows you to vary the spacing between lines, but unless your instructor agrees to different spacing, observe the conventions of academic writing and double-space all papers except those you write by hand. Generally, leave margins of 2.5 cm (or no more than 3.75 cm) on all sides of the text to give your reader room for comments and to prevent a crowded appearance. The ruled vertical line on notebook paper marks the left margin for handwritten papers.

(2) Indention

The first lines of paragraphs should be uniformly indented. You can set your word processing software to indent the first lines of all paragraphs 1.25 cm. (Indent 2.5 cm if writing by hand.) Indent block quotations 2.5 cm from the left margin. (See 20b.)

(3) Paging

Place Arabic numerals—without parentheses or periods— at the right margin, 1.25 cm from the top of each page. Unless you are using a format that requires running titles (e.g., APA), put your last name immediately before the page number in case a page gets misplaced.

The first page

Unless your instructor requests a title page, place your name, your instructor's name, the course and section number, and the date in the top left-hand corner (2.5 cm from the top and 2.5 cm from the left edge of the page), double-spacing after each line. You should also double-space between the lines of a long title and centre all titles.

Begin your first paragraph on the second line below the title (first double-spaced line). (See the models in chapters 29, 34, and 35.) Most research papers do not require a title page, but if you use one, follow your instructor's directions about the form.

Subsequent pages

Place your name and the page number in the upper right-hand corner, 1.25 cm from the top. Begin text at the left margin, 2.5 cm from the top and double-space throughout.

(4) Headings

Headings can make a long document easier to read. They can highlight the organization of a long block of information or make it easy to combine several brief statements to avoid choppiness. If you use headings, make them consistent throughout your document, and if you have two levels of headings, treat all occurrences of each level alike. For instance, headings in this book follow a pattern similar to that of an outline. The main rules are identified by a number and letter set against the left margin and followed by subdivisions marked by numbers in parentheses. Further subdivisions are set flush with the left margin and, depending on the level of the division, appear in bold type of various sizes.

26c The appropriate form for electronic documents can vary.

Electronic documents may be published on the Internet, on your campus network, on a class or organization's electronic bulletin board, or even on a disk that you hand to your instructor or fellow student. Electronic documents, which are usually easy to modify, permit new kinds of collaboration and use of materials.

(1) Electronic mail

E-mail, as a medium for communication, is much less formal than a letter or a memo, but more enduring than conversation in that it can be edited, saved, and filed. It also fosters very speedy communication and offers more convenience than either postal mail (called "snail mail" by those who use e-mail frequently) or voice mail. E-mail uses a format like that of an interoffice memo, with "TO" and "SUBJECT" lines for entering the address of the person you are writing to and the topic of your message. (See also 35b(1).)

Using e-mail puts concern for audience in the foreground and requires special care to communicate ideas clearly. Experienced users have developed guides (humorously referred to as netiquette) to help new users avoid some common hazards. Some standard advice appears below.

Checklist for Bulletin Board Postings and Electronic Mail

1. Keep line length short. Because some users have monitors that display only 40 characters in a line, it is considerate to keep your messages concise, your paragraphs short, and your subject focussed.
2. Make the subject line descriptive of your message so your reader(s) can find and file your message easily.

continued

continued from previous page

✓

3. Use a signature line at the end of each message. Your signature should include three things: your name, your position and affiliation (if any), and, if your e-mail program does not show your e-mail address in the "FROM" line, your e-mail address. It can also include your postal address and telephone number if you wish, but it should not be longer than four lines.

4. Use capitals as you would in an ordinary typewritten document; that is, use mixed upper- and lowercase letters. Full capitals in electronic communications is understood as shouting. If you wish to stress a word, you can enclose it in asterisks, but do so *sparingly.*

5. Use good sense regarding what you write about others. Like a bulletin board, e-mail is neither private nor secure, and while it is unlikely that anyone would snoop in your mail messages, it is possible that a recipient might forward your message without your knowledge, embarrassing you—or even making you liable. Regular Internet users advise, "If you wouldn't like to see it on the evening news, don't put it in e-mail."

6. Similarly, respect the privacy of others. Just as you would not distribute photocopies of personal notes or post them on a campus bulletin board, don't forward personal messages without the writer's permission. (And don't perpetuate chain letters. They use up electronic resources that may already be strained.)

7. Respect copyright. Anything not specifically designated as public domain is copyrighted, including messages from friends that you got in your electronic mailbox. Credit any quotations, references, and sources. (See also 33g.)

continued

continued from previous page

☑

8. Sarcasm and irony are frequently misunderstood in messages posted to bulletin boards, and even in personal e-mail. These strategies depend in large part on facial expression and tone of voice, so your joke may be seen as criticism, and what is meant to be irony is frequently confused with straightforward statement.

9. Consider carefully before you use emoticons or Internet jargon. Although people often follow an ironic statement with an emoticon to emphasize that it isn't to be taken seriously, others find those little faces (or *smileys*) constructed out of punctuation marks annoying (:−>). And although acronyms are widely used in informal electronic communication, they can be confusing and annoying to the uninitiated, who may not understand a statement such as BTW for "by the way," or "sorry for the flame" as an apology for antagonistic criticism.

(2) The World Wide Web

The World Wide Web is similar to a newspaper or magazine. It contains **pages** that a reader can view using a **browser**. (A browser is a computer program that fetches the text and graphic images that make up a Web document—a page—and enables the user to view them.) Web pages can be dynamically linked to other web pages to form a new sort of document set. It is as different from a book as a book is from an ancient papyrus scroll, but it can contain much the same information, just presented differently. Instructors increasingly ask students to construct web pages in lieu of submitting papers. While the details of such construction are beyond the scope of this handbook, a few tips might be helpful.

Checklist for Designing Web Pages ✓

1. Use graphics sparingly. Graphic files are typically very large and take a long time to transfer. Unless a reader has very fast equipment, he or she may well abandon your beautiful, graphics-rich document for one that is less lovely but faster to access.

2. Don't crowd your page with text. Just as books with narrow margins and dense type can be intimidating, so can a similarly constructed web page. Set pages up so that they can be read on a single screen and provide a link to other screens.

3. Understand the difference between a paper page and a web page. Each has its advantages and disadvantages. Quick access to dozens or even hundreds of topics is easier with a web browser than with a book, but few would care to curl up with a video monitor. Take advantage of the capabilities of the tool you are using.

26d Proofreading provides quality control.

Proofreading is different from revising or editing. (See 29b–d.) **Revising** requires you to reconsider and possibly reorganize your ideas. **Editing** makes sure your prose is as clear, accurate, and stylistically consistent as possible and pays particular attention to the conventions of grammar, mechanics, punctuation, and spelling. **Proofreading** checks for and corrects errors of layout, spelling, punctuation, and mechanics, and serves as a final check to make sure all necessary revising and editing have been done. Proofreading can be done manually or with a word processing program; doing both is insurance against error.

If you are using a word processing program, it is a good idea to print out a draft of your document so that you can check it carefully on paper and make any necessary changes before you print the final copy. If you have typed or handwritten your document, make any necessary corrections by neatly drawing a single line through the incorrect material, placing a caret (∧) where the correct material is to be inserted, and writing the correct information clearly above the typed or handwritten line or, if long, to the side with a line drawn to the caret if needed for clarity.

To use the proofreading checklist that follows, you should first make sure your paper is properly formatted as specified in **26b** (or by your instructor). Then you might try reading your paper backward, sentence by sentence, out loud, checking for accuracy as recommended in each of the other sections of the list. Read the words slowly, looking at and pronouncing each syllable carefully. Some people find it more efficient to read through the paper several times this way, checking for a different set of items on each pass. It helps to refer to the chapters and sections cross-referenced in this handbook and also to keep your dictionary handy (**13a**, chapter **22**) to look up any words you are uncertain about as you proofread.

Checklist for Proofreading

Layout
- Have you used proper margins? For paper documents, are all margins 2.5 cm wide or according to your instructor's specifications? For electronic documents, are margins consistent throughout the document? Are paragraphs formatted consistently?
- Is each page numbered?
- Does the first page have the appropriate title and heading?

continued

continued from previous page

- Is the first line of each paragraph indented 1.25 cm if word processed or 2.5 cm if handwritten?
- Is the print (or handwriting) dark, clean, clear, and legible?
- Are the lines double-spaced?
- Are all listed items numbered sequentially?

Spelling (22)
- Are all words spelled correctly? Have you run a spell checker program?
- Have you double-checked the words you frequently misspell or any the spell checker might have missed (e.g., homonyms or misspellings that still form words, such as *form* for *from*)?
- Have you consistently used the first spelling of words that have more than one option (*theatre/theater*)?
- Have you double-checked the spelling of all foreign words?

Punctuation (17, 18, 19, 20, 21)
- Does each sentence have appropriate closing punctuation, and have you used only one space after each period (21a)?
- Is all punctuation within sentences appropriately used and correctly placed (comma, 17; semicolon, 18; apostrophe, 19; other internal marks of punctuation, 21; hyphen, 22f)?
- Are quotations carefully and correctly punctuated (20, 33h)?

Capitalization and italics (23 and 24)
- Does each sentence begin with a capital letter (23e)?
- Are all proper names, people's titles, and titles of published works correctly capitalized (23a–c)?
- Are quotations capitalized properly (20a, 33h(2))?
- Are italics used properly (24)?

Larger Elements

Chapter 27

Working with Paragraphs

Although they are an essential unit of thought in writing, paragraphs rarely stand alone. They stand in relation to and in the context of all the other paragraphs that surround them in a composition. It is, however, occasionally useful to view them separately to observe how a single paragraph is organized and why it is or is not effective. Furthermore, many of the development patterns and strategies described in this chapter as paragraph strategies also apply to writing the whole essay. As you work through this chapter, you should keep in mind that the flow of information in your essay is one of your most important considerations and that you may want to revise paragraphs to support and reflect that flow.

Good paragraphs are **unified, coherent,** and **well developed,** and they can be said to contribute to the development of the main idea of a paper in ways similar to those in which sentences contribute to the development of an idea in a paragraph. (See **27c** and **d.**) Sentences and paragraphs are integral parts of the larger units—that is, the paragraphs and the essays—to which they belong. The beginning of a paragraph is indented to signal the reader that a new idea or a new direction for an idea follows. (Indention is also used in dialogue. (See **20a(4).**)

In paragraph 1, observe how the sentences relate to a single main idea (showing unity), how ideas progress easily from sentence to sentence (showing coherence), and how specific details support the main idea (showing development). (For easy reference, the paragraphs in this section are numbered—except for those needing revision. The topic sentences in paragraphs 1 to 6 are indicated by italics.)

1 *Dreams, fantasies of the life we would choose for ourselves, enlarge our horizons.* They represent the goals we pursue; they offer challenge, sustenance, self-esteem, an essential vision of tomorrow. Without them, the grind of daily life would be lacklustre and pointless, an unending round of effort without purpose. Achievement in the absence of dreams is impossible. —NEIL BISSOONDATH, "A Land Worth Loving"

Paragraphs have no set length. Typically, they range from 50 to 250 words and average perhaps 100 words. Paragraphs in books are usually longer than those in newspapers and magazines.

Although one-sentence paragraphs are occasionally used for emphasis, short paragraphs often indicate inadequate development. Long paragraphs, too, can reveal problems in your writing, especially if they exhaust one point or combine too many points.

Transitional paragraphs (page 313) as well as introductory and concluding paragraphs (chapter 28) serve other purposes.

ESL Some cultures find the directness and brevity valued in North American academic and business writing inelegant or even rude. If your culture values indirection, you will have to make an adjustment to this kind of directness in order to write to North American readers. (See also chapter 15.)

27a   Paragraphs should be unified.

In a unified paragraph, each sentence helps develop the main idea or the gist of the paragraph. The main idea often suggests a new, interesting relationship between two other ideas or facts not otherwise connected. Stating the main idea in a single sentence (often called a topic sentence) will help you achieve unity.

(1) Main idea and topic sentences

Writers usually convey the main idea of a paragraph in a topic sentence, which may appear at any point in the paragraph. For example, the topic sentence in paragraph 2 (in italics) announces that our aging population will bring about many changes in our society.

2   *The greater number of elderly in the population will call for changes and create conflicts in society.* Many of our myths about aging and the elderly will be changed. Older people are remaining vigorous and independent much longer as a result of health care advances. Because of improved pensions, fewer elderly people are now living in poverty. Thus we can expect an increase in "grey power." It is already reflected economically in the increasing number of television commercials aimed at older people. We can also expect pressure on governments to maintain, or even improve services like pensions and health care. —MARGARET WARD, *The Family Dynamic*

The main idea of a paragraph is frequently stated at or near the beginning, as in paragraph 2. It is sometimes also restated at the end to emphasize its importance, particularly in introductory paragraphs. In paragraph 3, compare "Society sends clear messages about the role that time plays in people's lives" with the final statement, "Whether we choose to fit with society's expectations about time, choose to ignore them, or fight against them, society has influenced the way in which we all view and manage time."

3   *Society sends clear messages about the role that time plays in people's lives.* On some TV channels, time is on constant display and viewers can set their watches to within a microsecond. We live in a culture in which time matters and success is often measured by speed. For many people the few weeks of the year when they are on holiday and can enjoy the slower pace of unhurried living are a welcome change from the fast pace of work and school. Others even prefer to vacation at a fast pace and get bored quickly if there is a lull in activities. Whether we choose to fit with society's expectations about time, choose to ignore them, or fight against them, society has influenced the way in which we all view and manage time.

—JOAN FLEET and DENISE REAUME, *Power over Time*

Occasionally, the topic sentence is stated near the end of the paragraph, especially when the writer progresses from specific examples to a generalization as in paragraph 4.

4   Ironically, I had to move to the United States, considered by Canadians to be more racist, to get a job as director of a research institute. I know it would have been hard, if not impossible, to get such a job in Canada. My brother, too, had to move to the United States to find a job more commensurate with his graduate business education, and he now works as a vice-president with a major bank in New York City. He tried many times to land a position with a Canadian bank but never did receive an interview. I know many Canadians of African origin who have also moved to the United States and found meaningful work, which is a shame. As Africans, some of us have worked very hard to integrate and become Canadian. Yet we were always racially defined as the "other." *No matter how much we tried, it appears that the standards for full membership as a Canadian are still related to whiteness.*

—HENRY MARTEY CODJOE, "Can Blacks Be Racist: Reflections on Being 'Too Black and African'"

A single topic sentence can serve for a sequence of two or more paragraphs.

5   *Contemporary legends differ from legends of the past in that they claim to be factual rather than fantastic.* These legends, although highly believable, are based on hearsay rather than fact. Some of them are horror stories reflecting urban fears, while some, like the trickster tales, are stories with a humorous, slightly ambiguous moral twist. An example of the first is the perennial legend of the Halloween candy poisoned (by strangers) that stirs up parental anxieties each October.

6   Most students have heard many legends spawned by essay anxieties, such as the one about the student who handed in a recycled essay and received a good mark on it, but with a note from the professor saying "I only got a C on this, but I always thought it was a lot better than that." Jan Harold Brunvand . . . has collected hundreds of these tales, which always betray their spuriousness by being told far too many times and with far too many embellishments and revisions, and always as told by a reliable source or a friend of a friend (FOAF). Urban legends deal with understandings of deviance and control. They tell us that certain ways of living (deviance) are likely to lead to grief or humiliation, and in the process they express our fears (and sometimes our sense of humour).
    —LINDA B. DEUTSCHMANN, *Deviance and Social Control*

Occasionally, a paragraph contains no topic sentence because the details unmistakably imply the main idea. For example, the author's love of plants, although never explicitly stated, is clearly the central idea of the following paragraph.

7   After work, I go walking and weed-inspecting. Weeds and wildflowers impress me as much as any cultivated plant. I've heard that in a year when the milkweed is plentiful, the Monarch butterflies will also be plentiful. This year the light pinkish milkweed flowers stand thick and tall, and sure enough, here are the dozens of Monarch butterflies, fluttering like

dusky orange-gold angels all over the place. I can't identify as many plants as I'd like, but I'm learning. Chickweed, the ragged-leafed lambs' quarters, the purple-and-white wild phlox with its expensive-smelling free perfume, the pink and mauve wild asters, the two-toned yellow of the tiny butter-and-eggs flowers, the burnt orange of devil's paintbrush, the staunch nobility of the huge purple thistles, and, almost best of all, that long stalk covered with clusters of miniature creamy blossoms which I finally tracked down in my wild-flower book—this incomparable plant bears the armorial name of the Great Mullein of the Figwort Family. It may not be the absolute prettiest of our wildflowers, but it certainly has the most stunning pedigree.

—MARGARET LAURENCE, "The Shack"

Exercise 1

Photocopy a page or two from a piece of writing you like and mark the topic sentences. Be prepared to share your work in class.

Exercise 2

Write a paragraph with a topic sentence at the beginning, another with the topic sentence at the end, and a third with the topic sentence at the beginning and restated at the end.

If you get stuck, here are a few suggestions to get you started.

1. Two benefits of peer editing are . . .
2. You know you are in trouble when . . .
3. Discrimination can be defined as . . .
4. Before speaking in front of others . . .

(2) Main idea and paragraph unity

The most common way to unify a paragraph is to make each sentence support the main idea. In paragraph 8, each sentence shows exactly what the writer means by the noisy village referred to in the topic sentence.

8   Her head was a noisy village, one filled with people, active and full of life, with many concerns and opinions. Children, including her own, ran about. Cousins twice removed bickered. A distant aunt, Maddie, decked out in two printed cotton dresses, a patched-up pair of pants and an old fuzzy sweater, marched up and down the right side of her forehead. Soon she would have a migraine. On the other side, a pack of idlers lounged around a heated domino game, slapping the pieces hard against her left forehead. Close to her neck sat the gossiping crew, passing around bad news and samples of malicious and scandalous tales. The top of her head was quiet. Come evening this would change, with the arrival of schoolchildren; when the workers left their factories and offices, the pots, banging dishes and televisions blaring would add to the noisy village.   —MAKEDA SILVERA, "Her Head a Village"

Each sentence in paragraph 9 supports the main idea that a writer needs time to rejuvenate, and each sentence also contributes to the **unity** of Richardson's essay as a whole by pointing toward the main idea of the next paragraph— that reading another writer's work encourages newness and a shifting of habits.

9   For the writer, winter is a time of growth and harvest, and summer is the time for sowing. Summer is the season for recharging the batteries, for replenishing the wellspring, for laying the table for the muse, for sterilizing the forceps used by literature's midwife. Or obstetrician. Legislation on this point varies from region to region across the country. While there is no guarantee that the hoped-for regeneration will take place, the surest way I know of facilitating such a fertilizing is through reading. Reading and writing are without doubt part of a continuum, and reading, even more than travel, is where writing begins.   —BILL RICHARDSON, "Dog-eared Days"

As you check your paragraphs for unity, revise or eliminate any information that does not clearly relate to the main idea. If the relationship between the main idea and the details is obvious to you but not to your reader, add a phrase or a sentence to make their relevance clear. If more than one major idea appears in a single paragraph, either refocus your main idea or develop each idea in a separate paragraph.

Exercise 3

Note how each sentence in the following paragraph expresses a different major idea. Select one sentence and use it as a topic sentence to develop a unified paragraph with specific details and examples.

[1]The games we played as kids were definitely more authentic and socially productive than the computer games played by kids today. [2]To begin with, we were not afraid to get dirty. [3]Street games such as ball hockey, tag, and kick the can were physically demanding. [4]They helped us to develop athletic abilities such as stamina and co-ordination that we would find indispensable in playing organized sports later on. [5]Secondly, these games required team effort. [6]By playing them, we learned various social skills like cooperation and the ability to manage interpersonal relationships. [7]In addition, our success as a team required us to communicate effectively in order to clarify our common goals and aspirations. [8]Most importantly, however, the games my generation played as kids taught us the importance of respect and personal responsibility. [9]We learned to value rules because we understood they applied fairly to everybody. [10]Cheaters were often shunned and warned that if they ever wanted to play with the gang again they'd have to play by the rules. [11]Loyalty was another principle that we learned through our games. [12]How many lifelong friendships were forged between the tattered nets of a street hockey game no one can say.

27b　Clearly arranged ideas and effective transitions foster paragraph coherence.

A paragraph is coherent when the relationship among the ideas is clear and the progression from one sentence to the next is easy for the reader to follow. To achieve this goal, arrange ideas in a clearly understandable order. If your paragraph emphasizes the main idea as paragraph 10 does, make sure that each sentence refers to the subject of the topic sentence. If your paragraph moves along like paragraph 11, the subject of each sentence should echo the predicate of the previous one. In either instance, link the sentences by effective use of pronouns, repetition, conjunctions, transitional phrases, and parallel structure. These transitional devices also ease the transitions between paragraphs.

(1) Patterns of coherence

Different kinds of writing use different patterns to establish coherence. In the humanities, the primary pattern establishes links between the subject of the topic sentence and all subsequent sentences in the paragraph. In this way, the subject is gradually *unpacked*. That is, we see the other ideas or details that the subject contains, as the following diagram illustrates.

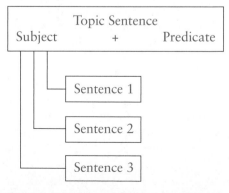

10 One Chinese man waiting for the passenger ship to dock at the pier at the foot of Granville Street stood out from the crowd by virtue of his nearly six-foot frame. He had a body that was all limbs, long even in his fingers, which gave his every gesture an elongated emphasis. A fedora graced his head, and he was attired in a custom-tailored three-piece gray suit. His shoes and wire-rimmed glasses were polished and his black hair meticulously combed to expose a high forehead, a physical trait the Chinese considered a sign of intelligence. He owned two suits—one gray, the other brown—and two fedoras. Believing one's appearance mirrored one's inner mind, his appearance today was, as always, immaculate. His manner, like his dress, was sober and serious. At thirty-seven, he was a year younger than the city of Vancouver.

—DENISE CHONG, *The Concubine's Children*

The pattern that dominates in the natural and social sciences links each sentence, chain-like, to the predicate of the preceding one. In these disciplines, it is important to convey a sense of method. That is, in addition to stating what is the case, the writer explains *why* or *how* it is the case and *what follows* from this state of affairs. See, for example, paragraph 11 and the diagram that follows.

11 Each of us perceives from a particular perspective that is shaped by our physiology, culture, standpoint, social roles, cognitive abilities, and aspects of ourselves and our personal experiences. This means that what we perceive is always partial and subjective. It is partial because we cannot perceive everything but instead select only certain aspects of phenomena to notice. We then organize and interpret those selected stimuli in personal ways that are necessarily incomplete.

—JULIA WOOD and ANGELA HENRY, *Everyday Encounters*

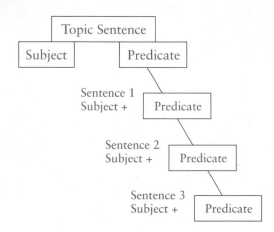

But writers generally match the pattern they use to the writing they do. Writers in the humanities who wish to move quickly over material are likely to use a chaining pattern. Similarly, writers in the sciences who wish to explain a single idea in depth will generally use the focussed pattern.

(2) Order of ideas

One of the simplest ways to arrange ideas in a paragraph is to use **chronological order**.

12   Color is what my mother wanted in her wine, so she and I spent the better part of the afternoon cutting the beets into little cubes and boiling them slowly for two hours until the pot appeared to be a kettle of boiling blood. Later I would hold cheesecloth across the mouth of a crock as my mother ladled the beet blood into the cloth to strain it. She would then add the sugar and raisins, orange and lemon peels, and float the slice of toast covered in yeast, yeast-side down, on the mixture. We would let this stand in the root cellar for a fortnight, stirring several times each day. Then my mother and

I would very carefully strain the beet wine and bottle it for
Mrs. Boulee.   —GAIL ANDERSON-DARGATZ,
The Cure for Death by Lightning

Descriptive passages are often arranged in **spatial order**.
Starting from a single point of reference, the description
can move from north to south, from near to distant, from
left to right, and so on. Note the movement from Vancouver's waterfront to Chinatown in paragraph 13.

13   From the pier it was a short, ten-minute ride east along
      Pender Street to Chinatown. Their taxi skirted the city's financial district. Its tall stone buildings and rhythmic flow of streetcars spoke of ordered calm. On the other side of the tram
      lines that ran between New Westminster and Vancouver, the
      western architecture suddenly gave way to a dense conglomeration of two- and three-story brick buildings bedecked with
      an assortment of awnings. Two tiny alleyways off Pender,
      Canton and Shanghai Alleys, both of which had been privately
      developed, were congested with tall, narrow tenements, dozens of businesses, shops, restaurants, even a public bath and
      an opera house. May-ying was vaguely reminded of the buildings she had seen in Canton.
                          —DENISE CHONG, *The Concubine's Children*

Another useful arrangement is **order of importance** (climactic), from most to least important or from least to most
important. (See also **11c**.) In paragraph 14, the author
focusses on a hierarchy of intelligence, moving from lower
to higher forms of life.

14   An ant cannot purposefully try anything new, and any ant
      that accidentally did so would be murdered by his colleagues.
      It is the ant colony as a whole that slowly learns over the ages.
      In contrast, even an earthworm has enough flexibility of brain
      to enable it to be taught to turn toward the left or right for
      food. Though rats are not able to reason to any considerable
      degree, they can solve such problems as separating round
      objects from triangular ones when these have to do with health

or appetite. Cats, with better brains, can be taught somewhat more, and young dogs a great deal. The higher apes can learn by insight as well as by trial and error.

—GEORGE RUSSELL HARRISON, *What Man May Be*

Sometimes the movement within the paragraph is from **general to specific** or from **specific to general**. A paragraph may begin with a general statement or idea, which is then supported by particular details, as in paragraph 14 above, or it may begin with a striking detail or series of details and conclude with a climactic statement as in paragraph 15, or a summarizing statement as in paragraph 16.

15   The ancient Greeks had the agora. The ancient Romans had the forum. In Spain, people still take an after-dinner ramble around the plaza, while in Italy, people wave and chat and sip their cappuccinos in the piazza. In modern Britain, people can yet get together to mix and mingle and murmur in gathering spots that range from the dinkiest village common to the hurly burly of Trafalgar Square. And here in Canada? What do we have here in Canada to compare to the agoras, the forums, the greens and commons and squares of the Old World?

Well, we have the Mall.

The shopping mall.

—ARTHUR BLACK, "Walk a Mall in My Shoes"

16   All my life I'd bought things with a mind to how well they would pack or store. I checked a shirt to be wrinkle-free before I tried it on, bought books but never paintings which would have to be crated for a move. I had borrowed furniture or made do with what could be left behind. Owning a house was a fantasy of stability beyond my imagining, and it frightened me. Only the reluctance of the mortgage broker to grant a mortgage to two women without the signature of a man restored my courage. What I discovered about owning a house was that it was a place where things could be left behind in their own places and returned to again and again. A trip to

Europe no longer meant an uprooting. Home was a place you could leave behind intact, and it would be there for you when you got back. —JANE RULE, "Choosing Home"

One common form of the general-specific pattern is **topic-restriction-illustration,** in which the writer announces the topic, restricts it, and illustrates the restricted topic. In paragraph 17, the writer announces the topic—the oddest artificial language—restricts it in the second sentence by giving a reason, and then illustrates it with examples.

17   One of the oddest artificial languages ever was Solresol, invented by François Sudre in 1827. The Frenchman reasoned that since music was the universal language, the seven notes of the musical scale were the perfect building blocks for an international vocabulary. Single notes were reserved for simple words (*do* for "no," *re* for "and"), double notes for pronouns, triple notes for everyday words (*do-re-la* for "year"), and longer combinations for more uncommon terms. In addition, opposites were expressed whenever possible by reversing the order of the notes: *do-mi-sol* for "God" means that "Satan" must be *sol-mi-do.* Sudre tinkered with the language for 45 years, but was never able to overcome the fundamental flaw: people would rather speak a conversation than whistle it.*   —GAVIN EDWARD

In the **question-answer** pattern, the first sentence asks a question that the supporting sentences answer.

18   Are we living in an overeducated society? One variant of the conflict approach argues that we are. In this view, recent recessions have eliminated jobs, depressed incomes, restricted career paths, and constrained upward mobility. Increasingly, obtaining high levels of education provides less and less assurance of entry into high-status jobs. Inflated admission requirements for jobs often necessitate that recruits be trained well

---

* Excerpt from "Dejpu'bogh Hov rur qablḷ! (Your Face Looks Like a Collapsed Star)," by Gavin Edward. Copyright © 1996 Condé Nast Publications. All rights reserved. Originally published in *Wired.* Reprinted by permission.

beyond the level actually necessary for satisfactory performance. Furthermore, restricted entry into occupations, coupled
with inflated admission requirements, means that many highly
trained people must find work not only at less challenging jobs
in their field, but also in less demanding positions outside their
area of expertise. Although overeducation may create problems of "underemployment," thereby diminishing the job satisfaction of those affected, the evidence presented earlier
suggests clearly that those with higher levels of education are
not nearly so hard hit by a worse fate—unemployment.

—IAN GOMME, "Education"

Another common paragraph arrangement is the **problem-
solution** pattern, in which the first sentence or two state
the problem and the rest of the paragraph suggests the
solution, as illustrated by paragraph 19.

19   That many women would be happier not pursuing careers
      or intellectual adventures is only part of the truth. The whole
      truth is that many people would be. If society had the clear
      sight to assure men as well as women that there is no shame
      in preferring to stay non-competitively and non-aggressively
      at home, many masculine neuroses and ulcers would be
      avoided, and many children would enjoy the benefit of being
      brought up by a father with a talent for the job instead of by
      a mother with no talent for it but a sense of guilt about the
      lack.   —BRIGID BROPHY, "Women"

Paragraphs 12 through 19 illustrate eight of the many
possible types of arrangement within the paragraph. Any
order or combination of orders is satisfactory as long as
the sequence of ideas is logical and clear.

Exercise 4

Find examples of three different kinds of paragraph development.
Identify the coherence pattern of each and its order of ideas
(chronological, spatial, climactic, general to specific, specific to

general, topic-restriction-illustration, question-answer, problem-solution). Explain in writing how each paragraph follows the pattern and organization you have identified.

Exercise 5

Examine paragraphs from your own writing in other projects and find two examples of subject-focussed paragraphs and two of chaining paragraphs. Revise each paragraph, converting the focussed paragraphs to chaining paragraphs and vice versa. What difficulties do you encounter? What happens to each paragraph?

(3) Transitional devices: pronouns, repetition, transitional words and phrases, and parallel structures

Many of the same kinds of transitions link sentences within paragraphs and paragraphs within a paper: pronouns, repetition of key words or ideas, conjunctions and other transitional phrases, and parallel structures. (See also chapters 8 and 10.)

Pronouns

In paragraph 20, the writer links sentences by using the pronouns *his* and *he*. Although these same two pronouns are used repeatedly, their referent, "Ryan," is always clear.

20   Ryan at six was underweight. He was a picky eater. He had allergies. He was afraid of the dark and occasionally wet his bed. He was always coming down with a cold or else getting over an earache. He cried easily, and couldn't bear to be scolded. He refused to look people in the eye, even the eyes of his father, especially the eyes of his father—the father who had left his wife and child, who'd packed a couple of suitcases late on a Winnipeg afternoon and moved out of the Lipton Street house, taking up residence in a crummy apartment over on Westminster Avenue.   —CAROL SHIELDS, *Larry's Party*

Repetition of words, phrases, or ideas

In paragraph 21, the repetition of the key word *wave* links the sentences. The repetition also provides emphasis. (See 11e.)

21   The weekend is over, and we drive down the country road from the cottage to the pier, passing out our last supply of waves. We wave at people walking and wave at people riding. We wave at people we know and wave at people who are strangers.

—ELLEN GOODMAN, "Waving Goodbye to the Country"

Conjunctions and other transitional expressions

Conjunctions and transitional phrases demonstrate the logical relationship between ideas. Notice the subtle changes in the relationship between two clauses linked by different conjunctions in the following sentences.

He laughed, and she frowned.

He laughed while she frowned.

He laughed because she frowned.

He laughed, so she frowned.

He laughed; later, she frowned.

Here is a checklist of some frequently used transitional connections arranged according to the kinds of relationships they establish.

Checklist of Transitional Connections	
• **Alternative and Addition**	or, nor, and, and then, moreover, besides, further, furthermore, likewise, also, too, again, in addition, even more important, next, first, second, third, in the first place, in the second place, finally, last

continued

continued from previous page

✓

• Comparison	similarly, likewise, in like manner
• Contrast	but, yet, or, and yet, however, still, nevertheless, on the other hand, on the contrary, conversely, even so, notwithstanding, in contrast, at the same time, although this may be true, otherwise, nonetheless
• Place	here, beyond, nearby, opposite to, adjacent to, on the opposite side
• Purpose	to this end, for this purpose, with this object
• Result or Cause	so, for, therefore, accordingly, consequently, thus, thereupon, as a result, then, because, hence
• Summary	to sum up, in brief, on the whole, in sum, in short
• Repetition	as I have said, in other words, that is, to be sure, as has been noted
• Exemplification	for example, for instance, in any event
• Intensification	in fact, indeed, to tell the truth
• Time	meanwhile, at length, soon, after a few days, in the meantime, afterward, later, now, then, in the past, while

Parallel structures

Parallelism is the repetition of a sentence pattern or of other grammatical structures. (See also chapter 10.) In paragraph 22, the first three sentences are structured the same way:

When you're three years old . . . , that's expected.

When you're six . . . , you deserve some credit. . . .

When you're nine . . . , you should be applauded. . . .

Repeating this pattern emphasizes the close relationship of the ideas.

22   When you're three years old and stick mashed potatoes up your nose, that's expected. When you're six and make your bed but it looks like you're still in it, you deserve some credit for trying. When you're nine and prepare the family meal but the casserole looks worse than the kitchen, you should be applauded for your effort. But somewhere along the line, some responsible adult should say, "You're too old for this nonsense."
                              —DAN KILEY, *The Peter Pan Syndrome:*
                              Men Who Have Never Grown Up

Exercise 6

Revise the following paragraph so the thought flows smoothly from one sentence to the next. Add pronouns and linking devices, and revise sentences to create parallel structure and to repeat key phrases.

23   ¹"Reality-based" TV programs have become very popular recently. ²They appear to capture spontaneous events on film. ³Most viewers are not aware that much of the action that transpires on these programs is staged. ⁴The shows' directors use dramatic lighting to convey mood. ⁵They employ soundtracks to heighten the atmosphere. ⁶They often incorporate sound effects like wild animals or blowing wind to give the sense of danger or seclusion. ⁷Participants on these programs are often selected because producers think they will appeal to the audience. ⁸The shows' producers isolate their target audience. ⁹They make sure that people on their shows reflect the desires of this target audience. ¹⁰Directors often script important pieces of dialogue at critical moments during production. ¹¹A tense confrontation that appeared to have erupted suddenly between two people who were once close allies was actually rehearsed before being filmed. ¹²The relationships that develop between participants on these shows are often as contrived as those between characters on a sitcom or a soap opera.

(4) Transitions between paragraphs

Transitions between paragraphs are as important as transitions between sentences and are achieved by many of the same devices—repetition of words or ideas, conjunctions and other transitional expressions, and parallel structures. Such devices are usually evident in the first sentence of a paragraph. (The italics in each of the following examples were added.)

You can repeat a word or idea from the last paragraph in the first sentence of the new one, as in paragraphs 24 and 25. (See also 27b(1).)

24 For those who pray or chant with great perseverance, there is the suggestion that their *waiting* has been converted into purposefulness.

25 Of course, we do not just *wait* for love; we *wait* for money, we *wait* for the weather to get warmer, colder; we *wait* for the plumber to come and fix the washing machine. . . .

—EDNA O'BRIEN, "Waiting"

In paragraphs 26 and 27, Anne Kingston picks up the idea of bacteria as a transition to her second paragraph.

26 It's like a thousand other upbeat cleanser commercials. A perky white-bread couple stand talking in a pristine kitchen. Only they're talking about their family's recent illness. At first, they thought it was the flu. But it may have been something more insidious. It might have been salmonella poisoning. Mom has a theory: "It might have come from bacteria [camera closes in ominously on a chicken wrapper on the counter] spread around our kitchen to other food." Her solution? Lysol Antibacterial Kitchen Cleaner, which, she says, "may help [keep] us from getting sick."

27 Germs are everywhere, it seems. Attacking, infiltrating, ingratiating themselves into everyday life. Most frightening are the unharnessable ones, the ones linked to very real, deadly

diseases. AIDS. Antibiotic-resistant bacteria, including the rare group A streptococci that killed the Muppeteer Jim Henson, and the necrotizing fasciitis that attacked Lucien Bouchard. Virulent strains of *E. coli* that left eleven dead and made close to 1,000 ill in Japan last summer. And then there are all of those killer microbes harboured in hospitals.

—ANNE KINGSTON, "Cleaning Up"

Paragraphs 28 and 29 show how you can use transitional words or phrases to connect paragraphs.

28   At the beginning of the 1920s, professional hockey was solely Canadian. The Pacific Coast League (formed in 1911), the Western Canadian League (begun in 1921), and the National Hockey League (NHL, inaugurated in 1917) alone competed for the coveted Stanley Cup. Then the NHL expanded into the lucrative urban market of the United States. By 1927, the NHL consisted of five American and five Canadian teams. The Ottawa Senators dominated the NHL in the early years of the decade, winning the Stanley Cup four times.

29   The NHL, in turn, dominated hockey throughout the 1920s. It paid the average player $900 a year, with a few exceptional players earning upward of $10 000. Although interest in amateur trophies—the Allan Cup and the Memorial Cup—continued in the smaller centres, the focus remained on the NHL even after the league shrank to six teams, with only the Toronto Maple Leafs and the Montreal Canadiens in Canada. Almost all the NHL players remained Canadian.

—R. DOUGLAS FRANCIS et al.,
Destinies: Canadian History Since Confederation

You can use parallel structures to demonstrate relationships between paragraphs, as in paragraphs 30 and 31.

30   I came to the sea because my heart was broken. I rented a cabin from an old professor who stammered when he talked. He wanted to go far away and look at something. In the cabin there is a table, a chair, a bed, a woodstove, an aladdin lamp. Outside there is a wall, a privy, rocks, trees and the sea.

(The lapping of waves, the scream of gulls.)

31   I came to this house because my heart was broken. I brought wine in green bottles and meaty soup bones. I set an iron pot on the back of the stove to simmer. I lit the lamp. It was no longer summer and the wind grieved around the door. Spiders and mice disapproved of my arrival. I could hear them clucking their tongues in corners.
      (The sound of the waves and the wind.)
                              —AUDREY THOMAS, "The Man with Clam Eyes"

Sometimes a transitional paragraph serves as a bridge between two paragraphs. Ordinarily, such a paragraph is short (often consisting of only one sentence) because the writer intends it to be merely a signpost, as in paragraphs 32 through 34.

32   Now you are expecting me to describe how I saw the folly of my ways and came back to the warm nest, where prejudices are so often called loyalties, where pointless actions are hallowed into custom by repetition, where we are content to say we think when all we do is feel.

33   But you would be wrong. I dropped my hobby and turned professional.

34   If I were to go back to the headmaster's study and find the dusty statuettes still there, I would arrange them differently. I would dust Venus and put her aside, for I have come to love her and know her for the fair thing she is. But I would put the Thinker, sunk in his desperate thought, where there were shadows before him—and at his back, I would put the leopard, crouched and ready to spring.
                              —WILLIAM GOLDING, "Thinking as a Hobby"

27c   Details and examples can develop paragraphs.

Many short paragraphs are adequately developed and supply enough information within the context of the essay to satisfy the reader. For example, the following paragraph, although only one sentence, contains considerable detail.

35   To have parents who are, as they say, dysfunctional—in this case, needy, infantile, self-indulgent, narcissistic, ruthlessly selfish hysterics who use up all the oxygen in the room and then gasp self-pityingly that they are having trouble breathing—is a maturing burden for a child, and a sad kind of discipline.   —LANCE MORROW,
      "Childhood in a Fishbowl: Having Famous Parents Can
      Be So Embarrassing. How's a Kid Going to Cope?" *Time*

Sometimes short paragraphs can be combined if they deal with the same idea. More often, however, short paragraphs need to be developed with more specific details or examples.

(1) Developing with specific details

Notice how the series of details in paragraph 36 supports the topic sentence (italicized).

36   . . . *twisters transfixed me with their bizarre violence, the random precision of their malevolence.* Half an apartment building is destroyed, yet an inch away from the vanished wall, the table remains set for dinner. A chequebook is snatched from a pocket. A man opens his front door and is carried two hundred feet above the treetops, landing unharmed. A crate of eggs flies five hundred feet and is set down again, not a shell cracked. All the objects that are transported safely from one place to another in an instant, descending on ascending air currents: a jar of pickles travels twenty-five miles, a mirror, dogs and cats, the blankets ripped from a bed leaving the surprised sleepers untouched. Whole rivers lifted—leaving the riverbed dry—and then set down again. A woman carried sixty feet then deposited in a field next to a phonograph record (unscratched) of "Stormy Weather."
      —ANNE MICHAELS, *Fugitive Pieces*

(2) Developing with examples

Use appropriate and specific examples to clarify your ideas. The following definition may be unclear without the italicized example.

> A euphemism is the substitution of a pleasant expression for an unpleasant one, *such as "passed away" for "died."*

Paragraph 37 uses several closely related examples (as well as details) to illustrate that countries that did not conduct witch trials were societies that resisted change in the 16th century.

37   Places that were sheltered from change did not develop the craze. For example, while the French in France were burning Huguenot heretics and witches, the stable French settlement in Canada was not affected; the belief in witches existed, but no panic was associated with it. The same was true of Ireland, whose Catholic people were unshaken in their ways and unwilling to make use of the oppressive courts imposed on them by the English. In Ireland between 1534 and 1711, only nine proceedings against witches were recorded, most of them initiated by English or Scottish immigrants, and less than half of these resulted in execution. Similarly, in confidently Catholic Italy and Spain, few witches were burned.
        —LINDA B. DEUTSCHMANN, *Deviance and Social Control*

You can also use one striking example, as in paragraph 38, to clarify your idea.

38   What is called the Georgia Viaduct in Vancouver is in fact a roadway accessing the downtown area. It is well illuminated, has a sidewalk, and is travelled by several thousand automobiles most hours of the day. It was on this thoroughfare one early evening last month that a young woman was brutally assaulted by two men, escaping with her life when she was able to leap over the pedestrian rail into the path of the oncoming traffic and a motorist finally stopped and picked her

up. The police estimate that several hundred cars passed her by as the attack took place. So did several pedestrians. The case has been widely deplored in the Vancouver media. What's wrong with people, they want to know. It's a good question. It should be asked, not just by police, but by those in a position to shape our culture: television producers, novelists, journalists, literature professors, and, above all, the people who plan the social studies curricula in the school system. Why is it, they should discover, that these people did not stop—"these people" being you and I?   —TED BYFIELD,

"Peace at Any Price on Vancouver's Georgia Viaduct"

Details and examples clarify and explain your point.

Exercise 7

Develop the following sentences with enough details and/or examples to make an interesting paragraph.

1. Many people wonder how _____ stays in shape.
2. It was the filthiest room I had ever seen.
3. The class was so boring I decided to cut.
4. I grew up in the friendliest neighbourhood in the world.

Exercise 8

Examine your own writing and select a paragraph you think needs additional details or an appropriate example. Rewrite the paragraph.

 27d   Writers use various strategies to develop paragraphs.

You can learn to write good paragraphs by studying the various techniques professional writers use to develop ideas. All the strategies for developing paragraphs discussed in the following pages are useful for developing whole compositions. (See also chapters **28** and **29**.)

The more you read, the more you will find that most paragraphs are developed by a combination of methods. Some good paragraphs almost defy analysis. Because these development strategies reflect the ways people think, we tend to use them in combination with each other. For example, the formal definition can be developed through both classification and contrast, or narration can be developed by using descriptive details. The important consideration is not that a specific method is used to develop the paragraph, but that the development is clear, complete, and appropriate. No one method or combination is better than another. Use the one—or ones—that best suit your purpose. As you study the following illustrations of good paragraphs, notice how each main idea is developed.

(1) Narrating a series of events

A narrative discusses a sequence of events, normally in the order in which they occur, that develop the point you are making. This form often uses time markers such as *then, later,* or *at a later date.* (Longer narratives often begin in the middle of a sequence of events and contain flashbacks to earlier events.) The narrative must be closely related to your main idea and must develop that idea. The writer in paragraph 39 uses narrative to develop the main idea stated in the first sentence in the paragraph.

39   In sharp contrast with the militancy displayed by suffragettes in Britain and the United States, female suffrage in Canada was achieved through a peaceful—and piecemeal—process. By 1872 women property owners in British Columbia, single or married, were permitted to vote in city elections.

The municipal franchise was won in Ontario in 1883, but only for spinsters and widows who met the prescribed property qualifications. Manitoba granted single and married women the municipal vote in 1887. The provincial franchise, however, came much later. The first province to grant female suffrage was Manitoba in 1916. All other provinces extended the franchise in the next few years except Quebec, which did not do so until 1940. Spurred by the suffragist agitation and the war, the Dominion government finally granted women the right to vote in the federal enfranchisement acts of 1917 and 1918.   —PAUL W. BENNETT and CORNELIUS J. JAENEN,
"The Canadian Women's Movement, 1880–1920s:
A Struggle for Political Rights or Social Reform?"

(2) Describing to make a point

Focus your description according to your purpose. In describing your car, you would emphasize certain features to a prospective buyer, others to a mechanic who is going to repair it, and still others to a friend who wants to borrow it.

Descriptive details should be clearly ordered—from near to far, from general to particular, from right to left, from top to bottom—thus providing an orderly scheme for the reader. In paragraph 40, Ann-Marie MacDonald uses a general-particular perspective to enable the reader to picture the town of New Waterford from the height of a church steeple. Notice also her use of imagery ("iron tower against a slim pewter sky" and "the silver sea rolls and rolls"). (See "Imagery" in 35a(4).)

40   Here's a picture of the town where they lived. New Waterford. It's a night bright with the moon. Imagine you are looking down from the height of a church steeple, onto the vivid gradations of light and shadow that make the picture. A small mining town near cutaway cliffs that curve over narrow rock beaches below, where the silver sea rolls and rolls, flattering

the moon. Not many trees, thin grass. The silhouette of a colliery, iron tower against a slim pewter sky with cables and supports sloping at forty-five-degree angles to the ground. Railway tracks that stretch only a short distance from the base of a gorgeous high slant of glinting coal, towards an archway in the earth where the tracks slope in and down and disappear. And spreading away from the collieries and coal heaps are the peaked roofs of the miners' houses built row on row by the coal company. Company houses. Company town.

—ANN-MARIE MacDONALD, *Fall on Your Knees*

Descriptions can appeal to more senses than just sight. Norma De Haarte in paragraph 41 makes her description of the flocks of birds vivid by blending visual and auditory images.

41   As the afternoon sun started to set, large flocks of showy macaws, parrots and parakeets congregated. Moving from tree to tree, they set up a chattering and squalling. Then upwards they would fly again, colourful in the dazzling light. Joined by flocks of herons, mallards, sea gulls and cranes that nestled on the seashore, they fluttered, picturesque against the sky-blue canvas, plumes bathed in the golden rays of sunset. Together, the birds filled the air with a warlike chattering, screeching, screaming, chirping, chirring. Swirling forward, then backward, then forward again, they would race westward, home.   —NORMA DE HAARTE,
"Little Abu, the Boy Who Knew Too Much"

(3) Explaining a process

Process paragraphs, in explaining how something is done or made, often use both description and narration. You might describe the items used in the process and then narrate the steps chronologically, as in paragraph 42.

42   The best of all scientific tricks with an egg is the well-known one in which air pressure forces a peeled hard-boiled egg into a glass milk bottle and then forces it out again

undamaged. The mouth of the bottle must be only slightly smaller than the egg, and so you must be careful not to use too large an egg or too small a bottle. It is impossible to push the egg into the bottle. To get the egg through the mouth you must heat the air in the bottle. That is best done by standing the bottle in boiling water for a few minutes. Put the egg upright on the mouth and take the bottle off the stove. As the air in the bottle cools it contracts, creating a partial vacuum that draws the peeled egg inside. To get the egg out again invert the bottle so the egg falls into the neck. Place the opening of the bottle against your mouth and blow vigorously. This will compress the air in the bottle. When you stop blowing, the air expands, pushing the egg through the neck of the bottle and into your waiting hands.

—MARTIN GARDNER, "Mathematical Games"

(4) Showing cause and effect

A paragraph that explores a cause raises the question Why? and must answer that question to the satisfaction of the reader. Be sure to avoid the fallacy of assuming that since one event precedes another it is necessarily the cause of that event. (See **31h(8)**, "False cause.") Paragraph 43 provides several reasons for the Red River flood of 1997.

43   Throughout the winter of 1996–97, long-term observers knew that a flood of some magnitude was in the works. All the warning flags were flying high. The recipe for a full-fledged Red River flood requires a number of carefully measured ingredients. The ground must be saturated by several consecutive years of heavy rainfall. Come autumn, the snow must hold off for as long as possible, so that the earth can develop an iron-hard frost layer that will remain impervious to melt-water in the spring. Once the ground is good and frozen, there must be plenty of snow. Finally, cold temperatures must persist well into April, trapping all the moisture in slush and snowbanks until the very last moment. Then, when the polar

air mass that squats so stubbornly atop Manitoba for most of the winter retreats, the moisture must let go all at once. The later the melt, the greater the resulting flood.

—JAKE MacDONALD and SHIRLEY SANDREL,
*Faces of the Flood: Manitoba's Courageous Battle
against the Red River*

Paragraphs can also demonstrate effects, as in paragraph 44, which discusses how unions benefit their members financially.

44   Unions benefit their members financially. Research by Canadian economists suggests that, on average, unionized workers earn about 10 percent more than non-union workers do. . . . However, unions negotiate for more than wages. Consequently, union members are more than twice as likely to have pension plans provided by their employer. And unionized workers receive more paid vacations and holidays, and are more likely to have dental and medical plans and better job security than are comparable non-union workers. Unions also contribute to reducing overall wage inequality in a nation's labour market. This is largely because union impact on wages is greatest for workers in the lower and middle ranges of the income, education, and skill distributions. In other words, without unions income inequality in Canada would most likely rise. Indeed, in the United States and Britain growing income inequality has been linked, in part, to declining union membership.   —HARVEY J. KRAHN and GRAHAM S. LOWE,
Work, Industry and Canadian Society

(5) Comparing and contrasting to develop an idea

A **comparison** points out similarities; a **contrast** points out differences. A comparison or a contrast can be organized in either of two ways (or a combination of them), the choice depending on the writer's purpose. Writers often use both methods for the sake of variation. Vivian Smith uses the **part-by-part method** in paragraph 45, in which she analyzes gender differences in the workplace by looking first at how male entrepreneurs define success, then female entrepreneurs, and next at the career assumptions that are made about men, then women.

45   Ms. Duxbury sees other gender differences played out in all kinds of workplaces, from academia to government to the private sector. A male entrepreneur, for instance, might want nothing less than for his fledgling company to go international as soon as possible, but a woman may define success in the same situation as providing enough income for herself and family, as well as enjoying the work. When men meet men on the job, each assumes the other is career-oriented, but a woman must prove that she is, says Ms. Duxbury. As individual managers are churned through jobs faster and oversee more and more people (as part of downsizing), they have less opportunity to act as mentors: And having a mentor appears to be a necessary ingredient for women's success.

—VIVIAN SMITH,
"Corporate Culture: A Delicate Balance for Women"

David K. Foot and Daniel Stoffman use a **unit-by-unit method** to compare approaches to shopping. In paragraph 46, they describe a young person's approach, then in paragraph 47 they describe a middle-aged person's approach.

46   A young person has little money and lots of time. If she wants to buy a new stereo, she checks out every store in town because every dollar saved is important and, what's more, she has plenty of time to hunt for bargains. Once she's made the purchase, she takes the system home and puts it together. It doesn't matter how long it takes.

47   A middle-aged person has more money but less time. He's got heavy responsibilities at work and at home. He is not going to spend his precious leisure hours doing comparison

shopping to try to save $50 on a pair of speakers. This person wants a top-quality stereo system from a store with a good reputation, and he wants it with a maximum of speed and a minimum of fuss. He may even pay extra to have it delivered and assembled, because the time saved is worth more than the additional cost. —DAVID K. FOOT and DANIEL STOFFMAN,
Boom, Bust & Echo: How to Profit from the
Coming Demographic Shift

Two valuable kinds of comparisons are analogy and metaphor. A **metaphor** is a figure of speech. (See **14a(5)**.) An **analogy**, often used in argument, makes a point by comparing a complex or unfamiliar concept to a simple or familiar one or by comparing two familiar concepts that are not ordinarily thought to be similar. In paragraph 48, Nelson Mandela draws an analogy between leadership and gardening.

48   In some ways, I saw the garden as a metaphor for certain aspects of my life. A leader must also tend his garden; he, too, plants seed, and then watches, cultivates, and harvests the result. Like the gardener, a leader must take responsibility for what he cultivates; he must mind his work, try to repel enemies, preserve what can be preserved, and eliminate what cannot succeed. —NELSON MANDELA,
"Raising Tomatoes and Leading People"

However, it is important that you do not assume that because two things are alike in some ways they are alike in all ways. (See **31h(6)**, "False analogy.")

(6) Classifying and dividing to develop an idea

To classify is to categorize things in large groups that share certain common characteristics. **Classification** is a way to understand or explain a large or diverse subject and discover the relationships within it. When you classify chocolate pudding as a dessert, you tell your reader that, like most desserts, it is probably sweet and high in calories. **Division**, in contrast, breaks objects and ideas into parts that are smaller and examines the relationships among them. A store manager might group books according to publisher for her own inventory or according to types— biography, science fiction, mystery, and so forth—for her customers.

Classification and division represent two different perspectives; ideas can be put into groups (classification) or split into subclasses (division) on the basis of a dividing principle. Classification and division most often work together because once you have placed something in a class, the next logical step is to explain the characteristics of that class, which is division. So you may find yourself using both classification and division to approach your subject. They work together to give a view that places the subject in a context and develops it in detail. Notice how Linda Deutschmann first establishes the classifications in paragraph 49 and then explains them in the two paragraphs that follow.

49   According to arousal theory, some people are *augmenters*. They see colours as brighter than other people see them, noises as louder, pain as more painful, and excitement as more exciting. Others are, physiologically, *reducers,* who perceive stimuli but do not react to them as much as average people do. These differences have been found to be associated with typical modes of behaviour including risk-taking types of deviance.

50   Augmenters quickly find a given level of stimulation "too much" and attempt to retreat from it. As infants, they show a greater "startle response" to noise and light, and as adults, they tend to seek reduced stimulation. They are more likely to be seen as introverts who seek quiet pastimes. If they become criminals, it will be in the less exciting, less risky forms of crime. . . .

51   Reducers take longer to "get the message" from pain or
pleasure (they are harder to train) and are more likely to enjoy
the physical sensations that accompany risk-taking actions.
Reducers who drink, for example, may drink hard, experiencing the drunkenness as an escape from boredom, and are less
likely to be deterred by a colossal hangover than are augmenters. Reducers are more likely to drive fast, engage in
unsafe sex, skydive, gamble, have criminal records, and
acquire serious injuries.   —LINDA B. DEUTSCHMANN,
                                          Deviance and Social Control

Analysis, like division, breaks an object or idea into its
elements. In paragraph 52, Aaron Copland analyzes three
ways to listen to music.

52   We all listen to music according to our separate capacities.
But, for the sake of analysis, the whole listening process may
become clearer if we break it up into its component parts, so
to speak. In a certain sense we all listen to music on three
separate planes. For lack of a better terminology, one might
name these: (1) the sensuous plane, (2) the expressive plane,
(3) the sheerly musical plane. The only advantage to be gained
from mechanically splitting up the listening process into these
hypothetical planes is the clearer view to be had of the way
in which we listen.
              —AARON COPLAND, "How We Listen to Music"

(7) Formulating a definition

Paragraphs of definition explain the meaning of a concept,
a term, or an object. Sometimes we define arbitrarily:
"They use the term 'pony' to refer to an equine of any
size." Or we may define by describing how something
works: "A security system is supposed to hinder burglars."
The effect of definition is to put a concept, a term, or an
object into a class and then differentiate it from other
members of the class: "A concerto [the term] is a
symphonic piece [the class] performed by one or more solo

instruments and orchestra [the difference]." The **difference**
distinguishes the **term** from all other members of the **class**.
Paragraph 53 defines discrimination by placing it in a class
("any act") and by distinguishing it ("the behavioural counterpart of prejudice") from other members of that class.
The definition is then clarified by details.

53   Discrimination is often defined as the behavioural counter-
      part of prejudice. In reality discrimination can exist without
      prejudice; conversely, prejudice can flourish without leading
      to discriminatory actions. Generally speaking, discrimination
      refers to differential treatment of individuals or groups
      because of their membership in a group, rather than as
      individuals or on personal merit. Intrinsic to all types of dis-
      crimination are the realities of power: Those with power pos-
      sess the capacity to put prejudice into practice in a way that
      denies, excludes, or controls. Discrimination can be thus
      defined as any act, whether deliberate or not, that has the
      intent or the effect of adversely affecting others on grounds
      other than merit or acquired skills.   —M. IBRAHIM ALLADIN,
                                          Racism in Canadian Schools

Definitions can be clarified and extended by details, examples, synonyms, or etymology (the history of the word).
Synonyms are often only one or two words enclosed in
commas immediately following the term.

> Enumerators, *people who compile a list of eligible voters before
> an election*, derive their name from a Latin word meaning
> "number."

27e   Editing can improve paragraph logic and effectiveness.

At some point in the process of writing your essay, you
may stop to assess the logic and effectiveness of a paragraph. Although this activity is a normal part of revising

and editing, it can also occur at almost any time during your writing, and it can be repeated as frequently as necessary. When you rework paragraphs, you should consider the points in the following checklist.

> **Checklist for Revising Paragraphs** ✓
> - Do all the ideas in the paragraph belong?
> - Are any necessary ideas left out?
> - Is the paragraph coherent? Do the sentences focus on the topic? Do they link to previous sentences? Is the order of sentences logical?
> - Are sentences connected to each other with easy, effective, and natural transitions? Is the paragraph linked to the preceding and following paragraphs?
> - Is the paragraph adequately developed? If there are problems, can analyzing the strategy used to develop the paragraph help solve the problem?

Exercise 9

Prepare for a class discussion of the following paragraphs (54, 55, and 56) by identifying main ideas (**27a**), transitions (**27b**), and methods of development (**27c** and **27d**).

54   One Aboriginal people's teaching that is having an impact on the world is the Seventh Generation philosophy/prediction. Simply put, it refers to how indigenous peoples make decisions with the Seventh Generation in mind. The present generation is responsible for leaving future generations with a continuous cycle of resources and a habitable and safe environment. This contrasts with Western planners, who once thought they were morally responsible only for a planning period, usually five years.

    —S. BRASCOUPE, "Aboriginal Peoples' Vision of the Future: Interweaving Traditional Knowledge and New Technologies"

55   A number of factors affected the socialization of the baby-boom generation. First, the country was in boom times, and

the general affluence led people to expect that life would be easy. Second, there was a mushrooming of technology. Third, institutions were weakened, and a loss of respect for authority resulted. Fourth, parents made Dr. Spock's *Baby and Child* a bestseller. His advice was for a much more permissive kind of care than that recommended in earlier years. . . . Some parents, however, took his advice to the extreme, and provided very little structure for their children. Fifth, the effect of being born into a large family meant that more of the process of socialization was carried on by children, and that teamwork and social skills were emphasized. These children also experienced more family instability because of an increasing number of broken marriages. Sixth, this is the first generation that never knew what it was like to live without television. Seventh, the period after World War II saw a swift migration from farm to town, and from town to city. Small towns tend to set and enforce standards more than cities do, but are also much more supportive to families. Finally, advances in medicine meant a rapid drop in infant and child mortality and a reduction of physical suffering.

—MARGARET WARD, *The Family Dynamic*

56   Barriers to mobility out of the secondary labour market may also be more subtle. For some individuals, a history of employment in marginal jobs may itself act as a barrier. In some regions of Canada, the prevalence of seasonal work means that many people are forced into an annual cycle where income is obtained from part-year jobs, employment insurance, and welfare assistance. A work record showing frequent layoffs or job changes may simply be reflecting the nature of the local labour market. But it could also be interpreted as an indication of unstable work habits. Similarly, a long sequence of temporary jobs, a common experience for many well-educated and highly motivated young Canadians, could nevertheless handicap them because employers might assume the problem originates with the job applicant rather than the labour market.   —HARVEY J. KRAHN and GRAHAM S. LOWE, *Work, Industry and Canadian Society*

Exercise 10

Write paragraphs using any of the strategies of development described in **27d**. Start with one of the following topic sentences.

1. The (largest, ugliest, most unusual, oldest, etc.) building I ever saw . . .
2. When we were 10 years old . . .
3. I like the kind of (car/truck/van, computer, camera, etc.) I have now better than the last (specific car/truck/van, computer, camera, etc.) I had because . . .
4. Let me explain why I can't stand . . .
5. My job is the very definition of (stress, pleasure, frustration, gratification, challenge, stupidity).

Chapter 28

Planning and Drafting Essays

Whenever you write an essay, you engage in a process of developing an appropriate topic (**28b**) for a certain audience. You often need to explore various possibilities to discover what you want to write (**28c(1)**), how to focus your subject (**28c(2)**), how to form a thesis (**28d**), and how to develop an appropriate plan of organization (**28e**). Your writing will benefit if you write more than one draft, rethinking and restructuring what you have written. If you try to engage in all of these activities simultaneously, you may become frustrated. Experienced writers understand that writing is a process, a process that usually requires a considerable investment of time.

As you move through this process, you may need to return to a specific activity several times. For example, drafting may help you see that you need to go back and collect more ideas, change your thesis, or even start over with a new one. Rather than seeing repeated effort as a sign of failure, experienced writers consider it an indication of commitment. Writing effective essays requires serious work, but the effort is worthwhile. Although the process of writing essays is seldom neat or straightforward, working out your ideas and making them clear to readers will help you gain new insights and enjoy a sense of genuine accomplishment.

28a Writers must understand their purpose, audience, and occasion.

Effective writers work to develop a clear sense of purpose, audience, and occasion.

Purpose	What a writer hopes to achieve in a piece of writing
Audience	Who will read the piece in question
Occasion	Where and when the exchange between writer and audience takes place

Your purpose should be appropriate for both the audience and the occasion. Consider, for example, how your speech changes depending on the audience and the occasion. You would not talk to a prospective employer the way you talk to your closest friend. Nor would you speak the same way to your friend regardless of the occasion—which means not only the immediate time and place of an exchange, but also how context influences that time and place. Meeting a friend for coffee when she is excited about getting a new job would generate words different from the ones you would say to her the first time you see her after she has suffered a serious loss. You should demonstrate similar flexibility when making appropriate choices for different essays. The combination of purpose, audience, and occasion is called your **rhetorical situation**. Assess your rhetorical situation when you are planning an essay and remember it when you are revising (chapter 29) your drafts.

(1) *Purpose* means why you are writing.

To decide your purpose, or why you are writing, it helps to ask yourself if you want to

- express how you feel about something
- report information to readers
- explain the significance of information
- persuade readers to agree with you
- convince readers to undertake a specific action
- amuse or entertain readers

When classified according to purpose, nonfiction writing is often described as expressive, persuasive, or expository.

Expressive writing emphasizes the writer's feelings and reactions to the world—to people, objects, events, and ideas. Expressive writing allows for, even encourages, departures from formal conventions and rules, allowing the writer to discover a personal voice. Such writing may lead to detailed reflection on the writing act itself and how this contributes to new self-understanding. In recent years, especially in the humanities and social sciences, interest in autobiographical writing—life writing in the form of personal letters, journal keeping, and so on—has increased. The following example comes from an essay by Mordecai Richler designed to depict the experiences of his father's life.

> My father came to Montreal as an infant, his father fleeing Galicia. Pogroms. Rampaging Cossacks. But, striptease shows aside, the only theatre my father relished, an annual outing for the two of us, was the appearance of the Don Cossack Choir at the St. Denis Theatre. My father would stamp his feet to their lusty marching and drinking songs; his eyes would light up to see those behemoths, his own father's tormentors, prance and tumble on stage. Moses Isaac Richler, who never marched, nor drank, nor pranced.
>
> —MORDECAI RICHLER, "My Father's Life"

Persuasive writing is intended to influence the reader's attitudes and actions. Most writing is to some extent persuasive; through the choice and arrangement of material, even something as apparently straightforward as a résumé can be persuasive. However, writing is usually called persuasive if it is clearly arguing for or against a position.

When you write persuasively, you need the critical and rhetorical skills discussed in chapters 31 and 32. Persuasion depends on both rational and emotional appeals. The reader's perception of a writer's honesty, fair-mindedness, and goodwill is as crucial as the writer's presentation of evidence and rational arguments. In turn, the writer needs to respond to a reader's concerns and doubts. In a paragraph from his essay "A Dead End for Humanity," which is about the extinction of languages, naturalist Wade Davis establishes a reasonable and moderate outlook.

> Every view of the world that fades away, every culture that disappears, diminishes the possibilities of human life. We lose not only knowledge of the natural world but also intuitions about the meaning of the cosmos. We reduce the human repertoire of adaptive responses to the common problems that confront all humanity.   —WADE DAVIS

Expository writing, or referential writing as it is sometimes called, focusses the reader's attention on the objective world—the objects, the events, and the ideas themselves—rather than on the writer's feelings about them. Textbooks, news accounts, scientific reports, and encyclopedia articles are often expository, as are many of the essays students are expected to write in university and college. When you report, explain, clarify, or evaluate, you are practising exposition. The following paragraph describes the differences between two cultural attitudes toward time.

> Cultures also differ in their orientations toward time. [One anthropologist] distinguished between cultures that have monochronic and polychronic orientations. Monochronic (one time) cultures, such as non-aboriginal Canada, view time as a

valuable commodity to be saved, scheduled, and carefully guarded. Within monochronic cultures, punctuality and efficiency are valued. Thus, people are expected to be on time for appointments, and classes, and they are expected to complete work quickly. In contrast, polychronic (many times) cultures take a more holistic systemic view of time. Members of these cultures assume that many things are happening simultaneously. Thus, punctuality is seldom stressed. Meetings may start late, with people joining in after discussions begin. Tangential discussions and social conversations are part of normal meetings in polychronic cultures. People may even cancel meetings without the dramatic reasons required for politeness in monochronic cultures. The belief that time is holistic leads members of polychronic cultures to assume that the rhythms of life—working, socializing, attending to personal matters— are interrelated. This becomes especially important for teachers to remember when First Nations children do not conform to time constraints. —JULIA WOOD and ANGELA HENRY,
Everyday Encounters

In addition to writing to express themselves, inform others, or persuade others, some people write primarily because they find satisfaction in the imaginative use of language. This purpose is often evident in fiction, poetry, and drama. (See 35a.) It can also be found in nonfiction writing, such as the following example from an essay describing the author's family's migrations across Canada.

They travelled by railway, and then from St. Norbert, which at the time seems to have been a kind of caravanserai for French-speaking Canadian settlers heading south, they started off one spring morning in their wagon filled to the ridge-pole, across the wild plain, following a faintly marked trail toward the rolling Pembina mountains. According to my grandfather, their irregular profile was supposed to console his wife for the loss of her native hills—but the very opposite happened: the sight of these pretentious little slopes was to

sharpen her regret at ever having left the steep slopes of her youth. This was the beginning of generations of divided love in our family, divided between prairie and mountain: a heartbreak, as I wrote in *The Road Past Altamont,* but also an inexhaustible source of dreams and confidences, of leavings and "travellations" such as few people knew to the extent we did, a family that was horizon-bound, if there ever was one. And of course it is in their divided loves that artists and others find their hurts and treasures. —GABRIELLE ROY,
My Manitoba Heritage

Writing that emphasizes the imaginative use of language is sometimes described as **literary** writing, whether it takes the form of a poem, an essay, or a joke.

Writers frequently have more than one purpose, choosing to write humorously, for example, to persuade readers to change a certain behaviour. There is nothing wrong with having more than one purpose. Indeed, your purpose may change or evolve in the course of writing. One way of engaging a reader's interest is to call attention to such changes as they occur. The reader gets a sense that the subject is dynamic, capable of being seen from several viewpoints. If you have more than one purpose, you should be using one to help you achieve another—which is very different from writing without a purpose or simply losing sight of your original purpose.

Exercise 1

Select one of the following subjects and write a description of how you would approach this subject if you were writing an essay that would be primarily (a) expressive, (b) persuasive, (c) expository, and (d) literary.

1. summer	4. computers	7. working
2. children	5. rain	8. music
3. cars	6. fast food	9. housing

(2) *Audience* means who will read your writing.

Understanding your audience will help you decide on the length and depth of your essay, the kind of language to use, and the examples that will be the most effective. Audiences vary considerably, and so do writers. Some writers like to plan and draft essays with a clear sense of audience already in mind; others like to focus on the audience primarily when they are revising their work (chapter 29). At some point, however, you must think clearly about who will be reading your writing and ask yourself if your choices are appropriate for this audience.

Specialized audiences

A **specialized audience** has considerable knowledge of the subject you are writing about and a keen interest in it. For example, if your subject is a new skiing technique, a group of ski instructors would obviously constitute a specialized audience. So would readers of *Ski* magazine, although in writing for this audience you would allow for a greater variation in the knowledge and interest of the reader.

When writing for specialized audiences, you need to consider how much and what kinds of information, as well as what methods of presentation, are called for. You can adjust your tone and the kind of language you use as you tailor your presentation to their expertise and attitudes. (See 13c(1).) The average reader would probably find the following example impenetrable, but it is written for a specialized audience of experts who understand linguistics and are familiar with the terminology.

> The notions of illocutionary force and different illocutionary acts involve really several quite different principles of distinction. . . . So we must not suppose what the metaphor of "force" suggests, that the different illocutionary verbs mark off points on a single continuum. Rather, there are several

different continua of "illocutionary force," and the fact that the illocutionary verbs of English stop at certain points on these various continua and not at others is, in a sense, accidental. For example, we might have had an illocutionary verb "rubrify," meaning to call something "red." Thus, "I hereby rubrify it" would just mean "It's red." Analogously, we happen to have an obsolete verb "macarize," meaning to call someone happy. —J. R. SEARLE, "Speech Acts: An Essay in the Philosophy of Language"

Many of the papers you write in university or college are for a specialized audience. When you write an essay for a course, you can assume that your instructor is already well informed about the material. No one is ever entirely expert, however, and a specialized audience is usually pleased to learn something new. However, writing for a specialized audience does not necessarily demand that you know more than specialists in that field. At times it may be sufficient to demonstrate that you understand the material and can use appropriate language to discuss it. Moreover, a specialized audience for one subject would be a non-specialized audience for another.

Non-specialized audiences

A **non-specialized audience** consists of readers not expert on your topic but presumably willing to read what you have to say about it. It is possible to identify certain characteristics even in a general audience so that you can shape your presentation accordingly. When writing essays, you can usually assume that your readers have many interests different from your own but share a willingness to learn about new material if it is presented clearly and respectfully. This assumed audience is not very different from the one articles in a general encyclopedia are written for. Think too of the popularity of books such as Stephen Hawking's *A Brief History of Time*. Hawking is an expert in the field he is writing about, but his intended audience is not. Still, his readers find his explanations of abstract concepts accessible, provocative, and useful. The success of Hawking's book highlights the importance of being able to write as an expert to a non-expert readership. Consider how the following description from an introductory linguistics textbook explains a concept that the author of the comparable passage on pages 336–37 assumed to be already understood by a specialized audience.

> The study of how we do things with sentences is the study of **speech acts**. In studying speech acts, we are acutely aware of the importance of the *context of the utterance*. In some circumstances *There is a sheepdog in the closet* is a warning, but the same sentence may be a promise or even a mere statement of fact, depending on circumstances. We call this purpose—a warning, a promise, a threat, or whatever—the **illocutionary force** of a speech act.
> —VICTORIA FROMKIN and ROBERT RODMAN,
> *An Introduction to Language*

Non-specialized audiences may be of quite different kinds and require some adjustment of subject matter and diction. For example, the author of an advanced textbook can assume an audience already familiar with basic concepts in the field, so one approach to envisioning a non-specialized audience is to think in terms of education level. You could ask yourself, for example, whether the audience you are writing for is composed of your peers or university graduates who majored in a field different from yours. An upper-level textbook in linguistics presents a somewhat more complete approach to speech acts than an introductory text:

> Every speech act has two principal components: the utterance itself and the intention of the speaker in making it.

First, every utterance is represented by a sentence with a grammatical structure and a meaning; this is variously called the **locution** or the utterance act. Second, speakers have some intention in making an utterance, something they intend to accomplish; that intention is called an **illocution**, and every utterance consists of performing one or more illocutionary acts. —EDWARD FINEGAN and NIKO BESNIER,
Language: Its Structure and Use

You could also envision a non-specialized audience defined by some other common ground—such as readers of the same gender. If you look through popular magazines, you can easily find articles written for either men or women. However, when writing for a gender-specific audience, do not make the mistake of thinking that all men—or all women—think the same way or share the same values. Further, there is a big difference between consciously choosing to write for a gender-specific audience and accidentally ignoring gender differences when writing for an audience that includes both men and women.

Sometimes you may not know much about your audience. When this is the case, you can often benefit from imagining a thoughtful audience of educated adults. Such an audience is likely to include people with different backgrounds and cultural values, so be careful not to assume that you are writing for readers who are exactly like you. A useful technique, in this case, is to imagine yourself in conversation with a small group of specific persons who have diverse backgrounds but nevertheless share an interest in your topic.

Multiple audiences

Writers often need to address multiple audiences. At work, for example, you might need to write a memo or a letter that will be read not only by the person to whom it is addressed but also by other people who receive copies. The readers in a multiple audience can have distinctly different expectations. If, for example, you are asked to evaluate the performance of an employee you supervise and send copies to both that person and your own boss, one part of your audience is probably looking for praise while the other is looking to see if you are a competent supervisor.

When writing essays in university or college, you may find yourself writing for multiple audiences. The most common example is drafting an essay that will be discussed in a small group of fellow students and read by your instructor. If you choose to write an essay for a general audience and submit it to a professor who is a specialist on your subject, you are, in effect, writing for multiple audiences. Writing effectively for multiple audiences requires you to consider a variety of attitudes and positions. (See 32c.) You can benefit from doing so when planning your essay and also by reading from different points of view as you prepare to revise what you have drafted. (See chapter 29.)

Exercise 2

Choose a recent class and write a description of it that would be read by (a) a member of your family, (b) the teacher of the class, or (c) the dean of your school. Then write a second description that would be read by all three of these audiences.

(3) *Occasion* means the circumstances under which writers and readers communicate.

Occasion is the context in which the writing occurs, the circumstances under which the exchange between a writer and a reader takes place: time, place, and climate. A letter written on the occasion of a friend's marriage is likely to differ from a letter written on the occasion of her divorce.

A message sent by e-mail—see 26c(1) and 35b(1)—is seldom written with precisely the same care as a letter sent to the same person. An essay written outside class may be very different from an essay written in a classroom even if both are written for the same audience and with the same purpose. Moreover, either of these essays could be influenced by climate or social context—whatever is happening in the writer's world. Students taking the same exam for the same teacher are to some extent influenced by external events. For example, a national economic crisis could either distract their attention or improve their motivation.

When you read the work of other writers, you will sometimes find examples in which the occasion is specifically stated, as in the following passage.

> In the twenty-second month of the war against Nazism we meet here in this old Palace of St. James, itself not unscarred by the fire of the enemy, in order to proclaim the high purposes and resolves of the lawful constitutional Governments of Europe whose countries have been overrun; and we meet here also to cheer the hopes of free men and free peoples throughout the world.
>
> —WINSTON CHURCHILL, "Until Victory Is Won"

Often, however, the occasion must be inferred. Whether or not you choose to state your occasion when writing an essay, it is essential that you consider it. For example, your instructor may have higher expectations for your final essay in a course than for your first. The occasion is different because the time and climate are different.

28b Writers need to find appropriate subjects.

If you are assigned a subject or if your situation clearly dictates one, you can move directly to considering the particular aspect of it you will emphasize (28c(2)), the expectations of your audience (28a(2)), and the method of organization best suited for your discussion (28e). If you must choose your own subject, you should consider not only your own interests but also your rhetorical situation. Of the various subjects that appeal to you, which would be the best for your purpose on this occasion for this audience?

When you are free to choose a subject, you can write an appealing paper on almost anything that interests you. Often the best subject is one drawn from your own experience—your personal knowledge, interests, and beliefs. Do you play a musical instrument? Enjoy sports? Like to travel? Do you have a job? Can you think of a particular place that is important to you? An interesting person you know? What ambitions do you have for yourself? What strong convictions do you hold? The challenge, of course, is to make what interests you interesting to your readers. Whether your purpose is to express, persuade, or inform, take this opportunity to share something that is important to you so that others will recognize its value.

Students are often asked to write essays about subjects outside their own experience. For instance, you may have to write a paper for a microbiology course. Although you are free to choose your subject, your purpose is to write an expository essay demonstrating your command of information (see pages 333–34) rather than an expressive paper revealing how you feel about microbes (see page 332). Just as you do when you write about personal experience, however, you should make an effort to find material of interest to you. Look in your textbook, particularly in the sections listing suggestions for further reading and study. Go through your lecture notes and examine the annotations you made in whatever you read for the course. (See 33f(2).) Ask yourself if there are any aspects of your subject that you feel certain about and any others about which you would like to learn more. Writing about a subject is one of the best ways to learn about it, so use this assignment not only to satisfy your audience but also to satisfy yourself.

Finding a subject can be difficult, and some writers become frustrated at this stage of the writing process. (See **30b**.) Do not be afraid to talk with your instructor or with other students. Discussing ideas with other people can help you generate new ones and decide on those likely to yield good essays.

Exercise 3

1. Choose a personal experience that might be an appropriate subject. Write a paragraph describing why you think it would be useful to share this experience with others. Identify your audience and write a second paragraph describing how much information you would need to include so that this audience would understand your experience. Then, for your own reference, set some limits for yourself by making a separate list of anything about this experience that you do not want to include because you wish to protect your privacy or avoid embarrassing your audience.

2. Select an academic subject from one of your courses and write a paragraph describing how you would approach this subject if you were writing for the instructor of that course and how you would approach the same material if you were writing for ninth graders.

 28c By exploring subjects, you can focus on a topic.

When you are free to choose your own subject, you can use a number of different methods to discover the best subject for your essay. If you already have one in mind, the same methods can be used to explore possibilities for focussing and developing it. As you explore, you will probably discover a number of paths that look as if they could take you where you want to go and others that you will choose not to follow.

(1) There are several ways to search for a subject.

If you have a hard time finding subjects to write about, try journalling or freewriting. If you have a subject in mind but are unsure of how to develop it, try listing, questioning, and applying perspectives. Use whatever methods produce results for you. Different methods may work best for different subjects; if you run out of ideas when using one method, switch to another. Sometimes, especially for an assigned subject remote from your own interests and knowledge, you may need to try several methods.

Journalling

Keeping a journal is a proven way to generate subjects for essays. Although there are many different kinds of journals, students often benefit from writing daily in a personal journal or a writer's notebook.

In a **personal journal**, you reflect on your experience. Instead of simply listing activities, meals, or weather reports, you use writing to explore how you feel about what is happening in your life. You might focus on external events, such as what you think about a book or a film, or focus on your inner life by exploring changes in mood or attitude. Writers who keep a personal journal usually write for a reader they trust. Your reader may be real or imagined, say a close friend or family member. Or perhaps the reader may be a version of yourself—a person you once were or might become. Even in personal writing, then, writers need to project a reader slightly removed from themselves writing *now,* so that new details and discoveries can be made. In the process of writing a journal—and reading it—writers not only explore themselves but also discover subjects that can be used for essays.

Like a personal journal, a **writer's notebook** also includes responses to experience. In this case, however, the emphasis is on sorting through what you are learning. Students often benefit from keeping a writer's notebook in which they respond exclusively to what they are reading. They record quotations that seem especially meaningful, evaluate the strengths and weaknesses of a particular text, summarize the material (33h(5)), note points they agree with, and jot down questions they would like to raise in class or pursue in an essay. In addition to helping you discover subjects for essays, a writer's notebook can help you become a better reader.

Some writers keep both a personal journal and a writer's notebook. Others keep only one—or create a combination of the two. In either case, they feel free to write quickly without worrying about spelling, grammar, or organization.

Freewriting

When freewriting, writers put down on paper without stopping whatever occurs to them during a limited period of time—often no more than 10 minutes or so. They do not worry about whether they are repeating themselves or getting off the track; they simply write to see what comes out. The process helps them discover ideas they did not realize they had. The entries in a personal journal or writer's notebook may be freewritten, but freewriting is not limited to journalling. You can take out a sheet of paper and freewrite whenever you have a few minutes to spare. Some writers use different-coloured marking pens or different types of underlining to identify different topics generated by this activity.

In directed freewriting, writers begin with a general subject area and record whatever occurs to them about this subject during the time available. When asked by his English teacher to write about whatever he knew about graffiti, Julien Mitchell wrote the following example of directed freewriting during five minutes of class time. This was the first step toward drafting the essay that appears later in this chapter (pages 371–74), the final version of which appears in chapter 29 (pages 411–15).

Write about graffiti? What do I say? I don't think it's all that bad? I see it everywhere when I'm walking in the city. There seems to be more around these days. When I was younger I hardly noticed it at all. Maybe I just didn't care. Am I getting old? Back to graffiti. Gangs tagging. Some people HATE it! Store owners especially, I imagine. The police, too. But what's the harm, really. It does cover up some pretty ugly buildings. Some of it is like a work of art. Imagine if people thought that Michelangelo's work was ugly? Maybe somebody did at one time! Artistic expression is important, isn't it? We should support freedom of expression. Banning it is censorship. Lots of colours in graffiti. Some of it's like art—better than art. Some of it can be ugly though. Different strokes for different folks, I guess. What's the history of graffiti? Where did it originate. When

I was in Pompeii, Italy, they were even making graffiti way back then. Are those who spray paint really all that bad? <u>I heard a story about a guy that had to repaint over his graffiti as part of his punishment when he was found out by the cops.</u> I wonder if it made him stop. <u>Kids should be able to be creative.</u> At least when they're spray painting, they're staying out of trouble. Maybe? What else about graffiti? Maybe some famous artists started by making graffiti. What's the name of that guy in N.Y.? He died a little while ago, but his work was really well respected after a while. People don't freak out when people paint images on sidewalks in chalk. How come? Because it's not permanent. I guess. I think graffiti can help society but I've got to figure out why and how. It makes buildings look better, promotes free speech. And it's creative!

As the underlinings show, this freewrite generated at least four possible writing topics about graffiti: it promotes creativity, it's a form of art that isn't appreciated, it encourages freedom of expression, and people are punished for doing it. Some of these topics overlap. It certainly is an art form that is largely not appreciated and perhaps that's why people are punished for doing it; it's a form of art and art forms are also usually creative. However, the focus could also be narrowed to a single topic. Within a few minutes, this writer has discovered that he has more to say than can be addressed in a single essay.

Listing

One way to gather ideas about your writing topic is to make an informal list. The advantage to listing is that, like an outline, it lets you see individual items at a glance rather than having to pick them out of a block of writing. It also encourages the establishment of relationships. Jot down any ideas that come to you while you are thinking about your subject. Do not worry if the ideas come without any kind of order, and do not worry about the form in which you write them down; grammar, spelling, and diction are not important at this stage. Devote as much time as necessary to making your list—perhaps five minutes, perhaps an entire evening. The point is to collect as many ideas as you can.

Julien made the following list after he had decided to focus his essay on graffiti as a form of artistic expression.

Michelangelo

not understood

people are threatened

youth need an outlet

right to freedom of expression

doesn't harm anyone

public is rewarded
    colourful
    covers old buildings
    free

artists called vandals

"different strokes for different folks"

gangs and violence

stuffy white-shirts

This list may appear chaotic, but earlier items suggest later ones, and a review of the whole list may suggest items that need to be added. As you look through the list, you will find some ideas that are closely related and might be grouped together. For instance, items about the type of people who are graffiti artists can be grouped together. Toward the end of his list, Julien began to establish some relationships by developing ways in which the public is rewarded by viewing graffiti. Order and direction are beginning to emerge.

For an example of a list written and revised under pressure, see page 422.

Questioning

Explore a subject by asking yourself questions. There are two structured questioning strategies you might use—journalists' questions and a similar approach known as the pentad that encourages seeing relationships. The **journalists' questions** ask *Who? What? When? Where? Why?* and *How?;* they are easy to use and can help you discover ideas about any subject. Using journalists' questions to explore the subject of graffiti could lead you to think about *who* creates graffiti and *who* hates graffiti, *what* it looks like, *when* it was created, *why* it is done and *why* some people dislike it, *where* it is found, and *how* it promotes creativity.

The **pentad** considers the five dramatic aspects of a subject: the *act* (what happens), the *actor* (who does it), the *scene* (the time, place, and conditions under which the event occurred), the *agency* (the method or circumstances facilitating the act), and the *purpose* (the intent or reasons surrounding the act). This method differs from journalists' questions by suggesting relationships among the various aspects of the subject. For instance, what relationships can be explored between the criminalization of graffiti and the people involved in this act—the actors, in this case the graffiti artists and those who dislike it? Or a writer could explore the relationship between the act and the scene by describing the types of graffiti and the places where it is found, both of which are conditions under which the act occurred.

Applying perspectives

Sometimes it is helpful to consider a subject in three quite different ways—as static, dynamic, and relative. A **static perspective** would focus your attention on what graffiti is. You might define it, describe the typical picture, analyze its components, or use a specific piece to provide an example.

The **dynamic perspective** focusses on action and change. You might examine the history of graffiti, how it has changed over the years, or how a certain piece of graffiti changed your perception of this art form.

The **relative perspective** focusses on systems and relationships. You could examine the relationship between a piece of art by a famous "accepted" artist and a graffiti artist's work or between street art and art in art galleries.

(2) Writers need to focus on specific material.

Exploring the subject will suggest not only productive strategies for development but also a direction and focus for your writing. Some ideas will seem worth pursuing; others will seem inappropriate for your purpose, audience, or occasion. You will find yourself discarding ideas even as you develop new ones. A simple analogy will help explain. When you want a picture of a landscape, you cannot photograph all that your eye can take in. You must focus on just part of that landscape. As you aim your camera, you look through the viewfinder to make sure the subject is correctly framed and in focus. At this point you may wish to move in closer and focus on one part of the scene or to change your angle, using light and shadow to emphasize some features of the landscape over others. You can think of your writing the same way—focussing and directing your ideas just as you focus and direct the lens of your camera—moving from a general subject to a more specific one.

For example, "graffiti" is too large and general a subject to make a good writing topic. However, some of the items that emerged in freewriting about this subject (page 346) and in the list that it elicited (page 348) can be grouped to form a topic that is both interesting and manageable. Or a single item, if well chosen, could lead to a sharply focussed essay of some depth. When you compare the draft of Julien Mitchell's essay on graffiti (pages 371–74) and the final version of it (pages 411–15), you will see how drafting and revising can sharpen a writer's focus.

Strategies for development, which are discussed in **27d** as ways to develop paragraphs, are natural thinking processes that are especially useful for shaping ideas about a subject. Remember that purpose, audience, and occasion, as well as the subject, must be considered when selecting a guiding strategy. Often the strategy emerges as you explore or draft; do not impose an inappropriate strategy. Refer to the explanations and examples in **27d** as you work through the various strategies. Here are questions that you might ask yourself.

a. *Narration*   When did I first see graffiti? What types of people would create graffiti?

b. *Process*   How do you create graffiti? What are the steps? What products/tools do artists need?

c. *Cause and effect*   Why do some people hate graffiti? What makes some people want to do it? What are the effects on our physical environment?

d. *Description*   What does graffiti look like? What do the neighbourhoods where graffiti exists look like?

e. *Definition*   How would I define graffiti? How would others define graffiti? What's the dictionary definition? What makes art better?

f. *Classification and division*   How can I clearly classify graffiti? Are there different types of graffiti? How is graffiti different from other forms of art? How is art classified? Does graffiti have different movements like other forms of art?

g. *Example*   What artists have created graffiti? How does their work differ from one another?

h. *Comparison and contrast*   How does graffiti differ from other forms of expression? How do artists differ from one another? How do the artists differ from those people who dislike graffiti?

The following introductory sentence suggests a focus on comparison and contrast:

> When I think of graffiti in relation to other art forms, I can see how all art forms, including graffiti, create controversy in the community.

This sentence suggests cause and effect:

> The negative attitudes about graffiti can be traced to uptight white-collar workers, fear of disenfranchised youth, and traditional notions of artistic expression.

Essays frequently combine several of these strategies to achieve yet another strategy. Kem Luther uses narration and comparison and contrast in the process of describing the wind in the trees.

> In the society of gossiping trees, the stiff conifers, the spruces and firs, are notorious liars. These trees have a way of transferring a motion caused by the wind through the whole tree. A trembling branch on the near side of such a tree may tell about a burst of wind on the far side of the tree, or even about a bird hopping through the interior. Other conifers are more committed to veracity. White pines and red cedars, for example, are straight talkers. Every branch of the white pine nearest me is waving, testifying to a motion of air inside the tree, next to the trunk. I reach my hand inside and feel a cool, ever so slight movement of air.
>
> —KEM LUTHER, "I Have Seen the Wind"

In the following introduction, Maude Barlow uses narration and description, but in the essay itself she adds definition, examples, and cause and effect to develop her discussion of the *maquiladora*.

> Many Canadians in the anti-free trade movement can remember with startling clarity the first time they toured a Mexican *maquiladora*. For me, it was a side-trip to the first Canada–Mexico coalition *Enquentro* in 1990, and it changed my life. I had seen terrible poverty before, but this was my first encounter with a deliberate policy of economic bondage. This was not some terrible remnant of the past; it was the shining city on the hill, the brave new world of economic globalization.
>
> —MAUDE BARLOW, "*Maquiladoras* of the North"

The exact focus you finally choose will be determined by your purpose, your audience, and the time and space available.

Exercise 4

Explore one of the subjects from Exercise 3 by writing down your answers to the journalists' questions (Who? What? When? Where? Why? and How?). Next use the three perspectives to explore by writing answers to the questions What is it? How does it change? and What is it related to (part of, different from, or like)? Finally, explore the subject by writing questions appropriate to the various development strategies. How would you limit your subject? What would you focus on?

28d A clearly stated thesis conveys your main idea.

If you have limited and focussed your subject, you have gone a long way toward developing an idea that organizes the content you include and the approach you take. Your organizing idea, or thesis, ensures that decisions you have made about purpose, audience, and occasion fit together.

(1) Essays usually include a thesis statement.

In academic and many other kinds of writing you will normally be expected to state your main idea succinctly. This **thesis statement** contains a single idea, clearly focussed and specifically stated, that grows out of your exploration of a subject. A thesis statement can be thought of as a central idea phrased in the form of an assertion. Usually, it embodies an interesting relationship or creative tension between hitherto unrelated or even opposed ideas or conditions that you have uncovered in your exploration. Since it takes the form of a claim (see **31b**) you are making, it connects the general, public aspects of a subject with the private. It expresses what you, as a writer, think is true, interesting, or valuable about the subject.

An explicitly stated thesis statement helps you keep your writing on target. It identifies the topic you are writing about, the approach you are taking, and in some cases the plan of development you are using. Note how the thesis statements below do all of these. The first is from an expressive essay:

> By the time that his children were growing up the great days of my father's life were over.
> —VIRGINIA WOOLF, "Leslie Stephen"

With this apparently simple statement, the author has established that the topic is her father and indicated that she will discuss both early accomplishments and later decline while focussing primarily on his life within the family.

The following thesis statement for an expository essay divides "discipline" into three kinds.

> A child, in growing up, may meet and learn from three different kinds of disciplines.
> —JOHN HOLT, "Kinds of Discipline"

The main idea in a persuasive essay usually carries a strong point of view—an argumentative edge.

> It always amazes me when people express surprise that there might be a "race problem" in Canada, or when they attribute the "problem" to a minority of prejudiced individuals. Racism is, and always has been, one of the bedrock institutions of Canadian society, embedded in the very fabric of our thinking, our personality. —ADRIENNE SHADD,
> "Institutionalized Racism and Canadian History:
> Notes of a Black Canadian"

You will probably try out several thesis statements as you explore your subject. Rather than starting with a preconceived thesis that you must then rationalize, let it develop out of your thinking and discovery process. (See 28c.) Your goal should be a claim that is neither self-evident nor too broad.

A clear, precise thesis statement will help unify your paper; it will guide many decisions about what details to keep and what to toss out. You can also use the thesis to guide your search for additional information you may need to strengthen your point. But it is important to allow your essay to remain flexible in the early stages. If you have information about your subject that is interesting but does not really help you make your point, including it in your early drafts might lead you to a better essay by indicating a more profitable focus. As you write, check your thesis statement frequently to see that it connects the several stages or divisions of your thought. Do not hesitate to change your thesis, however, if you find a more productive path or one you would rather pursue. Make whatever adjustments you need to ensure a well-linked essay. When you revise (chapter 29), test everything you retain in your essay against the thesis you have eventually decided on—your original or a new version you have developed.

In some cases a thesis might be stated in more than one sentence, but it is more often stated in a declarative sentence with a single main clause (1e)—that is, in either a simple or a complex sentence. If your thesis statement announces two or more co-ordinate ideas, as a compound sentence does, be sure you are not in danger of having your paper lose direction and focus. If you wish to sharpen the thesis statement by adding information that qualifies or supports it, subordinate such material to the main idea.

Beware of vague qualifiers such as *interesting, important,* and *unusual.* Often such words signal that you have chosen a subject that does not interest you much; you would do better to rethink your subject to come up with something you care about. In a thesis statement such as "My education has been very unusual," the vague word *unusual* may indicate that the idea itself is weak and that the writer needs to find a stronger subject. However, this kind of vague thesis may disguise an idea of real interest that simply needs to be made specific: "Our family grew closer after my parents decided to teach me at home." Sometimes thesis statements containing vague words can be made more effective by simply replacing the bland words with other, more meaningful ones. The following examples show ways to focus, clarify, and sharpen vague thesis statements.

> **Vague**   I have trouble making decisions.
>
> **Better**   Making decisions is difficult for me, especially when money is involved and most of all when such decisions affect other people.
>
> **Vague**   Summer is an interesting season.
>
> **Better**   Summer is the best season for losing weight.

Thesis statements appear most often in the introductory paragraph, although you can put them anywhere that suits your purpose—occasionally even in the conclusion. The advantage of putting the thesis statement in the first paragraph, however, is that your reader knows from the beginning what you are writing about and where the essay is going. Especially appropriate in academic writing, this technique helps readers who are searching for specific information to locate it easily. If the thesis statement begins the introductory paragraph, the rest of the sentences in the paragraph usually support or clarify it with more specific information.

> To be a Newfie is to be a survivor. Newfoundlanders are a great people because they have a way of surviving without ever becoming victims. There is about them an exhilarating, nose-thumbing air of tempting the fates that ceaselessly try to bring them down. Their great spirit, fed by muscular Darwinian impulses, has allowed them to claim with brassy validity that they are a race apart. But in the decade between 1985 and 1995, there was a real possibility they would become an endangered species. —PETER C. NEWMAN,
> *The Canadian Revolution, 1985–1995:*
> *From Deference to Defiance*

> In many ways a pool is the best place to do real swimming. Free water tends to be too tempestuous, while in a pool it is tamed and imprisoned; the challenge has been filtered out of it along with the bacteria.
> —JOHN KNOWLES, "Everybody's Sport"

(2) A main idea is necessary even when a thesis statement is not required.

Some kinds of writing do not require a formulated thesis statement, but they do contain a main, or controlling, idea. A memoir, for example, or a journal—such as the record you might keep of a camping trip—is a focussed piece of writing preserving your reflections and observations. In the example below, notice how Sasenarine Persaud captures the reader's attention by using the varying personalities and moods of Hindu gods as a controlling idea to describe the Demerara River in Guyana.

> But if the palms were the eyes, the river was god himself, full, calm, soft as Shiva meditating on *Kailash*. Sometimes it was sugar-brown, rain-muddied, flowing out to the Atlantic with branches, twigs, the fruits of the land, little pieces of gleaned wisdom flowing into the accommodating deluge of the ocean. Sometimes the quiet river lapping at the logs of the wharf before the tide turned sounded like the discourse of Arjuna and Krishna in the face of the two imposing armies about to destroy themselves in the great nuclear battle of the planet earth. Then the river pounded itself and everything else with a ferocity that was simultaneously bitter and sweet and it was as though Shiva had come down from Kailash with fire in his eyes, power, grace, poetry in his feet—the *Nataraja* dancing his eternal and unmatched dance of love, and destruction/creation. Sometimes there would be rain on the river and the other bank, the West bank, would be hidden in the silver wall of water—even ships in midstream would be hidden in the embrace of the falling water—and I would think;
> from water to water
> from cloud to river
> from sea to sky . . .   —SASENARINE PERSAUD,
> "When Men Speak That Way"

Expressive writing is sometimes characterized by a spirit of inquiry in which the writer plays with possibilities without necessarily coming to a conclusion or making a specific point. Rather than approaching the topic of a "national literature" as a definition, Pat Smart uses an inquiry approach, inviting the reader to consider the subject from various angles.

> What constitutes a national literature, and what role, if any, does literature play in the identity of a people? Has lit-

erature become completely cosmopolitan or international, as Salman Rushdie suggested in a recent issue of *The New Yorker*? Writing on the literature of India, Rushdie claimed that "literature has little or nothing to do with a writer's home address" and that the best Indian writers "are too good to fall into the trap of writing *nationalistically*." The same issue contained a photograph of "a gathering of India's leading novelists," including our very own Rohinton Mistry, with no reference to the fact that Mistry is a *Canadian* writer. Should we care?   —PAT SMART, "The 'Pure Laine' Debate"

Writing without a thesis statement is especially common when the main thrust of the development is narrative or descriptive. And reports of information, whether research papers (chapter 34) or business documents (35b), frequently do not require a thesis. Even in persuasive writing the thesis is sometimes implicit rather than explicit. Yet, even when your thesis is implied, your readers should be able to sense a clear direction and focus in your paper. You can make sure they will by articulating your main idea for yourself and then checking that your writing stays focussed on it.

 CAUTION Many university and college instructors expect every essay to have a clear thesis statement.

28e Arranging ideas requires choosing an appropriate method or combination of methods.

Many writers need a working plan to direct their ideas and keep their writing on course. Some follow a formal arrangement pattern; others use informal written lists or formal topic or sentence outlines. Such plans are especially helpful for lengthy papers and for writing under pressure. (See chapter 30.) Whatever method you choose for planning your writing, remember that you can always change your plan to suit any new direction your writing takes. The point is to have a means for directing your effort toward fulfilling your purpose.

(1) Informal working plans

An informal working plan need be little more than an ordered list that grows out of a collection of ideas. Look at the informal working plan that Julien Mitchell made as he prepared to write on graffiti as a form of artistic expression.

Before he started to write his first draft, Julien re-examined his freewriting (page 346) and his first list of ideas (page 348). He decided that he was right to focus on graffiti as an art form—passing over other topics such as the history of graffiti and its criminal associations. Reviewing the items on his list, he noticed that his concerns could be grouped into three categories: misinterpretation, freedom of expression, and the beauty and benefits of graffiti. He then formulated a tentative thesis and made an ordered list to chart the direction of his essay:

THESIS: Graffiti is a form of art that promotes freedom of expression and is beneficial to society, once it is embraced.

1. Physical description of graffiti
2. Definition of graffiti--not vandalism
3. Freedom of expression
4. Benefits to society
5. Graffiti's beauty
6. Decriminalization

When you make such a list, ideas might overlap. For example, it may not be possible to separate "the physical description of graffiti" from "the definition of graffiti." Some ideas may drop out, and others may occur as you draft. But you have the beginning of a plan that can guide you.

As Julien continued to work on his essay, he made several changes in his original plan. For example, he decided to discuss freedom of expression before the benefits of graffiti, added a conclusion, and then wrote an entirely different conclusion. Because writing is a process, changes of this sort are natural.

(2) Outlines

Writers sometimes find themselves required to follow a plan of organization that has been determined for them. The ancient Greeks, for example, developed a method of arrangement that helped audiences follow whatever a speaker was saying because certain aspects of a speech almost always occurred in the same sequence. Even today, this **classical arrangement** proves useful for many writers—especially writers trying to persuade. For a description of classical arrangement, see page 460.

Often, however, outlines grow out of the writing. Some writers can develop an excellent plan early in their writing process, turning a working list into a formal outline. Others discover that they need to rethink their original plan after they have actually done some writing. But whether it is written before the first draft or after it, a formal outline is often helpful when analyzing a draft and preparing to revise it. For example, if an outline shows only one subgroup under a heading, that section of the draft might need rethinking.

A structured outline uses indention and numbers to indicate various levels of subordination. Thus it is a kind of graphic scheme of the logic of your paper. The main points form the major headings, and the supporting ideas for each point form the subheadings. An outline of Julien's paper might begin as follows:

```
THESIS: Graffiti is a form of art that promotes
freedom of expression and is beneficial to
society, once it is embraced.
    I. Freedom of expression
       A. An artistic outlet
          1. Outlet for thoughts, feelings,
             desires
          2. Promotes creativity
       B. Informs others of different cultures
          1. Visitors to cities
          2. Increases knowledge of diversity
   II. Public is rewarded
       A. Aesthetically pleasing
          1. Covers up ugly walls
          2. Enlivens an alley
          3. Makes a person notice a nook
       B. Free art
          1. Museums, art galleries are
             expensive
          2. Colourful outdoor exhibits
  III. Needs to be embraced
       A. Store owners shouldn't be concerned
       B. Harmless expression
       C. Attitudes are changing--art
          commissioned
```

A decimal system can also be used:

```
1. Freedom of expression
   1.1 An artistic outlet
```

```
        1.11 Outlet for thoughts, feelings,
             desires
        1.12 Promotes creativity
    1.2 Informs others of different cultures
        1.21 Visitors to cities
        1.22 Increases knowledge of diversity
2. Public is rewarded
    2.1 Aesthetically pleasing
        2.11 Covers up ugly walls
        2.12 Enlivens an alley
        2.13 Makes a person notice a nook
    2.2 Free art
        2.21 Museums, art galleries are
             expensive
        2.22 Colourful outdoor exhibits
3. Needs to be embraced
    3.1 Store owners shouldn't be concerned
    3.2 Harmless expression
    3.3 Attitudes are changing--art commissioned
```

The types of outlines most commonly used are the topic outline and the sentence outline. The headings in a **topic outline** are expressed in grammatically parallel phrases, while a **sentence outline** presents headings in complete and usually parallel sentences. A topic outline has the advantage of brevity and highlights the logical flow of your paper; a sentence outline forces you to think through your ideas more thoroughly. Here is how a sentence outline for Julien's essay might begin:

```
THESIS: Graffiti is a form of art that promotes
freedom of expression and is beneficial to
society, once it is embraced.

I. Individuals, including graffiti artists,
   should be able to express themselves
   freely.
```

A. **Graffiti provides an artistic outlet.**
1. **Thoughts, feelings, desires are released.**
2. **Creativity is promoted.**
B. **Graffiti is helpful in that it informs others of different cultures.**
1. **Visitors to cities in Canada are witness to an unusual form of artistic expression.**
2. **Enables others to understand the diversity of the different cultures in our cities.**

The headings in a sentence outline can often serve as topic sentences when you draft.

Regardless of what type of outline you choose, you will need enough major headings to develop your subject fully within the boundaries established by your thesis. Outlines are also useful for summarizing the main ideas of lectures and reading material when you want to communicate ideas to other people in a brief, readily accessible form. When drafting an essay, however, do not let your outline become a straitjacket. If new ideas occur to you as you are writing, put them down as they occur. You may find that these ideas enrich your paper even though they did not appear in the outline. If you later find that you strayed off track, you can eliminate the digressive material as you revise.

28f Your first draft will not be your final draft.

Put your ideas on paper quickly. Matters such as spelling, punctuation, and usage are not as important in the first draft as they are in the final draft. Your first draft may be sloppy and tentative, but it gives you something you can improve on in another draft. Keep your plan in mind as you write. If you find yourself losing track of where you want to go, stop writing and re-read what you have. You may need to revise your plan, or you may simply need to re-orient yourself. If you are stuck and do not know what to write next, referring to your plan can help.

You may prefer to write chunks or blocks of your essay without worrying about the final order of those chunks. For example, if you have trouble writing the introduction, start with a supporting idea you feel sure of, and write until you reach a stopping point. When you are actually writing, you will probably think more efficiently. You can then move on to another part that will be easy to write—another supporting idea paragraph or even the introduction or conclusion. What is important is to begin writing, to write as quickly as you can, and to save your early work so that you can refer to it during revision.

(1) Introductions must be effective.

An effective introduction arouses the reader's interest and indicates the subject and tone of the essay. (See **28a** and **29a**.) For long or complex essays especially, a good introduction also charts the direction the essay will follow so that readers know what to expect.

The introduction often contains the thesis statement. (See **28d**.) Introductions have no set length; they can be as brief as a couple of sentences or as long as a couple of paragraphs or more. Although introductions appear first in the essay, experienced writers may compose them at any time during the writing process—even after they have drafted the rest of the paper.

You can arouse the interest of your audience by writing introductions in a number of ways.

a. Start with an interesting fact or unusual detail that catches the reader's attention.

> There are seven billion people on Earth. Only 10 per cent of them have telephones, and only 10 per cent of those are linked by personal computer.   —WILLIAM THORSELL,
> "Signposts in a Time of Bewildering Change"

b. Use an intriguing statement to lure the reader into continuing.

> After smiling brilliantly for nearly four decades, I now find myself trying to quit. Or, at the very least, seeking to lower the wattage a bit.
> —AMY CUNNINGHAM, "Why Women Smile"

c. Engage the reader's attention with an anecdote.

> It is 7:30 AM and there is a wild woman loose in my house. She is barking out one-word commands at two little children and one grown man, all of whom are not trembling in her wake. Yes, it's me, trying to wrestle our morning into submission. Mom vs. the volcano, one of my friends calls it.
> —JUDITH TIMSON, *Family Matters*

d. Begin with a question your essay will answer.

> Home. What is home? Where? That comfortable illusion of a house somewhere, a piece of land, a swinging gate, linear memories tied to physical objects, has always escaped me. I say illusion, not delusion. There are illusions worth having. We all need a bit of emotional comfort.
> —JOHN RALSTON SAUL, "Rivers"

e. Start with an appropriate quotation.

> "A Disturbance of Memory on the Acropolis" begins with Freud recounting the afternoon he and his younger brother decided spontaneously to divert their holiday travels from Corfu to Athens. Freud wrote the paper many years after his holiday, never having forgotten the experience: ". . . I stood for the first time on the hill of the Acropolis in Athens,

between the temple ruins, looking out over the blue sea. A feeling of astonishment mingled with my joy," and he thought "So all this really *does* exist, just as we learnt at school!"

—JEANNE RANDOLPH,
"Sacred and Secular Performance:
Psychoanalytic Reflections on Identity and Ritual"

f. Open with an illustration.

A few summers ago, VIA Rail offered an enticing 50 percent rate reduction for foreign visitors to Canada, but did not advertise the bargain, suspecting that it would anger Canadians whose taxes subsidize the corporation. I learned about the scheme while purchasing a ticket in Kingston, Ontario. The agent asked, stealthily, for my passport. I was puzzled. "What do you mean, my passport?" She then advised me about the discount for foreigners, specifying that my "American accent" marked me as an eligible passenger. I informed the agent that (as the *très* white beer commercial says), "I AM CANADIAN." But it's never been simple to be a black in Canada. —GEORGE ELLIOTT CLARKE, "The Complex Face"

g. Begin with general information about the subject or show how you came to choose it.

As a counsellor in a re-education program for abusive men, I recently worked with a man who was convicted of assault causing bodily harm. The charges stemmed from an incident where he beat his wife severely on Christmas Day with their children present. Asked to explain his actions, he told the court he was upset that morning because his wife allowed the children to open their presents before he got out of bed.

—RICK GOODWIN, "Power and Control:
Why Men Dominate Women"

h. Simply state your thesis.

No doubt about it, Canada's tenth prime minister was truly weird. Mackenzie King's diaries still have the power to shock, even though their contents have been known for a quarter of a century now. I recently trawled through some of the endless wash of words while I was researching the life of his mother, Isabel Mackenzie King. I can only echo the emotions of Reginald Whitaker, when he wrote in 1976 of staggering "shell-shocked and blinking from the Public Archives into the bright sunshine of an Ottawa afternoon." The professor of political science at York University asked himself, as subsequent readers of the diaries all ask themselves, "Can this be the man who was prime minister for twenty-two years? I am not a worshipper of power and I am more than ready to countenance stupidity, nastiness, and triviality in the holders of public office. But I am not prepared for a descent into delirium." —CHARLOTTE GRAY, "Crazy like a Fox"

Whatever type of introduction you choose to write, use your opening paragraph to indicate your subject, engage readers' attention, and establish your credibility.

(2) An essay needs an effective conclusion.

The conclusion often summarizes the main points and may also encourage the reader to action or further thought on the subject. An essay should not merely stop; it should finish. Some suggestions follow.

a. Conclude by rephrasing the thesis.

If the banks were more committed to their customers, they would focus more on how to bring their clients' profits in line with their own. With all the talk about mergers, global competition and the restructuring of Canada's financial services markets, our banks have to realize that being world-scale does not automatically mean being world-class. World-class companies are not satisfied with simply responding to customer demands. They aim to solve the business problems of their customers. World-class companies position themselves as an integral ingredient of their customers' success. Ultimately, world-class competitiveness means that in an era of global competition, even the break-even time of the banks will depend on their customers' bottom line.

—JAYSON MYERS, "They're Okay; You're Not"

b. Direct the reader's attention to larger issues.

Better fire alarms, more fire-resistant buildings and improved fire-fighting technology may all save lives, but the central problem remains the human brain, and its attitude toward fire. Killer fires continue to spring from carelessness or inattention—from discarded cigarette butts, overheated pots of cooking oil and creosote-choked chimneys. Deaths continue to occur because people fail to appreciate the power and speed of a blaze. Respecting the alarm is only the first step in changing the way humans see fire. Ultimately, fire must be seen as a formidable adversary rather than an unlikely threat— and then, perhaps, there will be fewer alarms to heed.

—RAY FORD, "Fire and the Human Psyche"

c. Encourage your readers, or others, to change their attitudes or to alter their actions.

Opera is a barometer of the health of the arts in any country because it combines so many art forms and because it is large and highly visible. I think that the arts in this country are, at the moment, pulling rabbits out of hats, and it is time that government at all levels faced up to what a civilized nation should contribute to the health of its soul.

—RICHARD BRADSHAW, "Two-Penny Opera"

d. Conclude with a summary of the main points covered.

All our giving carries with it messages about ourselves, our feelings about those to whom we give, how we see them as people and how we phrase the ties of relationship. Christmas giving, in which love and hope and trust play such an intrinsic part, can be an annual way of telling our children that we think of each of them as a person, as we also hope they will come to think of us.

—MARGARET MEAD and RHODA METRAUX, "The Gift of Autonomy"

e. Clinch or stress the importance of the central idea by referring in some way to the introduction.

Introduction   Why wasn't I surprised? "Federal labs to be shut down," blared *The Globe and Mail*'s front-page headline, and I stared at it with that same sick feeling I've had every time the big drug companies have won another victory. The federal government had announced it was closing its own drug research laboratories to save $2 million a year, leaving university research labs and drug companies themselves to advise federal regulators about drug safety and effectiveness.

Conclusion   . . . With the closing of the government labs, what guarantee do we have now that our publicly owned universities will do independent research? Or will they only work on projects financed by drug firms? Do I have to ask?
                                        —STEVIE CAMERON,
                                        "*Elm Street* Editor's Letter"

Whatever strategy you choose, provide readers with a sense of closure. Bear in mind that they may be wondering, "So what?" Your conclusion gives you an opportunity to respond to that concern. If there is any chance readers may not understand your purpose, use your conclusion to clarify why you asked them to read what they have just read.

(3) A good title fits the subject and tone of an essay.

The title is the reader's first impression and, like the introduction, should fit the subject and tone of the paper. Sometimes the title announces the subject simply and directly: "Montcalm and Wolfe" or "Political Satire." Often a title uses alliteration to reflect the writer's humorous approach, as in "A Pepsi Person in the Perrier Generation," or a twisted cliché, as in "The Right Wrong Stuff." A good title may also arouse the reader's curiosity by asking a question, as does "Who Killed the Bog Men of Denmark? And Why?"

Some writers like to choose a title before they draft because they find that a good title helps clarify their direction. Others choose the title later in the writing process. Whenever you decide to title your paper, a good way to begin is to try condensing your thesis statement without becoming too vague or general. Re-read your introduction and conclusion, and examine key words and phrases for possible titles. Try to work in some indication of your attitude and approach.

Exercise 5

Choose an article or chapter from a work you recently read and evaluate the introduction and conclusion. What writing strategies do they reveal, and how effective are they? Write an alternative introduction and conclusion using a significantly different strategy.

28g   Studying a first draft helps writers to see how it can be improved.

As you read the following draft, remember that it is only the first draft. Two later drafts—including the final draft—are reprinted in chapter 29.

```
Julien Mitchell
English 101
        Graffiti: Art Form or Vandalism?
    Not produced by Michelangelo or contained
in the Sistine Chapel, graffiti is still
considered an artistic representation. Graffiti
is a form of art, which provides freedom of
expression, a favour to society, and the
display of interesting works. Unfortunately
some may disagree, feeling that graffiti is
```

nothing more than vandalism. Entirely unlike
vandalism which is considered a criminal act,
graffiti is too often misinterpreted and
scrutinized. Existing for many years graffiti
is a form of art that may benefit societies
once it has been embraced.

It is important to note the history of
graffiti before diving into the whole art
versus vandalism debate. Graffiti is one of the
five elements of hip hop, the others being
deejaying, beatboxing, b-boying, and emceeing.
Much like the other elements, graffiti was an
opportunity to gain recognition and respect in
the streets. It started out as just tags where
writers would compete for how many times their
tag (writing name) would appear on walls,
inside or outside trains or anywhere it could
be seen by the general public. It also was the
silent means for street gangs to mark their
territory so that outsiders would know exactly
who's turf they were on. Although by no means
are these productive means to express one's
self but, to the disenfranchised innercity
youth of graf's early days, it gave them a
voice where there was once silence.

Each individual within society has a
right to freedom of expression. The acceptance
of graffiti as a form of art provides artists
with respect and the freedom to openly express
themselves. Alike many forms of art, graffiti
is an outlet for feelings, thoughts, desires,
and ideas. It enables artists to display
personal perceptions as well as significant
issues experienced throughout ones community
and worldwide. This outlet also enables the

portrayal of a specific culture, group, or
belonging experienced. Through graffiti an
artist is given the opportunity to display
group identities. These opportunities underlie
the concept of diversity and what it means to
live amongst diversity. In a diverse
community, everyone is given the right to do
whatever chosen so long as it does not induce
harm. Graffiti creates absolutely no harm to
any individuals and is therefore a human right
need to be decriminalized.

In addition to the benefits provided to a
graffiti artist, the public is also rewarded.
The allowance of graffiti is a favour to the
public. Creating a colourful exhibition
generates amusement and interaction about
society. Those passing by are given a sense of
life from graffiti images at no financial cost.
Graffiti art is exhibited for free and often
changes with the seasons. Unlike art galleries
graffiti may be widely viewed and interpreted
throughout many major cities for absolutely no
financial cost.

In addition to a free enlightening
exhibit, graffiti covers up bare, cracked, and
depleted walls. Fortunately for society
graffiti hides the unpleasant apperance of
buildings with lively and interactive works of
art.

Graffiti is not only freedom of expression
and a benefit to society, it promotes the open
display of interesting works of art. Graffiti
englightens any ally or wall with it's bright
colours, symbols, and characters. These
artistic expressions provide a viewer with

colourful interest and intrigue. A sense of the particular artist may be felt as well as a depiction of their feelings or perception on a specific idea or event. Education may be presented in many forms. Graffiti educates and perpetuates discussion, whether or not a viewer agrees with the artists' impression. Considered works of art, graffiti may also be referred to as an interesting, educational, and artistic form of expression.

Alike many forms of expression graffiti arises acceptance in only some persons. As controversial issue within society graffiti provides many benefits but is imagined to be a criminal act amongst some. Due to the fact that it is often committed without permission gives incentive to the idea that it may be considered vandalism. Graffiti enhances apperance not destroying it and therefore should be decriminalized. It is refreshing to note that graffiti has been elevated from its criminal status. Artists are now being commissioned to paint pieces of advertising and are being asked to create art for other businesses. Many of those that started out in the seventies and eighties have now established business enterprises involved in airbrushing for T-shirts, tattooing, and CD jacket design. And while artists like Lady Pink, Case or Duro will not be whispered in the same breath with Van Gogh, the progress that graffiti has made is truly remarkable.

! **CAUTION** The preceding paper is an early draft. Do not consider it a model essay. It is reprinted here so that you can see how it improved through revision. For later versions of this paper, see pages 406–11 and 411–15.

Here are some of the comments Julien received when he distributed this draft in a writing group.

I really liked your paper, especially the way that you've drawn out issues on graffiti that I'd never thought about. Although I'm no real fan of graffiti because I think it's ugly, you've managed to persuade me that it does serve a purpose in our world.

Good paper! I think that the part about the history of graffiti is great, but I don't think it is really necessary. After all, it doesn't really support your thesis, does it? You've taken an issue and made me reconsider my own ideas about it. Well done.

Great topic! Who would have thought that graffiti could be so interesting? Most think it's an eyesore. I loved your essay and wouldn't change a thing.

The only thing that bothered me about your paper was the ending. I think it could be shorter and you could maybe delete the information about graffiti being "elevated from its criminal status." I really like the last line of your essay, though.

Do you think you could make the title more interesting? I think if it showed what side of the debate you are arguing, this would be better. When I started reading your essay, I wasn't sure what you were going to say. Maybe you could let me know earlier on by creating a fantastic title. All in all, however, I really enjoyed your paper.

Before revising this draft, Julien had to weigh these comments and decide for himself which were the most useful.

Exercise 6

Re-read the draft of "Graffiti: Art Form or Vandalism?" and the comments it received. Identify the comments that you think are the most useful and then add two of your own.

Personal writing and writing about writing focus on the writing act.

Some forms of writing focus on the writing act itself, that is, the process by which writers come to an awareness of what they did not know before. Such writing may appear less schematic, less unified than what we are accustomed to. But its aim is to offer writers a chance to reflect on language as it rises out of specific social conditions, in direct collaboration with particular audiences. The spotlight, then, is on interactivity among all the elements of discourse: writer, reader, subject, and occasion. We speak not just of specialized writing forms such as the essay or report but of what is common to all forms, namely *text*.

Being aware of yourself as a writer means being involved in the construction of new knowledge. This is more than just discovering knowledge as something that exists, *out there*. It is selecting, rearranging, and re-evaluating existing knowledge in order to meet a current need. Having recourse to the personal, either as a form of writing in itself (see 28a) or as a prewriting activity (see 28c), is not just a matter of reporting on the day's activities or revealing your deepest feelings. Rather, it involves a reexamination of the self, of your beliefs, attitudes, and values under pressure, that is, as they are undergoing change. In a sense, we do not know exactly who we are until we write—until we let ourselves be created by the words we choose. In short, like other writing, personal writing expresses a need to be skeptical, to problematize, to question.

Here is the opening paragraph of a personally focussed essay in which the author confesses her confusion about whether or not to accept an academic appointment. Ironically, she has been preparing for this position much of her life, yet her moment of reward is also her moment of greatest fear. Her "self," then, is not a static entity; it is adapting to new circumstances, evolving new awareness.

> In the weeks before the English Department at Oberlin College was about to decide whether or not I would be granted tenure, I was haunted by dreams of running away—of disappearing—yes, even of dying. These dreams were not a response to fear that I would not be granted tenure. They were a response to the reality that I *would* be granted tenure. I was afraid that I would be trapped in the academy forever.
> —BELL HOOKS, *Teaching to Transgress*

bell hooks begins by *problematizing* her subject: she describes two diametrically opposed reactions (desire for success and fear of entrapment) to the same experience. This opening conflict leads to reflection on her personal past, as well as connecting her with history (she writes as a female and as Black).

In the following letter/essay, we see a similar opening confession of uncertainty, mystery. Maureen, the writer of "My Husband," has mixed feelings about returning to school. She is aware of the contrast between others' expectations of her and her expectations of herself. She feels simultaneously strong and weak, a doubled-up feeling that she recycles through the essay. Notice how she generates flow between ideas by anticipating reactions of her reader (her daughter) and responding to these—in advance.

Answering questions at strategic moments leads her to see the problem from different angles, which in turn allows her to *revise* her understanding of the problem as she goes along. So, in a sense, at the beginning of her essay she does not know what the ending will be. Nonetheless, there is a definite, though spontaneous, linkage between the question she poses at the start and the insight or decision she eventually arrives at. Along the way, she includes all kinds of informal, sometimes tangential, detail and personal anecdote. Of course, she must pay strict attention to her own words as she writes them down. It is this attention to her own writing that makes this exercise "writing about writing."

What appears at first glance as a very loose, discontinuous type of writing is really quite rigorous in its attention to detail, its awareness of language, its overall engagement with life issues at a concrete level. While the author delays stating a central idea (thesis), she preserves a mystery until the time seems right to solve it. Because it is a gradual, step-by-step investigation of a problem, this writing resembles a formal research process. In addition to revealing the writer as an agent in the writing process, thus enabling her to develop her voice as well as trust in her own point of view, this writing shows the importance of "breaking open" a subject (in this case the writer's husband and her relationship with him) and of having an actively engaged audience in mind to "converse" with. Setting up an issue to explore is, in more specialized forms of writing, a first stage in constructing a workable thesis statement. Relating ideas to a particular audience helps focus your attention on the impact your words are having on others, as well as build transitions from point to point (see 28a). Such skills are transferable to more formal, persuasive, or expository writing, at the first-year level and beyond.

Maureen Zaharychuk

Dr. A. Stubbs

ENGL-100-010

21 September 2001

My Husband

Dear Sydney (or should I say Peanut), *Addresses specific reader*

Refers to occasion of writing
I can't believe I'm back taking classes. Taking classes is a huge responsibility. You have to believe and trust in yourself enough to go after
States contradictory feelings
what you want. I know that you and others think I'm a big responsible grownup. Look, I'm a parent, a wife--so it's an automatic assumption I guess. I'm the person who is always there to give support. But right now I'm feeling very weak, insecure, absolutely terrified. Why? Because I don't know how I'm going to do this. I'm thinking,

maybe I can figure it out by telling you a few things about me, your dad, how we got where we are. I know you're going *Anticipates reader reaction* through some mixed feelings yourself about my going back to school. And what makes it even harder is you had those same feelings when Dad started back. So I hope that this letter will help a little.

Writes "backward" into the past

Two years ago, I was more proud of your father than I'd ever been. He decided to go to university. He wanted to become a teacher. But as proud as I was of him, I had some other feelings, the kind of feelings you wish you could wash away. Kind of like when you have *Uses analogy to appeal to* been digging in the mud and it starts to *reader's level of* get dry and itchy. Except the feelings I *understanding* had you couldn't just wash away, like doubt and fear. Feelings that have always made me go very quiet or--the opposite--say things I don't mean. Even though you're only eight years old, I hope you can relate. You do the same

thing. Like when you're afraid you hide
yourself away. Especially when a movie
is scary or you think you might be in
trouble for spilling a drink. The reason
I know this is, it's part of my job
as a mom. Our friends thought they
knew me. They thought I was mad that
Daddy was getting to go to school while
I was stuck working. Wrong! I guess our
friends didn't know me very well after
all. This will probably sound silly to
you, but I was scared Daddy would be too
smart for me and maybe I'd lose him to
someone who was, you know, more
intelligent. So I was jealous. And
that's something I know you've felt
recently. It's the feeling you got when
you saw Danielle's new house with the
trampoline in the backyard. Well, that's
what I went through when Dad started
telling me about all the new things he'd
learned at university that day.

   Your dad has such a great memory.
He can remember things from when we first

Uses conversational style to create flow from idea to idea

got married, which I can't (that's a
horrible feeling). A funny example is
the other night. Your dad remembered the
time Jonathon and Cara were at our
house. I'd say they were about four and
seven. They were a lot like you. They
were bored so we gave them a bath. Well,
we didn't have the hot tub back then,
but we did have this spa thing for the
tub. So Dad and I put them in the tub,
added the bubble bath, and guess what?
They vanished. All you could see were arms
waving about. It was funny but scary.
Your dad has a ton of memories like
that, good and bad. And like I say, he
retains everything he learns. Just like
you, by the way. Sydney, you are so good
at school. I want to say that now. You
are shown something once and you
remember it. I wish it were that easy
for me.

  It seems the knowledge I pick up
keeps disappearing somewhere. Whereas
everything I'd like to forget stays. But

Describes personal memory, anecdote

Calls attention to process, reminding reader of what has been said and pointing ahead

I do remember something your grandfather said: "If you want something bad enough you just have to work harder." I guess I just have to keep reminding myself of that.

Expands the issue, introduces new ideas

There's something else I'm jealous about when it comes to your dad. Your dad knows what he wants to do with his life. I can honestly say I don't know what I want. I talk about a career in marketing, but I'm not sure. You're very lucky you have a ways to go before you need to make a decision about all that.

It's funny when I look at your dad and see how much he has grown as a person in the past few years. You've probably noticed it too but in a different way. The reason I say that is I'm not looking at things through the eyes of an eight-year-old. As your mom, I'd like to try to paint you a picture of how he's changed. When I sit on the couch across from him, I see a face that has matured. (And before you say

Focusses on how subject and writer's perspective changed— process is as important as outcome

NEL

anything, it's not just the white hairs in his beard either!) You know how you can look at me and tell something is making me sad? Or how I can look at you and say you must not feel good because your freckles aren't sticking to your face any more? Well, it's the same when you look at your dad's face. I can see confidence, satisfaction, happiness, peace--all signs of a very strong human being. A good way to put it is this: he seems calmer inside, or maybe a better word would be "settled." His whole outlook on life is so much more positive. And when he's like that, it seems to just flow over us. All three of us. You can tell which days those are because we all seem happier--but that seems to be most of the time. He has become a doer, not just a talker or thinker. An example is when he says we're going skating today--we do it, we don't just talk about it. And that reminds me: I love to watch the two of

Uses parenthetical information to further the writer— reader relationship

you together. Whether it's reading stories, playing Spyro, or just watching the Simpsons. I love it because I look at him and he just glows with pride and love for you. And trust me, he makes sure that everyone knows it. You should see him when he tells people his daughter is in the U of R Conservatory Junior Choir.

Believe it or not, you're the reason for so many of the changes that have happened to him. One that I'm positive about is that he has way more patience now than he ever did before you came along. Well, most of the time anyway. (He's only human right? Oh, I forgot, he's "Super Dad" to you.) The scariest thing your dad has done is give up a Stanley Cup playoff game (on more than one occasion) to help you build a Lego house. Or let you watch one of those goofy kid shows. I look at your dad now and I see the person I fell in love with over fourteen years ago. (Yeah,

Explores ideas through parenthetical remarks, asides

Uses dialogue to help create flow from idea to idea

here comes some mushy stuff.) But I also see a person who has experienced a lot and learned how to handle it. What a realization to find that you've fallen in love again with the same person who at the same time isn't the same person. He's so much more. (Does that make sense to you? Maybe you need to be older. . . .) Just think of it like this: sometimes you and Bradley say you're not friends anymore because you can't agree on how to play Digemon, but two days later he does something nice for you and you become best friends again. Because of all these changes I've been telling you about, I've realized that I want to grow. I want to look towards the future again. Yes, I want to be a better mother, daughter, wife, and friend. But I also want something more.

Uses concrete examples to make subject accessible to reader

I need to tell you what your dad was like before you were born, and how he was in the first few years of your life. There was a time when I didn't see

all the good things in your dad I do
now. I can remember looking at him and
he'd be joking around, seeming so happy.
But I could tell by looking in his eyes
he wasn't, not really. Sydney, it was like
flower wilting. You know you've been
watering it but it isn't helping. So you
realize it needs something else. But
you're not sure what. You see, when I
first met your dad, "we" were important.
Then it seemed to become more about
"him." If something happened, it was how
it affected him, not us. He seemed
ticked off all the time. I wondered if
it was me or the world he was mad at.
Just like the times when you get mad and
when I ask you what's wrong you say "I
don't know." Well, I don't think your
dad was too sure back then either. I
don't mean he didn't love being your
father. It was more like he wasn't sure
how to be one, so he kept his distance a
bit. It's scary for a man having a
daughter. Your dad was a great guy, and

Uses simile to explain ideas

NEL

he was my best friend for a long time, but that seemed to change over the years. He was a person who needed to find himself. (Did you know grown-up people can get lost--and not just in the mall?) Or, as they say, at least let go of some baggage. It's strange, but it was one of the things that really attracted me to him--that mystery. But at the same time, I felt like I was part of the baggage. (You know, after writing that last sentence, I suddenly understand what you mean when you say, "I know you're busy with work and school, but can you make time for me." Well, Sydney, you're definitely not "baggage," and you never will be.) Overall, I think Daddy was someone who wasn't ready to grow up, whereas I was someone who wanted to be less grown up. (Now, as I write this, I'm wishing we'd gone through all this before you were born. That monster, guilt! You sure didn't need to be caught up in this.)

Catching herself in the act of writing—writer uses self-consciousness to come to a new realization

Writes "forward" into the future

On a bright note, when I look into the future, I picture your dad fulfilling his dreams (some of them anyway, the important ones). My grandmother always told me to keep dreaming, so I'm telling you to make sure you never stop, okay? Anyway, I find I really am beginning to believe there's a future for our family, even though I'm not totally sure of the direction we're heading in. I can tell you your dad will only continue to grow as a father, husband, and friend. He's proven this to us. I believe that the challenges waiting for him won't scare him the way they did before. In fact, he seems to look forward to them. I hate to tell you this, but the challenges you'll have to face won't always be good, or momentous, or exciting. Homework is the perfect way to explain this--sometimes fun, sometimes "oh no!" But I have to confess, I can't wait to see my family (Dad, me, you) graduate. (Wouldn't it be cool if your dad ended up teaching at the same high school you went to? Just think--he can keep an eye on the boys!)

I know you've said he'll be an awesome teacher, but you say that because he's your dad. As someone who has watched him through the years, I believe he will because, as I said before, he's got so much "real life experience." And every day he'll gain more. I believe he'll make a difference with his students. I can tell this by the way he coaches and hangs out with you and your friends, and that cocky, determined look he gets on his face. You know that look, right?

Reader becomes active participant in writer's process of exploring the subject

You're maybe going to ask, "Why did you write about Daddy?" Well, Sydney, there are a lot of people who've made a difference in my life (including you, especially you). I guess I could've written about any of them. If I hadn't written about your dad, it would have been Grandpa. Because, though they're different, he and Dad are also so much

Anticipates reader's question and responds

Introduces new subject to help solve overall problem

alike. They both had you. Grandpa had a lot of ghosts that haunted him and he never dealt with them. He just put them in a place where no one else could see them. But then, you were the joy of his life. When you were born, I never saw my dad so alive. I thank you for that. I wish you hadn't had to see Grandpa get sick, but I think your being there made it easier for him and all of us. I think it's the same for your dad. I believe you helped make it possible for him to go through all the changes I've been talking about.

New insight

Well, there's one thing I've learned from losing Grandpa and that is you can't keep your ghosts locked up. You have to let them out, whether you talk about them, or write about them, or whatever. You have to let go. I know you do it by drawing a picture, just like the one you drew of Grandpa as an angel. Grandpa didn't get a chance to let go of his ghosts, his demons. And they haunted him till the day he died, even during the happier times. I'm so thankful that your dad has dealt with them, found peace with some of them. In a strange way, I know Grandpa would have been proud of him for doing that.

I think about Grandpa quite a lot these days. Before you came along, Grandpa was a workaholic. It was work and more work, 24/7. The only time we got to spend time with him was on the three-week vacation we took every year. Even then, he'd pick the place, and everything we did was pretty much according to a schedule. It wasn't all bad. But I remember thinking it would've been nice to just let loose and talk once in a while. It always seemed like he wanted to be somewhere other than with us. As I say, that all seemed to change when we had you. Grandpa loved to spend time with you, whether it was sitting on his lap watching Barney and eating veggie thins, or out shovelling

snow back on the spots he'd just
cleaned.

Sydney, I thought the main reason I *Author identifies the moment her ideas changed*
chose to write about your dad was
because he's made me feel alive again. I
hadn't realized how big a part of me had
died inside till a little while ago. But
because of all the changes he's gone
through, I've found myself questioning
what I wanted and who I wanted to be.
Whether I wanted it or not, it was my
turn to deal with my ghosts. In fact,
I'm dealing with my ghosts just by
writing this to you. One of my fears has
been that I'd forget all the good
memories, dwell too much on the bad
stuff. Now I realize I'm not. Melo-
dramatic as it sounds, the tears in my
eyes tell me that. Gosh, whoever thought
a person could cry over "veggie thins"!
Also, I'm not so scared now that I don't
know what I want to do with the rest of
my life. It's just hit me that your dad
didn't decide overnight, and I shouldn't

have to either. I still have lots of time. That's comforting.

When I started writing this I thought I saw myself as weak. But you know what? I'm not. It feels so good to say that. A weak person would never have gone through this, all the doubts and insecurities. The flip side is, I realize I can't change what's happened or what's going to happen. Maybe you're strongest when you accept your own powerlessness. I can't change your getting hit by a car, or your being born eleven weeks early, or your dad and I separating for a year, or Grandpa suffering so long with Alzheimer's. But I can accept them as my memories, which means I can hang on to the past and still keep some distance between me and the pain.

Reaches a conclusion by reflecting on her writing process

Ironic insight (a new contradiction)

Most of all, I needed to tell you in the middle of all this that you are truly amazing. Because of you and your

father, I think I might even be able to
like "me." I'm starting to realize I'm
terrified of your being like me. Syd, I
was always scared of being like Grandpa.
Working the same job and never being
there for my family. Guess what? The
harder I tried not to be like him the
more I became him. The funny thing is, I
was proud of him but not of myself.
Explain that! How can you like yet not
like something or someone for the same
reasons? Grandpa's been gone a while
now, and maybe it's too late to be
wondering about the past. Then again,
maybe you have to lose something before
you realize it's important.

I hope when the time comes for you
to read this you'll understand the
things I'm trying to say and the
difference you made in my life, in all
our lives. And that it helps you get
through. But then, I also know this is

just words, and you'll have to learn it
all for yourself too. Over the next ten
to twenty years.

Love,

Mom

Chapter 29

Revising and Editing Essays

To **revise** means "to see again." This activity, which is at the heart of writing well, implies that you take a fresh look at your draft—rethinking what you have written and what you still need to write by distancing yourself from your work and evaluating it from a reader's point of view. To **edit** means to polish a piece of writing by making word choice more precise (**14a**), prose more concise (chapter **15**), and sentence structure more effective (chapters **11** and **12**), in addition to eliminating any errors in grammar, punctuation, and mechanics. Although these two activities can overlap, they are essentially very different. Inexperienced writers sometimes think they are revising when they are really editing. You need to do both, so be careful not to confuse one with the other.

Revising usually comes before editing, because you can waste time perfecting a paragraph that you later decide to delete. This does not mean that you cannot correct errors as you move along, especially if doing so makes you more confident or comfortable. But the more time and energy you invest in editing early on, the harder it may be to make major changes that would enrich your essay. When something looks perfect on the surface, it can be tempting not to touch it. Even if you do some editing as you draft, you should be willing to rearrange paragraphs and make significant cuts and additions as you revise.

29a   Your tone reveals your attitude.

Tone reflects your attitude toward your subject and must be appropriate to your purpose, audience, and occasion, whether for a personal essay or a lab report. Although humour might well be suitable in a letter to a friend telling her of trouble with your new car, it would be inappropriate in a letter of complaint to the manufacturer. Consider the difference in tone between the following two writers, both of whom are trying to persuade people to support capital punishment. The first is from a successful journalist who amused and provoked readers of his newspaper column. The second is from a book by a university professor. Both are discussing what they learned from Aristotle about anger and revenge.

> A keeps a store and has a bookkeeper, B. B steals $700, employs it in playing at dice or bingo, and is wiped out. What is A to do? Let B go? If he does he will be unable to sleep at night. The sense of injury, of injustice, of frustration will haunt him like pruritus. So he turns B over to the police, and they hustle B to prison. Thereafter A can sleep. More, he has pleasant dreams. He pictures B chained to the wall of a dungeon a hundred feet underground, devoured by rats and scorpions. It is so agreeable it makes him forget his $700. He has got his *katharsis*.   —H. L. MENCKEN, "The Penalty of Death"

> Anger is expressed or manifested on those occasions when someone has acted in a manner that is thought to be unjust, and one of its origins is the opinion that men are responsible, and should be held responsible, for what they do. Thus, as Aristotle teaches us, anger is accompanied not only by the pain caused by the one who is the object of anger, but by the pleasure arising from the expectation of inflicting revenge on someone who is thought to deserve it. . . . Anger is somehow connected with justice, and it is this that modern penology

has not understood; it tends, on the whole, to regard anger as a selfish indulgence.

—WALTER BERNS, *For Capital Punishment*

Exercise 1

1. Re-read the passages by H. L. Mencken and Walter Berns and then write a short analysis of how these men sound. Be sure to identify specific words or phrases that led you to attribute this tone to them.
2. Study the draft of Julien Mitchell's essay (pages 371–74) and then study his final version (pages 411–15). Write a short essay comparing the tone of these two versions.

29b Revision is essential to writing well.

In one way or another you revise throughout the writing process. For example, even in the earliest planning stages, as you consider a possible subject and then discard it in favour of another, you are revising. Similarly, after choosing a subject, you might decide to change your focus or emphasize some new part of it. That, too, is a kind of revision. And, of course, you are revising when you realize that a sentence or a paragraph you have just written does not belong where it is, so you pause to strike it out or to move it elsewhere.

Nevertheless, experienced writers usually revise after they have completed a draft—no matter how much they may have revised while planning and drafting. They not only revise and develop paragraphs (chapter 27), they review the draft *as a whole*. Although some writers do so immediately after drafting, while their minds are still fully engaged by their topic, they usually benefit from setting the drafts aside for a time so that later they can see their work more objectively. What looks good when you are excited does not necessarily look good the morning after. Whenever possible, plan your writing process so that you can put a draft aside, at least overnight, and then see it later with fresh eyes.

 Because revision is an ongoing process, writers often print several different versions when composing with a computer. By labelling each version—or at least dating each hard copy—you can keep track of how your work is evolving.

(1) Everything on the page benefits from reconsideration.

When you review your essay as a whole, ask yourself if the point of your essay comes through clearly and if you ever digress from it. Writers frequently get off the track as they generate ideas through the act of writing. Now is the time to eliminate those side trips. It is also wise to make sure that you are developing a point rather than simply repeating the same thing in different words—or, as sometimes happens, contradicting yourself by saying two very different things.

Revising also demands reconsidering your rhetorical situation (page 331). Have you provided examples or other details that will interest your audience? Are your ideas clearly expressed in language appropriate for your audience? Is your tone (**29a**) appropriate for this occasion?

Moreover, you should examine your paragraphs to make sure that they are unified, coherent, and well developed (chapter **27**). Assess how well each paragraph leads to the next, whether you need to rearrange any, and whether your transitions are effective (see **27b(4)**.)

! **CAUTION** When you move paragraphs, check to see if your new arrangement works and if you need to write new transitions.

(2) What is not on the page can be even more important than what is there.

One of the most challenging tasks in revision is to look for what you have left out that your audience might expect or that would strengthen your paper as a whole. Your best ideas will not always surface in your first draft; you will sometimes have an important new idea only after you have finished your draft and taken a good look at it. No matter how good a draft looks, ask yourself if something is missing.

Inexperienced writers sometimes end an essay prematurely because they cannot think of anything else to say. One way to get past this block is to use such strategies as questioning (pages 349–50), listing (pages 348–49), and applying perspectives (page 350). Another way is to share your work with other readers and ask them to let you know if there is anything they find confusing or want to know more about. Providing readers with this kind of specific direction can get you a much more focussed response than simply passing a paper to someone and asking, "What do you think?" When not given direction, some readers may keep reservations to themselves because they suspect they are being asked to approve a finished product.

Checklist for Revising Essays
- Is the purpose of the work clear (28a(1))? Does the work stick to its purpose?
- Does the essay address the appropriate audience (28a(2))?
- Is the tone (29a) appropriate for the purpose, audience, and occasion?
- Is the subject focussed (28c(2))?

continued

continued from previous page

- Does the essay make a clear point (28d)? Is this point well supported? Do the relationships expressed in the essay clearly relate to this point?
- Is each paragraph unified and coherent (27a–b)? Are the paragraphs arranged in a logical, effective order (28e)? (See the paragraph checklist on page 327.)
- Does the essay follow an effective method or combination of methods of development (28e)?
- Is the introduction effective (28f(1))?
- Is the conclusion appropriate for the essay's purpose (28f(2))?

29c   Editing improves your writing.

After you are satisfied with the revised structure of your paper and the content of your paragraphs, edit individual sentences for clarity, effectiveness, and variety. (See chapters 8 through 16.) Consider combining choppy or unconnected sentences and rework long, overly complicated ones. If you overuse some structures, say, introductory prepositional phrases, try to rework some of them into other patterns. Eliminate any needless shifts in grammatical structures, tone, style, or point of view.

Examine your diction, and make sure the words you have used are the best choices for this particular essay. If any words leap out as much more formal or informal than your language as a whole in the essay, replace them with words that are more consistent with your style. Eliminate any unnecessary words (chapter 15). If you have experimented with words new to your vocabulary, make sure that you have used them accurately.

Check whether your punctuation is correct and whether you have followed standard conventions for mechanics. Even if you have already used a spell checker (22a), use it again because new errors may have been introduced since you last checked. Remember also that such programs are never foolproof. Double-check that you are correctly using words like *there* and *their* or *who's* and *whose*—correctly spelled words that might be the wrong words in a specific context.

Checklist for Editing

Sentences

- Are ideas related effectively through subordination and co-ordination (9)?
- Are all sentences unified (8)?
- Do any sentences contain misplaced parts or dangling modifiers (5)?
- Is there any faulty parallelism (10)?
- Are there any needless shifts in grammatical structures, in tone or style, or in viewpoint (8e)?
- Are ideas given appropriate emphasis within each sentence (11)?
- Are the sentences varied in length and in type (12)?
- Are there any fragments (2)? Are there any comma splices or fused sentences (3)?
- Do all verbs agree with their subjects (7a)? Do all pronouns agree with their antecedents (6a)?
- Are all verb forms appropriate (7)?

Diction

- Are any words overused, imprecise, or vague (14c, 14a)? Are all expressions idiomatic (14b)?

continued

---

continued from previous page

- Have all **unnecessary** words and phrases been eliminated (15)? Have any **necessary** words been left out by mistake (16)?
- Is the vocabulary appropriate for the audience, purpose, and occasion (13, 28a)?
- Have all technical words that might be unfamiliar to the audience been eliminated or defined (13c(1))?

Punctuation and mechanics

- Is all punctuation correct? Are any marks missing?
- Are all words spelled correctly (22)?
- Is capitalization correct (23)?
- Are titles identified by either quotation marks (20c) or italics (24a)?
- Are abbreviations (25) appropriate and correct?

29d Proofreading can help make your papers error-free.

Once you have revised and edited your essay, carefully format it (chapter 26). It is then your responsibility to proofread it. Proofreading means making a special search to ensure that the product you submit is error-free. Your proofreading may alert you to problems that call for further editing, but proofreading is usually the last step in the process of writing an essay.

 Thanks to the computer, you can easily produce professional-looking documents with handsome fonts and perfect margins. Showing that you care about presentation indicates that you respect your audience and care about your work. Remember, however, that presentation is only one aspect of a successful project. A paper that looks good could still have problems. No matter how beautiful your paper looks when you print it out, proofread it carefully.

Be alert for minor errors that you could have missed—such as a misspelled word, a missing comma, or a book title that has not been italicized. Also watch for two common errors: accidentally leaving a word out or writing the same word twice. Errors of this sort are especially common now that so much writing is done on computers. A spell checker program can alert you to repeated words, but you have to proofread to see if deleting or moving material led to other errors. For example, when deleting a phrase you may have accidentally left one of its words in the text. Or when moving a sentence, you may have put it in the wrong spot.

Because the eye tends to see what it expects to see, many writers miss errors even when they think they have proofread carefully. It is usually wise to proofread more than once, and many writers find that they benefit from reading their work aloud as they proofread.

An extra pair of eyes can also be helpful, so you might ask a friend to help you. This is very different, however, from abdicating your own responsibility. If someone else helps you proofread, this check should be in addition to your own. Moreover, if you ask someone to proofread your work, remember that you are asking for only an error-check. If you want a more thoughtful response to your essay that could help you revise it, you need to ask for this kind of response at an earlier point in the process.

Use the Proofreading Checklist in chapter 26, pages 288–89, to check your format, spelling, punctuation, and mechanics. If your paper is to be in MLA or APA style, see chapter 34.

29e You can benefit from studying how other writers work.

After Julien Mitchell had time to reconsider the first draft of his essay on graffiti and to think about the responses he received from readers, he made a number of changes in his second draft. Here is what his paper looked like midway through its revision.

Julien Mitchell

I need to add a date and teacher's name

English 101

(centre)]**Graffiti: Art Form or Vandalism?**[*A better title?*

I need a more interesting first line. This is wordy.

Not produced by Michelangelo or contained in the Sistine Chapel, graffiti is still considered an artistic representation. Graffiti is a form of art, which provides freedom of expression, a favour to society, and the display of interesting works. Unfortunately some may disagree, feeling that graffiti is nothing more than vandalism. Entirely unlike vandalism which is considered a criminal act, graffiti is too often misinterpreted and scrutinized. Existing for many years

graffiti is a form of art that may benefit societies once it has been embraced.

Delete this paragraph!

~~It is important to note the history of graffiti before diving into the whole art versus vandalism debate. Graffiti is one of the five elements of hip hop, the others being deejaying, beatboxing, b-boying, and emceeing. Much like the other elements, graffiti was an opportunity to gain recognition and respect in the streets. It started out as just tags where writers would compete for how many times their tag (writing name) would appear on walls, inside or outside trains or anywhere it could be seen by the general public. It also was the silent means for street gangs to mark their territory so that outsiders would know exactly who's turf they were on. Although by no means are these productive means to express one's self but, to the disenfranchised innercity youth of graf's early days, it gave them a voice where there was once silence.~~

Each individual within society has a right to freedom of expression. ~~The acceptance of graffiti as a form of art~~ *off topic* ~~provides artists with respect and the freedom to openly express themselves.~~ Like many forms of art, graffiti is an outlet for feelings, thoughts, desires, and ideas. It enables artists to display personal perceptions as well as significant issues experienced throughout one's community and worldwide. This *awkward* outlet also enables the portrayal of a specific culture, group, or belonging experienced. Through graffiti‸ an artist is given the opportunity to display group identities. These opportunities underlie the concept of diversity and what it means to live amongst diversity. In a diverse community, everyone is given the right to do whatever chosen so long as it does not induce harm. Graffiti creates absolutely no harm to any individuals and is therefore a human right ~~need~~ *that needs* to be decriminalized.

In addition to the benefits provided to a graffiti artist, the public is also rewarded. The <u>allowance of graffiti</u> is a *awkward* favour to the public. Creating a colourful exhibition generates amusement and interaction about society. Those passing by are given a sense of life from graffiti images at no financial cost. *wordy* Graffiti art is exhibited for free and *Example —* often changes with the seasons. Unlike *cost of admission to* art galleries, graffiti may be widely *museums &* *galleries* viewed and interpreted throughout many major cities for absolutely no financial cost.

In addition to a free enlightening exhibit, graffiti covers up bare, cracked, and depleted walls. Fortunately for society graffiti hides the unpleasant appearance of buildings with lively and interactive works of art.

Graffiti is not only ‸*a* freedom of expression and a benefit to society, it promotes the open display of interesting *watch* *spelling* works of art. Graffiti (englightens) any

Is this the best way to present my ideas?
1) freedom of expression
2) public rewarded
3) promotes art

NEL

watch spelling (ally) or wall with it's bright colours, symbols, and characters. These artistic expressions provide a viewer with colourful interest and intrigue. A sense of the particular artist may be felt as well as a depiction of their feelings or perception on a specific idea or event.

¶ Education may be presented in many *Examples?* forms. Graffiti educates and perpetuates discussion, whether or not a viewer agrees with the artists' impression. Considered works of art, graffiti may also be referred to as interesting, educational, and artistic form of expression.

insert from next page → Unlike many forms of expression, graffiti arises acceptance in only some *unclear* persons. As a controversial issue within society, graffiti provides many benefits but is imagined to be a criminal act amongst some. Due to the fact that it is often committed without permission gives *Wordy* incentive to the idea that it may be considered vandalism. Graffiti enhances *sp*

apperance not destroying it and

therefore should be decriminalized. ~~It~~

move to previous page ~~is refreshing to note that graffiti has~~

~~been elevated from its criminal status.~~

Artists are now being commissioned to

paint pieces of advertising and are

being asked to create are for other

businesses. Many of those that started

out in the seventies and eighties have

now established business enterprises

involved in airbrushing for T-shirts,

tattooing, and CD jacket design. And

while artists like Lady Pink, Case or

Duro will not be whispered in the same

breath with Van Gogh, the progress that

graffiti has made is truly remarkable.

29f The final draft reflects the care the writer took.

Julien Mitchell

Professor Henrikson

English 101

14 December 2002

Graffiti: What's All the Fuss?
Graffiti has existed for thousands of
years. Etched in the walls of Pompeii,
Italy, are the crude writings of those
who felt the need to artistically
express themselves in 70 A.D. The marks
remain there to this day. Although
graffiti may never be as revered as the
work of Michelangelo, it is still an
important form of artistic
representation. Indeed, it is an art
form that benefits the community in
subtle and interesting ways.
Unfortunately, some disagree, feeling
that graffiti is nothing more than
vandalism. In fact, graffiti is too often
misinterpreted and scrutinized. It is a
form of art that benefits us all because
it gives to the community, and promotes
freedom of expression.

What would you rather look at: the
bare, cracked, and depleted walls of a
stuffy office building, or the eye-
catching picture of a talented artist?
Fortunately for us, graffiti hides much
of the unpleasant appearance of
buildings. It enlightens any alley or

wall with its bright colours, symbols, and characters. These artistic expressions promote interest and intrigue. A sense of the particular artist may be felt as well as a depiction of his or her feelings or perceptions on a specific idea or event. It is important to keep in mind that education may be presented in many forms. Graffiti not only helps train artists, but it educates and perpetuates discussion in the public, whether or not a viewer agrees with the artists' impression.

Many critics of graffiti neglect the benefits it provides to the community. Unlike art galleries, graffiti may be widely viewed and interpreted throughout many cities for absolutely no financial cost. When the average cost of entering a museum or art gallery is at least ten dollars, the art in the streets is a welcome reprieve. In fact, graffiti artists hope that the public will analyze their work and engage with it. Certainly these outdoor exhibits generate amusement and interaction in local communities. Those passing by are given a sense of life from graffiti images. They are encouraged to ask questions of the art in the same way they might of the Mona Lisa. But unlike the static art that is hung on the dull walls of a gallery, graffiti art is dynamic, for it lives in the vibrant and ever-changing streets. This makes artists change their works frequently, allowing viewers to recognize patterns and colours in the works of their favourite street artists.

Perhaps the most important issue related to this discussion on graffiti is the importance of freedom of expression. Each individual within our community has a right to free expression. Accepting graffiti as a form of art provides artists with respect and the freedom to openly express themselves. Like many forms of art, graffiti is an outlet for feelings, thoughts, desires, and ideas. It enables artists to display personal perceptions as well as significant issues that are experienced. This outlet also enables specific cultures to voice their concerns about societal issues. Through graffiti, an artist is given the opportunity to display group identities. These opportunities underlie the concept of diversity and what it means to live in diverse communities. Everyone must be given the right to express herself freely so long as it does not induce harm. Because graffiti does absolutely no harm to individuals, it should be decriminalized.

It is refreshing to note that only recently is graffiti being elevated from its criminal status. Artists are now being commissioned to paint pieces of advertising and are being asked to create art for bland business facades. Many of those graffiti pioneers who started out in the seventies and eighties have now established business enterprises that incorporate the skills they learned as street artists. And while artists like Lady Pink, Case, or Duro will not be whispered in the same breath with Van Gogh, the progress that graffiti has made is truly remarkable.

Exercise 2

Compare the two versions of "Graffiti: What's All the Fuss?" reprinted in this chapter, and summarize how Julien revised his work. If he showed this paper to you before handing it in for a grade, what would you tell him?

Chapter 30

Writing under Pressure

Some writers feel under pressure no matter how much time they have because they suffer from writing anxiety. Strategies for reducing such anxiety include freewriting frequently (28c), making writing a normal part of the day by keeping a journal (28c), and learning that most writing situations allow time for a process (chapters 28 and 29) rather than a one-time chance at perfection. The focus of this chapter, however, is how to write well under the pressure of time constraints.

It is not always possible to engage in a writing process that stretches over a period of weeks or even days. Sometimes writers must quickly respond to e-mail (35b(1)) or prepare a proposal for presentation at a hastily convened meeting. Working students and single parents are sometimes unable to devote as much time as they would like to every writing assignment. And almost all students are faced, at some point, with essay examinations that must be written in two hours or less. The key to succeeding in such situations is to use whatever time you have as efficiently as possible.

30a Preparing ahead of time helps you succeed.

When required to write under pressure, bring knowledge to the situation by preparing ahead of time. Although an essay exam may not occur until midterm, preparation should begin on the first day of class. Decide what is most important about the material you are learning, and pay attention to indications that your instructor considers certain material especially important. Ask questions whenever you are uncertain.

In addition to knowledge, you can bring writing experience to potentially stressful situations. Plan your time so that you write frequently for your own benefit, even when you are not required to do so. By regularly exercising your writing ability, you will be able to write more fluently when forced to write quickly.

If you are faced with a specific task that must be completed in a relatively short time, invest a few minutes in making a schedule. If the time allowed for this assignment has already been specified, as is usually the case with an in-class essay, divide that time into blocks. Give yourself time to study the assignment, plan your response, and then draft your essay. Also, be sure to allow time for revising and proofreading.

If you are writing outside class, follow essentially the same process. The key difference is deciding how much time you can allot to this task and whether you want to complete it in a single block of time or in separate blocks stretched over an afternoon or evening in which you engage in other activities. If a writing task is important, even the busiest people usually manage to find time to complete it.

30b There are ways to overcome writer's block.

Writer's block can occur at any time to any writer, no matter how experienced. When time is not an issue, writers sometimes overcome their block by stepping away from the work and doing something else that does not require a lot of concentration. Completing a physical task, such as washing dishes or shovelling snow, can help writers by getting them away from their desks without making them forget the writing entirely. Activities such as these can be completed while the mind is still playing with writing possibilities. Good ideas often arise when the mind is only half focussing on how to resolve a particular problem.

When writing under pressure, however, you may not be able to leave your desk. If you fear that pressure will lead to writer's block, several strategies can help reduce the risk.

Checklist for Overcoming Writer's Block
- Wear comfortable clothes. (If a particular pair of pants or shoes helps you feel relaxed, this is a good time to wear them.)
- Use writing implements that work best for you. (Some pens feel better in the hand than others; if you are accustomed to using a computer, see if this is an option when writing away from your usual workplace.)
- Keep near you anything you are likely to need. (Even if you do not use your dictionary, for example, knowing that it is close at hand can help you avoid unnecessary stress.)
- Position yourself carefully. (If you are working at home, choose the place where you usually work most efficiently. If you are in a classroom with open seating, choose a seat that suits you. Some people feel safest when tucked in a corner, for example; others like to sit in the front row so they can shut out the rest of the class.)

Once you are actually writing, try not to stop prematurely. If you are following an abridged version of your regular writing process, you know that you can revise after you have drafted as much as you can. You can employ a process even when writing a 50-minute in-class essay. By planning to save 10 minutes at the end of the period for eliminating irrelevant points, clarifying others, and correcting errors, you can draft without becoming obsessed with whether or not you are making mistakes.

Exercise 1

Write an essay of approximately 500 words in which you describe your ideal working conditions for writing and identify which of these conditions you could create when writing an in-class essay.

30c Essay tests require special preparation.

(1) Read instructions and questions carefully.

Students who normally write well sometimes do poorly when writing in-class essays and essay exams because they are in such a rush to begin writing that they do not read the instructions carefully or adequately consider which question best suits them. Before you start writing, read the instructions carefully and note specific directions. For example, realizing that you must "answer questions A *and* B" is very different from believing that you must "answer question A *or* B." If you are responsible for more than one question, note how many points each is worth. When no points are specified, you can tell which questions are the most important if an instructor recommends spending more time on one than on another. If one question will count more heavily than the others, pace yourself with this fact in mind.

Invest a few minutes in studying the questions so that you do not make a false start and waste time. Most questions contain specific instructions about how, as well as what, you are to answer. Be alert for words like *compare, define, argue,* and *cause* that identify your task and provide cues for organizing your response. Other terms like *discuss* or *explain* are less specific, but they may be linked to words like *similar* or *differ* (which signal a comparison or contrast), *identify* (which signals definition or description), or *why* (which signals the need to identify causes). Also note language indicating whether you are being asked to report information or to offer your own views. Words like *think, defend,* and *opinion* signal that you are expected to frame a thesis (28d) and support it. When asked to answer more than one question, decide whether they are likely to overlap. If you accidentally drift into answering more than one question at a time, you might find yourself with nothing more to say when you get to the next section of your exam.

(2) Decide how to organize your response.

Although time constraints may keep you from creating an outline, you should always be able to find time to draft an informal working plan (28e). Identify the thesis you will offer, then list the most important points you plan to cover. These points might occur to you randomly, and you might subsequently decide to rearrange them, but the first step is to create a list that does justice to your topic. When you have finished the list, you can review it: Delete any points that seem irrelevant or not important enough to discuss in the time allowed. Then number the remaining points in a logical sequence determined by chronology (reporting events in the order in which they occurred), by causation (showing how one thing led to another), or by order of importance (going from the most important point to the least important). An alternative plan is to arrange your points in order of increasing importance, but this can be risky when writing under pressure: if you run out of time sooner than you expected, you may not get to your most important point.

Here is an example of an edited list quickly composed during the first few minutes of an essay exam. It was jotted down in response to the following question: "Some readers believe that *The Merchant of Venice* is racist. Discuss the treatment of Shylock in this play. Do you think the play is anti-Semitic? If so, why? If not, why not?"

THESIS: Though the treatment of Shylock is racist, it must be understood in context.

if time allows →

6. play should be read by students mature enough to understand the context

~~Shylock's daughter~~

tie together

1. old stereotypes about Jews are reinforced

2. Shylock has many negative qualities: mention the "pound of flesh" — why he's asking for it

5. Shakespeare also shows the human, sympathetic side of Shylock, especially in the "Do I not bleed?" speech

3. other characters make comments about his being a Jew

4. treatment of Shylock is much milder than was common in Shakespeare's day

The language of an assignment sometimes tells you how to organize it. For example, consider the following task.

Discuss how the building of railroads influenced the development of Canada during the second half of the nineteenth century.

At first glance, this assignment might seem to state the topic without indicating how to organize a discussion of it. To *influence,* however, is to be responsible for certain consequences. In this case, the building of railroads is a cause and you are being asked to identify its effects (27d(4), 28e). Once you have recognized this, you might decide to discuss different effects in different paragraphs.

Here is another example:

Consider the concept of the unconscious as defined by Freud and by Jung. On what points did they agree? How did they disagree?

The reference to two psychoanalysts, coupled with words like *agree* and *disagree,* indicates that your task is to compare and contrast. You could organize your response to this question by first discussing Freud's ideas and then discussing Jung's—preferably covering the same points in the same order. Or you could begin by establishing similarities and then move on to differences. There is almost always more than one way to organize a thoughtful response. Devoting at least a few minutes to planning your organization can help you demonstrate what you know.

(3) State main points clearly.

Instructors who read essay exams and in-class essays are usually looking to see how well students have understood assigned material. Stating your main points clearly will help them make that evaluation. In a weak essay, important points may be buried where they can be overlooked while minor or irrelevant points are prominent. Make your main points stand out from the rest of the essay by identifying them somehow. For instance, you can use transitional expressions such as *first, second, third;* you can underline each main point; or you can create headings to guide the reader. By the time you have drafted most of your essay, you should know what your key points are. Because the act of writing often generates new ideas, these points may differ from those you had planned to make. Use your conclusion to summarize your main points. If you tend to make points that differ from those you had in mind when you started, try leaving space for an introduction at the beginning of the essay and then drafting your introduction after you have drafted the rest.

(4) Stick to the question.

Always answer the exact question as directly as you can. Sometimes you may know more about a related question than the one assigned. Do not wander from the question being asked to answer the question you wish had been asked. Similarly, make sure that you follow your thesis as you answer the question; do not include irrelevant material. If you move away from your original thesis because better ideas have occurred to you as you write, go back and revise your thesis (**28d**). If you drift into including irrelevant material, draw a line through it.

(5) Revise and proofread.

Save a few minutes to re-read your answer. Make whatever deletions and corrections you think are necessary. If time allows, think about what is not on the page by asking yourself if there is anything you have left out that you can still manage to include. Unless you are certain that your instructor values neatness more than competence, do not worry about making corrections. Doing so will allow you to focus on improving what you have written, whereas re-copying your answer just to make it look neat can be an inefficient use of time (and possibly leave you with only half your essay re-copied at the end of the exam). Make sure, however, that your instructor will be able to read your changes. Clarify any illegible scribbles. If you have added ideas in the margins, in each case draw a line to a caret (∧) marking the exact place in the text where you want them to be placed. Finally, check spelling, punctuation, and sentence structure (29d).

Exercise 2

Write three questions that you might be asked on an essay exam for a course you are currently taking. Then choose the question you like best and write a description of how you would organize your response.

Exercise 3

Bring in an old exam from another course. If the exam posed any difficulties for you, be prepared to identify them and discuss how you responded. If you liked this exam, be ready to explain why.

Chapter 31

Reading and Thinking Critically

To read and think critically means to distinguish between ideas that are credible and those that are less so. In addition to reading for content by identifying the key points in a text, critical readers think about what they read and evaluate it. Critical thinking is essential for critical reading. It is also essential when writing arguments (chapter 32) and undertaking other types of writing (chapters 34 and 35).

Critical readers know that they cannot believe everything they are told. They understand that different writers discussing the same topic and drawing on the same evidence can reach significantly different conclusions. Instead of routinely agreeing with the writer who seems to reinforce reassuringly familiar beliefs, critical readers are likely to discover that different writers have each revealed a part of what may ultimately prove to be true. The challenge for readers, then, is to identify which ideas make more sense than others and to determine the extent to which those ideas are reliable and useful. In addition, critical readers study language carefully because they understand that writers influence readers by using a range of rhetorical strategies that may not be apparent at first glance.

Because thinking and reading critically involve making well-reasoned choices, these closely related skills are among the most valuable you can acquire. You can master them through practice, just as you have mastered other skills.

31a Previewing can help you read a text critically.

To **preview** reading means to orient yourself to a text by assessing how difficult it will be and what you are likely to learn from it. When you understand what a task demands, you are more likely to complete it successfully. Comprehending what you read is the first step toward reading critically. After all, you cannot determine the merits of a text without understanding its content.

When you page through a magazine looking for articles that seem interesting, you are, in a sense, previewing it. A simple preview of this sort can help you identify what you want to read, but it might also lead you to an article that disappoints you. A more systematic preview can give you better results, especially when you are undertaking serious reading in university.

To preview reading assignments, ask yourself the following questions:

Checklist for Previewing a Text
- How long is this work, and how long is its average paragraph? How much time will I need to read this piece carefully?
- What do I already know about this subject? Can I keep this knowledge in mind as I read so I can establish some immediate connections with this text?
- Do I have any strong feelings about this subject that could interfere with my ability to comprehend how it is treated in this text?
- Do I know anything about this author? If this author is already familiar to me, can I trust what he or she writes? If this author is unfamiliar to me, does this source include

continued

continued from previous page

any biographical information that will help me assess his or her credibility? (See 31d.)

- What can I learn from the title? Is there a subtitle? If there are subheadings in the text, what do they reveal about the organization of this work?
- Does this book include a table of contents or an index? Does this article include an abstract? Are there graphs, figures, or other visual aids? If so, how can this material be useful to me?
- Is there a bibliography that will indicate how extensive and current the research is?
- Does the introduction or conclusion reveal the thesis of this piece?
- Has the author included a summary near the conclusion or at the end of any of the subsections?
- Would it be easier for me to understand this text if I read something else first?

In addition to asking yourself these questions, you can also benefit from scanning specific sentences and phrases. Although the central idea of a paragraph can occur anywhere within it (chapter 27), it often appears in the first or last sentence. By reading these sentences, you can get a sense of a work's content and organization. You can also scan for key phrases that writers use to signal important points. The phrase *in other words,* for example, signals that a writer is about to paraphrase (33h(4)) a point just made—probably because it is important. Other key phrases include *in the following article* (or chapter), which can signal a statement of the author's focus or purpose; and *in summary, in conclusion,* and *the point I am making,* which signal a restatement or clarification of the author's thesis. In addition, words like *therefore* and *thus* signal that a point is being made about the information just presented.

Previewing is a way to make reading easier and more meaningful. It can also help you select appropriate material when you do research (chapter 33). But remember that previewing a text is not the same as reading it fully and closely.

31b Critical readers distinguish between fact and opinion.

As you acquire information through reading, you may believe that you are acquiring **facts**—reliable pieces of information that can be verified through independent sources or procedures. Facts are valued because they are believed to be true. **Opinions** are assertions or inferences that may or may not be based on facts. When these ideas are widely accepted, they may seem to be factual when actually they are not.

Facts are not necessarily more valuable than opinions; a thoughtful opinion may have more merit than a page of random facts. But accepting opinions unsupported by facts can lead you to faulty conclusions that damage your credibility.

To distinguish between fact and opinion, ask yourself questions about what you have read: Can it be proved? Can it be challenged? How often is the same result achieved? (See 31c.) If a statement can consistently be proved true, then it is a fact. If it can be disputed, then it is an opinion.

Fact	Spinach contains iron.
Opinion	Canadians should eat more spinach.

To say that spinach contains iron is to state a well-established fact; it can be verified by consulting published studies or by conducting laboratory testing. But to say that Canadians need to eat more spinach is to express an opinion that may or may not be supported by facts. When considering the statement "Canadians should eat more spinach," a critical reader might ask, "What is spinach good for? How important is iron? Do *all* Canadians suffer from iron deficiency? Is spinach the only source of iron?" Exploring any of these questions could lead to discovering differences of opinion as well as learning some facts.

Because the facts themselves can change, critical readers and thinkers need to remain flexible as they distinguish between fact and opinion. The erroneous belief that the sun revolves around the earth was once considered a fact, and Newtonian physics was once believed to be indisputably true. Describing what can easily happen in research, a distinguished physician writes that a good scientist must be prepared for the day when his or her life work is suddenly called into question:

> All the old ideas—last week's ideas in some cases—are no longer good ideas. The hard facts have softened, melted away and vanished under the pressure of new hard facts.
> —LEWIS THOMAS, "The Art of Teaching Science"

No matter how knowledgeable, a reader who is unwilling to assimilate new information and question old ideas cannot expect to meet the challenges of a rapidly changing world. The collapse of the Soviet Union, for example, necessitated that other countries devise new approaches to foreign policy. Or, to take another example, researchers studying AIDS must maintain their intellectual dexterity so they can adapt their work as new information becomes available.

Exercise 1

Determine which of the following statements are fact and which are opinion. Explain your decisions in writing and be prepared to discuss your choices in class.

1. Toronto's CN Tower is taller than the Calgary Tower.
2. Toronto's CN Tower is a far more appealing structure than the Calgary Tower.
3. Albert Einstein donated his violin to the Mozart Appreciation Society.
4. Mozart's music lacks the emotional intensity of Beethoven's.
5. Finding a job without a post-secondary education is impossible these days.
6. It rains more in Victoria than in any other city in Canada.
7. The Dieppe raid, which took place during the Second World War, was a terrible tragedy for Canada.
8. The Canadian forces that took part in the raid on Dieppe during the Second World War suffered heavy casualties.
9. The Toronto Blue Jays were the best team in baseball in the early 1990s.
10. It is a known fact that men can handle pressure better than women.

31c   Critical readers look for evidence.

Critical readers expect writers to support their claims with ample evidence consisting of facts and other data such as personal experience and observation. When you are reading a work that makes a specific point, ask yourself whether the writer has provided evidence that is accurate, representative, and sufficient. Examine critically any information that writers present. Accurate information should be verifiable. Recognize, however, that a writer may provide you with data that are accurate but unreliable because they are drawn from an exceptional case or a biased sampling. If, for example, you are reading an argument about physician-assisted suicide that draws all its information from material distributed by a medical association, the evidence cited is unlikely to represent the full range of data available on this topic.

Similarly, examine polls and other statistics carefully. How recent is the information, and how was it gathered? For example, to calculate unemployment rates in Canada, the homes of a random sample of 50 000 families are visited to find out how many people have been temporarily laid off, are waiting to start a new job within four weeks, or do not have a job but have looked actively and unsuccessfully for paid work in the last four weeks. This method of measuring unemployment fails to consider those who are underemployed or who have given up looking for employment.

To decide how much evidence is appropriate, consider the size and originality of the claim. As a general rule, a writer who takes an unusual position on an issue will need to provide more evidence than a writer who has taken a less controversial stand. But in either case, a surplus is usually better than a deficit. Be sure, however, to consider the quality and significance of the evidence.

Exercise 2

Study the evidence in the following two excerpts. How accurate and reliable is the evidence in each? Explain your opinion in writing.

[1]Every television journalist soon learns that the picture comes first. [2]Words and other sounds, as well as the structure of a television news story, make an important contribution to the story's impact on the viewer, but only in a supporting role.

[3]Without dramatic and eye-catching images, even the most important news story is difficult to convey on television; conversely, a relatively insignificant and routine event, such as a highway accident, fire or incident of domestic violence, will rate prominence on television news if the camera has caught the action.   —PETER DESBARATS

[1]Still, the landscape is littered with mines that Aboriginal young people must somehow dodge in order to succeed: systematic racism, and higher rates of illness, disease, suicide, substance abuse, school drop-out levels and unemployment. [2]From the very moment of birth—even in the womb— Aboriginal children face infinitely more challenges than non-Native babies. [3]Higher rates of smoking, alcohol, and poly-drug use among Aboriginal mothers compromise the health and survivability of the fetus, as well as the child's long-term future. [4]Almost twice as many Aboriginal babies die in infancy than do other Canadian infants, despite a steady improvement in Aboriginal infant mortality over the last 40 years. [5]In the 1960s in Canada, 60 Aboriginal babies died for every 1000 live births. [6]That improved to 23.7 deaths for every 1000 Aboriginal births by 1980. [7]Today, the deaths of Aboriginal babies average about 12 to 14 per 1000 births, but that is still far higher than the national mortality rate of about 6 per 1000. [8]Premature births and low birth weight, both of which are far more common in Aboriginal babies, can impair an infant's ability to thrive and may even lead to lifelong health problems. [9]Aboriginal babies are three times more likely to die in the first six months of life from Sudden Infant Death Syndrome.
—SUZANNE FOURNIER and ERNIE CREY,
"We Can Heal: Aboriginal Children Today"

 31d   Readers must evaluate a writer's credibility.

Critical readers look for evidence that helps them determine whether an author is well informed and fair-minded.

To determine how credible a writer is, ask yourself the following questions:

> **Checklist for Evaluating Credibility**
> • Does the writer support claims with evidence?
> • Does the writer reveal how and where evidence was obtained?
> • Does the writer recognize that other points of view may be legitimate?
> • Does the writer use sarcasm or make personal attacks on opponents?
> • Does the writer reach a conclusion that is in proportion to the amount of evidence provided?
> • Does the writer have credentials that invest the work with authority?

Thoughtful writers support their claims with evidence (31c, 32c) and reach conclusions that seem justified by the amount of evidence provided. They reveal how and where they obtained this evidence (34a, 34b, and 34d), and their tone (29a) is appropriate for their purpose, audience, and occasion (28a). Moreover, they show that they have given fair consideration to views with which they disagree (32c(2)). As you evaluate credibility, question any writer who seems entirely one-sided, but also question any writer who seems overly anxious to please.

Exercise 3

Evaluate the credibility of the following excerpt from an argument against The Atlantic Groundfish Strategy (TAGS).

¹In thinking about both the failure of TAGS and the design of any future program, we must remember why a program is even needed. ²There are too many people trying to live from

the fishery, especially in Newfoundland. [3]Too many people means more fishing effort than the stocks will bear, plus politicized decision-making over access to the stocks, as politicians prefer short-term electoral success to prudent husbanding of the resource. [4]Add to this poisonous brew a corrupted unemployment insurance program that each year turns a meagre fishing income into a comfortable life. [5]Instead of the slow steady outflow of population that low incomes and dwindling resource would produce, the outcome is periodic collapse of the over-fished stocks and crisis in rural fishing communities. [6]The latest collapse gave rise, in 1992, to the Northern Cod Moratorium, which occasioned the largest industrial layoff in Canadian history.

—"A Farewell to TAGS," *The Globe and Mail* editorial

Exercise 4

Read a series of editorials or letters in a newspaper. Select one that is one-sided or inadequately supported; select another that is well supported and fair-minded. Your choices should be of similar length. Prepare to read them in class and to explain your evaluation of them.

31e Critical thinkers understand inductive reasoning.

When writers use **inductive reasoning,** they begin with a number of facts or observations and use them to draw a general conclusion. Inductive reasoning is commonly used in daily life. For example, if you get indigestion several times after eating sauerkraut, you might conclude that eating sauerkraut gives you indigestion. This use of evidence to form a generalization is called an **inductive leap,** and the leap should be in proportion to the amount of evidence gathered. It is reasonable to stop eating sauerkraut if it consistently makes you ill—especially if you had sampled sauerkraut from more than one source (since different preparations could change the effect). But if you conclude that no one should eat sauerkraut, your conclusion would be too general for the amount of evidence in question.

Because it involves leaping from evidence to interpreting it, inductive reasoning can help writers reach probable, believable conclusions, but not some absolute truth that will endure forever. Making a small leap from evidence to a conclusion that seems probable is not the same as jumping to a sweeping conclusion that could easily be challenged. Generally, the greater the evidence, the more reliable the conclusion.

Science's use of inductive reasoning is known as the scientific method. For instance, early medical studies equated diets high in fat with coronary disease. The scientific community reserved judgment since the early studies were based on small samplings, but later studies with broader sampling confirmed the early reports. Although all persons with coronary disease cannot be studied, the sampling is now large enough for scientists to draw the conclusion with more confidence. Nevertheless, a critical thinker would still examine the available evidence carefully and ask a number of questions about it. If the research had been conducted primarily on men, would the conclusions be equally applicable to women? Are the conclusions equally applicable to people of all races? To what extent have the researchers controlled all variables? Does the evidence support the conclusion that has been drawn, or should the conclusion be modified? Because they are critical thinkers who ask such questions, scientists are often motivated to do further research.

When used in persuasive writing (chapter 32), inductive reasoning often employs examples. When you cannot cite all the instances that support your well-reasoned conclusion, one or a few examples closely related to the point you are making will provide evidence. (See 27c.) In the following inductively organized paragraph, a number of examples support the last sentence.

> The 1990 Governor General's Awards established Ann-Marie MacDonald (who won the drama prize) and Nino Ricci (who won for fiction) as important, rising writers. Poet and travel writer Karen Connelly became a best seller on the strength of her 1993 non-fiction award; novelist Russell Smith first gained wide attention when he was shortlisted for the 1994 GG for fiction. The small presses that published these shortlisted books—Coach House, Cormorant, Turnstone and Porcupine's Quill, respectively—were able to profit from GG publicity because it did not cost them the promise of $1,250 to keep their unknown young writers in contention. The absence of any fee has permitted the GGs to create new stars, while the Giller has merely confirmed the status of writers already possessed of a wealthy publisher. The Giller's exclusive focus on English-language fiction, furthermore, curtails public awareness of other forms of writing. As we hear less about the GGs, we are also less likely to learn who wrote last year's best biography, play or book of poems—or to hear about French-language writing.
>
> —STEPHEN HENIGHAN, "Giller's Version"

How you organize your inductive reasoning varies with the situation. You may wish to provide your evidence first and then offer your conclusion. Or you may wish to reverse the order by stating the conclusion first, in the form of a topic sentence (27a(1)) or a thesis statement (28d), and then presenting the supporting examples.

31f Critical thinkers understand deductive reasoning.

When writers use **deductive reasoning**, they begin with generalizations (premises) and apply them to a specific

NEL

instance to draw a conclusion about that instance. For example, if you know that all licensed mechanics must complete an apprenticeship program and that Martha wants to be a licensed mechanic, then you could conclude that Martha must complete an apprenticeship program. This argument can be expressed in a structure called a **syllogism**.

Major Premise	All licensed mechanics must complete an apprenticeship program.
Minor Premise	Martha wants to be a licensed mechanic.
Conclusion	Martha must complete an apprenticeship program.

Sometimes premises are not stated.

Martha wants to be a licensed mechanic, so she must complete an apprenticeship program.

In this sentence, the unstated premise is that all licensed mechanics must complete an apprenticeship program. A syllogism with an unstated premise—or even an unstated conclusion—is called an **enthymeme**. Enthymemes are frequently found in arguments and can be very effective in writing, but they should be examined with care since the omitted statement may be inaccurate. "Samuel is from British Columbia, so he must like salmon" contains the unstated major premise that "Everyone from British Columbia likes salmon." This premise is unacceptable because there is no reason to assume that everyone from a particular region shares the same taste in food—even if the food in question happens to be a local specialty. As a critical reader, you must accept the truth of a writer's premises in order to agree with the writer's conclusion.

A deductive argument must be both true and valid. A **true** argument is based on generally accepted, well-backed premises. A **valid** argument is based on logical thinking.

The conclusion in the following syllogism is valid because the conclusion follows logically from the major and minor premises, but it is not true because the major premise is not generally accepted.

Major Premise	All redheads are brilliant.
Minor Premise	Jane is a redhead.
Conclusion	Therefore Jane is brilliant.

The following deductively organized paragraph, from an argument in favour of cloning, draws on the premise stated in the first sentence.

> We cannot afford to ignore the potential benefits of cloning by limiting our discussion to the possibility that this bold technique will be used by billionaires and celebrities to make copies of themselves. Children could be born free of genetic diseases, even though both their parents are carriers, because the flawed genes could be replaced in the embryo with normal DNA. Patients with leukemia, whose healthy cells are cloned, could receive fresh bone marrow without the danger of rejection. Burn victims could receive grafts of soft, new skin from cloned cells. Patients with Parkinson's or other brain diseases could be provided with neutral tissue that is genetically identical to their own. At a time when cloning of human DNA is routinely done in biomedical research and current medical practices are insufficient, new options must be considered. The benefits of cloning may outweigh the risks.

According to the reasoning in this paragraph, the benefits of cloning may outweigh the risks. This conclusion rests on the premise that we cannot afford to ignore the potential health benefits of cloning. If current medical practice is not ensuring people's health and if new techniques are being developed to bridge the gap, then it is logical to conclude that these new techniques should not be dismissed out of hand.

Exercise 5

Supply the missing premise in the following statements and determine if the reasoning is valid and true.

1. Frank's father was an alcoholic. Frank must be an alcoholic.
2. Jack's a great musician. He gets asked to play at clubs all the time.
3. Spring will be six weeks late this year. The groundhog saw its shadow.
4. All towns in Southern Ontario must test their drinking water for *E. coli* bacteria. Peterborough is a town in Southern Ontario.
5. All stockbrokers have to complete a course in ethics. Mani wants to become a stockbroker.

31g The Toulmin method is an alternative approach to reasoning.

Another way of using logic is through the method devised by Stephen Toulmin in *The Uses of Argument* (New York: Cambridge UP, 1964). To create a working logic suitable for the needs of writers, Toulmin drew on deductive reasoning but put less emphasis on the formal conventions of a syllogism. His approach sees argument as the progression from accepted facts or evidence (**data**) to a conclusion (**claim**) by way of a statement (**warrant**) that establishes a reasonable relationship between the two. For example, in the argument,

> Since mechanics are required to complete an apprenticeship program, and since Martha wants to be a mechanic, Martha must complete an apprenticeship program,

the claim is that Martha must complete an apprenticeship program, and the evidence (data) consists of the fact that she wants to be a mechanic. The warrant, that mechanics are required to complete an apprenticeship program, ties the two statements together, making the conclusion follow from the data.

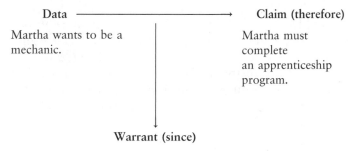

Data ⟶ Claim (therefore)

Martha wants to be a mechanic.

Martha must complete an apprenticeship program.

Warrant (since)

Mechanics must complete an apprenticeship program.

The warrant is often implied in arguments and, like the unstated premise in the syllogism, needs careful examination to be acceptable.

Of course, few arguments are as simple as this example. For instance, Martha may have been exempted from the apprenticeship program because she has a special skill for which there is an urgent need. In such cases, writers can make allowances for exceptions. Qualifiers such as *usually, probably,* and *possibly* show the degree of certainty of the conclusion, and rebuttal terms such as *unless* allow writers to indicate exceptions.

> **Since** Martha is a licensed mechanic, she **probably** completed an apprenticeship program **unless** an exception was made for her.

Notice that the boldfaced transitional words express logical relationships among ideas in the argument and corresponding elements in the sentence. Like inductive and deductive reasoning, the Toulmin model makes allowances for important elements of probability.

⚠️ **CAUTION** Too many qualifiers can make an argument seem hesitant and unconvincing.

In the following paragraph, the writer claims that we should let those with more money "pay for some of their non-essential medical care." His data are that these people already buy better cars and houses, retire earlier, travel first class, and take better vacations. His warrant is that "we would keep the private money in the country, we would create a new industry, and we would improve health care for everybody."

In Canada, those who have more money can buy better cars and houses, retire earlier, travel first class, and take better vacations. Why don't we let these people pay for some of their "non-essential" medical care? The money the state saves by not having to cover their costs could be spent enhancing the public system, or shortening waiting lists. As long as a proper mechanism is put in place to monitor this private industry (to ensure that a two-tiered system does not evolve), this is a "win-win" proposal. We could keep all the private money in the country, we would create a new industry, and we would improve health care for everybody. —CHRISTOPHER SIMPSON, "Saving Health Care by Privatization"

Exercise 6

Analyze the argument in the following excerpt by asking yourself the following questions:

a. What is the conclusion or claim?
b. What data support the claim?
c. What is the warrant that underlies the argument?

[1]When one person (or a group) is repeatedly hurtful to another, that's bullying. [2]We grownups have not been very good at stopping it at school, summer camp, clubs or in the neighbourhood. [3]Creative denial has been our strategy.

⁴Denial starts with dismissing acts of bullying as insignificant. ⁵We ignore little signs, we avoid making inquiries. ⁶Or we tell the victims to grow a thicker skin and stand up for themselves.

⁷In the obvious cases, we label the bully a bad seed, a wicked or damaged child who should be removed from the situation. ⁸And then we fall silent again, because we don't know what to do, and because to admit that bullying is common would be to admit that our beloved children might be getting hurt, and we aren't going to help them.

—JOANNE KATES, "It's Open Season on Bullies—at Last"

Critical thinkers recognize logical fallacies.

Fallacies are lapses in logic that can result from misusing or misrepresenting evidence, from relying on faulty premises, or from distorting the issues. They can be the result of poor thinking, but they can also be a deliberate attempt to manipulate—as suggested by the origin of the term *fallacia,* which is Latin for "deceit." Fallacies are common, especially in persuasive writing. (See chapter 32.) Here are some of the major fallacies. Be alert for them in your reading, and try to avoid them in your thinking.

(1) **Ad hominem:** A personal attack on an opponent that draws attention away from the issues under consideration.

> **Faulty** He is unfit to be a member of Parliament because he drank too much when he was a university student. [Whether or not this candidate drank too much when he was young may reveal something about his character, but voters might decide that he now has political skills and principles that could benefit the country.]

(2) **Appeal to tradition:** An argument that says something should be done a certain way simply because it has been done that way in the past.

  Faulty We should not allow women to join this club because we have never let women join before. [Times change; what was acceptable in the past is not necessarily acceptable in the present.]

(3) **Bandwagon:** An argument saying, in effect, "Everyone's doing or saying or thinking this, so you should too."

  Faulty Everyone else is cheating, so why shouldn't you? [The majority is not always right.]

(4) **Begging the question:** A statement that assumes what needs to be proved.

  Faulty We need to fire the thieves in the police department. [If there are thieves working in the police department, this point needs to be established.]

(5) **Equivocation:** An assertion that falsely relies on the use of a term in two different senses.

  Faulty We know this is a natural law because it feels natural. [When first used, *natural* means principles derived from nature or reason; when used again, it means easy or simple because of being in accord with one's own nature.]

(6) **False analogy:** The assumption that because two things are alike in some ways, they must be alike in other ways.

  Faulty Since the books are about the same length and cover the same material, one is probably as good as the other. [The length and coverage of the books cannot predict whether one is as good as the other.]

(7) **False authority:** The assumption that an expert in one field can be a credible expert in another.

  Faulty The transportation budget must be cut, as the country's leading pediatrician has shown. [Pediatric medicine is unrelated to economics or political science.]

(8) **False cause:** The assumption that because one event follows another, the first is the cause of the second. Sometimes called *post hoc, ergo propter hoc* ("after this, so because of this").

  Faulty The new tax assessor took office last January, and crime in the streets has already increased 25 percent. [The assumption is that having a new tax assessor caused the increase in crime, an assumption unlikely to be true.]

(9) **False dilemma:** Stating that only two alternatives exist when in fact there are more than two (sometimes called the *either/or* fallacy).

  Faulty We have only two choices: to build more solar power plants or to be completely dependent on foreign oil. [In fact, other possibilities exist.]

(10) **Guilt by association:** An unfair attempt to make someone responsible for the beliefs or actions of others.

  Faulty Senator James must be dishonest because she belongs to the same club as that judge who was recently disbarred. [People can belong to the same club—or live in the same neighbourhood—without engaging in the same behaviour.]

(11) **Hasty generalization:** A generalization based on too little evidence or on exceptional or biased evidence.

> **Faulty** Ellen is a poor student because she failed her first quiz. [Her performance may improve in the weeks ahead.]

(12) **Non sequitur:** A statement that does not follow logically from what has just been said—a conclusion that does not follow from the premises.

> **Faulty** Erik is honest; therefore, he will get a good job. [Many honest people do not get good jobs.]

(13) **Oversimplification:** A statement or argument that leaves out relevant considerations about an issue to imply that there is a single cause or solution for a complex problem.

> **Faulty** We can eliminate hunger by growing more food. [Increasing the amount of food produced does not guarantee that the hungry will have access to it.]

(14) **Red herring:** Dodging the real issue by drawing attention to an irrelevant issue (sometimes called *ignoring the question*).

> **Faulty** Why worry about overcrowded schools when we ought to be trying to attract a professional hockey franchise? [Professional sports have nothing to do with overcrowded schoolrooms.]

(15) **Slippery slope:** The assumption that if one thing is allowed it will be only the first step in a downward spiral.

> **Faulty** A guide that shows surgeons' success rates will lead to surgeons' turning away more severely ill patients. [U.S. states with similar guides report an increase in the number of critically ill patients being treated.]

Exercise 7

Identify the fallacies in the following statements. For each statement, write one or two sentences in which you explain the flaw in reasoning.

1. The last time the Toronto Blue Jays won a World Series, the NDP was in power in Ontario; therefore, if we want the Blue Jays to win another World Series, we have to vote the NDP back into power in Ontario.
2. If we don't strengthen censorship, we will eventually have pornography on prime-time TV.
3. Fred's car is the same colour and size as Mort's, so they probably have similar performance.
4. We shouldn't sponsor girl's hockey because boys have been the only ones who've played hockey in Canada.
5. I intend on voting for the Rhinoceros Party this year because everybody I know voted for them last year.
6. As one of the country's wealthiest men, Conrad Black condemned the art exhibit for its lack of colour and style.
7. The real problem in our cities is not homelessness; it's the fact that decent, hard-working people are paying too much for their parking permits.
8. Who cares whether or not she's studied economics? Helen wouldn't make a good councillor because she's lazy.
9. We can curb the increase in cases of asthma in this city by giving everybody gas masks.
10. He was wearing a brown corduroy jacket with suede patches on the elbows, so he must be an English professor.

Exercise 8

Examine several recent magazine advertisements and study the claims the ads make. Look specifically for examples of logical fallacies. Choose one ad that seems especially illogical. Bring a copy of it to class, as well as a paragraph in which you explain why the ad is unconvincing.

Exercise 9

Read the following paragraph and identify the logical fallacies you find in it. Then, adopting the point of view of someone opposed to animal experimentation, write two or three paragraphs responding to the argument offered here.

[1]As the Oscar-winning director Scavan Kleck has argued, "Animal experimentation saves lives." [2]Isn't the life of a little girl more important than the life of a chimpanzee? [3]We have to choose: we can either experiment on animals to find cures for life-threatening diseases or we can stand by helplessly while thousands of children die. [4]Experimentation is necessary because research is important. [5]And why should we worry about what happens to animals in laboratories when the real problem is how people treat their pets? [6]Advocates of animal rights are a bunch of sentimental vegetarians who don't care what happens to children, and they will never be satisfied with banning painful experiments on animals. [7]If they succeed in getting legislation passed that restricts experimentation, it's only a question of time before the sale of meat is prohibited. [8]Just look at the trouble they've already caused. [9]The cost of research has soared since people started protesting against animal experimentation.

Chapter 32 | Writing Arguments

When you are planning to write an argument, you begin by following the same process you use to write other essays. You consider your purpose, audience, and occasion (**28a**), find an appropriate subject (**28b**), explore that subject (**28c**), establish a thesis (**28d**), and organize your ideas (**28e**). In addition, you use logic (chapter **31**), provide evidence to support your claims (**31c**), establish your authority to be writing on the subject you have chosen (**31d**), and determine whether it would be appropriate to appeal to the feelings of your audience (**32d**).

As you proceed, you should understand the importance of arguing ethically and treating your opponents with respect. Argument is a way to discover truth and negotiate differences. It should not be used to punish or ridicule people with whom you happen to disagree.

32a Different arguments have different purposes.

When writing an argument, you should consider your purpose. It may be to pursue the truth until you have formed an opinion that seems reasonable. It may be to convince an audience of readers that your position has merit. Or you might go farther and seek to persuade your audience to undertake a specific action that follows from the position you have taken. Just as important, your purpose could be to establish a consensus that brings people with differing views together. You can have a single purpose or more than one, but one purpose should predominate.

When you are writing to pursue the truth, you are writing **to inquire**. In conversation, you probably have ample experience with argument as a means of inquiry. When two or more people engage in conversation to explore what they think, they are engaging in inquiry. Two friends who meet to talk about a decision one of them needs to make are using argument as inquiry. Such an argument does not involve quarrelling; it is shaped instead by the give-and-take of dialogue as different ideas are exchanged. Philosophers and rhetoricians call this kind of serious conversation **dialectic**. Many of the great works of ancient philosophy take the form of a dialogue written along these lines. You might practise dialectic by actually writing a dialogue between two speakers or by simply weighing the pros and cons of differing views until you arrive at a conclusion that seems true to you.

If you have already reached a conclusion to which you are committed, then your purpose is probably **to convince** other people to accept your position to some extent. This purpose can take at least four different forms. If there is little likelihood that you can convince an audience to change a strongly held opinion, you could be achieving a great deal by simply convincing them that your position deserves to be taken seriously. If the members of your audience are not firmly and absolutely committed to a position, then you might write in the hope of convincing them to agree with you. If they agree with you in principle, then you might convince them to undertake a specific action—such as voting for the candidate you are supporting. Finally, if there are fundamental differences within your audience, you might write to reduce the extent of their conflict by establishing common ground and negotiating a compromise.

Exercise 1

Study the following paragraph and decide what the author's purpose seems to be. Then write a paragraph stating that purpose and the grounds that led you to your conclusion.

[1]The only potentially effective Canadian alternative is an appointed Senate, consisting of nonpartisan individuals chosen on the basis of their records as jurists, business or union representatives, community leaders, educators, and similarly qualified people from a variety of backgrounds. [2]They may be chosen in a manner similar to that used to appoint the judiciary, or the membership of the Order of Canada. [3]Above all, the basis for selection must primarily be competence, rather than region of residence or overt political affiliation.

—JOHN D. DENNISON, "Where the Triple-E Argument Fails"

32b Argument assumes the existence of differing views.

If there are no differences, then there is no need to argue. The first step toward finding a subject for argumentation is to consider issues that inspire different opinions. If most people already share the same opinion—believing, for example, that it is nice to sit by a fireplace on a cold winter night—then there is little point in writing an argument espousing this view. Widely held opinions could become topics for expressive or informative essays (28a), such as "Why I Love Fireplaces" or "How to Build Your Own Fireplace," but they lack the element of controversy found in an appropriate topic for argumentation.

Behind any effective argument is a question that can generate more than one reasonable answer. If you ask "Is there poverty in our country?" almost anyone will agree that there is. But if you ask "Why is there poverty in our country?" or "What can we do to eliminate poverty?" you will hear very different answers. When you write an argument, you are either looking for an answer to a question or showing that you have found the answer. Choose a question that needs an answer, then focus (28c) on the part of this question that you will address in your essay.

A good subject may occur to you if you note how you respond to the views of others. Your response to a class discussion or material you have read for class could lead to a good essay. When you are free to choose your own subject, you should be able to think of many suitable ones if you stay abreast of current events by reading newspapers and magazines. Even if you are doing something as simple as listening to a television commentator, you might find yourself agreeing or disagreeing with what you hear, and a good essay could be developed from this response. To find a subject, you can also try freewriting and listing (28c(1)).

When you think you have found a suitable subject, you can benefit from asking yourself a series of questions:

Checklist for Evaluating a Subject
- Is there more than one possible response? Would anyone be likely to disagree with me?
- Do I know enough about this subject? Can I find out what I need to know?
- Have I narrowed the subject so that I can do justice to it in the space I have available?
- Do I have a purpose in writing about this subject?
- Are the subject and purpose appropriate for my audience?

If you can answer "yes" to all these questions, you can feel confident about your subject and move further into the writing process.

32c Argument requires development.

You will sometimes need to do research to find information on your subject. (See chapter 33.) At other times you will be able to write directly from your own experience and observations. In either case, you should explore your subject in enough depth to have a number of reasons to support your conclusion and enough evidence to support these reasons. In addition, you should consider the reasons why other people might disagree with you and be prepared to respond to them.

(1) Effective arguments are well supported.

If you have an opinion or thesis (28d) that you wish to argue, you must have at least one reason for believing as you do. That reason must be established in your paper. Although it is possible to base your case on a single reason, doing so is usually risky. If your audience does not find this reason persuasive, you have no other support for your case. When you show that you have more than one reason for believing as you do, you increase the likelihood that your audience will find merit in your case. For example, suppose you believe in capital punishment and write an argument favouring it on the grounds that it deters crime. Readers who are aware of evidence showing that the death penalty does not deter crime could find your argument well written but dismiss it nevertheless. If you introduce other reasons for supporting the death penalty, then you make a more complex case that cannot be dismissed so readily.

When you are exploring your subject, make a list of the reasons that have led to your belief without trying to edit them. (See 28c(1).) When you are ready to begin drafting (28f), think critically (chapter 31) about the reasons on your list. Some may need to be eliminated because they overlap; some may need to be eliminated because you would have trouble supporting them or because they seem trivial compared with the others. You can then base your argument on the remaining reasons. If additional reasons occur to you as you draft, you can easily add them to your list or incorporate them immediately into your draft.

(2) Effective arguments respond to diverse views.

In addition to listing reasons for believing as you do, you should make a list of reasons why people might disagree with you. Good arguments are never one-sided. If you want to be persuasive, you must demonstrate that you are familiar with views other than yours. The most common strategy for doing so is to introduce reasons why others believe differently and then show why you do not find these reasons convincing. In classical rhetoric, this strategy is called **refutation**. By showing not only the reasons for your position but also the weakness of the objections that can be made against it, you bolster your case significantly.

As you consider opposing views, you are likely to discover some you cannot refute. Do not be surprised to discover that there is merit in other people's views. Issues are often controversial precisely because good arguments can be made by different sides. When you find yourself agreeing with a point raised on another side of the issue in question, you can benefit from offering a **concession**. By openly conceding that you agree with opponents on a specific point, you show that you are fair-minded (31d) and increase your credibility. Concessions also increase the likelihood that opponents will find merit in your case. It is hard to persuade people to agree with you if you insist that they are entirely wrong. If you admit that they are partially right, they are more likely to admit that you could be partially right as well.

E S L   Although it is inappropriate in some cultures to disagree openly with authority or to state your own views frankly, North American readers are accustomed to such directness. Consider the expectations of your audience (28a) and write with these expectations in mind.

Exercise 2

The following paragraph is taken from an argument in an editorial in *The Globe and Mail* in which the authors respond to the widely held view that Canada is a culturally diverse country. Write a short analysis of this paragraph in which you note (a) an opposition argument to which the authors are responding, (b) a refutation that they offer to this argument, (c) a concession that they make, and (d) any questions that this excerpt raises for you.

[1]Even our much-discussed ethnic differences are overstated. [2]Although Canada is an immigrant nation and Canadians spring from a variety of backgrounds, a recent study from the C.D. Howe Institute says that the idea of a "Canadian mosaic"—as distinct from the American "melting pot"—is a fallacy. [3]In *The Illusion of Difference*, University of Toronto sociologists Jeffrey Reitz and Raymond Breton show that immigrants to Canada assimilate as quickly into the mainstream society as immigrants to the United States do. [4]In fact, Canadians are less likely than Americans to favour holding on to cultural differences based on ethnic background. [5]If you don't believe Mr. Reitz and Mr. Breton, visit any big-city high school, where the speech and behaviour of immigrant students just a few years in Canada is indistinguishable from that of any fifth-generation classmate.

—"The Myth of Diversity," *The Globe and Mail,*
June 13, 1994

32d   Different kinds of appeal are often necessary.

If people were entirely rational, persuasion could be achieved through logic alone (chapter 31). But because people are often caught up in their own concerns, feel threatened by differences, or see argument as a kind of combat, they may not even hear what you are saying—no matter how logical it may be. Getting a fair hearing is essential if you want your views to be understood. Theories of argument, from the ancient world to the present, offer advice on how to gain this hearing.

(1) There are three classical appeals.

Aristotle and other important thinkers in the ancient world believed that persuasion is achieved through a combination of three appeals: ethos, logos, and pathos. **Ethos** means demonstrating that you are fair-minded and well informed so that readers can trust what you say. **Logos** is the effective use of critical thinking (chapter 31) and the judicious use of information. It is what you employ when you support your claims, make reasonable conclusions, and avoid logical fallacies (31h). Both logos and ethos are essential to effective argumentation. **Pathos**, or using language that will stir the feelings of your audience, is also an option. Although it can be misused by people who wish to obscure thought, it can be effective when used to establish empathy. When you are trying to be persuasive, remember that human beings have feelings as well as thoughts. Appeal to these feelings if you can, but do not rest your entire case on them.

(2) Rogerian appeals emphasize showing other people
   that you understand them.

Rogerian argument derives from the work of Carl R. Rogers, a psychologist who believed that many problems are the result of a breakdown in communication. In his book *On Becoming a Person* (1961), Rogers argues that people often fail to understand each other because of a natural tendency to judge and evaluate, agree or disagree. He emphasizes the importance of listening carefully to what others say and understanding their ideas. His model calls for having the courage to suspend judgment until you are able to restate fairly and accurately what others believe. When each person in a conflict demonstrates this ability, the likelihood of misunderstanding is significantly reduced. One of the advantages of this model is that it can be initiated by a single person in a potentially explosive situation. Another advantage is that it can help foster personal growth. Skills such as paraphrasing and summarizing (33h) are essential to Rogerian argument. Although this model can be used to achieve a number of goals, it is especially useful when building consensus. An argument organized along Rogerian principles would begin with a careful restatement of other people's views, then offer concessions, and only then introduce the position the rest of the essay will support.

32e There are several ways to organize an argument.

To organize your argument, you can begin by outlining or by writing your first draft and then deciding how to improve its organization as you revise (chapter 29). In either case, you can organize your argument deductively (31f) by working to a conclusion that is entailed by your premise or inductively (31e) by moving toward a conclusion that is not entailed by your premise.

Whether you choose to use induction, deduction, or another form of logic (31g), your decision is rhetorical. In other words, unless your instructor asks you to demonstrate a particular type of organization, no one type is unquestionably right for every written argument. The decisions you make about organization should be based on what would be most effective when writing about your subject on this occasion for the audience you have in mind.

There are, however, a few basic principles that are useful to remember.

(1) Introductions can vary.

You can begin by providing background, establishing your premise, offering a quotation, raising a question, or providing a relevant anecdote or example. (See 28f(1).)

(2) Separate reasons are best discussed in separate paragraphs.

You will usually need at least a full paragraph to develop any reason for your opinion, but some reasons could easily take several paragraphs. You might need two paragraphs to explain one reason and only one to explain another because one is more important or because you have more to say about one than the other. But if you try to discuss two separate reasons in the same paragraph, your audience may not follow you or the paragraph may lack unity and coherence (chapter 27).

(3) You can begin a paragraph with a view different from yours.

If you follow this strategy, the rest of the paragraph is available for your response and readers make only one shift between differing views. If you begin a paragraph with your view, then introduce an opponent's view, and then move back to yours, readers must shift direction twice and may miss the point. If you wait until the very end of a paragraph to respond to a different view, you could deny yourself the space you need to respond.

(4) Refutation and concessions are most effective when placed where readers will welcome them.

If you wait until the end of your argument to recognize views that differ from yours, some readers may have already decided that you are too one-sided—and may even have stopped reading. When writers are taking a highly controversial stand on a subject that has inspired strong feelings, they sometimes begin by responding to these strongly held views. Under other circumstances, however, an audience may react negatively to a writer who responds to opposing arguments before offering any reasons to support his or her own view. It is often best to offer at least one strong reason to support your case before turning to opposing views. If you keep at least one other reason in reserve, you can discuss it after your refutation and before your conclusion.

(5) Your conclusion can reinforce your purpose.

If you are writing to inquire, you might conclude with the truth you have reached. If you are writing to convince others, you might end by restating your position and summarizing your reasons for holding it. If you are writing to persuade readers to undertake a specific action, your conclusion should emphasize this point. (See 28f(2).)

Another way to organize your argument is to follow the plan recommended by classical rhetoric:

Introduction	Introduce your issue and capture the attention of your audience.
Statement of Background	Report information the members of your audience need to know before they can understand the position you are going to take.
Exposition	Interpret the information you have included and define any key terms.
Proposition	Introduce the position you are taking.
Proof	Discuss the reasons why you have taken your position.
Refutation	Show why you are not persuaded by the arguments of people who hold a different position.
Conclusion	Summarize your most important points and appeal to your audience's feelings.

Use this plan if it seems appropriate for your rhetorical situation (28a).

32f You can improve your ability to write persuasively by studying the arguments of other writers.

The following paper illustrates one student's response to an assignment in persuasive writing. As you read it, consider whether the author has argued her case effectively.

Janet Kowolsky
Professor Hayes
English 200, Section 1
25 April 2002

Making the Grade

Now that I am finishing my second term in university, I can see that I do much better on some exams than on others. Last term I had four midterm exams and three finals. This term I have already had another three exams, and more will be coming up in a few weeks. The results have been all over the place even though I studied hard for each of these tests. Part of the problem is that I've always tended to do better in some subjects than in others. But that doesn't explain everything. Some of my worst results have been in my best subjects. Performance on an exam is determined not only by how much you study for it and what the questions are like. It is also determined by the circumstances under which the exam is given.

Of the ten exams I've had so far, eight were taken in class and two were taken outside of class. The eight in-class exams differed in terms of how they were set up. Three of these involved studying like crazy without having a clear sense of what I'd be asked to do. My teachers pretty much said, "Make sure you review everything we've covered so far, because this exam is cumulative." Most of them did specify whether they would ask objective or essay questions--although my history teacher last term wouldn't even do that when someone asked. ("I'm still thinking about it," he said.) Also, they did let us know things like whether we could bring a dictionary or calculator to class. But that was about it.

The other exams were a lot less stressful. My history teacher this term gave us a list of six questions a week before our midterm and told us she would choose three of them for our test. This was helpful because I could tell what the exam was going to be like. I still had to study a lot, because I wanted to be able to do a good job with any of these questions, but I had a lot less anxiety preparing for the test. When I was preparing for exams in December, my psychology professor and my biology professor distributed copies of previous exams so that my classmates and I could have a rough idea of what our exam was going to be like. That was also helpful.

Unfortunately, each of these exams had to be taken in a room crowded with other students and filled with tension. Whenever I wanted to pause to think, I'd look around and see other people scribbling away and worry that I was falling behind. When people would start to leave early, I'd stress out completely--thinking something must be wrong with me because I needed all the time that still remained. Then there were a range of irritations and distractions: Losing concentration when someone arrived late and squeezed into the seat next to me, listening to people rummage in their backpacks for supplies, being asked if I had an extra pen, catching sight of other students passing material between them, and feeling like I was some kind of laboratory rat under the eye of the teacher monitoring the room.

Two other tests that I had were entirely different because they were take-home exams. One of these was in my introduction to literature class; the other was in calculus. Although these two exams were set up somewhat differently, they were both excellent. I think more professors should assign take-home exams.

The big advantage of a take-home exam is that you can work on it in a quiet place where you feel safe and comfortable. The questions on my two take-homes were really challenging, but I did well on both of them because I was in my own space. Because the circumstances of a take-home exam are more comfortable doesn't mean that the exam itself has to be easy. If professors eliminated some of the stress of exam taking, they would be able to tell more accurately how much their students really know. Isn't that the purpose of exams?

Some professors may be concerned that students will cheat if they take their exams at home. I have to admit that cheating could be a problem. On the other hand, students who really want to cheat can usually find a way of doing so on regular exams and other assignments. So avoiding take-home exams does not mean that cheating goes away. And take-home exams can be designed to minimize cheating. My literature exam, for example, was an open-book essay exam. It was really useful to be able to look up quotes to back up what I wanted to say, but there's no way I could have passed the exam if I hadn't read the material and thought about it in advance. Theoretically somebody could probably get a friend to take an exam like this for him. But the same thing could happen when we have to write papers. When somebody cheats this way, the professor should be able to tell even if she wasn't there watching the person do it.

Another common argument against take-home exams is that they could become big productions. I've heard some students say that they'd rather get an exam over with in two hours than have a take-home that takes as much work as writing another big paper. I understand these concerns. My literature teacher told us that we could take as long as we wanted on the exam just as long as we handed it in on time, and I ended up spending a whole morning on it. But my calculus professor insisted that we limit ourselves to the two hours we would get during the standard final exam period. We got to choose which two hours we would devote to the exam--and where we would take it--but the exam itself took no longer than any other exam. In other words, take-homes can be designed in different ways to make them appropriate for different classes.

There are a number of other advantages to take-home exams. Finals aren't scheduled during the hours the class met, and this can be a problem for students who have jobs or who have children to take care of. The take-home provides flexibility for such students by being sensitive to their needs. And just as they are more student-friendly, they are also more professor-friendly. Teachers don't have to hang around monitoring a classroom when they've got lots of other things they could be doing. And more important, they get to read better exams. Wouldn't professors be happier to see their students doing well than to see them doing poorly?

Take-home exams can be well designed or badly designed--just like any other assignment. But the flexibility they offer makes them preferable to traditional exams. Professors who have never offered a take-home exam should experiment with them. They will get a chance to do so soon, and I hope they will take advantage of it.

Exercise 3

Write an evaluation of the preceding argument. What is its purpose? What strategies has the author used to satisfy this purpose? How well is it supported, and how well is it organized? Is there anything the author has failed to consider?

32g Non-traditional writing: In writing to persuade, you can use reader response to advantage.

One way to gain the support of an audience is to delay stating your position until the last moment. This tactic opens up the argument to various views, enabling you to present alternate sides of an issue fairly, seemingly without prejudice. This is an especially effective strategy when your audience is hostile or skeptical. Being open to a number of different positions shows that you think there is equal value in all, implying that you have faith in the intelligence, knowledge, goodwill, and so on of persons concerned in the ongoing public debate. These are positive traits. A reader tends to like being seen in a becoming way and often rises to conform to the image you have projected.

Of course, you must ultimately take responsibility and make a tough choice from among several available viewpoints. But if you have written to empower your readership, you will find that many people may be more open to a need to change. The following persuasive essay explores the subject of rink rage, a subject chosen because it is topical and many-sided. The writer, Lisa, begins by setting up a creative dilemma: while we accept that rink rage is objectionable, we disagree about how to deal with it. One solution might be to force responsibility on parents by getting them to sign a "good behaviour pledge." But this means limiting individual freedom. Another possibility is to change the way hockey is played, which of course might offend the hockey purist. Lisa is careful to show at the start that both possibilities are viable and ethical, though both have their downsides. Indeed, this can be called a persuasive essay precisely because it involves moral attitudes, not simply practical choices. We could choose to sacrifice a degree of freedom in order to curb violence. Or we could advocate preserving the integrity of the game—but at the risk of endangering human life. The question is not which view is right or wrong because both are right and, ironically, wrong. The writer's task is to decide, and to help her readers decide, which course of action is better *at this particular time.*

This choice can only be made in light of the audience's deeper concerns, loyalties, and temperament. Therefore, having a clear, concrete idea of who the *local* audience is and how to appeal to this group (both logically and emotionally) is crucial. Note that the writer reveals herself, her own values, biases, or point of view. She does not hide herself from her readers in the interest, say, of achieving a false objectivity, of arriving at an ultimate, univocal truth. She makes no claim to such truth. By letting her audience see that she herself is touched by the issue, she presents herself as a member of a concerned group, and as an agent of change.

In turn, she establishes herself in her audience's mind as someone qualified to speak, to provide leadership, on this subject. Again, this type of writing does not try to adopt an omniscient stance, preferring to negotiate with readers. (See **32d(2)**.) Many of the decisions we reach in real life are tentative and subject to revision in light of changing circumstances or new information. Lisa follows this pattern in her essay. This does not mean she is indecisive or, on the other hand, that she uses personal opinion to browbeat the reader into submission. She accepts that many decisions are partial, based on incomplete data, but that they are shared among several individuals. The challenge of persuasive writing here is to create the possibility for, and motivate people to accept, consensus.

Lisa presents her essay as a conversation going on *now* among people involved in the issue, not just as a series of undeniable facts or timeless verities. Every statement she makes, then, is open to subjective interpretation. Authentic persuasion is marked by this underlying sense of the instability of the situation, which, admittedly, may make you feel somewhat insecure as a writer. Remember, though, that you are looking to build your audience's trust and support in reaching an agreement that has appeal to most parties.

At the end of her essay, Lisa includes an audience analysis that describes some attributes of the people she is addressing. Note how this description makes the audience into a kind of coauthor. Audience members are more likely to be convinced when they feel they have participated in the decision reached. This approach to argument characterizes the audience in, again, positive terms, as individuals who are unselfish, willing to discuss and reflect, in order to come to a communal consensus. The writer mounts a concession: since both viewpoints are equally informed and concerned, there is no loser in this debate. The effectiveness of this writing lies in its management of audience reaction—in process. To influence an audience in this way, you need a close-up, detailed awareness of its unique attributes.

Lisa Belyea

Dr. A. Stubbs

English 351-001

24 March 2002

Rink Rage

Ask just about anybody to name a violent
sport and they'll probably say hockey.
It's not just that it's a fast
game played with sticks and blades.
There's a lot of body thumping down on
the ice, and a lot of it is perfectly
legal. For those Canadians who watch
hockey only occasionally, this physical
roughness can be somewhat alarming. True
hockey fans like me don't deny that
hockey's a tough sport. Yes, hockey <u>does</u>
provide a forum for behaviours that
might get you arrested outside of the
stadium. And yes, a particularly good
game <u>is</u> rather like a war. But this is
the paradox of sport. Since the Olympics
of ancient Greece and the tournaments of
medieval times, sport has been a

*Establishes
paradox:
hockey
violence is
both
acceptable
and unaccept-
able,
depending on
one's viewpoint*

microcosm of human struggle and conflict. It's a theatre that lets us play at battle, celebrate the heroic aspects of warfare without having to pay the tragic cost. Hockey in particular calls for a healthy helping of these warlike qualities: strength, determination, and, most importantly, raw guts. And whether we approve of warfare or not, we still admire these qualities. (I personally became a Toronto Maple Leafs fan after watching Dougie Gilmour play a game against the Vancouver Canucks with a severed tendon in his leg.)

Uses personal anecdote to establish rapport with reader

Uses transition to join ideas, show sequences in evolution of thought

However, though there *are*, I suppose, some among us who are just bloodthirsty, hockey fans in general understand that the violence of hockey, or of any sport for that matter, has meaning only when it takes place within a protective covering of rules. That's why you're allowed to check only the guy who has the puck, or who's just shot it. And why crosschecking and slashing are penalized. And why spearing will get you kicked out of the game. When everybody's in agreement about the boundaries, you have a framework for aggressive behaviour that, ironically, guarantees safety. And games can't be fun if they're not safe (unless you happen to be into death sports). Therefore, like other fans who respect rules, I'm disturbed by the recent rash of incidents known as "rink rage," a term that's somewhat misleading since these incidents usually happen in the stands, not on the ice. Rink rage refers to uncontrollable outbursts of anger by fans, who get too caught up in the excitement of what they're viewing. These incidents are particularly common among parents, perhaps because at the junior levels of the sport, the guy getting hip-checked into the boards isn't some NHL superstar--he's somebody's

Elaborates the issue by uniting contradictory ideas, paradox

Answers the question that naturally arises here: What is rink rage? Furthers connection with audience

little boy. It's only natural that
parents feel protective of their
children, and want them to do well. So
maybe they can be forgiven if they fail
to appreciate that body checking's a
normal part of hockey--when it's their
kid who's getting plowed into the ice.
Strangely, however, some of these same
parents express their horror at the
violence by adopting similarly violent
measures themselves.

Shows sympathetic awareness of other points of view

Fortunately, the issue of rink rage
is now being addressed by parents,
coaches, and referees in junior-level
hockey. In fact, a couple of interesting
solutions have been put forward. One
appears in "Rink Rage," a cover
story appearing in the March 2001 issue
of <u>Maclean's</u>. The other is discussed in
Gary Mason's article "Lawsuit only the
tip of the ice for berserk hockey
parents," originally published in the
<u>Vancouver Sun</u> and now available on the
Hockey Regina web page. The question I

States sources. Makes it clear the issue is current and still undecided want to address isn't which plan is more effective, in practical terms, but the larger ethical issue of which is in the best interest of the players, not to mention the sport as a whole.

The Maclean's article is more interested in exploring the problem of rink rage than coming up with a cure for it. This is likely because the authors are journalists and thus slightly removed from the world of hockey (compared with players and their parents at least). Also, its target audience is people across the entire country, not just a select group of sports enthusiasts. It aims, then, to focus broad public attention on an increasingly serious social problem. A version of rink rage, as the article points out, can be found in sports other than hockey. And it can be tied to other phenomena such as "road rage" and "air rage." Noting that unruly behaviour by parents "poisons the atmosphere and drives volunteer coaches and low-paid referees out of the game," the article describes a plan that has been recommended by experts, one that has already been successfully implemented by several sports organizations. The plan is to make parents sign a "good behaviour pledge," in effect a promise to conduct themselves in an appropriate manner at games and respect the decisions of coaches and referees, even if they don't agree with them. Parents who refuse to sign are simply not allowed to attend games.

The Mason article on the other hand seems to be addressed specifically to hockey parents, for it discusses the problem of rink rage only briefly, focusing instead on the need for answers. Mason argues that the best way to deal with the problem is, at lower levels of hockey, to give all players equal ice time. Only in cases of overtime or championship games, he says,

Transitional marker shows how ideas evolve and connect, creating gradualism— i.e., the points are made one at a time should this rule be waived. Mason argues that this solution will alleviate parents' "single biggest source of frustration," namely their child's lack of ice time. It will also provide coaches with "a tool to . . . motivate players who need motivating." That is, it will make ice time a reward for those who are disciplined and hard-working while setting up a deterrent for players who are consistently irresponsible. Thus, instead of "reforming" parents to fit the game, as the pledge plan does, we change the game to fit the parents.

Broadens context by referring to the history of the problem, showing how it has changed

Although the discussion of rink rage is relatively recent, the problem itself, as the <u>Maclean's</u> article mentions, has been around since "the good old days." However, it has come to the attention of the Canadian and American public because of the steady rise in incidents so outrageous they might be funny if their results weren't so frequently tragic. For example, Mason talks about the case of Helene Canuel, a Quebec woman who sued for damages because her son, a goalie, "didn't start a game he expected to." The Canuel incident is trivial compared with a peewee game in Port Dover, Ontario, in which officials ejected all 200 fans for shouting abuse and hurling debris on the ice. Passions ran so high that referees had to be escorted from the arena under police guard.

Both articles cite other instances of rink rage, each made all the more alarming because they took place in front of children. They agree, though, that the most disturbing case of all is the recent tragedy in Reading, Massachusetts, where a hockey dad, Thomas Junta, beat to death a volunteer supervisor, Michael Costin, for ejecting him from the game for abusive behaviour. Though previous cases may have been regarded as the concern of the sports world alone, the Junta/Costin incident

Cites specific case— creates emphasis

has, as I say, dropped the issue squarely in the lap of the general public. All of us must now recognize that rink rage is our business, simply because violence in society affects us all. Perhaps with this realization comes an added sense of urgency: the problem isn't going to go away. One reason, as Mason points out, is bigger and bigger NHL salaries--the greater these become, the higher parents will set their sights. And, as a natural consequence, the more frustrated parents will become when they think someone is standing in their child's way to stardom.

Direct address to reader helps link ideas, points to next stage of discussion

Let's consider the pledge plan in a bit more detail, in terms of its implications for players, parents, and the game itself. At first glance, it seems totally reasonable. Presumably, parents who care about their children would, as a first priority, want to safeguard them from unruly fan behaviour. It's logical to assume they'd be totally behind this measure. And wouldn't parents resistant to signing a pledge, for whatever reason, likely be the very ones we'd want to keep away?

Possibly, but not necessarily. After all, why should *any* parent have to sign a piece of paper just to get permission to watch a child take part in a sporting event? Couldn't parents say attendance at their children's games belongs to them by right? And what happens if parents have a grievance that's genuine? Will their right to watch their child play be taken from them if they make trouble? Finally, what sort of precedent would we create if we gave coaches and supervisors--not parents--ultimate control over children?

Mason's proposal has advantages and disadvantages too. Its most significant benefit, perhaps, is that it offers greater opportunity for players who are eager to play but lack hot-shot status. It lets them develop their skills without feeling pressure to compete with the superstars. That should make some parents happy. But what about the players who are gifted? What about the ones who have talent, who could make it to the pros? Shouldn't they have every conceivable opportunity to develop their skills, which means not having to give up their ice time to other kids, who may be playing only because their parents made them? Furthermore, wouldn't a game in which third-rate players got as much playing time as first-rate players be much less exciting to watch? Wouldn't we be undermining the integrity, the spectacle of the sport merely to suit the increasingly petulant demands of some (not all) parents? And what kind of precedent is that to set?

Uses question-and-answer to develop and link points

I must admit to being of two minds about this issue. I confess I'm not in a position to judge once and for all whether parents' rights outweigh equal opportunity. After all, I don't even

Writer is aware of two sides to issue; includes personal viewpoint to create community with audience have children (though I hope to some day). I am, however, a hockey fan. And what affects "my" sport affects me. Then, too, I'm a Canadian. Even if I took no interest in sport, the escalation of emotions into violence is my concern. It's everyone's concern. For, generally speaking, as civilized people I think we have a duty to ensure that children--not just our own but all children--grow up in a society where it's made clear that certain violent behaviours are not acceptable.

The decision isn't an easy one. On reflection, though, while I hesitate to endorse any plan that requires parents to sign a paper in order to participate in a process that should be theirs by right, I'm in favour of the pledge plan. My reason is that it's a long-term solution, one that considers both the child <u>and</u> the game. Though the equal ice time plan certainly benefits second- and third-string players, it is,

Writer sympathizes with audience's predicament

unfortunately, only a temporary solution. Also, it speaks to only one issue: playing time. While it doesn't infringe on the rights of parents, as the pledge plan does, it doesn't really provide a sure means of stopping other problems (such as bad calls by a referee) from turning into major incidents. And we need above all to take action to curb the violence. When you think about it, giving equal ice time could, over time, have an opposite effect from what it intends. By leaving room for future episodes of rink rage, it may actually prove harmful to the very children it has been put in place to protect. The pledge plan on the other hand, though I recognize that it sets a dangerous precedent in regard to the rights of parents with respect to their own children, gets at the root of the problem: the parents themselves. And though it hardly seems fair to punish all parents for the actions of a few

Writer decides that of the two "goods" at stake, protecting children outweighs personal freedom

ruffians, isn't it better for all
concerned that parents swallow their
pride and sign the pledge? This is
surely better than allowing any more
children to be put in danger.

Works Cited

Deacon, James, Brenda Branswell,
   Susan McClelland, and Daryl Smart.
   "Rink Rage." Maclean's 26 Mar. 2001.
   Online posting. 26 Feb. 2002
   < http://personal.nbnet.nb.ca/rhealr/
   sources/rinkrage.html>.

Gary Mason. "Lawsuit Only the Tip of
   the Ice for Berserk Hockey Parents."
   Vancouver Sun 14 Dec. 2001.
   Online posting. 26 Feb. 2002
   < http://www.hockeyregina.sk.ca/pages/
   news/lawsuit/php3>.

Reader Analysis

I am writing to Canadians who watch
hockey only occasionally, i.e., to the

casual fan. These are people who may not understand hockey as well as Don Cherry, but would be familiar enough with the game to know some of the hockey terms I have used, particularly in the first few paragraphs. I am writing to those who are uncomfortable with the violence of hockey and alarmed by the rise in incidents off the rink. Ideally, these people are parents who are also in some way involved in the world of youth hockey, whether as fans, referees, coaches, or supervisors, but this is not absolutely required. I say that "ideally" I am writing to parents because I think that they are most likely to put the interests of the children first and, thus, while they may be opposed to restrictions on the rights of parents, they may eventually be convinced that it is in the best long-term interest of the kids to stop rink rage right now once and for all. I have, however, tried to keep my focus broad enough that any Canadian could be influenced by my argument. Hence the passage near the end about how violence in our society is everyone's responsibility, whether or not we have children or watch hockey.

Chapter 33

Research: Finding and Evaluating Sources

Although writing from research usually takes more time than writing essays based on information already familiar to you, the process involves many of the same skills. The distinctive feature of a research assignment is that it requires you to develop a subject by drawing on outside resources and acknowledging them properly. Improving your ability to work with sources may subsequently help you with other writing assignments as well, since you may need to obtain information from sources even when you are not specifically required to do research.

Further, writing from research involves many of the same skills that you use to write essays based on familiar information.

33a Information from sources is basic to most writing.

Rather than considering the research paper as a special assignment unrelated to other kinds of writing, you should recognize that almost anything you write requires you to acquire and use information. On some occasions, you may discover that you have sufficient information from your own experience or observations. On other occasions, you may need to explore the resources of a library to discover the work of other writers or researchers who can help you. In either case, remember that you are a writer, not simply a compiler of data. No matter how many sources you use, you are the most important presence in a paper that has your name on it. Think of the paper as a **researched** paper—that is, written from research that you have evaluated and then used to advance a **thesis** (28d).

(1) Analyzing the rhetorical situation

A researched paper, like any other paper, requires that you consider occasion, purpose, audience, and subject.

Writing that responds to events in the world around you—a wedding, a birthday, a job application—takes account of one of the elements of **occasion** (28a(3)), perhaps the most obvious element. But occasion involves much more than that. Is the writing you are doing something you have been asked to do? Did someone ask you to do research? What kind of research is expected? For example, some papers require you to interview people, while others concentrate on print or electronic sources. What is the scope of the project? When is your deadline? What is your rhetorical stance?

Will the **purpose** (28a(1)) of your paper be chiefly expository (to report, analyze, or explain) or persuasive (to prove a point)? Are you writing to understand the information better? To show someone else that you understand? To solve a problem?

Your **audience** (28a(2)) may or may not be expert on your subject, but you should usually envision a reader who is intelligent, fair-minded, and interested in what you have to say. Similarly, you should present yourself as a writer who is thoughtful, fair-minded, and responsive to the views of others, because any sign of bias can undermine your credibility (31d) as a researcher. Your audience will also determine to a great extent how formal your paper will be, what level of language you will use (expert vocabulary, longer or shorter sentences), and what the format of the paper will be (MLA, APA, documentation styles adopted by a particular company, and so on).

You find a **subject** for a researched paper in much the same way as you find a topic for any piece of writing: you are assigned the topic (as you may be in the workplace as well as in a university class), you find a subject that interests you, or you are moved to answer a question. (See 28b.) An inquiring mind is the best equipment you can bring to this task: Choose a subject that interests you and is appropriate for your audience. If you are stuck for an idea, consider some of the methods mentioned in 28c(1). You might also try browsing on the **World Wide Web**, staying alert for sites and categories that interest you.

Once you have a subject in mind, the exploration methods discussed in 28c(1)—journalling, freewriting, listing, questioning, considering perspectives—will almost certainly help you find an interesting focus. Limiting the topic is especially important for a researched paper, since one of your main objectives is to show your ability to treat a subject in some depth within the time allowed and (usually) the length specified. But even if you begin research with a thesis, be prepared to revise it if your research findings do not support it. (See also 31b.)

A quick Web search using keywords from a subject you have in mind will help establish whether there is enough (or too much) material on your subject. (The amount of pertinent material in your university library is also an important test.) If you find dozens of relevant sources, you should probably narrow the subject to one with a more manageable scope. However, if you have difficulty finding sources, chances are that your subject is too narrow and should be broader. Because the best researched papers usually draw on different kinds of material, you should also reconsider any topic that would force you to rely exclusively on one type of source. A paper based only on newspaper articles, for example, could easily lack depth, and research drawn exclusively from books might overlook current information in the field. Similarly, relying solely on electronic sources is unwise, since the technology is so new that much excellent material is not yet in electronic form.

Exercise 1

Evaluate the following subjects for a 10-page researched paper. If any seem too broad, suggest a narrower topic. For example, "Canadian Poetry" should be narrowed to something like "Twentieth-Century Maritime Poets." If any seem too narrow, suggest a broader subject—for example, "Raising Wheat in Brazil" could be expanded to "The Variety of Crops in Brazilian Agriculture." Eliminate any subject that you would be unable to find reliable sources for.

censorship of the Internet	opening more abortion clinics
safe sex	animal experimentation
legalization of marijuana	tofu-based salad dressings
puns in Shakespeare	feminism

(2) Developing a research problem and analyzing your own knowledge

An important step in doing research is to envision your topic as a research problem and then to establish what you already know about it. This step should help considerably in avoiding accidental plagiarism (see 33g) since you will have a record of what you already know before you began researching. A **research problem** might be a question or an issue that can be resolved at least partly through research. It may be argumentative, but it may not be a matter of opinion. For example, the thesis "animal experimentation is wrong" is not a research problem because research cannot prove a moral judgment. Research, however, can prove whether a policy is effective. The thesis "animal experimentation is necessary for medical research" is a hypothesis suitable for research.

Establishing what you already know about a topic takes freewriting and brainstorming several steps farther. Try to write down everything you know about your topic. Try to convince someone else of your thesis and write down all the information you bring to your argument. Think about where you have seen your thesis discussed and search your memory for all the information you can remember about the subject. Use the thinking strategies in chapters 31 and 28, then examine what you think you know to see if your points are matters of opinion or if they are independently verifiable. (See also 31b.)

(3) Establishing a research routine

A few words of advice: Scheduling your time is especially important because researched papers are usually assigned several weeks before they are due, and the temptation to procrastinate may be strong. Make sure to allow enough time for the long process of choosing a subject (28b), preparing a working bibliography (33b), reading extensively, taking notes (33f(2)), developing a thesis (28d), outlining (28e), drafting (28f), and revising (29b). Begin early and keep your schedule flexible. As you write your paper, you may need to return to a part of the research process that you thought you had completed. For example, when drafting your essay, you may discover that you need additional information—you may need to conduct a personal interview or return to the library for further research.

Another tool that can be very helpful is a research log, which can help you stay on schedule and keep you from having to do tasks over. It is somewhat like a journal in that you can record in it everything you do: ideas for subjects, ways to refine topics, what you already know. Not only will a research log provide a central location for recording your research activities, but it can also keep your schedule right in front of you and help keep track of tasks you have not yet completed. Further, it can be vital if you have to do any backtracking.

Here is a sample form that can help you make a realistic schedule. You may need more (or less) time for each of these activities. Adjust your schedule to conform to the way you work best.

Activity	Days Needed	Date Completed
1. Explore the campus library	1	_____ ☐
2. Find a topic and develop a working hypothesis	1	_____ ☐
3. Establish a search strategy	1	_____ ☐
4. Develop a working bibliography	6	_____ ☐
5. Take notes	6	_____ ☐
6. Develop the thesis and outline	2	_____ ☐
7. Draft the paper	4	_____ ☐
8. Seek peer review	2	_____ ☐
9. Revise the paper	1	_____ ☐
10. Prepare the works cited	1	_____ ☐
11. Prepare the final draft	1	_____ ☐
12. Proofread	1	_____ ☐

33b A working bibliography lists sources.

A working, or preliminary, bibliography contains information (titles, authors, dates, and so on) about the materials you think you might use. Write down the most promising sources you can find. Often the sources you consult will have helpful bibliographies. Draw on them, but do not use them exclusively, or else the research will no longer be yours and you will miss other sources. Some researchers find it convenient to put each entry on a separate index card, which makes it easy to add or drop a card and to arrange the list alphabetically without recopying it. Others prefer to use a computer, which can sort and alphabetize items automatically. It is also a good idea to follow consistently from the very beginning the bibliographical form you are instructed to use. The MLA bibliographic style can be found in 34a and APA style in 34d. Using the specified style from the start will save you valuable time later, when you must compile a formal list of works cited that will appear at the end of your paper. Be sure to note the address for Internet sites in case you need to visit the site again to link to other sites. Note the call number of books you consult in case you need to re-check a book after you have returned it or want to see if there are similar books shelved near it.

Primary and secondary sources As you look for sources, be aware of which ones are primary and which are secondary. Primary sources for topics in literature and the humanities are generally documents and literary works. In the social sciences, primary sources can be field observations, case histories, and survey data. In the sciences, primary sources are generally empirical—measurements, experiments, and the like. Secondary sources are commentaries on primary sources. So a critique of

McKellen's adaptation of Shakespeare's *Richard III* would be a secondary source, as would results of a survey of a representative population of 20- to 30-year-olds or a report of the results of an experiment. Sources that summarize and explain secondary sources, such as most textbooks, are sometimes called **tertiary sources**. Learn to evaluate the quality of secondary and tertiary sources. Many are excellent commentaries, although all involve some degree of interpretation. However, some secondary sources, particularly field resources and electronic documents, may not be reliable. Unlike print sources, these are often not peer-reviewed before the information is published. That does not mean you should avoid these sources completely; it does mean you must use them carefully. (See also 33e.) Generally speaking, the closer you get to primary sources, the more reliable your information.

33c   Library research requires a strategy.

University and college libraries are organized to make research as efficient as possible. Usually a map or diagram—either printed for handing out or posted on the wall—shows where various kinds of materials are located. Reference books, encyclopedias, and indexes—materials that cannot usually be checked out of the library—are located in the **reference collection**, which may also include indexing information for electronic databases, either online or on CD-ROM. Other books are located in the **stacks** or at the **reserve desk** and can be checked out for a specified length of time. If your library has a closed-stack policy, you request the books you need by call number from the **circulation desk**. You can find the call number in the **main catalogue**. If the stacks are open, however, it may be useful to browse among the books shelved near those you have located through the catalogue. **Periodicals** (magazines, journals, and newspapers in print or microform) are usually stored in a special section of the library. If your library does not have a book or periodical that you need, bear in mind that your university may participate in an inter-library loan program, which is an arrangement among local or regional university libraries for the exchange of books and periodicals. You may also be entitled to use the facilities of other university libraries in your area. If you have difficulty locating or using any research materials, do not hesitate to ask a **reference librarian** for help.

Remember also that unless an instructor has asked you to confine yourself to printed information, your search does not need to be limited to a library. You might use information drawn from radio, television, and the Internet; from conducting interviews with experts on your topic; or from observations you have acquired through personal experience. Much of the research people do in their daily lives involves more than one approach to the issue in question. If you plan to buy a new car, for example, you may read reviews published in various magazines available in your library, interview people familiar with the cars that interest you, and take a test drive or two. A similar strategy may be appropriate for research assignments in school or at work: read, interview, and observe.

(1) Books and periodicals

Books

The first place to look is usually the **main catalogue**, which can take the form of cards or computer files. The main catalogue lists all books owned by the university or college and shows whether a book is in the general library or elsewhere in a special collection. Some libraries still maintain a **card catalogue**, which consists of cards arranged alphabetically in drawers. Cards for each book are filed alphabetically by author, by title, and by subject or subjects. Most libraries, however, have **computerized catalogues**, which save space and make research more efficient. (See 33e.)

A library catalogue, then, whether computerized or maintained on cards, identifies books by author, title, and subject. Some computerized catalogue programs also allow researchers to locate sources by supplying the computer with other information, such as a keyword that may appear in the title or even a book's call number.

Although there may be a slight visual difference between the format of the computerized entry and its equivalent on a catalogue card (see the following illustrations and 33e), both provide essentially the same information: author, title, place of publication, publisher, date of publication, the length and size of the book, and any special features such as a bibliography. You will also be given the book's call number, which tells you exactly where in the library the book is located.

If your library provides you with access to both card and computer catalogues, check with a librarian to see which is more current. Libraries that have computerized their catalogues may have stopped including new acquisitions in their card catalogues, and libraries that have only recently computerized their catalogues may not yet have their entire collection online. (See also 33e(2).)

An entry from a computerized catalogue In addition to providing all the data found on the printed card, a computerized catalogue entry usually reveals the location and status of the book—information that can save a researcher time when looking for a book that has been moved to a special collection or checked out by someone else. Libraries use a number of different systems for computerizing catalogues, so expect to encounter variations on this example.

```
        Online Catalogue—BRIEF DISPLAY (1 of 1 titles)

                                    Number of holdings :1
AUTHOR          :Coursen, Herbert R.
TITLE           :Shakespearean performance as
                 interpretation / H.R. Coursen
PUBLISHER       :Newark :
                 University of Delaware Press ;
                 London :
                 Cranbury, NJ :
                 Associated University Presses,
                 c1992
LANGUAGE        :ENGLISH

   LIBRARY      LOCATION     COLLECTION/         STATUS/
                             CALL NUMBER         DUE DATE
   --------     ---------    ----------------    ----------
1. MAIN         MAIN         PR3091.C69 1992     In Library
 Last Page
Options:                              ⟨ENTER⟩ = scroll options
 FD = Full display  P = Prior screen   E = Extend search
  L = Limit list    O = Output         M = MARC
```

This is an example of an author card for the same source. Cards filed by title and by subject will have the same information under different headings.

```
PR
3091 Coursen, Herbert R.
.C69 Shakespearean performance as interpretation / H.R.
     Coursen.—Newark:
1992 University of Deleware Press, 1992.
       Bibliographical references (p. 253-262).
       Includes index.
       ISBN 0-874-13432-3 (alk. Paper)

    1. Shakespeare, William, d 1564-1616—Stage history.
    2. Shakespeare—Film and video adaptations. 3. Shake-
    speare—Criticism and interpretation—History.
    I. Title
```

Library of Congress Subject Headings If you are uncertain about how to search for information on your topic and if your library uses Library of Congress numbers for cataloguing books (most academic libraries do), you can first look for your subject in the **Library of Congress Subject Headings** (*LCSH*). If your subject is indexed by that catalogue, you will find a specific catalogue number for books on your subject, as well as cross-references to related subject areas that may help you sharpen your focus. If you find a number indexed, write it down; then find that number in your library's own **shelf list**, which lists all the books in the library by call number. The first part of a call number indicates the subject (for example, the PR in PR3091 stands for British literature). Therefore, when you look up the call number of a book, you should find adjacent to it the call numbers of other books the library owns on that subject.

Periodicals

Since periodicals (magazines, journals, newspapers) are published frequently, they often contain some of the most recent information on your subject. A variety of periodical indexes (usually located in the reference section of the library) do for articles what the main catalogue does for books. Since each index includes many publications not listed in the others, you may need to consult a number of indexes to find the information you need. Most of the print indexes listed in this section are also available electronically. For information on using these, see pages 499–500.

Indexes for general-interest periodicals If you think that articles on your subject have appeared in Canadian mainstream or academic periodicals or in Canadian news-papers, you might want to consult the *Canadian Periodical Index* (*CPI*) and the *Canadian Index*. *CPI* is a bilingual index that lists over 400 periodicals, many of them Canadian. The *Canadian Index* is a consolidation of the *Canadian Business Index*, the *Canadian News Index*, and the *Canadian Magazine Index*. Some overlap does occur between *CPI* and the *Canadian Index*, but only the *Canadian Index* covers Canadian daily newspapers.

MOVIES

Cross-references	*See also* Animation; Children's movies; Cinematography; Experimental films; Film editing; Movies, Documentary; Screenplays and screenplay-writing; Television broadcasting—Movies; Violence in movies; Women in film
Article summary	McKellen wards off purists' discontent [Richard III movie] . *VS* Ja 12'96 pC1,C2 A Shakespearean purist takes liberties: actor Sir Ian McKellen logged more than 300 stage performances of Richard III before bringing the play to the screen. *G&M* Ja 24'96 pC1

The *Canadian Index* excerpt above shows that *The Vancouver Sun* published an article on *Richard III* on pages C1 and C2 of the January 12, 1996, edition. *The Globe and Mail* also published an article on the film. At the front of each volume of the *Canadian Index* is a key to abbreviations and a sample entry.

CPI arranges its entries alphabetically rather than sequentially. Movie reviews are listed by film title.

MOVIE REVIEWS

Restoration.
> *Maclean's* 109 no 6 (F 5 '96): p56

Richard III.
> *Maclean's* 109 no 6 (F 5 '96): p56
> *New Republic* 214 no 7 (F 12 '96): p30–1
> *Time (Can ed)* 147 no 3 (Ja 15 '96): p44–5

Ridicule.
> *24 Images (Fr)* no 83–84 (automne '96): p92–3

Subtopics
arranged in
alphabetical
order

The Canadian edition of *Time* published a review of *Richard III* in volume 147, number 3 (January 15, 1996) on pages 44 and 45.

For older articles of general interest, you can consult *Poole's Index*, 1802–1907; *Nineteenth Century Reader's Guide*, 1890–99; or, for specifically Canadian articles, the *Index to Pre 1900 English Language Canadian Cultural and Literary Magazines* on CD-ROM.

Indexes for special-interest periodicals Virtually every specialized field has its own periodicals, which usually provide much more detailed information than can be found in magazines or newspapers aimed at the general public. When conducting research, you should be familiar with indexes that cover periodicals within various professions. Some of the most useful ones are listed below.

Applied Science and Technology Index. 1958–.

Art Index. 1929–.

Biological and Agricultural Index. 1946–.

Business Periodicals Index. 1958–.

Canadian Business Index. 1975–1992.

Canadian Education Index. 1965–.

Cumulative Index to Nursing and Allied Health Literature (CINAHL). 1982–.

Education Index. 1929–.

Humanities Index. 1974–.

Index to Canadian Legal Literature. 1961–.

Index to Legal Periodicals. 1908–.

Medline. 1985–.

Music Index. 1949–.

Public Affairs Information Service (Bulletin). 1915–.

Social Sciences Index. 1974–.

The print versions of these indexes (becoming increasingly rare as libraries replace them with CD-ROM versions and discard the paper volumes) are organized like the *Canadian Periodical Index.* Consult the front of any volume for a key to the abbreviations used in individual entries. A similar format is also used by the *MLA Bibliography,* which is essential for doing research in literature. The *MLA Bibliography* includes books as well as periodicals, and each volume is divided into separate sections covering research on the literature of different languages and time periods. Like most indexes to special-interest periodicals, the *MLA Bibliography* can be consulted in printed volumes, through a CD-ROM disk covering several years, or through an on-line database search. When they publish electronic versions of their indexes, some publishers change the title: *Current Index to Journals in Education (CIJE)* and *Resources in Education (RIE)* are the print volumes for research in education, while *Educational Resources Information Center (ERIC)* is the electronic version.

Electronic databases of scholarly materials are much easier to search and update than print versions, so most libraries have switched to them. All the CD-ROM databases in your library will probably look very much alike and can probably be searched using much the same set of commands. A different library, however, may subscribe to the same databases through a different service, and the commands and the screen designs may differ from what you are used to. The more familiar you are with the versions your library subscribes to, the easier it will be to learn how to use those in other libraries.

Abstracting services   In addition to providing the bibliographical information necessary for locating sources, an abstracting service provides short summaries of the articles and books it indexes. Your library may have CD-ROM disks for such abstracts as *Academic Abstracts, Biology Abstracts, Chemical Abstracts,* and *Psychological Abstracts,* as well as for *PsychLit* or *PsychINFO,* which are both available in electronic form only, and *CARL,* which contains the tables of contents for most scholarly journals. (See 33e for more complete information on electronic sources and resources.) When using one of these services, you can quickly scan the short summaries and decide which seem likely to be the most useful. You may also be able to print out a list of citations, a list of citations with abstracts, and even the full text of some of the articles you discover. Here is a citation and abstract from *Academic Abstracts,* a service that covers many widely available periodicals.

Computerized abstract

```
Subject: RICHARD III     (Motion picture);
   RICHARD III Foundation
  Title: Historical Richards.
 Author: Geier, Thom
Summary: Points at the criticism received by
   the film 'Richard III' for its historical
```

```
      inaccuracy. New Jersey based Richard III
      Foundation's complaints; Details of the
      movie, including Richard III portrayed like
      Hitler.
   Source: (US News & World Report, 1/22/96,
      Vol. 120 Issue 3, p14, 1/5p, 1c)
      ISSN: 0041-5537
Item No: 9601167647

         (We subscribe to this magazine.)

      ** FullTEXT Available — Press F7 **
```

(2) Reference works

When doing research, you may need to consult a variety of reference works. A general encyclopedia, such as *The Canadian and World Encyclopedia* (on CD-ROM) or *Encyclopaedia Britannica* can provide useful information, especially at an early stage in your research. And you will almost certainly need to consult a dictionary. (See 13a and 33e.) For a list of reference books useful when writing about literature, see page 638. A few of the most widely used reference books are listed here with abbreviated bibliographical information. Note that these are reference sources: refer to them for help, but do not rely on any of them as a principal source for a university or college paper.

Special dictionaries and encyclopedias

Chronicle of Canada. Ed. Elizabeth Abbott. 1990.

Bercuson, David J., and J. L. Granatstein. *Collins Dictionary of Canadian History*. 1988.

Canadian & World Encyclopedia. [CD-ROM]. 1995–.

Dukelow, Daphne A., and Betsy Nuse. *The Dictionary of Canadian Law.* 2nd ed. 1995.

Encyclopedia of Philosophy. Ed. Paul Edwards. 4 vols. 1972.

Encyclopedia of Psychology. Ed. Raymond J. Corsini. 4 vols. 2nd ed. 1994.

Encyclopedia of Religion. Ed. Mircea Eliade. 16 vols. 1986.

Encyclopedia of World Art. 15 vols. 1959–68. Supp. 1983, 1987.

International Encyclopedia of the Social Sciences. Ed. D. L. Sills. 8 vols. 1977. Supplements.

McGraw-Hill Encyclopedia of Science and Technology. 15 vols. 6th ed. 1987. Yearbooks.

The New Grove Dictionary of Music and Musicians. Ed. Stanley Sadie. 20 vols. 1980. Reprinted with corrections in 1995.

Biographies

Biography and Genealogy Master Index. CD-ROM. 1998.

Canadian Who's Who. 1910–.

Collins Biographical Dictionary of Scientists. 4th ed. 1994.

Contemporary Authors. New Revision Series. 1981–

Contemporary Canadian Authors. 1995.

Dictionary of Canadian Biography. Ed. Ramsay Cook. 14 vols. 1966–.

Dictionary of National Biography (British). 22 vols. 1882–1953. Rpt. 1981. Supplements.

Discovering Authors. CD-ROM. Cdn. ed. 1996. Updates.

Who's Who in America. 1899–. (See also Marquis's *Who's Who Publications: Index to All Books,* revised annually.)

Who's Who in Canada. 1909–.

Almanacs and yearbooks

Britannica Book of the Year. 1938–.

Canadian Almanac & Directory. 1847–.

Canadian Global Almanac.

Information Please Almanac. 1985–.

World Almanac and Book of Facts. 1868–.

33d Field research requires special skills.

Research in the field involves interviewing, observing, experimenting, and conducting surveys.

Depending on your topic, you may want to include one or more of these other types of research. The most common alternative to library research is an **interview.** The faculty members at your university or college, business and professional people, and even relatives and friends can be appropriate subjects for an interview if they have relevant first-hand experience with the subject you are researching.

Since well-informed interviewers usually ask the best questions, you should consider an interview only after you have done some reading on your subject. Schedule interviews well ahead, and if you plan to use a tape recorder, ask permission. Take a professional approach to the interview: Have pens or pencils and paper ready for taking notes and fresh batteries and blank tapes for your tape recorder. Dress appropriately and be punctual. Record the time and date of the interview on tape or, if you do not use a tape recorder, at the beginning of your notes.

Begin with questions that are broad enough to give people room to reveal their own special interests; then follow up with more specific questions. Be prepared to depart from your list of planned questions whenever your subject says something of particular interest that would be useful to pursue. After the interview, send a letter thanking the interviewee. A courtesy of this sort is especially appropriate when someone has made time for you in a busy schedule or has been genuinely helpful during the interview itself.

Closely related to the interview is the **survey**, in which you ask a number of people the same set of questions and then analyze the results. You can administer the survey orally in interview fashion, or you can distribute a written questionnaire by mail or in person. Once you have a clear idea of what you want to find out, you may find the following checklist helpful in constructing a good survey questionnaire.

Checklist for Creating Survey Questions
- Does each question relate directly to the purpose of the survey?
- Are the questions easy to understand?
- Are the questions designed to elicit short, specific responses?
- Are the questions designed to collect concrete data that you can analyze easily?
- Are written questions designed to give respondents enough space for their answers?

In addition to interviews and surveys, you may also have occasion to draw directly on your own **experience** or **observations**. In the paper reprinted on pages 572–92, for example, Katie Frushour incorporated her own experience viewing both the Olivier and McKellen film versions of *Richard III* with the information from her library search—a strategy appropriate for comparing the two films. For a different topic, observation might involve arming yourself with a still or video camera and/or tape recorder, writing out a plan for observing, rehearsing the observation, and taking written notes (in addition to tape) during the actual observation. But check with your instructor to see whether field research is appropriate for your research project and what kind of field research would be most productive.

33e Electronic resources are fast and efficient.

Electronic research tools enable researchers to find more information faster than ever, but the quality of the results can be uneven. Electronic research techniques require knowing how to evaluate sources as well as how to find them.

(1) Developing a research strategy

Publicly available information is stored electronically in **on-line information storage and retrieval systems** (for example, *Dialog*), on CD-ROMs, and on the Internet. To locate and retrieve information in each of these you need a basic set of skills, as well as a group of skills particular to the kind of storage medium.

As with library sources, electronic research demands that you follow a basic search strategy.

BASIC SEARCH STRATEGY TIPS

1. Frame the topic as a thesis statement.
2. Identify main ideas and concepts.
3. Determine databases to be searched.
4. Identify the keywords.
5. Check the controlled vocabulary thesaurus (if there is one).

---

6. Apply a basic search logic.
7. Check system documentation on file structure and format information.
8. Log on and perform the search.
9. Identify citations to keep.
10. Refine the search strategy if the first search returned too many, too few, or irrelevant citations.

Focussing on a topic and **identifying concept areas,** the beginning steps in this strategy, echo the beginning steps for locating information in libraries. **Selecting a database** to use according to type and subject area is similar to deciding whether to consult the *MLA International Bibliography* or the *Canadian Periodical Index.* Will you use a database stored on a CD-ROM (which has the advantages of being inexpensive and relatively easy to use) or do you need to do an online search (which can be expensive and tricky to execute efficiently)? **Identifying keywords** is also not much different from deciding on a list of subject headings to look up in a library.

When you use print sources, you check your main concepts against the *LCSH.* (See 33c(1).) When you use a database (a collection of machine-readable information that you can retrieve using a computer), you must **check your keywords against the database thesaurus**—a list of the controlled vocabulary or official descriptors used for retrieving information. If a keyword is not part of the controlled vocabulary, a database search will turn up no **records** (units of stored information). That means no information can be found using the terms you have tried, not that the database contains no information on that subject. Use the controlled vocabulary for your search terms.

Basic search logic enables you to guard against retrieving too many or too few records. A search result that says, "Found: 2,493,508 records containing the descriptor 'film' " is as useless as one that reports, "Sorry, no records found." You can use certain words (called **logical** or **Boolean operators**) to broaden or narrow your search:

or   broadens a search—**young adults or single adults** finds all records that contain information about either category;

and   narrows a search—**young adults and single adults** returns only those records that contain both categories;

not   excludes specific items—**young adults and single adults not homeless** will exclude any records that mention homeless young single adults;

near   prevents inclusion of widely separated terms—**young adults near single adults** instructs the database to list only those references to both young adults and single adults that occur within a preset number of words (this option is often not available).

After you have logged on and performed your search, evaluate the records you have retrieved and discard any that are irrelevant. If you need to narrow or broaden your search, revise your selection of keywords and use them with logical operators.

(2) Your university or college library as a gateway

Many university and college libraries offer students access to major electronic information storage and retrieval systems such as *FirstSearch* or *Dialog,* which allow you to search in a large number of databases. Although some universities offer free access to these systems, students will often need to purchase access cards. If your school does not grant access to one of these, check to see if you have free access to *Academic Abstracts* or *InfoTrac.* Other databases that may be available for you to use are *ingenta* (which indexes a large number of periodicals) and *Canadian Books in Print* as well as some full-text search and retrieval databases such as *LexisNexis* for newspapers and legal documents, respectively. These systems allow users to search by keyword, author, and title. Most permit users to restrict searches to a specific time period, language, and type of record.

Sample search: *MLA* (using *FirstSearch* system)

```
***** Topic Area Selection ***************
TOPIC AREA NUMBER (or Action):1
TOPIC AREA: Arts & Humanities
NO. DATABASE                    DESCRIPTION
|1 WorldCat        Books and other materials in libraries
|                  worldwide.
|2 Article1st      Indexes nearly 12,500 journals.
|3 Contents1st     Tables of contents of nearly 12,500
|                  journals.
|4 FastDoc         Index of articles with text online or by
|                  e-mail.
|5 ArtAbstracts    Leading publications in the world of the
|                  arts.
|6 HumanitiesAbs   Abstracts of articles in the humanities.
|7 MLA             Literature, languages, linguistics,
|                  folklore
DATABASE NUMBER (or Action): 7
******** MLA BIBLIOGRAPHY **************+
COVERAGE: Literature, languages, linguistics, and folklore
from over 4,000 journals and series published worldwide,
1963 to the present. Updated ten times per year.
© 1996 The Modern Language Association of America

+************* List of Records ***************+
DATABASE: MLA              LIMITED TO: /English
SEARCH: su:shakespeare film criticism FOUND 6 Records
NO.        TITLE                        AUTHOR       YEAR
|1 Screening Shakespeare          Pilkington, Ace   1990
|2 Criticism and the Films of     Felheim, Marvin   1986
|  Shakespeare's P...
```

```
| 3 Shakespeare on Film: Some German    Bies, Werner       1983
|   Appro
| 4 The Spiral of Influence: 'One       Kliman, Bernice    1983
|   Defect' in H...
| 5 Sight and Space: The Perception     Styan, J.L.
|   of Shakesp
| 6 Criticism for the Filmed            Homan, Sidney R    1977
|   Shakespeare
```

```
HINTS: View a record.................type record number.
    Decrease number of records....type L (to limit) or A (to
    'and').
    Do a new search.................type S or SEARCH.
RECORD NUMBER (or Action): 5
************* Full Record Display ***************
Record 5 of 6
```

```
|  NUMBER: Accession: 78-1-4052. Record: 78104052.
|  UPDATE CODE: 7801
|  AUTHOR: Styan, J.L.
|  TITLE: Sight and Space: The Perception of Shakespeare on
|      Stage and Screen
|  SOURCE: Bevington, David; Halio, Jay L.; Muir, Kenneth;
|      Mack, Maynard.
|      Shakespeare, Pattern of Excelling Nature:
|      Shakespeare Criticism in Honor of America's
|      Bicentennial from The International Shakespeare
|      Association Congress, Washington, D.C., April 1976.
|      Newark: U of Delaware P, London: Associated UP. 304
|      pp.
|  PAGES: 198-209
|  LANGUAGE: English
|  PUB TYPE: book article
|  DESCRIPTORS: English literature; 1500-1599; Shakespeare,
|      William themes and figures; Film
```

Many of the same databases are available on CD-ROM: *ERIC*, *PsychLIT*, and *MLA*. If your library has a database you need on CD-ROM, you can use the basic search strategy to find out what is indexed there. But CD-ROM searching has one disadvantage in common with print searching: Once published, the information cannot be updated without issuing a continuation. If you need up-to-the-minute information, you might need to search through one of the online information storage and retrieval systems to supplement what you find on CD-ROM. The advantage of CD-ROM searching is that it is usually free, whereas there is often a charge for using the same databases online.

(3) Using the Internet

The use of the Internet, and the World Wide Web in particular, is similar to other kinds of student resources. However, because it has transformed the way we conduct research and, indeed, the way we learn and teach, it deserves a special mention. A detailed discussion for gaining access to and using the Internet is beyond the scope of this handbook, but convenient help is readily available. The academic computing centre at your school might offer workshops on how to access the World Wide Web, send an e-mail, or sign up to a newsgroup. You may also want to consult some of the following sources for more detailed information and assistance:

Ackermann, Ernest, and Karen Hartman. *The Information Searcher's Guide to Searching and Researching on the Internet and World Wide Web.* 2000.

Berkman, Robert. *The Scholar's Guide to Research in the Digital Age: How to Make the Most of the Internet, Digital Libraries, E-Journals, and More.* 2000.

Branscomb, H. Eric. *Casting Your Net: A Student's Guide to Research on the Internet.* 2000.

Carroll, Jim, and Rick Broadhead. *Carroll and Broadhead's Canadian Internet Guide 2002: Canada's Most Comprehensive Guide to Doing Research on the Internet.* 2002.

Clegg, Brian. *Mining the Internet: Information Gathering and Research on the Net.* 1999.

Heckman, Grant. *Nelson Guide to Web Research 2001–2002.* 2001.

Page, Loraine. *Super Searcher, Author, Scribe: Successful Writers Share Their Internet Research Secrets.* 2002.

E-mail is one of the most commonly used features of the Internet. It is no exaggeration to state that widespread use of e-mail has changed the way we communicate with friends, colleagues, and educators. E-mail can also function as a convenient tool for research. Assuming you know the address of a well-known researcher or academic, you can correspond with him or her, asking them questions that relate directly to your own work. Any replies that you receive can be saved on your hard drive and printed off whenever you want; thus, they can form the basis of primary research for a documented essay.

Listservs, newsgroups, chats, and **bulletin boards** are other interactive tools of the Internet. Listservs are interactive mailing lists. Messages on a certain topic are sent by e-mail to a group of subscribers. You can read the message and respond to either the author or to the whole group. Newsgroups and chats are online discussion groups. Messages on a particular topic are posted publicly and available to anyone who calls up the site. Everyone is free to respond. Hundreds of newsgroups and chats are recreational, but many can be of use to researchers. A directory of scholarly and professional electronic conferences can be found at <www.kovacs.com>. There is also a search engine devoted to newsgroups called Google Groups <groups.google.com>, and one devoted to listservs called Liszt <www.liszt.com>.

To find out whether there are any lists that might discuss the problems of young adults living with their parents, Adrienne Harton (see 34e) could have sent an e-mail message to listserv@listserv.net, leaving the subject line blank and including this phrase: "list global/multiple-generation household." A return message would list all groups listserv can identify with that keyword. If Adrienne had not gotten the results she wanted, she could have sent another message requesting "list global/young adult."

There are other methods of retrieving information from the Internet, some of which are not as frequently used as they once were. Technologies such as **Gopher, File Transfer Protocol (FTP)**, and **Telnet** (see **Glossary of Terms**) have been largely eclipsed in popularity by the **World Wide Web**. The Web refers to a particular network of servers (computers that store information) that connect data and resources through hypertext. (Hypertext is a form of text that contains links to other texts; it also makes possible transferral of digitized images and other types of files.) The Web is growing at an unimaginable rate, and its capabilities are becoming ever more sophisticated with the advent of new technology. This growth has made the Web the vastest and most uncontrolled body of information that has ever existed.

Planning and refining a search on the Web is a student's first step in exploiting the benefits it offers. Websites are viewed on a browser, which is a software program that renders HTML (hypertext mark-up language—the computer code with which web pages are created) into an intelligible format. Most educational institutions have access to high-speed Internet connections that can retrieve information from the Internet almost instantaneously. A sample page looks much like the one Katie Frushour found on *Richard III*.

This page is on a new film about Richard III and is sponsored by the Richard III Society, an organization devoted to rehabilitating the memory of England's most maligned king—a fact that Katie had to consider when evaluating the information she found there.

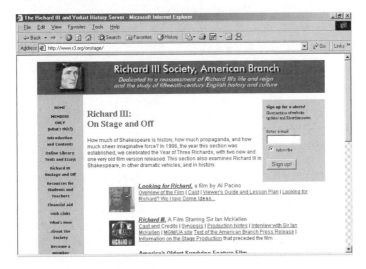

Search engines and **directories** are the two most common means of finding information on the Web. A search engine scans millions of web pages for the presence of keywords, links, and other information; essentially, you enter your query on your subject, and its Web-crawling software examines the sites in its database, returning with a list of "hits," or links to sites. An example of a pure search engine is Google.

Directories, on the other hand, organize an edited collection of websites by subject. Using a directory to find information on Picasso, you would select the "Arts & Humanities" menu category, and then perhaps the option "Criticism and Theory" from the subsequent menu, and so on, until you end up with a series of web pages devoted to the specific aspect of Picasso you are exploring.

The picture of the Yahoo! Canada home page also illustrates that the distinction between search engines and directories has become blurred: many search engines have some sort of directory on their home page. Following is a

list of the most common directories (Canadian versions have been supplied where available):

Yahoo!   <www.yahoo.ca>

- Allows users to search by category or by website
- Often provides links to other more specialized directories

Internet Public Library   <www.ipl.org>

- A specialized directory organized by librarians with an online text collection of 14 000 titles
- Offers a "reference collection" including dictionaries, thesauri, books of quotations, etc.

Below is a list of home pages of popular search engines and some of their characteristics:

AltaVista   <www.altavista.ca>

- Can translate pages into or out of a number of languages; these translations are done by a software program, not by a qualified human translator, and should be used only to glean a general idea of the content of a particular text.
- AltaVista also operates an all-purpose translation site called Babel Fish at <babelfish.altavista.digital.com>.

Google   <www.google.ca>

- A fast and efficient search engine with a database of over 1.3 billion pages
- Evaluates sites based on the number and nature of links that point to them as well as on the presence of keywords

Northern Light <www.northernlight.com>

- Sorts results by "relevance" or "date and time"
- Supports natural language searching
- Offers GeoSearch, which searches for local websites within a specified radius of a chosen location

Metasearch tools enable you to conduct a search on a number of search engines at once. The advantage of this is that you dramatically increase the size of the database you consult. On the other hand, metasearches usually take longer. Some examples of metasearch tools are listed below:

Ixquick <www.ixquick.com>

- Eliminates duplicate sites
- Awards sites stars for each search engine that has placed them in its top 10 returns, providing users with an instant popularity ranking

Dogpile <www.dogpile.com>

- Allows users to customize searches
- Uses 15 search engines and several specialty engines for images, news, audio, and other forms of information

Ask Jeeves <www.askjeeves.com>

- Allows searches in natural language
- Responds to questions posed with a list of similar questions, from which you can choose one to be answered

There are also some specifically Canadian search tools, such as Canada.com <www.canada.com> and Maple Square <www.maplesquare.com>.

Once you have found relevant material in your search, a good idea is to **bookmark** the site. Also called "Favourites," bookmarks allow you to go directly to a web page without having to type the address in your web browser all the time. Bookmarks can also be saved to floppy disks, which is particularly useful if you are using a publicly accessible computer in a library or student centre or if you use more than one computer. It is also a good idea to print off material from every source you consult. Online sources are ephemeral; a particular page may be readily located one day but have moved to a different address the next. A printout also includes a record of the date that you retrieved the information, which is essential for properly documenting the source in a research paper bibliography. You also have the option of saving a web page onto your computer. If the page uses a lot of text, you may want to save it in a "text only" (**.txt** file extension) format to reduce the amount of space it occupies on your disk. As a text only file, it will also be available for viewing in your word processing program.

Using the Internet is an exciting, seductive way to find and use information. People are used to the idea that they have to document information they take from books and periodicals; be sure also to give proper credit for information you take from the Internet. The Internet is a new medium, and it presents new temptations and new dangers.

! CAUTION Caution #1 Guard against computer viruses. They lurk in every part of the Internet and they can be extremely destructive to your own and your school's data. Fortunately, good, free virus checkers are available.

Caution #2 Be conscious of security. Do not give out your telephone number or address over the Internet. Do not tell anyone your password.

Caution #3 Pay for what you use unless the material is clearly freeware or in the public domain.

Caution #4 Give proper credit. *Freeware* and *public domain* mean you do not have to pay, not that you can use images or text as if they were your own.

Caution #5 The Internet offers extensive information, but **not all information**. Plenty of good sources still exist in print.

Caution #6 Check reliability. Evaluate the source critically. Are there errors? Is the site monitored? (Many are not.) Is the author identified and are his or her credentials given?

 33f **Evaluating sources requires thought; taking notes demands accuracy.**

(1) Testing reliability, bias, and integrity

When you are doing research, one important consideration always is the reliability of your sources. (See 33b.) Ask the following questions about the sources you discover:

Checklist for Evaluating Sources
- What are the author's credentials?
- Do others speak of the writer as an authority?
- Does the work contain evidence indicating that the author is well informed?
- Does the work contain evidence that the author is prejudiced in any way?
- Is the work recent enough to provide up-to-date information?
- Is the work published by a reputable company?
- Does the work provide documentation to support important points?
- Does the work include a bibliography that can help you to identify other sources?

Canadian Book Review Annual and *Book Review Digest,* which contain convenient summaries of critical opinion on a book, could help you decide which books are most dependable. *The Book Trade in Canada,* published by *Quill & Quire;* the *UK Publishers Directory,* edited by Ellen Rocco; and Bowker's *Literary Marketplace* will provide basic information about publishers. You can usually assume that university presses demand a high standard of scholarship. As for periodicals, an article published in an academic journal (as opposed to a popular magazine) has usually been reviewed by experts before publication. Be alert for bias that may be built into a source, even if it is not obvious when you are reading. For example, an article on malpractice suits in the *Canadian Medical Association Journal* is likely to be sympathetic to physicians.

Some periodicals are straightforward about identifying their affiliations. For instance, editors of the left-leaning *Briarpatch* describe their magazine as offering

> an alternative view on issues and events. It offers essential reading on the labour movement, the environment, Aboriginal and women's rights, and international affairs. We don't pull punches when exposing the dirty dealings of corporations and governments.   —*Great Canadian Magazines*

On the Internet version of the right-leaning weekly newsmagazine *Alberta Report,* the editor clearly shows the periodical's bias when introducing a new "Family" section:

> The newspapers have been . . . [providing information about family life] in their "Life" sections for years, but we suspect our readers have little use for the relentlessly liberal homilies on teen self-esteem, elementary sex-ed, grief counselling and herbal remedies served up by the papers.   —PAUL BUNNER

As you read your sources, learn how to find and evaluate useful passages with a minimum of time and effort. Seldom will a whole book, or even a whole article, be of use for any given researched paper. You will usually find that you must turn to many books and articles, rejecting some altogether and using others only in part. You cannot always take the time to read each book completely. Use the table of contents and the index of a book, and learn to skim the pages until you find the passages you need. When you find them, read critically. (See chapter 31.) Ask yourself if you agree with what you are reading and if the material raises any unanswered questions.

Although the use of the Internet as a student resource has grown tremendously in recent years, students should be made aware of some of its limitations. To begin with, the amount of academic information on the Web is by no means exhaustive; it still represents only a small fraction of the resources available in, say, a typical reference library. The Web, thus, is but one source of information; it should not be considered to give the last word on a subject.

The Web is best utilized when searching for the most up-to-date information on a topic. New knowledge will appear far more quickly on the Web than it will in a book. However, information on the Web has an ephemeral nature and is less stable; unlike a book, information on the Web changes quickly and moves around. Thus, an article that was easily found one day might not be the same tomorrow—if it is there at all. Generally speaking, the Web is especially useful for finding facts and statistics; it is not well suited to locating, for example, a hard-to-find controversial piece of criticism or obscure political theory.

Finally, because of its accessibility, more responsibility falls on the researcher to evaluate the quality, relevance, and credibility of the material he or she finds. To be sure, the majority of the websites that are helpful to students are associated with academic, government, or other institutions that can be utilized confidently. Before using a website in your research, ask the following questions:

Checklist for Evaluating Websites
- Who is the author and/or the site's sponsor? Does the site appear under the sponsorship of a reputable institution?
- Can you confirm the authority of the author?
- Is the site well presented? Is the writing well edited and free of spelling errors? Is it well organized and designed?
- Is the site intended for the scholar or the general public?
- At what difficulty level is the text?
- Does the author refer to other important sources in the discipline?
- Is the documentation adequate?
- How does this resource compare to others you've found on the topic?
- Can factual material be verified from another source?
- Would you evaluate the links in the site as useful and relevant?
- Can you confirm facts or statistics mentioned in the site?
- Does the site show evidence of frequent maintenance?

Exercise 2

Do preliminary reading on your research subject. Identify one source that seems reliable and another that seems biased. Write a two-paragraph evaluation in which you assess the credibility of each.

Exercise 3

Evaluate the following sources for reliability and/or bias about the war on terrorism and about Aboriginal rights:

1. *Maclean's*
2. *Saturday Night*
3. *Canadian Living*
4. *The Globe and Mail*

(2) Taking notes

There are probably as many ways to take notes as there are note takers; some note takers are more comfortable taking notes on 8½-by-11-inch (21.6-cm-by-27.9-cm) paper, others on index cards, and still others using the computer. Each system has advantages and disadvantages, and you should match your choice to your project and your own work style. Whatever you use to create your notes, keep the following points in mind:

Checklist for Taking Notes

- Does every note clearly identify its source?
- Is an author/title code for each source noted in the working bibliography and on every page of your notes?
- When a source has sparked your own thoughts, have you identified both the source and the fact that the note is your own idea? Mistakenly attributing your ideas to someone else is a kind of documentation error that gets far too little attention.
- Have you put the full bibliographic citation on the first page of every photocopy and a short form on the following pages?
- Is the bibliographic information for the source of every note accurate? Double-check to be sure. Scrupulous care now can prevent a multitude of problems later on—such as being forced to abandon important information because you lost track of exactly where it came from.
- Have you taken down verbatim—that is, copied every word, every capital letter, and every punctuation mark exactly as it was in the original—any useful passage that

continued

continued from previous page

you think you may later quote, being especially careful to put quotation marks around any words you use directly from a source? Failure to do so as you take notes may lead to unintended plagiarism when you draft your paper.

- On photocopies, have you clearly indicated passages you intend to quote directly, passages you intend to paraphrase, and those you plan to summarize?

- Have you used different typestyles or different colours in computer files to make source identification of quoted text easy?

Using a notebook

A ring binder into which you can insert pages of notes as well as photocopies is an excellent organizational tool, particularly if you arrange it to keep your working bibliography separate from notes and photocopies and if you have a system for sorting notes into the main subject categories your work covers. Identify the source on every page of notes, and use a fresh page for each new source.

Using notecards

One of the best ways to take notes is to use cards of uniform size. (Many researchers use larger cards for notes than for bibliographic references because notes often require more room. Different sizes of cards also help a writer keep the cards' functions separate.)

Show the author's name (and a short title for the work if the bibliography contains more than one work by that author) on each card, and include the exact page number(s) from which the information is drawn. If you put no more than a single note, however brief, on each card and a heading of two or three keywords at the top, you can easily arrange your cards as you prepare to write your paper.

Using photocopies

Another way to take notes is to use photocopies of short excerpts from materials you think you might quote directly. On a photocopy you can mark quotable material and jot down your own ideas as you study the source. Make sure you document the source on the photocopy.

Photocopied source with notes

para- phrase?

Olivier's use of the direct address to the camera, which *important point!*

defies the naturally assumed aesthetic laws of the medium, is

another of those brilliant strokes whereby he brings a dis-

tinctly theatrical action to film and then gives it an impact

tried to make film reflect R's char. which only cinema can. The success of its effect depends upon

the fact that it amplifies elements which are implicit in the

play in the character of Richard. The boldness with which he

affronts the aesthetic laws of the medium is consonant with

the assuredness with which Richard challenges the accepted

procedures of royal succession and affronts the apparent spir-

itual order of the real.

Using computer files

If you have good keyboarding skills and are familiar with a word processing program, you may find it more efficient to use your computer for taking notes. One problem with this method, however, is that it is tempting to take down too much information verbatim. Another is that you may go too fast and make mistakes. As a result, you may not digest the information in your source well enough to use it skilfully, and you certainly run the risk of inadvertently failing to cite the source.

TIPS ON USING A COMPUTER TO TAKE NOTES

1. Create a separate master folder (or directory) for your paper.
2. Create folders within the master folder for your bibliography, notes, and portions of drafts.
3. Keep all the notes for each source in a separate file.
4. Use distinctive fonts and/or differentiators for notes on different source materials.

Using a computer to take notes makes it easy to copy and paste information into subject files and ultimately from subject files into the finished paper. But this method also makes it easy to lose track of where the note came from and increases the potential for inadvertent plagiarism.

! **CAUTION** Systematically identify the source of each note you cut and paste. As you work the information smoothly into your text, document your sources accurately and responsibly.

Exercise 4

Select a subject that you would like to become more knowledgeable about. Consult the main catalogue in your library and at least one periodical index. Propose two different ways of narrowing the subject. Write a paragraph in which you (a) report these two possibilities, (b) explain which of the two you have selected for further research, and (c) determine the number and quality of the sources that seem available. Then prepare at least four bibliography entries using cards or other means as your instructor requires.

33g Plagiarism is a serious offence.

Taking someone else's words or ideas and presenting them as your own leaves you open to criminal charges. In the film, video, music, and software business this act of theft is called **piracy**. In publishing and education it is called **plagiarism** and/or **cheating**. Whatever it is called and for whatever reason it occurs, it is wrong.

! **CAUTION** Plagiarism is a serious offence. Carelessness is no excuse. Although the act may escape criminal prosecution, employers generally fire an employee who uses material illegally, and teachers often fail careless students.

The *MLA Handbook for Writers of Research Papers,* 6th edition (New York: MLA, 2003) advises:

> To guard against the possibility of unintentional plagiarism during research and writing, keep careful notes that always distinguish among three types of material: your ideas, your summaries and paraphrases of others' ideas and facts, and exact wording you copy from sources. . . . [F]orms of plagiarism include the failure to give appropriate acknowledgment when repeating or paraphrasing another's wording, when taking a particularly apt phrase, and when paraphrasing another's argument or presenting another's line of thinking. (70–71)

One purpose of this chapter is to help you to use the ideas and thoughts of others responsibly—to avoid plagiarism.

ESL Some cultures view borrowing information much differently than North Americans do. For instance, in some cultures, anyone who has purchased a book and decides to quote from it can do so without citing the source or requesting (or paying for) permission. In North America, authorship is equated with ownership of any new information, and acknowledgment of the source must be made.

You must give credit for all information you borrow except for two kinds: common knowledge and your own ideas. Common knowledge includes such information as "December has 31 days," and well-known proverbs ("a penny saved is a penny earned") or historical information such as the dates of the battle at Vimy Ridge.

After you have read a good deal about a given subject, you will be able to distinguish between common knowledge in that field and the distinctive ideas or interpretations of specific writers. When you use the ideas or information that these writers provide, be sure to cite your source.

As for your own ideas, if you have been scrupulous in noting your own thoughts as you took notes, you should have no difficulty distinguishing between what you knew to begin with and what you learned in your research and so must give credit for. The information in your research log that shows what you were aware of knowing before you began research can help. (See 33a(3).)

Source   (from "Returning Young Adults," in *Psychology and Marketing*, 11, 1994, by J. Burnett and D. Smart, page 254)

Both generations want their rights. The RYAs want the autonomy they have grown accustomed to and expect their parents to treat them like adults. The parents, meanwhile, have come to recognize their own rights. They may resent that the time, money, and emotional energy they planned to invest in themselves after the child's departure are instead allocated to the RYA.

Undocumented copying

```
They may resent that the time, money, and
emotional energy they planned to invest in
themselves after the child's departure are
instead allocated to the RYA.
```

Appropriate citation

```
Marketing professors John Burnett and Denise
Smart note that parents "may resent that the
time, money, and emotional energy they planned
to invest in themselves after the child's
departure are instead allocated to the RYA"
(254).
```

Quotation marks show where the copied words begin and end, and the number in parentheses at the end tells the reader the exact page on which the quotation appears. In this case, the sentence that includes the quotation identifies the authors and establishes the context for the quotation. An alternative, more common technique for sources of lesser importance is to provide the authors' names within the parenthetical reference: (Burnett and Smart 254). If, after referring to the following checklist you cannot decide whether you need to cite a source, the safest policy is to cite it.

Checklist for Kinds of Information to Cite
- Writings, both published and unpublished
    by direct quotation
    by indirect quotation
    by reference to ideas

continued

---

continued from previous page

- Opinions and judgments not your own
- Arguable points and claims
- Facts (unless widely known)
- Images and graphics such as

works of art	drawings	tables and charts
film/video	maps	advertisements
photographs	music	statistics and graphs

- Personal communication
  - private
  - public
- Electronic media
  - broadcasts
  - recordings
  - computer-generated materials

33h   Integrating sources fosters mastery of information.

A research project that is a patchwork of snippets from others (even when meticulously cited) indicates that you are, at the very least, an inexperienced writer. The foundation of researched writing is always the writer's own ideas, which flow from point to point, supported and guided by research. Understanding how to evaluate sources, take notes accurately, and integrate ideas is essential.

(1) Mastering information

Digesting information has long been acknowledged as an excellent way to master what you read. However, digests are most useful when they focus on larger issues rather than details. A pattern for a research digest may help you stay on track.

Typically, depending on whether its source is an article or a book, such a digest contains from three to a dozen sentences. Each of these sentences should use a rhetorically strong verb (such as those in the list on page 532). The first sentence gives the author's name, the title, and the main idea of the work. The second sentence or set of sentences identifies the main points of the thesis and includes information about the methodology and kind(s) of support or argument the author used to develop these points. The third sentence or set of sentences identifies the rhetorical context—audience, occasion, facts of publication, and so on. Finally, the last sentence states the author's purpose.

(2) Integrating sources

When good research writers use borrowed material, they introduce it to readers by establishing the context from which the material came; for example, in a researched paper about the value of vitamin C, readers might find it useful to know that the author of a quotation praising the vitamin is a Nobel laureate in chemistry. Similarly, you can introduce a paraphrase by making clear why the information is important. An excellent way to introduce research is to use a phrase that indicates the author's attitude or the importance of the information. The following list of verbs that introduce quoted, paraphrased, or summarized information can be helpful in deciding how to integrate that information with your own ideas.

SIXTY-FOUR LEAD-IN VERBS

acknowledge	complain	explain	reason
add	concede	express	refute
admit	conclude	find	reject
advise	concur	grant	remark
agree	confirm	illustrate	reply
allow	consider	imply	report
analyze	contend	insist	respond
answer	criticize	interpret	reveal
argue	declare	list	see
ask	deny	maintain	show
assert	describe	note	speculate
believe	disagree	object	state
charge	discuss	observe	suggest
claim	dispute	offer	suppose
comment	emphasize	oppose	think
compare	endorse	point out	write

Writers of researched papers borrow information in three ways: quoting the exact words of a source, paraphrasing them, or summarizing them. With any of these methods, your writing will benefit if you are careful to integrate the material—properly cited, of course—into your own sentences and paragraphs. Whatever option you choose, make sure that you use sources responsibly.

! **CAUTION** Words or ideas borrowed from other writers must not be distorted in any way, and credit must be given when borrowing occurs.

The following examples of quotation, paraphrase, and summary show APA documentation style. For additional information on documentation, see **34a**, **34c**, and **34d**.

(3) Using direct quotations

A quotation should contribute an idea to your paper. Select quotations only if (a) you want to retain the beauty or clarity of someone else's words or (b) you plan to discuss the implications of the words in question. Keep quotations as short as possible and make them an integral part of your text. (For examples of ways this can be done, see 34b, sample MLA research paper; 34e, sample APA research paper; and 35a, writing about literature.)

Quote **accurately**. Enclose every quoted passage in quotation marks. Any quotation of another person's words except for well-known or proverbial passages should be placed in quotation marks or, if longer than four lines, set off as an indented block. (See 20b.)

Cite the exact source for your quotation. If you think your audience might be unfamiliar with a source, establish its authority by identifying its author the first time you refer to it. (Note that this citation is in APA style.)

Family science researcher Judith S. Peck (1991) defines the "launching" stage as "one of the most complex stages of the family's life cycles" (p. 150).

Checklist for Direct Quotations
- Have I copied all the words accurately?
- Have I copied all the punctuation accurately? (See 20f.)
- Do I need to observe a special form or special spacing? (See 20a and b.)
- Have I used ellipsis points correctly to indicate anything that is left out? (See 21i.)
- Have I avoided using ellipsis points *before* quotations that are clearly only parts of sentences?

continued

continued from previous page

- Have I used square brackets around everything I added to the direct quotation? (See 21g.)
- Have I used too many quotations? (Using too many quotations in a paper suggests an inability to think independently or to synthesize material.)

(4) Paraphrasing

A **paraphrase** is a restatement of a source in about the same number of words. Paraphrasing enables you to demonstrate that you have understood what you have read; it also enables you to help your audience understand. Paraphrase when you (a) use someone else's content but not his or her specific words or (b) simplify difficult material.

Your restatement of someone else's words should honour two important principles: your version should be almost entirely in your own words, and your words should accurately convey the content of the original passage.

Using your own words

Unless you enclose an author's words in quotation marks, do not mix them with your own even if the sentence structure is different. Equally important, do not make the mistake of thinking that you can substitute synonyms for an author's words while you preserve his or her sentence structure. Both of these are plagiarism, even if you cite the source.

As you compare the source below with a paraphrase that follows, note the differences in sentence structure as well as word choice.

Source (from "Returning Young Adults," *Psychology and Marketing, 11,* 1994, by J. Burnett and D. Smart, pages 253–269)

In general, contrary to assumptions about RYAs amassing large amounts of disposable income, the findings suggest that economic deprivation is the primary factor distinguishing the RYA from a single cohort. RYAs have an appreciably higher unemployment rate and lower income than a comparable singles group. Thus, the notion characterizing the modern RYA as a somewhat spoiled individual who wants to maintain his or her earlier lifestyle is not supported in this study.

Inadequate paraphrasing

`Although many think that RYAs have large`
`amounts of money to spend, research has shown`
`that RYAs differ from single young adults`
`mainly because more RYAs are unemployed or`
`have lower incomes. Research shows that the`
`general impression that RYAs are lazy`
`parasites is not correct (p. 267).`

Although this passage ends with a parenthetical reference to the original sources, the reference does not reveal the size of the debt. The author could be giving credit to Burnett and Smart for the whole passage or only the last sentence—it is hard to tell. And when you compare this "paraphrase" with the original source, you will find that the author has followed the same structure. Although the wording has changed, the paraphrase in this case is so close to the original that it could be considered plagiarism.

Adequate paraphrasing

`Burnett and Smart report research showing`
`that RYAs, contrary to opinion, have a more`
`difficult time meeting their bills than other`
`single young adults. Therefore, attitudes that`
`view them as lazy parasites are incorrect (p.`
`267).`

In this example, the page reference establishes where the paraphrase ends; the introductory "Burnett and Smart report" establishes where it begins. When you paraphrase, make sure that your audience will be able to tell whether you are paraphrasing a single sentence or more. As a general rule even in the hard sciences, which often tolerate fairly close paraphrasing in the interests of scientific accuracy, begin paraphrases with a few words indicating that you are about to restate another writer's words.

! **CAUTION**   If you simply change a few words in a passage, you have not adequately restated it. You may be charged with plagiarism if the wording of your version follows the original too closely, even if you provide a page reference to the source you used. A page reference after an inadequate paraphrase would acknowledge the source of your idea but not the extent of your debt to another writer's language.

Maintaining accuracy

Any paraphrase must accurately maintain the sense of the original. Compare the original statement below with the paraphrases.

Original	Owning a boat is like standing in the shower tearing up $1000 bills.
Inaccurate	Boat owners would feel comfortable "tearing up $1000 bills." [Changes the focus of the original.]
Accurate	Owning a boat is an expensive way to get wet. [Changes the language of the original but remains faithful to the sense, even though the humour is lost.]

Of course, deliberately changing the gist of what a source says is unethical.

Unethical Boat owners are financially irresponsible masochists who enjoy being uncomfortable. [Shifts focus from the experience of boat owning to an indictment of boat owners' personalities.]

(5) Summarizing

When you summarize, you condense the main point(s) of your source as you restate them in your own words. A summary is shorter than the original source and lacks the kind of detail that fleshes out the original; it is telegraphic. Summarizing, an essential skill for writing researched papers, enables writers to report the work of others without getting bogged down in unnecessary detail. Paraphrase when you want to restate a passage so that it is easier to understand, and summarize whenever you can save space by condensing a passage (or, in some cases, an entire work).

Source (from "Young Adults Returning Home: Implications for Social Policy," by B. A. Mitchell and E. M. Gee, pages 61–71, in B. Galaway and J. Hudson [eds.], *Youth in Transition: Perspectives on Research and Policy*, Toronto: Thompson, 1996)

> Table 7.1 presents the distribution of the main reason for the last return home. Economic reasons clearly take precedence over non-economic reasons. Economic reasons account for about 81% of the total reasons for returning home; 26% reported that they had boomeranged because of financial problems, 19% returned to save money, 13% stated that they returned due to transitional or temporary reasons such as finished travelling, and 13% returned for school-related reasons

such as to attend university. Only 17% of all reasons for returning fall into a non-economic category.

Summary

In their study of Vancouver-area RYAs, Mitchell and Gee (1996) found that the majority of RYAs cited economic reasons for returning home (p. 63).

⚠ **CAUTION** When you are summarizing, you may find it useful to retain a key phrase from your source; but if you do, put quotation marks around the words in question.

Exercise 5

Find a paragraph in two important sources that you may want to cite. After you read both paragraphs carefully, write a one-sentence summary of each. Then paraphrase the same paragraphs. Avoid using the same sentence patterns as the source. Choose your words carefully to convey the source's ideas exactly.

Exercise 6

Summarize Janet Kowolsky's argument paper, page 461, and answer the following questions:

1. What is the most important sentence?
2. What are the key points of Janet's argument?
3. What was her purpose?

Chapter 34

Research: Using and Citing Sources

To write well from sources is a complex process that requires writers to perform a number of diverse tasks. These include activating the creative imagination (chapter 28), integrating it with the ability to think critically about one's own ideas and those of others (chapter 31), developing a sophisticated mastery of complex information (chapters 27, 31, and 33), and demonstrating skill at managing time and materials (chapters 26 and 33). But all that effort can be lost if a writer does not document sources accurately, a skill that demands meticulous attention to details (chapters 20, 28, and 33). Different disciplines usually employ different documentation styles, so there is no single way to document or to prepare a bibliography that can be used in every department of a college or university. Use the style your instructor specifies. The manuals listed below discuss documentation forms in detail. If you are asked to use one of these manuals, look for it in your library's reference collection, study it carefully, and make sure your notes and bibliography correspond exactly to the examples it provides.

Style books and manuals

American Chemical Society. *The ACS Style Guide: A Manual for Authors and Editors.* Washington: Amer. Chem. Soc., 1997.

American Institute of Physics. *AIP Style Manual.* 4th ed. New York: Amer. Inst. of Physics, 1990.

American Mathematical Society. *AMS Author Handbook.* Providence: Amer. Mathematical Soc., 1997.

American Medical Association. *American Medical Association Manual of Style.* 9th ed. Baltimore: Williams, 1998.

American Psychological Association. *Publication Manual of the American Psychological Association.* 5th ed. Washington: Amer. Psychological Assn., 2001.

The Canadian Style: A Guide to Writing and Editing. Rev. and exp. ed. Toronto: Dundurn, 1997.

The Chicago Manual of Style. 14th ed. Chicago: U of Chicago P, 1993.

Council of Biology Editors. *Scientific Style and Format: The CBE Manual for Authors, Editors, and Publishers.* 6th ed. New York: Cambridge UP, 1994.

Editors' Association of Canada. *Editing Canadian English.* 2nd ed. Toronto: Macfarlane Walter & Ross, 2000.

Gibaldi, Joseph. *MLA Handbook for Writers of Research Papers.* 6th ed. New York: Modern Language Assn., 2003.

International Organization for Standardization. "ISO 690: Documentation—Bibliographic References—Content, Form and Structure." *Documentation and Information.* 2nd ed. Geneva: Inter. Org. for Standardization, 1987.

———. *ISO 690-2: Electronic Documents or Parts Thereof.* Geneva: Inter. Org. for Standardization, 1997.

Linguistic Society of America. *LSA Bulletin,* Dec. issue, annually.

McGill Law Review. *Canadian Guide to Uniform Legal Citation.* 4th ed. Scarborough, ON: Carswell, 1998.

Turabian, Kate L., et al. *A Manual for Writers of Term Papers, Theses, and Dissertations.* 6th ed. Chicago: U of Chicago P, 1996.

If your instructor does not require a specific documentation style, follow the style set forth by the discipline appropriate for your paper. When you do not know what type of documentation is appropriate, go to the periodical room of your library and model your documentation on the style you find used in one of the journals in your field.

To provide you with further help, the rest of this chapter discusses the two documentation styles most widely used in university and college writing: MLA style, most frequently used for papers in English (34a), and APA style, most often used for papers in psychology and other courses in the social sciences (34d). Some disciplines prefer to use the footnote or endnote system of documentation, so samples of this style are provided in 34c.

34a MLA-style documentation is appropriate for research papers in literary studies and foreign language courses.

As you draft a researched paper, remember that it is *your* paper. Using the headings on your cards (see page 524) and arranging your notes to follow your working plan or outline can make writing your paper easier than simply plunging in might be. Make sure to use your own words and your own style. Integrate your source material— paraphrases, summaries, quotations—with your own statements rather than making the paper a patchwork of other people's comments.

(1) Using parenthetical citations

Give proper credit by citing your sources. Traditionally, such citations took the form of notes numbered consecutively throughout the paper and placed either at the bottom of the appropriate page (footnotes) or all together at the end of the paper (endnotes). Although some disciplines still use a note system (see 34c), the MLA recommends placing citations in parentheses directly in the text. These parenthetical citations refer the reader to a list of works cited at the end of the paper. The advantage of this system is that it is easy for both writers and readers to use. The MLA suggests reserving numbered notes for supplementary or explanatory comments. The numbers are inserted in the appropriate places in the text, and the notes are gathered at the end of the paper. See page 588.

The basic elements of the parenthetical citation are the author's last name and the page number of the material used in the source. However, it is not necessary to repeat any information that is already clearly provided. In other words, omit the author's name from the parenthetical citation if you have identified it in the text of the paper, shortly before the material being cited. As you study the following examples, observe that common sense determines the information that must be included in a parenthetical citation and that this system is easy to use. (The first example is taken from the researched paper in 34b so you can see how a citation refers readers to a source listed alphabetically in the list of works cited at the end of the paper.) See also the details of punctuation and mechanics below.

A work by one author

`Olivier creates `Richard III`'s "central device of coherence" by using a cyclical theme of the crown (Brown 133).`

In this citation, the author's name is included within the parentheses because it is not mentioned in the text. Since there is only one work by Brown in the list of works cited (on page 590), there is no need to place a title in the parentheses. However, a page number is included because the reference is to a specific passage. Note how the citation changes if the text includes more information about the source:

Constance Brown argues that in <u>Richard III</u>, Laurence Olivier uses a cyclical theme of the crown to create "the central device of coherence" (133).

A work by two or three authors

The Internet is "simply one of the central characters in the play, a play in which all the information around us is being converted into digital form and in which the digital 1s and 0s of that information are regularly exchanged" (Carroll and Broadhead 9).

Provide the last name of each author, punctuating as you would for items in a series. Commas are not necessary in a citation involving only two authors, for example: (Carroll and Broadhead 9).

A work by more than three authors

For a work with more than three authors, follow the bibliographic entry, giving either the first author's last name followed by *et al.* or all the last names. (Do not italicize or underline the Latin phrase.)

In one important study, women graduates complained more frequently about "excessive control than about lack of structure" (Belenky et al. 205).

OR

```
In one important study, women graduates
complained more frequently about "excessive
control than about lack of structure"
(Belenky, Clinchy, Goldberger, and Tarule
205).
```

A multi-volume work

When you cite material from a multi-volume work, include the volume number (followed by a colon and a space) before the page number.

```
As Katherine Raine has argued, "true poetry
begins where human personality ends" (2: 247).
```

If your list of works cited includes only one volume of a multi-volume work, then you do not need to include the volume number in the parenthetical citation.

More than one work by the same author

When your list of works cited includes more than one work by the same author, your parenthetical citations should include a shortened title that reveals which of the author's works is being cited in a particular instance. Use a comma to separate the author's name from the shortened title when both are in parentheses.

```
According to Gilbert and Gubar, Elizabeth
Barrett Browning, Emily Dickinson, and
Virginia Woolf considered poetry by women to
be forbidden and problematic (Shakespeare's
Sisters 107). That attitude was based on the
```

```
conception that male sexuality is the "essence
of literary power" (Gilbert and Gubar,
Madwoman 4).
```

This passage cites two different books by the same authors, Sandra M. Gilbert and Susan Gubar: *Shakespeare's Sisters: Feminist Essays on Women Poets* and *The Madwoman in the Attic: The Woman and the Nineteenth-Century Literary Imagination*. The authors' names are not necessary in the first citation since they are mentioned in the text; they are included in the second citation because their names are not mentioned in connection with *Madwoman*.

You can often avoid cumbersome references by including information in the text that might otherwise have to appear parenthetically:

```
In The Madwoman in the Attic and Shakespeare's
Sisters, Sandra M. Gilbert and Susan Gubar
argue that the infrequent appearance of
women as literary figures is a result of
the repression imposed by male sexuality.
```

Works by different authors with the same last name

Occasionally your list of works cited will contain sources by two authors with the same last name—for example, rhetoricians Theresa Enos and Richard Enos. In such cases, you must use the first name as well as the last.

```
Richard Enos includes a thirteen-page
bibliography in Greek Rhetoric before
Aristotle (141-54). In her collection of
articles by prominent figures in modern
rhetoric and philosophy, Professing the
New Rhetorics, Theresa Enos mentions the
```

```
considerable contemporary reliance on pre-
Aristotelian rhetoric and includes an essay on
the subject by Michael Halloran (25, 331-43).
```

In these references, the citation of more than one page "(141–54)" identifies continuous pages while "(25, 331–43)" indicates that the reference is to two separate sets of pages.

An indirect source

If you need to include material that one of your sources quoted from another work, but you cannot obtain the original source, use the following form:

```
The critic Susan Hardy Aikens has argued on
behalf of what she calls "canonical
multiplicity" (qtd. in Mayers 677).
```

A reader turning to the list of works cited should find a bibliographic entry for Mayers (which was the source consulted) but not for Aikens (because the quotation was obtained secondhand).

Poetry, drama, and the Bible

When you refer to poetry, drama, and the Bible, you must often give numbers of lines, acts, and scenes, or of chapters and verses, rather than page numbers. This practice enables a reader to consult an edition other than the one you are using. Nonetheless, your list of works cited should still identify your edition.

Act, scene, and line numbers (all Arabic) are separated by periods with no space before or after them. The MLA suggests that biblical chapters and verses be treated similarly, although some writers prefer to use colons instead of periods in scriptural references. In all cases, the progression is from larger to smaller units.

The following example illustrates a typical citation of lines of poetry.

F. R. Scott deeply opposed the belief that if a poem depicted the maple leaf it was automatically worthy of support. This idea is evident in "The Canadian Authors Meet":

> O Canada, O Canada, Oh can
> A day go by without new authors springing
> To paint the native maple, and to plan
> More ways to set the selfsame welkin
> ringing? (25-28)

The following citation shows that the famous "To be, or not to be" soliloquy appears in act 3, scene 1, lines 56–89 of *Hamlet*.

In <u>Hamlet</u>, Shakespeare presents the most famous soliloquy in the history of the theatre: "To be, or not to be . . ." (3.1.56-89).

Chapter 35 contains additional examples of how to quote and cite literary works.

Biblical references identify the book of the Bible, the chapter within the book, and the pertinent verses. In the following example, the writer refers to the creation story in Genesis, noting that the story begins in chapter 1, verse 1 and ends with chapter 2, verse 22.

The Old Testament creation story (Gen. 1.1-2.22), told with remarkable economy, culminates in the arrival of Eve.

Names of books of the Bible are neither italicized—underlined—(see chapter 24) nor enclosed in quotation marks (see chapter 20), and abbreviation is desirable (see chapter 25). The *MLA Handbook* provides a list of abbreviations for parts of the Bible.

Punctuation and mechanics

Punctuation and numbers Commas separate the authors' names from the titles (Brown, "Olivier's *Richard III:* A Reevaluation") and indicate interruptions in a sequence of pages or lines (44, 47). Hyphens indicate continuous sequences of pages (44–47) and lines (1–4). Colons separate volume and page numbers (Raine 2: 247); one space follows the colon. Periods separate acts, scenes, and lines in drama (3.1.56–89). Periods (or colons) distinguish chapters from verses in biblical citations (Gen. 1.1 or Gen. 1:1)—see 21d.

Ellipsis points (21i) indicate omissions within a quotation: "They lived in an age of increasing complexity and great hope; we in an age of . . . growing despair" (Krutch 2). Brackets (21g) indicate interpolations within quotations: "Unlike our more revered and well-bought writers, [Greg] Hollingshead's narrative perspective [in *The Roaring Girl*] was distinctly wonky, working a really calm and intelligent sense of humour and displacement into the very essence of the stories and characters he was creating" (Archer N16).

When a question mark ends a quotation (21b), place it before the closing quotation mark; then add a period after the parenthetical citation: Paulo Freire asks, "How can the oppressed, as divided, unauthentic beings, participate in developing the pedagogy of their liberation?" (33).

The MLA favours Arabic numbers throughout, except when citing pages identified by Roman numerals in the source itself (such as the front matter of a book: page vi).

Placement of citations Wherever possible, citations should appear just before a mark of punctuation in the text of the paper.

```
Richard Enos provides a bibliography of
sources for the study of Greek rhetoric before
Aristotle (141-54), and Theresa Enos's edited
collection, Professing the New Rhetorics,
includes Michael Halloran's essay "On the End
of Rhetoric, Classical and Modern" (331-43).
```

Richard Enos's citation falls just before a comma; Theresa Enos's just before a period. However, in a sentence such as the following, the citations should follow the authors' names to keep the references separate.

```
Richard Enos (141-54) and Theresa Enos (25)
address classical rhetoric from very different
perspectives.
```

Lengthy quotations When a quotation is more than four lines long, set it off from the text by indenting 2.5 cm (or 10 typewritten spaces) from the left margin (20b). The citation in this case follows the final punctuation, to avoid making it seem part of the quotation:

```
Brantley further stresses the effectiveness
of Loncraine's setting as a device to
emphasize the image of tyranny. He says:
        Setting the work in Fascist Europe,
        with Richard's Black Shirt presence
        playing on memories of Oswald Mosley
        and Edward VII's alleged Nazi
        sympathies, always made a certain
        sense. It immediately set up echoes
```

> of what is still perceived as the
> greatest historical example of evil
> in the 20th century: Hitler's
> Third Reich. (1)

When quoting more than one paragraph, indent the first line of each paragraph by an additional 0.75 cm (or three typewritten spaces). Do not indent if you are quoting only one paragraph (or if the first sentence quoted is not the first sentence in a paragraph).

(2) Listing the works cited—MLA style

For MLA papers, the list of sources from which you have cited information is called the **Works Cited**. (Other documentation styles differ from MLA in how they arrange and name their reference lists—see, for example, 34d.)

When you are ready to produce your final draft, eliminate from your working bibliography the cards for the items you have not cited. Arrange the remaining cards in alphabetical order by the authors' last names. If you do not use cards, number your list or have the computer sort them alphabetically. You are now ready to prepare the list of works cited that will conclude your paper. As you make your final revisions, check your citations against this list to ensure that they are complete and correct.

Arrange the list of works alphabetically by author. If a source has more than one author, alphabetize by the first author's last name. Type the first line of each entry flush with the left margin and indent subsequent lines 1.25 cm (or five typewritten spaces—a hanging indentation); double-space throughout.

As you study the following MLA style entries, which cover most of the types of sources you are likely to list, observe both the arrangement of information and the punctuation. (See also pages 271–72 for a list of abbreviations that are used in works cited, notes, and tables.)

Books

Most book entries consist of three units separated by periods:

Author	Title	Publication data
Lastname, Firstname.	Title Underlined.	City: Publisher, date.

1. *Author.* Give the last name first, followed by a comma and the first name.
2. *Title.* Underline the title of the book (see 24a), and capitalize all major words. (See 23c.) Always include the book's subtitle.
3. *Publication data.* Provide the city of publication, the brief name of the publisher, and the latest copyright date shown on the copyright page. Type a colon after the city and a comma after the publisher. To shorten the name of the publisher, use the principal name: McClelland & Stewart becomes McClelland; Nelson Thomson becomes Nelson; Oxford University Press becomes Oxford UP; University of British Columbia Press becomes U of British Columbia P.

One author

MacLeod, Alistair. <u>No Great Mischief</u>. Toronto:
    McClelland, 1999.

More than one work by the same author

Tremblay, Michel. <u>Hosanna</u>. Rev. ed. Trans.
    John Van Burek and Bill Glassco.
    Vancouver: Talon, 1991.

```
---. Marcel Pursued by the Hounds. Trans. John
      Van Burek and Bill Glassco. Vancouver:
      Talon, 1996.
```

If you use more than one work by the same author, alphabetize the works by the first *major* word in each title. Give the author's name with the first title, but substitute three hyphens for the name in subsequent entries.

Two authors

```
Beal, Bob, and Rod Macleod. Prairie Fire: The
      1885 North-West Rebellion. Edmonton:
      Hurtig, 1984.
```

Invert the name of the first author (or editor) and place a comma after it. Do not invert the second name. Use a colon to separate a main title from a subtitle.

Three authors

```
Tate, Gary, Edward P. J. Corbett, and Nancy
      Myers, eds. The Writing Teacher's
      Sourcebook. 3rd ed. New York: Oxford UP,
      1994.
```

To cite books published by universities, abbreviate "university" and "press" without periods.

More than three authors

```
McGuire, Mary, et al. The Internet Handbook
      for Writers, Researchers, and
      Journalists. Toronto: Trifolium, 1997.
```

OR

McGuire, Mary, Linda Stilbourne, Melinda
    McAdams, and Laurel Hyatt. <u>The Internet</u>
    <u>Handbook for Writers, Researchers, and</u>
    <u>Journalists</u>. Toronto: Trifolium, 1997.

Corporate author

Canadian Securities Institute. <u>Bottom Line</u>
    <u>Guide to Investing</u>. Toronto: Canadian
    Securities Institute, 1998.

Anonymous author

<u>The Perils of Anonymity</u>. Smithville: Jones,
    1998.

In the case of anonymous authors, begin the entry with the
title. Do not use "Anonymous" or "Anon."

Editor as author

Taras, David, and Beverly Rasporich, eds. <u>A</u>
    <u>Passion for Identity: Canadian Studies</u>
    <u>for the 21st Century</u>. Toronto: Nelson,
    2001.

Edition after the first

Henry, Angela, and Julia Wood. <u>Everyday</u>
    <u>Encounters: An Introduction to</u>
    <u>Interpersonal Communication</u>. 2nd Canadian
    ed. Toronto: Nelson, 2002.

Work from an anthology

King, Thomas. "The One about Coyote Going
    West." <u>Anthology of Canadian Native
    Literature in English</u>. 2nd ed. Ed. Daniel
    David Moses and Terry Goldie. Toronto:
    Oxford UP, 1998. 203-10.

Use this form for an article or essay that was first published
in an anthology; use it also for a story, poem, or play
reprinted in an anthology. For an article or essay that was
published elsewhere before being included in an anthology,
use the following form:

Taylor, Drew Hayden. "There's a Trickster
    behind Every Nanabush." <u>Toronto Star</u> 3
    June 1995: J6. Rpt. in <u>Class Act:
    Readings for Canadian Writers</u>. Ed. Gary
    Webb and Donna Kerrigan. Toronto:
    Harcourt, 1996. 123-25.

Note where the essay first appeared and then show where
you read it. Use the abbreviation "Rpt." for "reprinted."
Both forms require you to cite the pages where the material
can be found. In the second example, you must cite both
the pages of the original publication and the pages of the
anthologized version.

Translation

Blais, Marie-Claire. <u>These Festive Nights</u>.
    Trans. Sheila Fischman. Concord, ON:
    Anansi, 1997.

Reprint

```
Mistry, Rohinton. A Fine Balance. 1995.
    Toronto: McClelland, 1997.
```

The original hardcover edition was published in 1995. The paperback version appeared in 1997. Use this form for books—even relatively recent ones—that have been reissued in a new format. (For reprinted articles, see "Work from an anthology.")

A multi-volume work

```
Kalman, Harold. A History of Canadian
    Architecture. 2 vols. Don Mills, ON:
    Oxford UP, 1994.
```

Cite the total number of volumes in a work when you have used more than one volume. If you use only one volume, include the number (preceded by the abbreviation *Vol.*) after the title. If the number of volumes in the complete work is important, include it at the end of the entry.

```
Clarkson, Stephen, and Christina McCall.
    Trudeau and Our Times. Vol. 2. Toronto:
    McClelland, 1994.
```

Encyclopedias and almanacs

```
C[lench], M[ary] H., and O[liver] L. A[ustin].
    "Birds: Strigiformes (Owls)." New
    Encyclopedia Britannica. 1998 ed.
```

```
Hile, Kenneth S. "Rudolfo Anaya." Contemporary
     Authors. New Rev. Ser., 1991.
```

When an author's name is indicated only by initials, check the table of contents for a list of contributors. When an article is anonymous, begin your entry with the article title and alphabetize according to the first important word in the title. Full publication information is not necessary for a well-known reference work organized alphabetically.

For sources that are more unusual, you should reveal more about the source:

```
Dreyer, Edward L. "Inner Mongolia."
     Encyclopedia of Asian History. Ed.
     Ainslee T. Embree. 4 vols. New York:
     Scribner's, 1988.
```

A book in a series

```
Frye, Northrop. The Educated Imagination. CBC
     Massey Lecture Ser. Concord, ON: Anansi,
     1993.
```

When citing a book that is part of a series, provide the name of the series and the number designating the work's place in it (if any).

A book with a title within its title

```
McHaney, Thomas, ed. William Faulkner's Go
     Down Moses: A Critical Casebook. New
     York: Garland, 1990.
```

When citing a book title containing another book title— that is, a title that would normally be underlined—do not underline the internal title. If the title within the title would normally appear in quotation marks, retain the quotation marks and underline the complete title. (See chapter 24.)

An introduction, foreword, or afterword

```
Bowering, George. Afterword. Swamp Angel. By
     Ethel Wilson. Toronto: McClelland, 1990.
     238-39.
```

Pamphlets and bulletins

```
Don't Play the Fool. Toronto: Canadian Cancer
     Society, 1995.
```

Titles of pamphlets are underlined.

Government publication

```
Krever, Horace. Commission of Inquiry on the
     Blood System in Canada: Final Report.
     Vol. 3. Cat. no. CP32-62/3-1997E. Ottawa:
     Minister of Public Works and Government
     Services, 1997.
Citizenship and Immigration Canada. A
     Newcomer's Introduction to Canada. Cat.
     no. Ci63-19/1997E. Ottawa: Minister of
     Public Works and Government Services
     Canada, 1997. (Also available in French:
     Le Canada et les nouveaux arrivants)
```

The citing of government publications is complicated because so much information is involved. If no author is given, list the name of the general division responsible for the publication first, followed by subdivisions in descending order of size. The decision as to whom to list as author is frequently arbitrary (for example, the second entry above could have been listed as "Canada"). Try to treat similar bodies similarly.

Follow the title of a government publication with any other information that might help a reader to find it, including the catalogue number. Note that many federal government publications are printed by Supply and Services Canada (sometimes listed simply as Supply and Services), but the responsible ministries and departments also publish some documents themselves. Most U.S. federal government publications are printed by the Government Printing Office (GPO).

Articles

The documentation format for articles differs slightly from that for books. The three units are the same, and they are still separated by periods, but note the differences in treatment for titles and publication information.

Author	Titles	Publication data
Lastname, Firstname.	"Title of Article." Periodical	day/month/year: pages.
Lastname, Firstname.	"Title of Article." Journal	volume (year): pages.

1. *Author.* Give the last name first, followed by a comma and the first name.
2. *Article title.* Type the article title in regular (Roman) face, and put it in quotation marks with the period inside the final quotation marks. Capitalize all major words in the title. (See 23c.)
3. *Publication data.* The exact kind of information differs according to the type of periodical, but all references provide the periodical title, the date of publication, and the page numbers on which the article appeared. Continuously underline the periodical title, and capitalize all major words in the title.

(See 23c.) Note that no punctuation follows the periodical title and that a colon introduces the inclusive page numbers. If the periodical provides both a volume number and a date, put the date in parentheses.

Weekly magazine or newspaper

Sheppard, Robert. "Brains over Brawn."
   Maclean's 22 Apr. 2002: 20.

Burkeman, Oliver. "Mafia Trial Ponders
   Startling Recovery of 'Mad' Vinnie the
   Chin." *Guardian Weekly* [Manchester] 25
   Apr. 2002: 23.

When it is not part of the newspaper's name, the city's name should be given in brackets after the title: *Guardian Weekly* [Manchester]. MLA style abbreviates the names of months (except for May, June, and July). Volume numbers are unnecessary because specific dates are given. (To compare with APA style, see page 603.)

Daily newspaper

Sokoloff, Heather. "Study Finds Cancer Agent
   in Comfort Foods." *National Post* 25 Apr.
   2002: A1, A16.

If a specific edition is not named on the masthead, put a colon after the date and then provide the page reference. Specify the section by including the section letter next to the page number as it appears in the newspaper: A7 or 7A. If the section is numbered, insert the section number preceded by sec. and followed by the page number: sec. 1: 8.

Editorial

```
Simpson, Jeffrey. "Why We Ended Up Dead."
     Editorial. Globe and Mail 20 Apr. 2002:
     A21.
```

If the editorial is not signed, begin the citation with the title.

Monthly magazine

A *journal* is a scholarly publication written for a specific profession, whereas a *magazine* is written for the general public.

```
Selim, Jocelyn. "The Sum of All Fears."
     Discover Apr. 2002: 22-23.
```

Magazine articles are often interrupted by other articles. If the first part appears on pages 45–47 and the last on pages 213–21, give only the first page number followed by a plus sign: 45+.

Journal with continuous pagination

Journals often list volume and issue numbers. A volume is a series of issues of a periodical, usually covering one calendar year. An issue is a single copy of a periodical. In the example that follows, the number 241 is the volume number of the periodical.

```
Clark, Lorna J. "A Contemporary's View of Jane
     Austen." Notes and Queries 241 (1996):
     418-20.
```

Citing a specific issue (e.g., Sep. 1996) is not necessary when a journal's pages are numbered continuously throughout the year.

Journal with separate pagination

Harris, Jonathan. "Art Education and Cyber-
Ideology: Beyond Individualism and
Technological Determinism." Art Journal
56.3 (1997): 39-45.

When an issue is paged separately (each issue begins with
page 1), put a period after the volume number and add the
issue number.

Non-print sources

Motion picture

The Sweet Hereafter. Dir. Atom Egoyan.
Alliance, 1997.

When you cite a particular performance, a screenplay, and
so on, put the person's name first:

Holm, Ian, perf. The Sweet Hereafter. By
Russell Banks. Screenplay by Atom Egoyan.
Dir. Atom Egoyan. Alliance, 1997.

Radio or television program

"Weather Guru." [Interview with David
Phillips]. Pamela Wallin Live. Prod.
Rebecca Eckler. CBC. 12 Dec. 1997.

Wachtel, Eleanor. Writers and Company. CBC,
Toronto. 23 Apr. 2002.

Play Performance

Wingfield's Folly. By Dan Needles. Dir. Doug
    Beattie. Perf. Rod Beattie. Citadel
    Theatre, Edmonton. 5 Apr. 1997.

Recording

Coldplay. A Rush of Blood to the Head. EMI,
    2002.

· If you are not using a compact disc, specify the type of
recording immediately after the title.

 Electronic media

The information required to cite sources such as software
programs or databases that can be distributed on diskettes
or CD-ROMs and the information required to cite online
sources differ in two important ways. Citations to CD-
ROMs and diskettes generally should identify the publisher, the place, and the date of publication. Citations for
information obtained online should state the electronic
address and the date of access. The date is vital because
online information can change daily or a site can disappear
between when you used it and when your reader attempts
to look at it. Furthermore, because the electronic address
is often the only way online information can be retrieved,
it must be absolutely precise.

The main reason for citing any source is to give your
readers enough information so that they can consult the
source on their own. Because there is not yet complete
agreement on how to cite electronic sources, and because
they change more frequently than print sources do, the
date given for the creation or latest modification of the site

and the date on which you accessed it are both important. Further, because sites may disappear overnight, it is wise to make a copy of any site you use as a source.

The *MLA Handbook for Writers of Research Papers*, 5th edition, cautions scholars to evaluate carefully the quality of any sources that they intend to use, print or electronic. You can find helpful information for evaluating general sources on page 519 and electronic sources on page 522.

E-mail

E-mail is treated much the same way personal letters and memos are treated. Give the name of the writer, a description of the message (usually the subject line), the receiver of the message, and the date.

```
Poteet, Louis. "Re: Research on Canadian
    Argots." E-mail to Kathryn Lane. 9 June
    1997.
```

Although the following example is not MLA style, you can enclose the e-mail address in angle brackets and insert it after the name.

```
Poteet, Louis. <lpoteet@antispam.ca> "Re:
    Research on Canadian Argots." E-mail to
    Kathryn Lane. 9 June 1997.
```

CD-ROM

For a source on CD-ROM, provide the author (if available) and the title (underlined), the publication medium, the place of publication, the publisher, and the publication date. Add the date of access last, if it is pertinent.

```
"Canadian Cancer Society." The 1998 Canadian &
     World Encyclopedia. CD-ROM. Toronto:
     McClelland, 1997.
```

CD-ROM (information published periodically)

For full-text articles that exist in print form, give bibliographic information about the text first, followed by full bibliographic information about the CD-ROM.

```
Persky, Stan. "Essays Show What's at Stake in
     Fight for Academic Freedom." Vancouver
     Sun 20 June 1997, final ed.: A23. Canadian
     NewsDisc. CD-ROM. Micromedia. June 1997.
```

Publication on diskette

For publications on diskettes, provide the title, the version number, a descriptive label, the publisher or distributor, and the copyright date. Add other information at the end of the entry, including, if pertinent, the operating system and units of memory necessary for running the program. When a program is attributed to an author, insert the author's name (last name first) immediately before the title.

```
Hieatt, Constance, Brian Shaw, and Duncan
     Macrae-Gibson. Beginning Old English:
     Exercise Disk. Diskette. Vers. 6.4.
     Binghamton: OEN Subsidia, 1994.
```

More than one medium

```
English Poetry Plus. CD-ROM, diskette. New
     York: Films for the Humanities &
     Sciences, 1995.
```

Electronic texts

Many literary and historical works are available in electronic form, but not all electronically available versions are equally reliable. Be sure to use the most authoritative source and state the title, date, and editor of the source for the electronic version. The date of access precedes the relevant URL. Be judicious about how much material you quote from sources. Although many electronic texts are prepared from sources now in the public domain, more are not, and you may have to get the publisher's permission to quote.

Shakespeare, William. The Life and Death of
    Richard the Third. The Complete Works of
    William Shakespeare. Aug. 1995. The Tech.
    MIT. 20 Feb. 2003 ⟨http://the-tech.mit.edu/
    Shakespeare/richardiii/⟩.

Electronic full-text articles accessed through a computer service

For full-text articles with a print counterpart give full bibliographic information about the article, followed by information about the service.

Graziose Corrin, Lisa. "Jeff Wall
    (Exhibition)." Parachute 88 (1997): 70.
    Online. Canadian Periodical Index. Gale
    Canada. Feb. 1997.

Electronic journal

Martin, Randall. "Isabella Whitney's
    'Lamentation upon the Death of William
    Gruffith.'" Early Modern Literary Studies

```
3.1 (1997). 19 Jan. 1998 ⟨http://
www.humanities.ualberta.ca/emls/03-1/
martwhit.html⟩.
```

An article in an online newspaper

```
"Food Banks Want Old Cellphones." Globe and
    Mail 27 Feb. 2003. 28 Feb. 2003
    ⟨http://www.globetechnology.com/servlet/
    story/RTGAM.20030227.gtb/GTStory⟩.
```

A review article in an online newspaper

```
Koeppel, Fredric. "A Look at John Keats." Rev.
    of Keats, by Andrew Motion. Nando Times
    News 16 Apr. 1998. 27 Aug. 1998 ⟨http://
    www.nando.net/newsroom/ntn/enter/041698/
    enter30_20804.html⟩.
```

Academic discussion list

Whenever possible, cite an archived version of a posting to a discussion list to make it easier for your readers to find your source.

```
Schipper, William. "Re: Quirk and Wrenn
    Grammar." Online posting. 5 Jan. 1995.
    Ansaxnet. 12 Sep. 1996 ⟨http://www.mun.ca/
    Ansaxdat/⟩.
```

World Wide Web page

```
Richard III: On Stage and Off. 22 Nov. 1995.
    Richard III Society. 28 Feb. 2003 ⟨http://
    www.r3.org/onstage/index.html⟩.
```

Gopher

To cite material retrieved by Gopher, use the uniform resource locator (URL), which shows the protocol to be used (Gopher), followed by a colon, two slashes, and the electronic address. Any page, paragraph, or section numbers follow the date of publication.

```
Page, Melvin E. "Brief Citation Guide for
    Internet Sources in History and the
    Humanities." 20 Feb. 1996. 9 pp. 7 July
    1996 ⟨gopher://h-net.msu.edu/00/lists/
    h-africa/internet-cit⟩.
```

FTP

To cite material retrieved by File Transfer Protocol (FTP), use the uniform resource locator, which shows the protocol to be used (FTP), followed by a colon, two slashes, and the electronic address. Any page, paragraph, or section numbers follow the date of publication.

```
"Beowulf, fol. 192 verso." The Electronic
    Beowulf Project. Ed. Kevin Kiernan.
    27 Aug. 1996. U of Kentucky. 12 May 1998
    ⟨ftp://beowulf.engl.uky.edu/pub/beowulf⟩.
```

This form reports that an image of manuscript page 192v is archived at beowulf.engl.uky.edu and can be downloaded from the directory pub/beowulf.

Newsgroup

```
Moraes, Mark. "Rules for Posting to Usenet."
    Online posting. 12 Jan. 1998. 20 Jan.
    1998 ⟨news:announce.newusers⟩.
```

Most newsgroups have no moderator to ensure the quality of the postings, and messages are not usually retrievable after a few weeks. Ask whether your instructor wants you to make your source retrievable by including the e-mail address of the person who posted the item.

Synchronous communications

To cite a synchronous group discussion, include the writer's name, event description, original date, forum (e.g., MediaMOO), access date, and telnet address.

```
Galin, Jeff. Netoric's Tuesday Café discussion
     "Teaching Writing in the Digital Age:
     What Makes Teaching Good These Days?"
     10 Sep. 1996. MediaMOO. 10 Sep. 1996
     ⟨telnet://purple-crayon.media.mit.edu/
     8888⟩.
```

If the discussion is archived, substitute the electronic address of the archive, for example, a World Wide Web site.

```
Galin, Jeff. Netoric's Tuesday Café discussion
     "Teaching Writing in the Digital Age:
     What Makes Teaching Good These Days?"
     10 Sep. 1996. MediaMOO. 12 Sep. 1996
     ⟨http://www.cs.bsu.edu/homepages/siering/
     netoric.html⟩.
```

Linkage data

Data about hypertext links can help establish the credibility of a source. Although the *MLA Style Manual* does not make a recommendation, the following format allows readers to retrace your steps.

```
Schipper, William. ⟨schipper@morgan.ucs.mun.ca⟩
    "Re: Quirk and Wrenn Grammar." 5 Jan.
    1995. ⟨ansax-1@wvnvm.wvnet.edu⟩ via gopher
    cwis.ucs.mun.ca (12 Sep. 1996). Lkd.
    ⟨http://www.georgetown.edu/labyrinth⟩.
```

Oral sources

Lecture

```
Haberman, Arthur. "Fantasy and Politics."
    Class lecture. Modes of Fantasy 241. York
    U, North York, ON. 14 Mar. 1995.
```

Use the title if available or provide a descriptive label for an untitled lecture and give the location and date.

Interview

```
Day, Michael. Personal interview. 31 May 2002.
```

For samples of citations of other non-print sources—such as games, filmstrips, microscope slides, and transparencies—consult Eugene B. Fleischer's *A Style Manual for Citing Microform and Nonprint Media* (Chicago: American Library Assn., 1978).

(3) Final revising, editing, and proofreading

After writing and carefully documenting the first draft of your paper, make needed revisions. Check your outline to make sure the organization is logical and unified (28e). Revise each paragraph to make its purpose clear, and edit each sentence to support its paragraph. Refer to chapters 26 and 29 as needed, particularly the revising, editing, and proofreading checklists. As you revise, make sure you continue to use your sources carefully and responsibly (33g). If you have questions about final manuscript form, refer to chapter 26 and to the sample research papers in 34b and 34e.

Some instructors ask their students to submit outlines, notes, and drafts along with the final paper. Other instructors require a title page and a final outline along with the text of the paper. A title page usually gives the title of the paper, the author, the name of the course and its section number, the instructor's name, and the date—all attractively centred on the page. The MLA recommends using no title page and giving the identification on the first page before the title of the paper: see page 572. (For a sample title page that can be modified for an MLA-style paper, see 34e, Sample APA research paper.)

34b Sample MLA research paper

When submitted with the text of a research paper, the final outline serves as a table of contents. In this case, a title page is advisable.

Exercise 1

Read the following paper and create an outline for it (review 28e if necessary). Your instructor will indicate whether you should create a sentence outline or a topic outline.

Exercise 2

Write a 200-word response to the following questions about the MLA paper: (a) Does the paper have a clear thesis? (b) Where is it first introduced? (c) How well is the paper organized? (d) Could it be organized in another way? (e) How well has the source material been included? (f) How well does the author include ideas of her own?

Katie Frushour

Professor Thompson

English 200, Section 5

8 May 1998

Using Cinematic Techniques to Emphasize Theme:
     Olivier's and Loncraine's Richard III

1   Shakespeare's plays are popular targets
for film adaptations, and Richard III is no
exception. With his 1995 release of Richard
III, Richard Loncraine is the newest addition
to the field of Shakespearean directors,
joining Laurence Olivier, who directed a
version of the same play in 1955. While the
films are true to the play's central theme of
tyranny, the cinematic techniques of the two
versions of Richard III are dramatically
different. In order to demonstrate the tyranny
of Richard, Olivier uses more traditional
techniques, such as a cyclical theme, artful
use of the shadow, and a careful film
adaptation, while Loncraine relies on an
unusual setting, clever casting, and creative
film adaptation. Therefore, although different
methods are employed to illuminate the common
theme of tyranny, they are utilized
effectively so as to emphasize the cinematic
appeal of both films.

2   Olivier's traditional cinematic methods,
which were groundbreaking in his time, bring
the complexity of Richard, Duke of Gloucester,
to life by highlighting his malice and desire
to control the crown of England. Olivier
cleverly uses the cyclical theme of the crown
being handed from king to king to symbolize

Comments

A. The identification, double-spaced, begins 2.5 cm from the top of the page and flush with the left margin. A double-spaced line precedes the centred title of the paper. A margin of 2.5 cm is provided at the left, right, and bottom.

B. Double-space between the title and the first line of the text. (A title consisting of two or more lines is double-spaced, and each line is centred.)

C. All pages (including the first one) are numbered with Arabic numerals in the upper right-hand corner, 1.25 cm from the top. The page number is preceded by the author's last name. Notice that no period follows the page numbers.

the rise and fall of Richard III, what
Constance Brown justly calls "the central
device of coherence" (133). Jack Jorgens
concurs with Brown's assertion as he states
that there "is no question that the theme of
the crown is important to the film" (137).
Jorgens identifies the theme of the film as the
"fall and rise of state" and argues that the
fall and rise are represented by the image of
the crown (137). The film opens with the
crowning of Edward IV, after which the
audience learns of Richard's self-serving lust
for the throne. The audience increasingly
becomes a party to Richard's malevolent
actions and his growing tyranny in his quest
for power, which culminates in his possession
of the crown of England. Soon after obtaining
the throne, however, Richard's tyrannical
methods lead to his death and the surrender of
the crown to Richmond, the rightful heir. This
common cycle of events creates a sense of
balance in the film, which is both central to
the theme and cinematically appealing.

3   Another cinematic technique employed by
Olivier is the artful use of the shadow. As
Richard confides his plots to kill Clarence and
to marry Lady Anne, his shadow slowly grows
until it consumes the whole screen. This use
of shadow symbolizes Richard's dominance and
his growing tyranny. Likewise, while the
audience watches Clarence describe the
horrible nightmare that he sees through the
window of his cell in the Tower, the camera

Comments

A. All three quotations in paragraph 2 are cited with only a page number because the authors' names are included in the text.

B. The second reference to Jorgens includes both a direct quotation and a paraphrase. Both are cited with a reference to page 137.

C. Notice how Frushour integrates the information from Jorgens into her own analysis.

D. Frushour uses her own viewing of Olivier's film for this information, and so nothing need be cited (paragraph 3).

slowly reveals the shadow of Richard on the
cell door. Through this action, Anthony Davies
suggests, the audience becomes an accomplice
to Richard's eavesdropping and thus a
confidant to his plotting (70). This action is
cinematically advantageous because it involves
the audience in the film, while developing
Richard's tyranny. Finally, the shadow is used
to emphasize the intertwining of Richard with
the Duke of Buckingham, a vital alliance in
Richard's quest for the crown. Jorgens
describes this powerful scene: "Buckingham's
shadow merges with Richard's . . . and the
shadow of the murderers falls upon the crucifix
in Clarence's cell as they enter to kill him"
(146). The shadows of both men are shown side
by side as they exit a room after plotting to
meet the young Prince of Wales' escort. This
visual representation of the alliance of
Richard and Buckingham reinforces their ties
to one another and provides a strong contrast
centred on Richard's tyranny when he and
Buckingham are estranged. Therefore, through
the clever and inventive use of the shadow,
Olivier is able to emphasize the theme of his
film, while making it cinematically appealing
at the same time.

4   Perhaps the most important of Olivier's
cinematic techniques is his adaptation of the
play. Shakespeare plays are never performed in
their entirety, as actor/screenwriter Ian
McKellen states in the "Production Notes" of
Loncraine's version of <u>Richard III</u>. Olivier

Comments

A. Because the quotation from Jorgens in paragraph 3 is brief, it can be run in with the text instead of being indented.

B. In paragraph 4, Frushour identifies McKellen's dual roles in the film—as main character and as the writer of the screenplay.

generally uses traditional methods of
adaptation, such as cutting characters and
occasionally dialogue, which serve to clarify
the plot by eliminating minor characters. He
also maintains the stereotypes of the
characters that were defined by Shakespeare.
Robert Wilson points out that Olivier uses
Shakespeare's archetypal clichés of Lady Anne
and Richard III (83-84).[1]

5   However, Olivier also adds scenes to the
film that are not in the play. One of these
key additions is described in Magill's Survey
of Cinema:

> [Olivier] interpolated the
> coronation of Edward IV from the end
> of Henry VI, Part 3 (the play that
> preceded Richard III in
> Shakespeare's history cycle) into
> the beginning of the film. This
> accomplished two things: it gave the
> audience a bit of welcome background
> to the action commencing on screen,
> and it also gave Olivier a framing
> device to use . . . ("Richard
> III")

6   This adaptation is important to the theme
of the film because it provides an insight into
the events that lead to Richard's coronation,
and it provides the cyclical theme of the
three crownings, which is important to the film
both thematically and cinematically. Olivier
also adds Mistress Shore to the opening
scenes. Her presence at the coronation and
brief interaction with Edward IV emphasize

Comments

A. The citation to Wilson's article, (83–84), at the end of paragraph 4 indicates that the summarized information appears on two pages.

B. Because Robert Wilson engages in a lengthy discussion about the archetypal clichés in *Richard III,* a summary of the remainder of his thesis is included in the notes and is indicated by a superscript numeral. The discussion is not included in the text because it is not directly relevant to Frushour's analysis.

C. The long quotation in paragraph 5 from *Magill's Survey of Cinema* is set off as a block, indented 2.5 cm from the left margin, because it is longer than four typed lines. The ellipsis points that appear at the end of the quotation indicate that the remainder of the quoted sentence is omitted.

D. No page number is cited in the parentheses because *Magill's Survey of Cinema* is an electronic source and has no pages. Instead, the quotation can be found by searching for a distinctive phrase.

E. When using an anonymous source such as *Magill's Survey of Cinema,* use a shortened version of the title. Frushour uses the title of the article in the work: "Richard III."

Edward's lasciviousness (Brown 14), which parallels Richard's lust for power. These brief scenes work to enforce the image of Richard as tyrant and are an important part of the cinematic beauty of Laurence Olivier's Richard III.

7   Loncraine's release of Richard III in 1995 takes a more contemporary approach to Shakespeare. Fuelled by a renewed interest in Shakespeare resulting from Kenneth Branagh's success in bringing the playwright to the big screen (Stark), the film sparked a controversy concerning Loncraine's choice of setting. Loncraine uses a fictional, fascist, art deco London circa 1930 for the setting of his film, which adds to its cinematic capabilities. Although critics such as Stanley Kauffmann complain that Loncraine's setting is unbelievable,[2] Jack Kroll states in his article concerning the recent release, "Loncraine gives you true movie visuals and rhythms as Richard rises to power . . . in an England of art deco and prewar tensions" (58). The setting parallels the tyranny of Richard. It becomes more militaristic as his obsession for the crown drives him to greater tyranny. Richard's tyranny fuels his rise to power, which "parallels Nazi Germany . . . with his introduction at a Nuremberg-style rally just prior to his coronation" (Kersey). Ben Brantley further stresses the effectiveness of Loncraine's setting as a device to emphasize the image of tyranny. He says:

Comments

A. The reference to Brown in paragraph 6 includes Brown's name because the name is not mentioned in the text immediately preceding the reference.

B. The reference to Stark in paragraph 7 acknowledges that Frushour got the idea that there is renewed interest in Shakespeare because of Branagh's productions from Stark's article. No page is cited because Frushour used the online version of the source.

C. Kauffmann's complaints about the film are given in a footnote because they are not directly relevant to Frushour's analysis.

D. In paragraph 7, ellipsis points in the quotations from Kersey and from Kroll (see original text below) show that nonessential information is omitted.

> **Source:** Kroll, Jack. "Richard III—My Kingdom for a Movie." *Newsweek* 29 Jan. 1996: 58.

> Loncraine gives you true movie visuals and rhythms as Richard rises to power, polishing off all the men, women, and children in his way, in an England of art deco and prewar tensions.

E. The citation to Kersey in paragraph 7 refers to a newsgroup posting for which no page number is available. The Works Cited list, however, gives the full electronic address for the source.

> Setting the work in Fascist Europe,
> with Richard's Black Shirt presence
> playing on memories of Oswald Mosley
> and Edward VII's alleged Nazi
> sympathies, always made a certain
> sense. It immediately set up echoes
> of what is still perceived as the
> greatest historical example of evil
> in the 20th century: Hitler's Third
> Reich. (1)

8   This setting, complete with "a wild boar
on the flags instead of a swastika" (Kersey)
and modelled from the modern image of tyranny
and fascism--Hitler's Germany--intensifies the
audience's perception of Richard III's rule.
The altered setting makes the film more
appealing to audiences with a strong mental
picture of Hitler's rule. McKellen states, "We
weren't trying to bring the play Richard III
to as many people as possible, but trying to
make a film . . . that would appeal to as
many people as possible" (Sime 1C). The
audience relates Richard to Hitler through the
cinematic images Loncraine creates, enforcing
both the theme and the cinematic appeal of the
film.

9   From a cinematic standpoint, Loncraine
also makes a few casting decisions that relate
the plot (and in turn the theme) of the film to
the audience. The "Production Notes" from
Richard III explain:

> [Robert] Downey [Jr.] and Annette
> Bening play Americans. Their casting
> . . . grew out of the fact that in

Comments

A. Notice that the page number for the block quotation from Brantley in paragraph 7 comes after the final period, whereas for quotations that are run into the text, such as Kroll's, the page number comes before the period.

B. Newspapers are cited by giving both the page number and the section in which the article appears. (Sime 1C) in paragraph 8 is an example.

C. Brackets in the block quotation in paragraph 9 indicate that the production notes include only the actor's surname.

the play Queen Elizabeth and her
brother, Earl Rivers, are outsiders.
They are not members of the
aristocracy and Loncraine and
McKellen wanted to find a twentieth-
century equivalent. (Paragraph 15)

Loncraine's choice to cast two Americans in
the small but important roles of Queen
Elizabeth and her brother emphasizes the role
of both characters as outsiders by equating
their exclusion from the aristocracy to an
average American's exclusion from royalty in
Britain today. Thus, a seemingly minor part of
the cinematic production, casting, enables
Loncraine to demonstrate a crucial element of
the plot, further enhancing the film's theme
and cinematic appeal.

10   Finally, like Olivier's film, the most
important technique emphasizing the theme of
Loncraine's film while making it cinematically
favourable is adaptation. Ian McKellen, who
wrote the screenplay in addition to playing
Richard, makes numerous character cuts,
rearranges or drops lines, and combines scenes
to adapt Shakespeare's play. Characters like
Lords Dorset, Grey, and Northumberland and
Queen Margaret are eliminated, and their lines
are given to other characters in the play. To
increase the pace of the film, McKellen
combines two scenes between Richard and Lady
Anne (Loncraine, Richard III), so that she is
successfully wooed in one scene rather than
two (Olivier, Richard III). This reduction in
scenes emphasizes the power that Richard has

Comments

A. No page number is necessary for the block quotation in paragraph 9 because it is a citation to a web page. In this instance, a paragraph number is given instead, according to advice (rather than a requirement) in the *MLA Handbook*. However, the full electronic address appears in the Works Cited.

B. The citations in paragraph 10 refer to the two identically authored and titled films. The director's name is included to distinguish one version from the other.

over Anne and allows the audience to compare it to the power he acquires as the movie gains momentum. This scene is so powerful that even in his negative review of Loncraine's film, Kauffmann describes the scene between Anne and Richard as intrinsically interesting (30). Yet, despite the major alterations that McKellen makes to reduce the four-hour play to just under one hundred minutes, he insists on preserving the spirit of Shakespeare. He says, in an on-line interview, "I will not betray his words." McKellen emphasizes the fact that although the characters are changed, lines rearranged, and scenes added or dropped, the words remain true and convey the proper image to the audience ("Richard III: Interview with Sir Ian McKellen"). This dedication to the spirit of Shakespeare's Richard III, while making cinematically advantageous alterations to the text, enables Loncraine to focus on the tyranny of Richard.

11   Forty years allows for numerous cinematic improvements, yet in Olivier's version of the play, Richard's tyranny is stressed using traditional methods that are just as cinematically appealing today as they were in 1955. Likewise, Loncraine's Richard III introduces a dramatic twist to the film, opening it for cinematic reinterpretation while preserving the tyrannical theme. Therefore, it is this artful and careful presentation of the films that allows both directors to successfully emphasize the

Comment

A. The citation in paragraph 10 to the interview with McKellen includes the title to avoid confusion with other electronic sources that quote McKellen. Since the reference is to a web page, there is no page number.

tyranny of Richard III while employing vastly
different, yet equally effective, cinematic
techniques.

Notes

[1]Wilson states that Lady Anne continues to
represent the angel image that is set in
opposition to the devil image represented by
the character of Richard III (83-84). He
further explains that as the angel, Lady
Anne's assigned duty is to reform the fallen
man, Richard III. Richard III, the devil, is
defined by his symbolic rape of the weakened
victim, Lady Anne.

[2]Kauffmann argues that by changing the
setting to Fascist times, Loncraine succeeds
only in creating an unbelievable story line
and distorts Shakespeare's original
intentions. Kauffmann says, "Are we to believe
that this power-greedy homicidal malcontent
was a fascist? Nonsense. He had nothing in his
head except schemes for personal advancement"
(30).

Comments

A. Notes are usually put at the end of the text and titled *Notes*. They are co-ordinated with their location in the text by a superscript number that comes before the indented first line of the note and also at the appropriate location in the text.

B. Footnotes fell out of general use because of the difficulty of arranging text around them. Rather, the information was placed on a separate page at the end of the text, which has the additional advantage of making it easy for a reader to set the notes side by side with the page being read. In-text citation is even easier to manage, and in an electronic source, a hypertext link (which generally offers fuller information) often accomplishes the same purpose as a note.

Works Cited

Brantley, Ben. "Mesmerizing Men of Ill Will."
    New York Times 21 Jan. 1996, late ed.:
    1+.

Brown, Constance. "Olivier's Richard III: A
    Reevaluation." Focus on Shakespeare
    Films. Ed. Charles W. Eckert. Englewood
    Cliffs: Prentice, 1972. 131-45.

Davies, Anthony. Filming Shakespeare's Plays:
    The Adaptations of Laurence Olivier,
    Orson Welles, Peter Brook, and Akira
    Kurosawa. Cambridge: Cambridge UP, 1988.

Jorgens, Jack J. Shakespeare on Film.
    Bloomington: Indiana UP, 1977.

Kauffmann, Stanley. "Stanley Kauffmann on
    Films: Shrinking Shakespeare." The New
    Republic 12 Feb. 1996: 30-31.

Kersey, Alan. "Review: Richard III (1995)."
    Online posting. 6 May 1995. 9 July 1996
    ⟨news:rec.arts.movies.reviews⟩.

Kroll, Jack. "Richard III--My Kingdom for a
    Movie." Newsweek 29 Jan. 1996: 58.

Richard III. By William Shakespeare.
    Screenplay by Ian McKellen. Dir. Richard
    Loncraine. MGM/United Artists, 1995.

Richard III. Dir. Laurence Olivier. British
    Broadcasting Company, 1955.

"Richard III: Interview with Sir Ian
    McKellen." Richard III On Stage and Off.
    20 Dec. 1995. Richard III Society Home
    Page. 3 July 1996 ⟨http://www.r3.org/
    mckellen/film/mckell.html⟩.

Comments

A. All works cited as sources in the paper and only those should be included in the list of works cited.

B. Alphabetize entries according to the author's last name. Works with more than one author are alphabetized under the name of whichever writer is listed first in the source itself.

C. Observe the use and placement of periods and commas, especially in relation to parentheses and quotation marks. A colon separates a title from a subtitle and the place of publication from the publisher's name. A colon also precedes page numbers of articles from periodicals. Use angle brackets to set off an electronic address in citations to electronic sources.

D. Citations to Usenet newsgroup postings should include the writer's name, a title taken from the subject line and enclosed in quotation marks, the description "Online posting," the original date of the posting, the date of access, and the prefix "news" followed by a colon and the newsgroup name, all enclosed in angle brackets. See the Kersey citation on page 590.

E. Notice that the citation to the interview with Ian McKellen is anonymous. Like anonymous print sources, anonymous electronic sources are alphabetized by title.

"Richard III." Magill's Survey of Cinema. CD-
     ROM. Salem: Salem, 1996.

"Richard III: Production Notes." Richard III
     On Stage and Off. 20 Dec. 1995. Richard
     III Society Home Page. 3 July 1996 ⟨http://
     www.r3.org/mckellen/film/notes.html⟩.

Sime, Tom. "Now Is McKellen's Winter of
     Content: Acclaimed Shakespearean Finally
     Wins Film Stardom in Richard III." Dallas
     Morning News 4 Feb. 1996: 1C.

Stark, Susan. "His Naked Villainy: Sir Ian
     McKellen Is No Garden-Variety Richard
     III." Detroit News 20 Jan. 1996. 3 July
     1996 ⟨http://www.detnews.com/menu/stories/
     32720.htm⟩.

Wilson, Robert F., Jr. "Shakespeare and
     Hollywood: Two Film Clichés." Journal of
     Popular Film and Television 15.2 (1987):
     83-84.

Comments

A. An anonymous source (such as *Magill's Survey of Cinema* or "*Richard III*: Production Notes") is alphabetized under the first important word in the title.

B. The citation for "Production Notes" is substantially the same as that for "Interview with Sir Ian McKellen" (page 590), but notice that the file name (notes.html) is different. That indicates a different World Wide Web page.

C. Inclusion of the issue number and date indicates that each issue of the *Journal of Popular Film and Television* is paged separately.

34c Some disciplines use the note style of documentation.

Although the MLA has recommended parenthetical documentation since 1984 (and the influential *Chicago Manual of Style* since 1982), some disciplines in the humanities still use either footnotes or endnotes for documentation. The information is provided here in case you are instructed to follow a note style of documentation.

Both footnotes and endnotes require that a superscript number be placed wherever documentation is necessary. The number should be as near as possible to whatever it refers to, following the punctuation (such as quotation marks, a comma, or a period) that appears at the end of the direct or indirect quotation.

Footnotes should be single-spaced four lines below the last line of text on the same page where the documentation is necessary. Double-space between footnotes if more than one appears on any one page. **Endnotes** should be double-spaced on a separate page headed *Notes*.

The following notes use the same sources as those used for "Listing the works cited—MLA style" on pages 550–69. By comparing the model footnote with its corresponding works cited entry, you will see differences between the two forms. (These numbered notes are arranged in a pattern for your convenience. They are numbered sequentially, as your notes would be for documentation. But your notes would not necessarily begin with "a book by one author" followed by "a book by more than one author," etc.)

A book by one author

[1] Alistair MacLeod, <u>No Great Mischief</u> (Toronto: McClelland, 1999) 47.

Indent 1.25 cm (or five typewritten spaces), then give the
note number (without punctuation) as a superscript, followed by a space. Additional lines in a note should be flush
with the left margin. Note that an abbreviation for "page"
is not used before the page number at the end of the note.

A book by more than one author

² **Harvey J. Krahn and Graham S. Lowe,
Work, Industry and Canadian Society (Toronto:
Nelson, 2002) 124.**

If the book has more than two authors, use commas to
separate the authors' names.

³ **Mary McGuire, Linda Stilbourne, Melinda
McAdams, and Laurel Hyatt, The Internet
Handbook for Writers, Researchers, and
Journalists (Toronto: Trifolium, 1997) 51–71.**

A multi-volume work

⁴ **Harold Kalman, A History of Canadian
Architecture, vol. 1 (Don Mills, ON: Oxford
UP, 1994) 241.**
⁵ **Stephen Clarkson and Christina McCall,
Trudeau and Our Times, vol. 2 (Toronto:
McClelland, 1994) 2 vols. 315.**

An edited book

⁶ **Robyn R. Warhol and Diane Price Herndl,
eds., Feminisms: An Anthology of Literary
Theory and Criticisms (New Brunswick: Rutgers
UP, 1993) 165.**

A work in an anthology

[7] Thomas King, "The One about Coyote Going West," <u>Anthology of Canadian Native Literature in English</u>, 2nd ed., eds. Daniel David Moses and Terry Goldie (Toronto: Oxford UP, 1998) 203-10.

An introduction, preface, foreword, or afterword

[8] George Bowering, afterword, <u>Swamp Angel</u>, by Ethel Wilson (Toronto: McClelland, 1990) 238-39.

An article from a newspaper

[9] Heather Sokoloff, "Study Finds Cancer Agent in Comfort Foods," <u>National Post</u> 25 Apr. 2002, A1, A16.

An article from a magazine

[10] Robert Sheppard, "Brains over Brawn," <u>Maclean's</u> 22 Apr. 2002: 20.

An article from a journal with continuous pagination

[11] Lorna J. Clark, "A Contemporary's View of Jane Austen," <u>Notes and Queries</u> 241 (1996): 418-20.

34d APA-style documentation is appropriate for research papers in psychology and most social sciences.

(1) Using parenthetical citations

In APA style, the basic elements of a parenthetical citation in the text are the author's last name, the year of publication, and the page number if the reference is to a specific passage in the source. If the author's name is mentioned in the text of the paper, give the date alone or the date and the page number in parentheses. In the following examples, note the details of punctuation and the treatment of the page number.

A work by one author

One writer has stated, "Views about contemporary families and family change are conditioned by beliefs about what families used to be like, as well as by an ideology of the modern 'ideal family'" (Gee, 1995, p. 79).

OR

Gee has stated, "Views about contemporary families and family change are conditioned by beliefs about what families used to be like, as well as by an ideology of the modern 'ideal family'" (1995, p. 79).

OR

> `Gee (1995) has stated, "Views about`
> `contemporary families and family change are`
> `conditioned by beliefs about what families`
> `used to be like, as well as by an ideology of`
> `the modern 'ideal family'" (p. 79).`

Unlike MLA style, APA style requires the abbreviation *p.* (or *pp.* for "pages") before the page reference. Use commas to separate the author's name from the date and the date from the page reference.

A work by two authors

> `There is a disproportionately high rate of`
> `high-school dropouts and street youth among`
> `lesbian and gay youth who experience familial`
> `prejudice and discrimination (O'Brien & Weir,`
> `1995).`

Use the ampersand (&) to separate the authors' names.

A work by more than two authors

> `The fact that people perceive the world in`
> `different ways is one of the main sources for`
> `conflict in a relationship (Berko, Rosenfeld, &`
> `Samovar, 1998).`

For works with *three to five authors*, cite all the authors in the first reference, but in subsequent references give only the last name of the first author followed by *et al.* ("Berko et al." in this case). For works with *six or more authors*, provide only the last name of the first author followed by *et al.*, even in the first citation.

Anonymous works

Use a shortened version of the title to identify an anonymous work:

`Chronic insomnia usually requires medical`
`intervention ("Sleep," 1993).`

In this case, the author has cited a short article identified in the bibliography as "Sleep disorders: What can be done about them."

Two or more works within the same parentheses

`After a divorce, the amount that a custodial`
`mother's standard of living will drop depends`
`on the non-custodial father's pattern of`
`financial support and on the legal processes`
`that enhance or detract from that support`
`(Grassby, 1991; Pask, 1993; Rogerson, 1991).`

Use a semicolon to separate different studies, and arrange them in alphabetical order.

(2) Listing the references—APA style

Format the "References" (alphabetical list of works cited) in the APA style your instructor specifies. (See the commentary on final manuscript style, pages 608–9.) As the fifth edition of the *Publication Manual* asserts, "APA publishes references in a *hanging indent* format, meaning that the first line of each reference is set flush left and subsequent lines are indented. If a hanging indent is difficult to accomplish with your word-processing program, it is permissible to indent your references with paragraph indents. The chosen format should be consistent throughout the references" (p. 299). Some instructors prefer that you indent the first line of each entry 1.25 cm (or five typewritten spaces) and type subsequent lines flush with the left margin. Instructors should specify the style they prefer for the final manuscript.

The reference entries below have a hanging indent.

Books

Most book entries consist of four units separated by periods:

1. *Author.* Give the author's last name and use initials for the first and middle names. For entries that contain more than one author, invert all names and put an ampersand (&) before the last one. (If two authors have the same last name and initials, spell out their first names and list the references in the alphabetical order of their first names.)
2. *Date.* Put the date in parentheses after the author's name. By including the date near the beginning of the entry, APA style draws attention to its importance.
3. *Title.* Capitalize only the first word in titles and subtitles. Do not capitalize other words (except for proper names that would be capitalized in other contexts). Separate titles and subtitles with a colon, and underline the title.
4. *Publication data.* Give only enough of the publisher's name so that it can be identified clearly.

Book by one author

Riordan, C. H. (1997). <u>Equality and</u>
        <u>achievement: An introduction to the</u>

sociology of education. New York:
Longman.

More than one work by the same author

If you use more than one work by the same author, list the works in order of the publication date, with the earliest first. Repeat the author's name for each work.

Saul, J. R. (1995). The unconscious
    civilization. Toronto: Anansi.

Saul, J. R. (1997). Reflections of a Siamese
    twin. Toronto: Viking.

Book by two or more authors

Krahn, H. J., & Lowe, G. S. (2002). Work,
    industry and Canadian society (4th ed.).
    Scarborough, ON: Nelson.

Contrast APA style with MLA style, which inverts only the name of the first author in a multi-author work. (See page 552.)

An edition after the first

Deutschmann, L. B. (2002). Deviance and social
    control (3rd ed.). Scarborough, ON:
    Nelson.

Translation

Freud, S. (1960). Jokes and their relationship
    to the unconscious (J. Strachey, Trans.).
    New York: Norton. (Original work pub-
    lished 1905)

Cite the date of the translation and include the date of the original publication at the end of the entry. In text, use the following form: (Freud, 1905/1960).

A government document

```
Statistics Canada. (1999). Overview of the
    time use of Canadians in 1998 (Cat. no.
    12F0080XIE). Ottawa: Author.
```

When the author and publisher are identical, use the word *Author* as the name of the publisher. Include a catalogue number (but not a library call number) if it is printed on or in the document.

Works with no author

Use the first significant words of the title to cite anonymous materials in the text, underlining the title of a book. Unless Anonymous is specifically designated as the author of a work, do not use it for in-text citations or the list of references.

```
Canadian donor's guide to fund raising
    organizations in Canada. (1998). (13th
    ed.). Toronto: Third Sector.
```

Articles

Capitalize only the first word and any proper nouns in article titles, and do not put quotation marks around titles. (If the article has a subtitle, use a colon to separate the title and the subtitle and capitalize the first word of each.) For an article in an edited book, provide both the title of the article and the title of the book in which it appears. Give the name of the editor and the complete page numbers of the article. For an anonymous article, place the article title where the author's name would normally appear, and alphabetize by the first important word in the title.

```
Crimes and war. (2002, April 22). Maclean's,
     13.
```

Unlike an article or book title, each main word of a journal title is capitalized. Do not precede the page reference by *p.* or *pp.*

Journal: Continuous pagination

```
Lenfant, C. (1996). High blood pressure: Some
     answers, new questions, continuing
     challenges. JAMA, 275, 1605-1606.
```

Journal: Separate pagination

```
Kolakowski, L. (1992). Amidst moving ruins.
     Daedalus, 121(2), 43-56.
```

Place the issue number in parentheses immediately after the volume number but do not underline it.

Monthly or weekly magazine

```
Selim, J. (2002, April). The sum of all fears.
     Discover, 23, 22-23.
```

For a monthly magazine, give the year first, followed by a comma and the full spelling of the month. For a weekly magazine, provide the exact date: (1998, February 18).

Newspaper

Simpson, J. (2002, April 20). Why we ended up
    dead. <u>The Globe and Mail</u>, p. A21.

Work in an anthology

Couture, J. E. (2000). The role of Native
    elders: Emergent issues. In D. Long &
    O. P. Dickason (Eds.), <u>Visions of the
    heart: Canadian Aboriginal issues</u>
    (pp. 33-48). Toronto: Harcourt.

Book review

Kuitenbrouwer, K. (2002, March 2). Heroes (and
    zeros) of science [Review of the book
    <u>Servants of the map: Stories</u>]. <u>The Globe
    and Mail</u>, p. D6.

When a review is titled, place the subject of the review in
brackets after the review title. When a review is untitled,
use the material in brackets as the title, but retain the
brackets to show that this "title" is a description.

Pyles, A. R. (1997) [Review of <u>Pre-Adolescent
    Female Friendships</u>]. <u>School Psychologist,
    2</u>, 57-59.

Non-print sources

Motion picture

Doran, L. (Producer), & Lee, A. (Director).
    (1995). <u>Sense and sensibility</u> [Film].
    London: Mirage.

Recording

```
Fellows, W. (Speaker). (1993). Nutritional
    needs for women with AIDS (Cassette
    Recording No. 8294). Madison, WI:
    Nutritionworks.
```

Electronic media

The APA offers updated guidelines to citing electronic sources in their 2001 edition of the *Publication Manual of the American Psychological Association*. To cite Internet sources, the APA recommends following two basic guidelines: to direct readers as closely as possible to the actual information being cited—to specific documents rather than home or menu pages—and to provide working addresses (p. 269). Each Internet reference should include a document title or description, a date (the date of publication and/or of retrieval), a URL, and an author when possible. The APA provides information about their electronic citation style at <http://www.apastyle.org/elecref.html>.

Periodicals

Most periodical articles now available online are the same as the print version, so the same basic information should be provided.

```
Raynor, H. A., & Epstein, L. H. (2001).
    Dietary variety, energy regulation, and
    obesity. Psychological Bulletin, 127,
    325–341.
```

If you have seen the article only in its electronic form, add "[Electronic version]" after the title.

If you have reason to believe that an online version of an article isn't the same as its original print version, then you need to add the date you retrieved the article, along with the URL. The URL should take the reader directly to the article, if possible.

Patz, J. (1994, Summer). The defective wife
     syndrome. <u>Stepfamilies</u>. Retrieved January
     25, 2002, from http://www.stepfam.org/
     education/articles/prof/patz.htm

For an article in an Internet-only journal, cite as follows:

Haythornthwaite, C. (2002, July-August).
     Computer-mediated communication and the
     "liberated" sociologist. <u>Canadian Journal
     of Sociology Online</u>. Retrieved October
     21, 2002, from http://
     www.arts.ualberta.ca/cjscopy/newmill/
     haythorn.html

Non-periodical Internet Documents

<u>APA Citation Guide</u>. (2002). Retrieved October
     21, 2002, from Mount Allison University
     Libraries, http://www.mta.ca/library/
     apa.htm

Report on a private organization website

Canarie., Inc. (1997, September 27). <u>Towards a
     Canadian health IWAY: Vision,
     opportunities and future steps</u>. Retrieved
     January 25, 2001, from http://
     www.canarie.ca/press/publication/pdf/
     health/healthvision.doc

Sierra Club of Canada. (n.d.) <u>Ten popular
     myths about the Kyoto Protocol</u>. Retrieved

```
October 21, 2002, from http://
www.sierraclub.ca/national/climate/
ten-myths-kyoto.html
```

Article retrieved from a database

```
Demont, J. (1997, August 11). Fontaine's
    vision: The new Grand Chief aims for
    unity. Maclean's, 110(32), 12-14.
    Retrieved October 22, 2002, from Canadian
    Periodical Index database.
```

Article retrieved via File Transfer Protocol (FTP)

```
Plato. (1901). The republic (Benjamin Jowett,
    Trans.). New York: Collier. Retrieved May
    31, 2002, from ftp://ftp.std.com/obi/
    Plato/The.Republic.z
```

Message posted to online forum or discussion group

```
Plant, S. (2002, April 8). Evolutionary
    algorithm for PC robot [Msg 1126].
    Message posted to http://groups.yahoo.com/
    group/artificialintelligencegroup/
    message/1126
```

Message posted to an electronic mailing list

For messages posted to a mailing list, include the name of the list and the address where the message is archived, as in this fictitious example:

```
Graves, N. (2002, August 24). Styles of
    calligraphy. Message posted to Graphic-
    Design electronic mailing list, archived
```

```
at http://www.liszt.com/lists/
Graphic-Design/mail-archive/topica/
msg000112.html
```

Personal e-mail messages should be treated as a personal communication; that is, they should be cited in the text as a personal communication, including author and date, but not included in the reference list.

34e Sample APA research paper

The APA *Publication Manual* specifies two different styles of manuscripts, the **copy manuscript** and the **final manuscript**. The *Manual* explains,

> The author of a thesis, dissertation, or student paper produces a "final" manuscript; the author of a journal article produces a "copy" manuscript (which will become a typeset article). The differences between these two kinds of manuscripts help explain why the requirements for theses, dissertations, and student papers are not necessarily identical to those for the manuscripts submitted for publication in a journal. (p. 321)

The copy manuscript style is used for a document that will be sent to a publisher and set in type. The final manuscript style should be used for such documents as student papers, lab reports, master's theses, and doctoral dissertations.

Copy manuscripts, the APA *Publication Manual* explains, "must conform to the format and other policies of the journal to which they are submitted" (p. 321). Final manuscript style, however, permits a "number of variations from the requirements described in the *Publication Manual*" (p. 322) and should conform to the requirements of an individual university, department, or instructor. The *Manual* further advises that it is not intended to cover scientific writing at an undergraduate level, because preferences for style at that level are diverse. Instructions to students to "use the *Publication Manual*" should be accompanied by specific guidelines for its use. (p. 322)

Generally speaking, a **title page** includes three elements, all of which are double-spaced. The **running head** is a shortened version of the **title** and appears in the upper left-hand corner of the title page. It will also appear in the upper right-hand corner of every page, including the title page, which is counted as page 1. (If you use this title page as a model for a paper in MLA style, do not include the running head or the page number.) The title appears next in upper- and lowercase letters and is centred. The **author's name** or **byline** appears below the title and is followed by the author's affiliation. If an instructor asks that the course number be included, it will generally appear as the affiliation. Unless the instructor specifically requires it, the instructor's name and the date the paper is due are not included. (A final manuscript may also include an **abstract**, a 100- to 200-word summary of the paper. This is the length of most abstracts in APA journals.)

The body of the paper, the **discussion**, should normally be double-spaced and include in-text citations as specified in the *Publication Manual*. Variations in spacing to promote readability, however, are not only permitted, but encouraged.

A fourth essential component of the final manuscript, the **references**, is a list of all the references cited in the text. It does not usually include any references not cited. However, any material that is especially pertinent or that informs the whole paper may be included if it is considered essential. When that is the case, the reference list becomes a bibliography. For additional examples of APA-style documentation, see the following student essay and the commentary on it printed on the right-hand pages.

Generation X 1

Generation X: Moving Back Home

Adrienne Harton

Soc 100, Section B

Comments

A. Student papers should be prepared in **final manuscript style** (see pages 608–9), double-spaced with in-text citations as specified in the APA *Publication Manual*. Depending on the particular requirements of your department or instructor, requirements for final copy may differ from those for copy manuscript style described in the body of the *Manual*.

B. A **title page** includes three double-spaced elements: running head, title, and author's full name and affiliation. Centre the title and author horizontally (but not necessarily vertically).

C. The **running head** is a shortened version of the title. It appears in the upper right-hand corner of every page and the upper left of the title page, which is counted as page 1.

D. If an instructor asks that the course number be included, it generally appears instead of the affiliation. Unless specifically required, the instructor's name and the date the paper is due are not included.

Generation X 2

Abstract

Young adults are residing in their parents'
homes in record numbers. Research indicates
that education, occupation, and personal
lifestyles all contribute to the economic
hardships of young adults. The generation born
between 1960 and 1976 faces financial
difficulties just like previous generations,
but parents of this generation seem more
willing, almost obligated, to support their
adult children.

Comments

A. An abstract is a short summary of a paper. The APA *Publication Manual* requires that an abstract be supplied on the second page of any essay that is to be submitted for publication (copy manuscript style). Check with your instructor to see if an abstract is required for your paper.
B. Harton's abstract is slightly over 60 words, a reasonable length for a short paper. The usual length is 100 to 120 words.

Generation X: Moving Back Home

1 Jim and Carole Wilson appear to be a comfortable couple in their 50s, married for 30 years. The Wilsons own a home, drive nice cars, and were able to pay for a university education for all three of their children. The Wilsons deviate from the stereotypical couple, though, because one of their university-educated children has moved back home. Scott, the oldest child, quit his temporary job (waiting tables "while I look for something better") and resumed residence in his old bedroom. Unfortunately for parents like the Wilsons, this syndrome has become increasingly common in the past 10 years. Grown children are returning to the nest or sometimes never leaving at all. The primary impetus for this phenomenon is economic: Young adults are moving back home because of educational opportunities or the lack of them, occupational difficulties, and personal lifestyle choices.

2 The RYA (Returning Young Adult) phenomenon is a family development syndrome looked at as circular in the family's attempt to "launch" the young adult members into independence. The young adult leaves home to experience adult independent living, returns home, hopefully to leave again, this time successfully. The act of emerging from the core family home and assuming responsibilities and, in essence, finding a place in the world can often be unsuccessful financially for many young adults. Peck (1991) defines the

Comments

A. In her opening paragraph, Adrienne Harton draws on personal experience to catch her audience's interest.
B. At the beginning of paragraph 2, Harton explains what RYA means. Thereafter, she uses the abbreviation without explanation.

"launching" stage as "one of the most complex stages of the family's life cycles" (p. 150). According to Natalie Swartzberg (1991)

> [North] American family young adulthood can be defined as usually beginning in the early twenties . . . when the young person is launched from the family of origin, and ending sometime in the early thirties, when the young adult is firmly ensconced in a job and is capable of intimacy. (p. 77)

For the most part, the reason for the RYA syndrome is economics.

3   Before analyzing the financial reasons why people in their 20s are returning to their parents' homes, researchers first determine the characteristics of this group. Burnett and Smart (1994) define RYAs: "To be a true RYA, both the individual and parents expected the child to leave home, the child actually did leave home but, because of the need for economic support, returned" (p. 255). The RYA phenomenon is also called the crowded nest or "boomerang effect." According to calculations based on the 1995 General Social Survey, 27 percent of all Canadian young adults have returned home for at least one period of four months (Mitchell, Wister, & Gee, 1998). Although not a staggering statistic, the implications for Canadian family structure are many, especially when considering the number of young adults who postpone leaving the nest in the first place. Statistics Canada found

Comments

A. Paragraph 3 describes RYAs by using demographic evidence.

B. Note that the long quotation—a quotation of more than 40 words—in paragraphs 2, 7, 9, and 11 is indented 1.25 cm (or five typewritten spaces) only, per APA style. (See 20b.)

that between 1981 and 1991 the number of adult children over 25 living at home rose 62 percent. In the 30-34 age range, the number rose by 83 percent (Carey, 1995, p. A1). The numbers are particularly alarming among young men between 25 and 29 years old. In 1985, one-fifth of men in this age group lived at home. Ten years later, the proportion rose to one-third (Carey, 1995, p. A1). There is little doubt that high unemployment rates among young people and the diminishing purchasing power of entry-level wages, along with escalating rents in urban centres, have created a hostile living environment that is pushing young adults back to their parents' nests.

4   Determining the characteristics of the RYA's family is another important control. Children from poorer families are more likely to return home than those from well-off households (Mitchell & Gee, 1996, p. 68). Because parents with high socio-economic status tend to have higher achievement expectations of their children, a potential RYA may be dissuaded from returning home. Young adults from wealthy families may also be receiving financial support from their parents to provide for their independent living arrangement (Gee, Mitchell, & Wister, 1995, pp. 126-127). Parents of young adults actually wield great influence in determining whether or not the child becomes an RYA. However, the economic circumstances of RYAs are almost

Comments

A. Paragraph 4 includes citations to sources with two and three
   authors.

always the deciding factor in moving back home. Knowing these characteristics of RYAs and their families leads to a more in-depth analysis of financial considerations and the RYA syndrome.

5   Education affects young adults in two ways with regard to moving home. Either the RYA is attending college or university and cannot afford to live on his or her own, or the RYA chose not to further his or her education and cannot be self-sustaining on the pay cheque alone. In the first case, research shows that Canadians are attending college and university as never before. Between 1971 and 1991, the number of Canadians with at least some postsecondary education almost doubled (Pratt, 1995, p. 71). Many students are doubling up their qualifications and, as a result, spend more time in school (Barlow, 1996). Living with one's parents effectively decreases a student's financial burden. These RYAs have sound and smart reasons for living with their parents, but what about the RYAs who are not continuing their education?

6   Some RYAs simply cannot afford to live away from home on a small salary. For them and for those who are unemployed or completing their education, returning to one's childhood home makes sense, whether the young adult is trying to save money or to maintain a particular lifestyle. As one young Gen X'er put it: "Those theories I got in college were

great, but now that reality is here, I need to figure out if they really work."

7   Jobs obviously affect economic situations of young adults. Some RYAs hold jobs and some do not, but for both groups, the dilemma is not having enough money to maintain a desired lifestyle and pay the bills too. The shifting economy means that most low-skill and entry-level jobs are in the services sector and not the traditional higher-paying manufacturing fields. For example, in British Columbia the Ministry of Skills, Training, and Labour has found that as those over the age of 35 are seeing increases in real earnings, young people are experiencing a disproportionate drop in their real earnings (Mcmartin, 1995, p. A1). Another problem relates directly to postsecondary education and choosing a major. As the business and technology sectors grow faster than areas grounded in liberal arts, students should plan for long-term job security by selecting a marketable major. Although unemployment seems to be an undesirable predicament, RYAs have a parental safety net, as illustrated by E. L. Klingelhofer (1989):

> The inability to find appropriate work has not been as catastrophic a burden as it once might have been because the parents were able to support the child, to help out, to tide him or her over. And, as the individual quest for work wore on

Generation X 8

and, eventually, wore out, what had been
thought of as a temporary arrangement
imperceptibly became a permanent one.
(p. 86)

Whereas unemployment once meant failure,
embarrassment, and perhaps even homelessness,
now it seems to be an opportunity to return
home.

8   Even for young adults with jobs, moving
home can be a solution to financial problems.
RYAs change careers with great frequency. A
full 30 percent of Canadians in the work force
are self-employed or flexibly employed, and so
rely on unstable contract and non-standard
work, resulting in high job mobility and lack
of security (Lowe, 1995, 10.11). Apparently,
grown children choose to live with their
parents to find some stability during
professional uncertainty. Furthermore, the
jobs that young adults, even when college- or
university-educated, obtain may not yield
enough money to survive away from home. A
postsecondary education can be very expensive.
Some young adults who shoulder their entire
college or university debts cannot afford to
live away from home while paying student loans
(Kuttner, 1995, p. M5). Regardless of whether
an RYA has a job or not, the economic sense of
moving back home exceeds the need for
independence.

9   The final financial reason why grown
children are returning to the nest encompasses
personal lifestyle decisions: delayed marriage
and middle-class comfort. The average age of
marriage has steadily increased since the
1970s. Littwin (1986) concludes:

> Commitment to a relationship is just as
> difficult for them as commitment to a
> career or point of view. It is one act
> that might define them and therefore limit
> their potential. Besides, it is difficult
> to be in a relationship when you still
> don't know who you are. (p. 219)

10   With the option of moving home, young
adults do not feel the pressure or the
necessity to marry early. Even when people do
marry early and divorce, research shows that
many young adults return to their parents'
homes to recover and stabilize (Klingelhofer,
1989, p. 86). RYAs can opt to live with their
families as an alternative to marriage or to
reestablish themselves after a divorce. In
either scenario, the RYA is more financially
stable than if he or she lived alone.

11   Some RYAs return to the nest to attain
the material comforts of a middle- to upper-
class home that they enjoyed and expected as
dependents. Adult children now receive
allowances, their own rooms, telephones, cars,

personal freedom. Why should they leave the nest? For wealthier families, adult children moving home is a particular problem. Littwin (1986) says:

> The affluent, perfect parent is the ideal target for rebellion-and-rescue. . . . The young adult resents that he has been given so much that he cannot give himself. He has been cared for too well and too conscientiously. (p. 140)

A potential RYA, still a student at university and for whom his parents pay all expenses, recently complained about the constraints his full-time summer job placed on his lifestyle, "I don't see how you and Dad get anything done when you have to work 40 hours a week" (K. James, personal communication, August 15, 1996). In an instant-gratification-seeking generation, returning to the nest is just easier than earning comfort.

12   In conclusion, young adults are moving back home for a variety of reasons. Of course, people of the 20-something generation would not be able to return home without parental acquiescence. Future research will reveal if RYAs develop a pattern of adult dependence on their parents, but for now, research proves that grown children are moving back home for a myriad of financial considerations. And,

Comments

A. Harton cites the personal communication from Karl James in paragraph 11 in the text but, as with other non-recoverable sources such as personal letters and e-mail, does not list it in the references.

B. Harton's concluding paragraph follows the traditional model of summarizing the preceding points and suggesting a direction for future study (**28f(2)**).

Generation X 10

perhaps, as one Gen X'er bemoans: "We as a
generation have yet to produce any defining
traits, except perhaps to show a defeatist
belief that we will do worse than our parents"
(Janoff, 1995, p. 10).

Comment

A. A strong final statement, the quotation Harton uses to conclude her essay contains an implicit challenge to Generation X. Note also that it is introduced by a colon (21d(1)).

Generation X 11

References

Barlow, J. (1996, February). Generation next: Meet some dynamic "Gen-X" entrepreneurs whose energy and enthusiasm put many top CEOs to shame. Report on Business Magazine, 12(8), 68-70, 72+. Retrieved March 21, 1997, from Canadian Periodical Index database.

Burnett, J., & Smart, D. (1994). Returning young adults. Psychology and Marketing, 11, 253-269.

Carey, E. (1995, June 30). "Kids" in their 30s returning to nest. Toronto Star, p. A1 (final ed.). Canadian newsdisc. Micromedia. [1996, June].

Cipriano, E. (1996). Who is this generation formerly known as x? Seriously, 6(1). Retrieved December 13, 1997, from ftp:// spc.5yr.edu/seriously/generation

Gee, E. M., Mitchell, B. A., & Wister, A. V. (1995). Returning to the parental "nest": Exploring a changing Canadian life course. Canadian Studies in Population, 22(2), 121-144.

Holtz, G. T. (1995). Welcome to the jungle: The why behind "Generation X." New York: St. Martin's Griffin.

Janoff, J. B. (1995, April 24). A gen-x Rip Van Winkle. Newsweek, 127, 10.

Klingelhofer, E. L. (1989). Coping with your grown children. Clifton, NJ: Humana Press.

Kuttner, R. (1995, June 25). The new elite: Living with mom and dad. Los Angeles Times, p. M5.

Comments

A. The reference list is organized alphabetically and begins on a new page. The last name is always given first, and initials are provided for first and middle names. The date of publication is always given parenthetically, immediately after the author's name. (See 34d(2).)

B. Observe the use of periods and commas, the style of capitalization for book and article titles, and the different capitalization style for journal titles. Underline book and journal titles, and also the volume number of periodicals.

C. If Harton's instructor had specified a final manuscript format that called for the first line of each entry to be indented 1.25 cm (or five typewritten spaces), the first two entries would look like this:

Barlow, J. (1996, February). Generation next: Meet some dynamic "Gen-X" entrepreneurs whose energy and enthusiasm put many top CEOs to shame. <u>Report on Business Magazine, 12</u>(8), 68-70, 72+. Retrieved March 21, 1997, from Canadian Periodical Index database.

Burnett, J., & Smart, D. (1994). Returning young adults. <u>Psychology and Marketing, 11</u>, 253-269.

Generation X 12

Littwin, S. (1986). <u>The postponed generation:
Why American youth are growing up later</u>.
New York: William Morrow.

Lowe, G. S. (1995). Work. In R. J. Brym (Ed.),
<u>New society: Sociology for the 21st century</u>
(pp. 10.1-10.28). Toronto: Harcourt.

Mcmartin, P. (1995, January 21). Talking 'bout
my generation: From boomers to busters,
from blessed ones to angry gen Xers,
we're all prisoners of demography:
Prisoners of time. <u>Vancouver Sun</u>, p. A1
(final ed.). Retrieved June 6, 1996, from
Canadian Newsdisc database.

Mitchell, B. A., & Gee, E. M. (1996). Young
adults returning home: Implications for
social policy. In B. Galaway & J. Hudson
(Eds.), <u>Youth in transition: Perspectives
on research and policy</u> (pp. 61-71).
Toronto: Thompson.

Mitchell, B. A., Wister, A. V., & Gee, E. M.
(1998, July). <u>The cultural dimensions and
pathways of returning home among Canadian
young adults</u>. Paper presented at the 14th
World Congress of Sociology, Montreal, PQ.

Peck, J. S. (1991). Families launching young
adults. In F. H. Brown (Ed.), <u>Reweaving the
family tapestry: A multigenerational approach
to families</u> (pp. 149-168). New York: Norton.

Pratt, L. (1995, March). Boomer envy. <u>Canadian
Living</u>, 65-71.

Schwartzberg, N. (1991). Single young adults. In
F. H. Brown (Ed.), <u>Reweaving the family
tapestry: A multigenerational approach</u>
(pp. 77-93). New York: Norton.

Chapter 35 | Writing for Special Purposes

The information conveyed throughout this handbook will benefit you in different writing situations. The essentials of English grammar (1–7) and the principles of effective sentence structure (8–12)—as well as conventions for using appropriate diction (13–16), punctuation (17–21), and mechanics (22–26)—are always relevant. Advice about planning and drafting (28), developing (27d, 28c), and revising and editing (29) applies to most writing that you will need to do in university or college and in your profession. Other advice, such as how to write arguments (32) and work with sources (33, 34), applies to specific purposes. This chapter will introduce you to principles that govern two additional situations: writing about literature (35a) and effective business communication (35b).

 Writing about literature increases understanding of it.

Like all writing in specialized fields, literature has its own vocabulary. When you learn it, you are not just learning a list of terms and definitions. You are grasping concepts that will help you understand literature and write about it effectively. This section introduces these concepts and provides basic guidelines for writing about literature. Your instructor can give you further help.

Writing about literature involves using the principles of good writing. Consider the rhetorical situation, especially your audience and your purpose (28a), and explore, limit, and focus your subject (28c) as you read and write. Work toward formulating a thesis statement (28d) that can be supported from the work itself, and plan how to organize your thoughts so that your essay will have a sound structure.

(1) Prepare for writing by reading, reflecting, and planning.

You cannot write effectively about a literary work that you have not read. Begin the process of writing about literature by reading carefully and noting your personal response. Think critically about these impressions and be open to new ideas as you plan your essay.

(a) Explore your personal response to literature.

As you read, take notes and jot down ideas. Trust your own reactions. What characters do you admire? Did the work remind you of any experience of your own? Did it introduce you to a world different from your own? Were you amused, moved, or confused? These first impressions can provide the seeds from which strong essays will grow. You may find that you need to modify your initial impressions as you study the work more closely or as writing takes you in a direction that you did not originally anticipate. But writing about literature begins with active, personal engagement with what you read.

You can facilitate this engagement by freewriting (see 28c) or by keeping a journal in which you record your reactions and questions. These methods of exploring a subject can help you discover what you think or what you want to understand. In addition to generating topics for writing, they provide a useful method for identifying questions you could raise in class. Here is a piece of freewriting on "The Miller's Tale," one short tale of many in Chaucer's *Canterbury Tales*. "The Miller's Tale" is discussed in the paper that begins on page 645. The author quickly wrote whatever came to mind, confident that doing so would help her discover a topic for an essay.

> The language in "The Miller's Tale" — hard to understand the story the first time through! The glossary and footnotes helped a lot the second time. Surprising that even though it was written in the 1380s, the story is hilarious to me today. The characters seem real, even for the modern world. Lust, adultery, farce, slapstick. All about ordinary people. Was it common in Chaucer's day to write that way? Absolon is the insulted lover who tries to get revenge. He is a fool but interesting to watch as he tries everything he knows. Nicholas is a good contrast for him. The story is so ribald. Isn't it strange that it is told by people on a pilgrimage? How does Chaucer make the characters in the story seem so alive, especially when it's a story within a story?

After briefly noting how the story made her feel, the author of this excerpt then moves on to ask three questions, each of which could lead to an essay through the exploration of possible answers. Another essay, for example, could compare and contrast "The Miller's Tale" with another piece of writing from the same period. Note also that this excerpt does not consist entirely of grammatically correct sentences. When you freewrite about literature, write whatever comes to mind without worrying about whether or not you are correct. You are thinking on paper, not editing an essay.

(b) Analyze, interpret, explicate, and evaluate.

Although you may have occasion to write papers in which you simply explore your personal response to a work of literature and relate it to your own life, writing papers about a literary work usually requires you to focus on the work itself. Your personal response may help you discover a direction you want to explore, but as you explore you will often need to look at a work by analyzing it, interpreting it, or evaluating it. A short paper may do only one of these; a long paper may do all three.

Analyze (see **27d(6)**) a work of literature by breaking it into elements and examining how such elements as setting, characters, and plot combine to form a whole. How do the elements interact? How does one element contribute to the overall meaning of the work? For example, in her paper on *King Lear* (beginning on page 653), Susan Ferk demonstrates how the characters in the subplot comment on and intensify the main plot and theme.

Interpret a work by asking what it means, bearing in mind of course that a work may have more than one meaning. Support your interpretation by referring to elements in the work itself. For example, in her paper on "The Miller's Tale" (beginning on page 645), Fran Valeni cites evidence to support her belief that the characters in Chaucer's story are more than just the stereotypes that are usually found in short, farcical tales, and that Chaucer, through his characters, comments on the foibles and strengths of human nature. Interpretation is closely related to analysis and allows writers to draw freely on any part of a work that can be used to explain its meaning.

An interpretation that attempts to explain every element in a work is called an **explication** and is usually limited to poetry. When explicating William Wordsworth's "A Slumber Did My Spirit Seal," a writer might note that the "s" sound reinforces the hushed feeling of sleep and death in the poem. But it would also be necessary to consider the meaning of "slumber," "spirit," and "seal," as well as why the words in this line are arranged as they are (as opposed to "A Slumber Sealed My Spirit" or "My Spirit Was Sealed by a Slumber").

Evaluate a work by asking how successful the author is in communicating its meaning to readers. Like interpretation, evaluation is a type of argument in which a writer cites evidence to persuade readers to accept a clearly formulated thesis. (See chapter 32.) In her paper on Christina Rossetti (beginning on page 664), Jane Wattam argues that Rossetti's elegies distort and re-define this genre. An evaluation of a literary work should consider both strengths and weaknesses if there is evidence of both.

⚠ **CAUTION** Although **summarizing** a literary work can be a useful way to make sure you understand it, do not confuse summary with analysis, interpretation, or evaluation. Those who have read the literary work are unlikely to benefit from reading a summary of it. Do not submit a summary unless your instructor has asked for one.

(c) Choose a subject and decide how you want to develop it.

If your instructor asks you to choose your own subject, your first step should be to reflect on your personal response (35a(1a)). Reviewing your response may enable you not only to choose a subject but also to formulate a tentative thesis. The purpose of your paper in this case would be to persuade readers to agree with your view. Also try some of the methods suggested in 28c to explore the work in question. If you generate more than one possible topic, decide which one seems most original.

Choose a topic that would be interesting both to write and to read about. Readers are usually interested in learning what *you* think. If you choose an easy topic, you may find yourself repeating what many others have already said. As a rule, try to avoid writing the obvious. However, do not let the quest for originality lead you to choose a topic that would be too hard to develop adequately.

Apply strategies of development (27d). You might **define** why you consider a character heroic, **classify** a play as a comedy of manners, or **describe** a setting that contributes to a work's meaning. Perhaps you could **compare and contrast** two poems on a similar subject or explore **cause-and-effect** relationships in a novel. Why, for example, does an apparently intelligent character make a bad decision?

(d) Re-read carefully.

Experienced readers understand that a literary work can provoke different responses from different readers. You can also have a significantly different response when rereading a work—even a work you think you understand already. Whenever possible, re-read any work that you are planning to write about. If its length makes doing so not feasible, at least re-read the chapters or scenes that impressed you as especially important or problematic.

If you have a tentative thesis, re-reading a work will help you find the evidence you need to support it. You are likely to find evidence that you did not notice on your first reading or that will require you to modify your thesis. To establish yourself as a credible source (31d), use evidence appropriate for your purpose (31c) and present it fairly.

A good way to note evidence, ideas, and concerns is to annotate as you read. Because experienced readers are actively engaged with their reading, they often keep a pen or pencil at hand so they can mark passages they may wish to study, ask about, or draw on when writing.

(e) Do research when appropriate.

Both writers and readers often favour papers that are focussed on a person's individual response, analysis, interpretation, or evaluation. But by reading criticism that reveals what other readers think of a given literary work, you can engage in a dialogue. When you draw on the ideas of other people, however, remember that you must use those sources responsibly (33g), and that even when you incorporate them you must still advance a position that is clearly your own. Few readers enjoy papers that offer little more than a collection of quotations.

When you read criticism, remember that a work of literature rarely has a single meaning. Three different critics may offer three radically different interpretations. Your responsibility is not to determine who is right but to determine the extent to which you agree or disagree with the differing views you encounter. Read critically (chapter 31) and formulate your own thesis (28d).

Chapter 33 explains how to do research. To locate material on a specific writer or work, consult your library's catalogue (33c) and the *MLA Bibliography,* an index of books and articles about literature. Like most indexes to special-interest periodicals (pages 498–99), the *MLA Bibliography* can be consulted in printed volumes, through an online database search, or through access to a CD-ROM covering several years.

You may also locate useful information in the following reference books:

Atwood, Margaret, ed. *The New Oxford Book of Canadian Verse in English*. Toronto: Oxford UP, 1984.

Benson, Eugene, and William Toye, eds. *The Oxford Companion to Canadian Literature*. 2nd ed. Toronto: Oxford UP, 1998.

Cambridge History of English Literature. 15 vols. Cambridge: Cambridge UP, 1907–33.

Cuddon, J. A., ed. *The Penguin Dictionary of Literary Terms and Literary Theory*. 4th ed. London: Penguin, 1998.

Drabble, Margaret, ed. *The Oxford Companion to English Literature*. 6th ed. New York: Oxford UP, 1998.

Evory, Ann, et al., eds. *Contemporary Authors*. New Revision Series. Detroit: Gale, 2001.

Hart, James D., and Phillip Leininger, eds. *The Oxford Companion to American Literature*. 6th ed. New York: Oxford UP, 1995.

Hazen, Edith P., ed. *The Columbia Granger's Index to Poetry*. 11th ed. New York: Columbia UP, 1997.

Howatson, M. C., ed. *The Oxford Companion to Classical Literature*. 2nd ed. 1989. London: Oxford UP, 1997.

Kamboureli, Smaro, ed. *Making a Difference: An Anthology of Ethnic Canadian Writing*. Toronto: Oxford UP, 1996.

Literary History of Canada: Canadian Literature in English. 2nd ed. 4 vols. Toronto: U of Toronto P, 1976, 1990.

New Cambridge Bibliography of English Literature. 5 vols. Cambridge: Cambridge UP, 1983.

Serafin, Steve. *Encyclopedia of World Literature in the 20th Century*. 3rd ed. 4 vols. New York: Saint James, 1998.

For an example of a paper that incorporates research about literature, see the essay by Jane Wattam (beginning on page 664).

! **CAUTION** Research is not appropriate for all assignments. Your instructor may want only your own response or interpretation. If your instructor has not assigned a researched paper, ask if one would be acceptable.

(2) Write essays about fiction.

Although the events have not happened and the characters may never have existed, serious fiction expresses truth about the human condition through such components as **setting**, **character**, and **plot**. In the *Canterbury Tales* (1380s), pilgrims on the long road to Canterbury entertain each other with stories. In "The Miller's Tale," two men each make their best effort to seduce the young wife of a carpenter. Nicholas gains her promise to spend the night with him if the opportunity arises. Absolon, on the other hand, continues in vain to serenade her, send her gifts, and stand hopefully under her window—until she plays a cruel joke on him.

Nicholas creates his opportunity by convincing the carpenter that Noah's flood is about to happen again and that the carpenter should be ready for it by sleeping in his boat, which is suspended by ropes from the ceiling of his shed. That night, all goes well until Nicholas goes to the window where Absolon, bent on revenge, is waiting. Absolon, in a case of mistaken identity, burns Nicholas's bottom, causing Nicholas to cry out in pain, "Help! Water! Water! Help for Goddes herte!" The carpenter, hearing the cries of "Water," thinks that Noah's flood has begun, chops the ropes that were holding the boat, and falls to the ground. Here is an excerpt from the conclusion:

> This carpenter out of his slomber sterte,
> And herde oon° cryen "Water!" as he were   *someone*
>   wood,°   *crazy*
> And thoughte, "Allas, now cometh Noweles
> flood!"
> He sette him up withoute wordes mo,

And with his ax he smoot the corde atwo,
And down gooth al: he foond neither to selle
Ne breed ne ale til he cam to the celle,[1]
Upon the floor, and ther aswoune° he lay.   *in a faint*
. . . .
   The neighebores, bothe smale and grete,
In ronnen° for to gauren° on this man   *came running /*
                                               to gape

That aswoune lay bothe pale and wan,
For with the fal he brosten° hadde his arm;   *broken*
But stonde° he moste° unto his owene harm,   *stand up / must*
For whan he spak he was anoon° bore   *quickly*
   down°   *refuted*
With° hende Nicholas and Alisoun: *by*
They tolden every man that he was wood—
He was agast° so of Noweles flood,   *afraid*
Thurgh fantasye, that of his vanitee°   *folly*
He hadde ybought him° kneeding-tubbes   *himself*
   three,
And hadde hem hanged in the roof above,
And that he prayed° hem,° for Goddes love,   *begged /*
                                               Nicholas and
                                               Alisoun

To sitten in the roof, *par compaignye.*°   *to keep him*
                                               company

   The folk gan laughen at his fantasye.
Into the roof they kiken° and they cape,°   *peer / gape*
And turned al his harm unto a jape,°   *joke*
For what so that this carpenter answerde,°   *no matter what*
                                               the carpenter
                                               said

It was for nought: no man his reson° herde;   *argument*
With othes grete he was so sworn adown,
That he was holden° wood in al the town,   *considered*

---

[1] He found time to sell neither bread nor ale until he arrived
at the foundation, i.e., he did not take time out.

For every clerk anoonright heeld with other:
They saide, "The man was wood, my leve
  brother,"
And every wight° gan laughen at this strif.°   *one / fuss*
Thus swived° was the carpenteres wif   *slept with*
For al his keeping° and his jalousye,   *guarding*
And Absolon hath kist hir nether° yë,   *lower*
And Nicholas is scalded in the toute:
This tale is doon, and God save al the
  route!°   *company*

Setting **Setting** involves time—not only historical time, but also the length of time covered by the action. It also involves place—not only the physical setting, but also the atmosphere created by the author. Because "The Miller's Tale" is a story within a story, there is more than one time sequence and more than one physical setting. The time sequence is in one sense very brief: the miller tells the tale in under a half hour. The sequence of events in the story, however, happens over a few days or weeks. The time sequence of the *Canterbury Tales*, in which "The Miller's Tale" appears, lasts as long as it takes the pilgrims to reach their destination. There is more than one physical setting, as well. In the larger story, the pilgrims are making their way along the road to Canterbury. Within it, "The Miller's Tale" takes place in a small town not far from Oxford. For the pilgrims listening to the story, the setting would lend a sense of immediacy and reality to the tale.

Plot The sequence of events that makes up the story is the **plot**. Plot is how and why events and actions connect with one another through time. Narrative, as distinct from plot, concerns the *telling* of events. An author may record events in an entirely different order from that in which they are imagined as taking place. Narrative uses flashback and foreshadowing, for example, to create a sense that the occasion of telling a story is separate from the story itself.

Plot   Arthur left home because he felt that his family didn't understand his need to succeed as an actor.

Narrative   I first met Arthur in a bar. He hold me about how he'd run away from home. Later I got a sense of how much he missed his family and wanted to impress them.

Depending on the author's purpose, a work of fiction may have a complicated plot or almost no plot at all. The plot of "The Miller's Tale" is simple, yet deftly woven from the intersecting experiences of the two lovers bent on wooing the carpenter's wife. In this story, the plot is less an end in itself than a vehicle for humour and character.

Characters   The **characters** carry the plot forward and usually include a main character, called a **protagonist**, who is in conflict with another character, with an institution, or with himself or herself. In "The Miller's Tale," Nicholas is the protagonist, in conflict with the carpenter, with Absolon, and, in his efforts to win her, with the carpenter's wife. By examining a character's conflict, you can often discover a story's **theme**, in this case, human weakness and comeuppance.

Point of view   The position from which the action is observed—the person through whose eyes the events are seen—is the **point of view**. It may be that of a single character within the story or of a narrator who tells the story. Many works of fiction are told from a single point of view, but some shift the point of view from one character to another. "The Miller's Tale" is told from the miller's point of view, as told through the author's point of view (because it is a story within a story). In this case, the narrator is **omniscient**—that is, all-knowing. A narrator who knows his or her own thoughts throughout the story but not those of other characters is **partially omniscient**. A story told by a character who refers to herself or himself as "I" employs the **first-person** point of view. (Do not confuse this character with the author.) When the narrator does not reveal the thoughts of any character, the story is being told from the **dramatic** or **objective** point of view.

Tone   Conveyed by point of view—as well as by diction and sentence structure—**tone** is the author's attitude toward the events and characters in the story or even, in some circumstances, toward the readers. The tone of the narrator in "The Miller's Tale" is brash, crude, and tongue-in-cheek, creating a humorous effect. Another story could have an ironic, bitter, or sombre tone. By determining a work's tone and the impact it has on you as a reader, you can gain insight into the author's purpose. (See **29a**.)

Symbolism   A common characteristic of fiction, **symbolism** is also used in drama and poetry. A **symbol** is an object, usually concrete, that stands for something else, usually abstract. On one level, it is what it is; on another level, it is more than what it is. In writing about a particular symbol, first note the context in which it appears. Then think about what it could mean. When you have an idea, trace the incidents in the story that reinforce that idea. In "The Miller's Tale," the name Absolon comes from the biblical name Absolom. Absolom was the vain son of David; he met his death when his long, curly hair became entangled in a tree as he rode his horse beneath it, giving his enemies their chance to kill him.

Theme The main idea of a literary work is its **theme**. Depending on how they interpret a work, different readers may identify different themes. To test whether the idea you have identified is central to the work in question, check to see if it is supported by the **setting, plot, characterization, tone,** and **symbols.** If you can relate these components to the idea you are exploring, then that idea can be considered the work's theme. In her paper on "The Miller's Tale," Fran Valeni looks at how Chaucer uses characterization to advance his theme—the foolishness and foibles of human nature, especially where lust is involved.

As you read and write, ask yourself the following questions:

Checklist for Analyzing Fiction
- From whose point of view is the story told?
- What is the narrator's tone?
- Who is the protagonist? How is his or her character developed?
- With whom or what is the protagonist in conflict?
- How does one character compare with another?
- What symbols does the author use?
- What is the theme?
- How does the author use setting, plot, characters, and symbolism to support the theme?

Sample student paper about fiction

In the following paper, a student interprets "The Miller's Tale," arguing that the theme is conveyed through characterization. Her assignment was as follows:

Re-read "The Miller's Tale," then using two important characters from the story, analyze how Chaucer uses characterization (a) for humour, (b) to advance the plot, and (c) to convey his theme. Your essay should be approximately four pages in length. Be sure to support your interpretation with evidence from the story.

Fran Valeni
Professor Johnson
English 100B, Section 3
12 January 1998

Two Contrasting Portraits in Chaucer's
"The Miller's Tale":
Chaucer's Art of Characterization

In "The Miller's Tale," Chaucer's art of   1
characterization lends an air of plausibility
to an otherwise silly farce. Despite the
barrier of centuries and the changes in
language that have taken place since Chaucer's
day, we can sympathize with his characters and
perhaps see ourselves in them. He achieves
this effect through masterful use of detail,
while at the same time treating his characters
both sympathetically and humorously. Just
enough information is revealed about them for
the tale to advance as it should and for the
reader to understand the motives and actions
of each one. Nicholas and Absolon, the two
rival lovers in the tale, provide good
examples of Chaucer's art.

"Hende" Nicholas smells good and looks   2
"lik a maide meeke for to see" (line 94).
Chaucer gives no other physical description of
him, yet we can imagine him as young and
attractive. He is a poor scholar who is very
interested in astrology, and who likes to sing
and play the psaltery. His room is elegant and
neat and his possessions (such as his
astrology books) reflect his intellectual
pride. He is a self-confident and scheming
man, well enough versed in "derne love" and

"solas" (line 92) to outwit a carpenter and seduce his wife. Unlike Absolon, his is not the lovesick, heart-on-his-sleeve approach to romance. Rather, he is direct and almost violent: "And he heeld hire harde by the haunche-bones" (line 171). All in all, Nicholas is an unprincipled individual whose scruples do not restrain him from bedding a married woman, boastfully deceiving her husband, or living at least partly on the money of his friends (line 112). Yet we may like him for his ingenuity, and for his talents as an actor and persuader. As a result, we might feel sorry for his painful "end" even while laughing at it.

3   Throughout the tale Nicholas demonstrates great self-control. He postpones his lust until a whole night can be spent with Alisoun; he shuts himself in his room for days to advance his scheme; and he thoroughly convinces John of impending disaster. In spite of these examples of his self-discipline and control, it is an act of <u>impulse</u> that brings him so much pain when he takes Alisoun's place at the window.

4   Nicholas's conspiracy and lovemaking with Alisoun, and his deception of John, illustrate how adept he is at manipulating others. It is plausible that his weather predictions and astrological skills might lead others to

imagine that he can also manipulate his environment.

As the protagonist of the tale, we see 5 Nicholas as the poor scholar, then the master of intrigue, and finally the successful seducer and trickster (although at some cost to himself). As the events unfold, so do the aspects of his character. Yet Chaucer announced early in the tale how well Nicholas knew the ways of secret love. Therefore, since his personality did not really change or grow in the tale, Nicholas must be called a static character, as is often seen in farce.

In contrast to Nicholas, Absolon's 6 physical appearance is described in minute detail. Each item contributes to the picture of "joly" Absolon as a foolish, overdressed, affected fop, from his intricately carved shoes to his curly, golden hair, "strouted as a fanne large and brode" (line 207). Like his namesake, Absolom, in the Bible "there (is) no blemish in him" (2 Sam. 14:25) and his hair is his crowning glory.

Absolon is the parish clerk, who also 7 knows how to clip and shave, let blood, and do legal papers and maps. These details make Absolon seem very realistic.

Humour, too, abounds in Chaucer's 8 descriptions of Absolon: dancing "with his legs casten to and fro" (line 224) or singing in his trilling falsetto, with his voice "gentil and smal" (line 252). His affected

Valeni 4

aversion to body odours is also hilarious. He chews licorice for his breath and is "somdeel squaimous" of passing wind (lines 229-230). Later, of course, it is that very act of Nicholas's that sparks the final scene.

9   As a lover, Absolon is again very funny. He is persistent and elaborate. His mouth, ready for kissing, "icches . . . all this longe day" (line 574), thus hinting at events to come. He sees himself as a great romantic and tries to speak in fancy words of love that emerge as crude and silly instead: "That for your love . . . I swelte and swete: / I moorne as doth a lamb after the tete" (lines 594-595).

10   Unlike Nicholas, Absolon is very impulsive and acts almost entirely on his emotions. He woos Alisoun directly under her husband's nose and later in the tale wreaks his revenge without taking time to think it over. He is also a powerless character, unable to win Alisoun or develop a relationship with her. Even her husband is not much affected by Absolon's persistence.

11   As the antagonist in the tale, Absolon moves from the lovesick fool to the sad and insulted lover, and finally to the angry and outraged avenger. As the tale unfolds, Chaucer allows Absolon to change and develop. Within the narrow limits of a short farce, Absolon is a dynamic character.

12   By looking at two contrasting portraits in "The Miller's Tale," the reader can

Valeni 5

appreciate Chaucer's art of characterization, not only for its sympathy and humour, but especially for its remarkably appropriate choice of details. More than that, by creating such lifelike characters, Chaucer paints their very humanity, so that we can recognize ourselves, and others, in them.

Valeni 6

Work Cited

Chaucer, Geoffrey. "The Miller's Tale." The Norton Anthology of English Literature. Vol. 1. 6th ed. Ed. M. H. Abrams. New York: Norton, 1993. 101-17.

In this paper, Fran Valeni argues that, in "The Miller's Tale," Chaucer uses characterization not only for humour but also to reveal human nature. This thesis is first introduced at the end of paragraph 1 and is restated in the final paragraph. The rest of the first paragraph establishes the basic structure of the essay: a close examination of two of Chaucer's characters. The references to Chaucer's use of details, humour, and sympathy are elaborated on in the body of the essay, first in terms of Nicholas and then Absolon. The final paragraph restates the thesis and helps the reader relate his or her own humanity to that of the characters.

Exercise 1

Write an outline for this paper. Compare your outline with the assignment given on page 644. Write a comment of approximately 100 words in which you evaluate how successfully the paper fulfils the assignment. Imagine that the author of this paper will read your comment. Try to be specific and helpful.

Exercise 2

In consultation with your instructor, choose a short story other than "The Miller's Tale" and complete the assignment on page 644.

(3) Write essays about drama.

Although it is written to be filmed or performed on a stage, drama can also be read, which is probably the way you will encounter it in your course work. In a performance, the director and the actors imprint the play with their own interpretations; in a book or script, you have only the printed word and the imagination you bring to it. Drama has many of the same elements as fiction, but they are presented differently.

Dialogue Dialogue is the principal medium through which we see action and characterization when reading a play. Examine dialogue to discover motives, internal conflicts, and relationships among characters.

Characters Often identified briefly in a list at the beginning of the play, the **characters** are developed largely through what they say and what is said about them and to them. In Ibsen's *A Doll's House,* for example, Nora's development can be traced through her gestures and her speech. The play opens with her saying such things as "Me? Oh, pooh, I don't want anything." It concludes with her deciding to leave her husband and declaring, "I must educate myself." In writing about drama, you might compare characters or analyze their development and its significance through their dialogue and their actions.

Plot   **Plot** in drama is similar to plot in fiction and is usually advanced by conflict between characters. Although there may be time lapses between scenes, the story line must be developed within the place constraints of the play. **Subplots** similar to the one outlined in the sample student paper that follows may reinforce the theme of the main plot.

You might examine in a paper how dialogue, characterizations, setting, and stage directions for gestures and movement further the action.

As you read and write, ask yourself the following questions:

Checklist for Analyzing Drama
- How are the characters depicted through dialogue?
- What is the primary conflict within the play?
- What motivates the characters to act as they do?
- Are there any parallels between different characters?
- How does setting contribute to the play's action?
- What is the theme of the play?
- If there is more than one story in the play, how do they relate to one another?

Sample student paper about drama

The following student paper discusses the significance of the subplot in *King Lear*. The writer chose to respond to the following question:

Does the conflict between Edmund and Gloucester contribute to the meaning you find in *King Lear*, or is this conflict an unnecessary distraction from the main action of the play?

Susan K. Ferk
Professor Dorgan
English 211
10 April 1998

The Subplot as Commentary in King Lear

To a careless eye, the subplot involving   1
Gloucester, Edgar, and Edmund in Shakespeare's
King Lear may appear to be trivial, unnecessary, and a simple restatement of the theme of
the main story. On close examination, however,
it is clear that Shakespeare has skilfully
introduced a second set of characters whose
actions comment on and intensify the main plot
and theme.

The first scene of King Lear sets up   2
comparison and contrast between Lear and
Gloucester. Gloucester jokes about his bastard
son while Lear angrily banishes his favourite
daughter. By the end of the second scene, we
realize how important their children are to
both men and yet how little they really know
them. Both are easily deceived: Lear by
Goneril and Regan, who convince him of their
love with flowery words, and Gloucester, who is
convinced by very little evidence of Edgar's
plot against his life. The audience is set up
to accept Lear and Gloucester as old fools.
Neither takes responsibility for what has
happened. Gloucester says "these late
eclipses" (1.2.96) have brought about these
changes, and Lear blames Cordelia for her
losses. Neither realizes or acknowledges that
his own foolishness has brought about these
events.

3   Gloucester, however, does comment on Lear's actions in scene 2. He is amazed that the king has limited his power so suddenly. When Edmund suggests that "sons at perfect age, and fathers declined, the father / should be as ward to the son, and the son manage his / revenue" (1.2.68-70), Gloucester is enraged by what he thinks are Edgar's words. He calls Edgar unnatural, and since this is exactly the action taken by Lear with his daughters, we can assume that he thinks Lear's act was unnatural also.

4   At Goneril's palace Lear foreshadows Gloucester's fate when he says "Old fond eyes,/ beweep this cause again, I'll pluck ye out" (1.4.278-79). In the same way that Lear fears for his eyes because of Goneril, so does Gloucester lose his eyes because of Edmund. At the end of act 1, Lear foreshadows his own destiny, "Oh, let me not be mad, not mad, sweet heaven!" (1.5.38).

5   Shakespeare brings together the two plots in act 2, scene 2, when Regan, Cornwall, Gloucester, and Edmund meet at Gloucester's castle. Cornwall's offer of employment to Edmund, made on the pretence of his royal service, seems logical to the members of the audience, who know the similarity of their true natures. It is interesting to note that Gloucester calls Edmund his "loyal and natural boy" (2.1.85), while Lear names Goneril a "degenerate bastard" (1.4.230).

6   Lear arrives at the castle and is outraged when Cornwall and Regan do not meet

him. However, Lear decides that perhaps Cornwall is ill and unable to come. Likewise, throughout the remainder of act 2 Lear tries to imagine that Regan and Cornwall love and respect him, and he makes excuses for them when their actions do not conform to his expectations. Lear has more at stake here than Regan's love. If she proves as evil as Goneril (and she proves even more so), then Lear cannot deny that he was wrong in supposing these two daughters more loving than his banished Cordelia. Lear soon acknowledges that the disease of his daughters is in his own blood. The realization of his errors and his loss of power and Cordelia drive him to the madness seen in act 3.

Gloucester and Lear meet in scene 4 of act 3 in the midst of a raging storm, Lear's madness, and Gloucester's despair. Gloucester has not suffered the worst, but his words begin to echo those of Lear in earlier scenes. He says, "Thou sayest the King grows mad: I'll tell thee, friend, / I am almost mad myself" (152-53). Gloucester helps the king into the hovel and cares for him like a child, similar to the way Edgar later helps Gloucester after his eyes are plucked out. 7

Death begins in act 3, scene 7. A servant dies defending Gloucester, and Cornwall is fatally wounded. In the confusion, Gloucester realizes his mistakes and his former blindness. After losing his sight, he can now see. When he is turned out, his wanderings in the country remind us of Lear in the storm. 8

Ferk 4

Likewise, in his despair, Lear has learned to
see.

9   Gloucester and Lear share many
similarities at this point. Both men at the
height of their afflictions desire the company
of Tom o'Bedlam, who represents wisdom. They
also acquire a sense of justice and care for
less fortunate men. Lear looks after his fool
in the storm, and Gloucester calls for clothes
for Tom. Their similarities intensify the pain
and change in each man. Also, Shakespeare's
use of a king and a nobleman both suffering
from their foolishness emphasizes the
universality of man's suffering. On the other
hand, they do not suffer in the same way.
Gloucester does not lose his mind, and Lear
does not try suicide.

10   In the end, the story comes full circle.
Edgar tells Gloucester his identity and asks
his father's forgiveness, thus causing
Gloucester's heart to break "Twixt two
extremes of passion, joy and grief" (5.3.202).
Lear also dies, with Cordelia in his arms,
trying so hard to believe her alive that it
strains his heart as well. These men have
learned much, but as in real life, wisdom in
old age and recognizing one's children for
what they are do not always bring peace and
happiness. The dismal final scenes of this
play, in which almost everyone dies, serve to
emphasize Shakespeare's intent to show two
unfortunate characters who suffer from
foolishness and Fortune's wheel.

Work Cited

Shakespeare, William. <u>The Tragedy of King
  Lear</u>. <u>The HBJ Anthology of Drama</u>. Ed.
  W. B. Worthen. Ft. Worth: Harcourt, 1993.
  174-214.

Susan Ferk supports her thesis by comparing and contrasting the characters of Lear and Gloucester as they move through the play. In act 1, the plots are separate, but she points out how they move together in act 2 and proceed along parallel lines, crossing only occasionally. She traces this progression throughout the play, following the characters' actions and dialogue while emphasizing the significance of each plot in reinforcing and intensifying the other.

Exercise 3

Select a recent film or television drama. Write a short essay in which you identify the theme and show how the actions of the characters reveal that theme.

(4) Write essays about poetry.

Poetry shares many of the components of fiction and drama. It too may contain a narrator with a point of view, and dramatic monologues and narrative poems may have plot, setting, and characters. But poetry is primarily characterized by its concentrated use of connotative **diction, imagery, allusions, figures of speech, symbols, sound,** and **rhythm.** Before starting to write a paper about a poem, try to capture the literal meaning of the poem in a sentence or two; then analyze how the poet transfers that meaning to you through the use of the following devices.

Speaker   The first-person *I* in a poem is not necessarily the poet. It may be a character, or **persona**, that the poet has created to speak the words. In some poems, such as Earle Birney's "Moon Down Elphinstone," there may be more than one speaker. Although there are times when the poet may be the speaker, you often need to distinguish between the two when writing about poetry.

Diction   The term **diction** means "choice of words," and the words in poetry convey meanings beyond the obvious denotative ones. (See **14a**.) As you read, check definitions and derivations of key words in your dictionary to find meanings beyond the obvious ones. How do such definitions and derivations reinforce the meaning of the poem? How do the connotations of these words contribute to the poem's meaning?

Imagery   The **imagery** in a poem is a word or phrase describing a sensory experience. Notice the images in the following lines from the poem "Meeting at Night," by Robert Browning, about a lover journeying to meet his sweetheart.

> Then a mile of warm sea-scented beach;
> Three fields to cross till a farm appears;
> A tap at the pane, the quick sharp scratch
> And a blue spurt of a lighted match,
> And a voice less loud, through its joys and fears,
> Than the two hearts beating each to each!

The feeling, the smell, and the sound of the beach; the sounds of the tap at the window, the scratch of a match being lighted, the whispers, and the hearts beating; and the sight of the two lovers in the match light, embracing—all are images conveying the excitement and anticipation of lovers meeting in secret.

Allusion   An **allusion** is a brief, unexplained reference to a work or a person, place, event, or thing (real or imaginary) that serves to convey meaning compactly. In his poem "Terence, This Is Stupid Stuff," A. E. Housman says with tongue in cheek that writing poetry is not half so valuable an activity as dance or drink.

> Oh many a peer of England brews
> Livelier liquor than the Muse,
> And malt does more than Milton can
> To justify God's ways to man.

In this small excerpt, Housman alludes to the poet John Milton and a line from his epic poem *Paradise Lost* in which he recounts the story of Adam and Eve and their expulsion from Eden. In fact, that poem contains the words "justify God's ways to man." The humour lies in Housman's assertion that drinking helps us understand the world better than does the poetry of Milton.

Paradox   A **paradox** is a seemingly contradictory statement that makes sense when thoughtfully considered. In a poem about searching for religious salvation, John Donne writes, "That I may rise and stand, o'erthrow me. . . . " At first glance, the wish to be overthrown seems to contradict the desire to "rise and stand." On reflection, however, the line makes sense: the speaker believes that he will rise spiritually only after he has been overwhelmed by the God he is addressing.

Personification   The attribution to objects, animals, and ideas of characteristics possessed only by humans is called **personification**. In the following lines from "The Persistent Suitor," Dave Margoshes personifies death, portraying it as a persistent suitor.

Three days into the treatment,
the chemical teeth gnawing
their way through her veins,
she passes a bad night,
wrestling with Death, who slips
not *under* her bed as the demons
she feared as a child liked to do
but *into* it, cozying right up
beside her, cuddling, hands all over her
breasts and backside, foul breath
singeing the tender flesh below her
earlobes, hardly a gentleman,
she thinks . . .

Simile A **simile** is a comparison using *like* or *as* to link dissimilar things. (See **14a(5)**.)

You fit into me
like a hook into an eye

a fish hook
an open eye

In these lines (from "You Fit into Me"), Margaret Atwood uses sewing and fishing items to describe a disturbing personal relationship.

Metaphor **Metaphor** identifies one thing with another without using *like* or *as*. It is one of the figures of speech most frequently used by poets. (See **14a(5)**.) In the following example, from "Walking Our Boundaries," Audre Lorde uses a metaphor to describe how it feels to wait for a lover's touch.

my shoulders are
dead leaves
waiting to be burned to life.

Overstatement Also called **hyperbole**, **overstatement** is a deliberate exaggeration used for ironic or humorous effect. In "To His Coy Mistress" by Andrew Marvell, the speaker describes how much time he would invest in courting the woman he admires if life were not so short.

> An hundred years should go to praise
> Thine eyes, and on thy forehead gaze;
> Two hundred to adore each breast,
> But thirty thousand to the rest.

Understatement Like **overstatement**, **understatement** is used for ironic or humorous effect. In this case, however, a serious matter is treated as if it were a small concern. Writing in "Musée des Beaux Arts" about indifference to human suffering, W. H. Auden describes a painting in which a boy with wings is falling from the sky.

> In Breughel's *Icarus,* for instance: how everything turns away
> Quite leisurely from the disaster; the ploughman may
> Have heard the splash, the forsaken cry,
> But for him it was not an important failure; the sun shone
> As it had to on the white legs disappearing into the green
> Water; and the expensive delicate ship that must have seen
> Something amazing, a boy falling out of the sky,
> Had somewhere to get to and sailed calmly on.

Sound Sound is an important element of poetry. **Alliteration** is the repetition of initial consonants, **assonance** is the repetition of vowel sounds in a succession of words, and **rhyme** is the repetition of similar sounds either at the end of lines (end rhyme) or within a line (internal rhyme). When you encounter such repetitions, examine and analyze their connection to each other and to the meaning of a line or a stanza or a poem. For instance, notice how the repetition of the *f* and *b* sounds in the following lines from Gwendolyn MacEwen's "Poem Improvised around a First Line" sound like small explosions, emphasizing the violence and the wonder of the image she describes. Notice, too, how the repeated *s* sound in the last line imitates the sound of the flames as they come in contact with the water.

> now I long to see you fullblown and black
> over Niagara, your bike burning and in full flame
> and twisting and pivoting over Niagara
> and falling finally into Niagara
> and tourists coming to see your black leather wings
> hiss and swirl in the steaming current—

Rhythm   The regular occurrence of accent or stress that we hear in poetry is known as **rhythm,** and the rhythm is commonly arranged in patterns called **metres.** Such metres depend on the recurrence of stressed and unstressed syllables in units commonly called **feet.** The most common metrical foot in English is the **iambic,** which consists of an unstressed syllable followed by a stressed one (procéed). A second common foot is the **trochaic,** a stressed syllable followed by an unstressed one (fífty). Less common are the three-syllable **anapestic** (overcóme) and the **dactylic** (páragraph). A series of feet make up a line to form a regular rhythm, as exemplified in the following lines from Coleridge's "Frost at Midnight."

> The Frost performs its secret ministry,
> Unhelped by any wind. The owlet's cry
> Came loud—and hark, again! loud as before.

Note the changes in rhythm and their significance—the ways in which rhythm conveys meaning. The second line contains a **pause (caesura)**, which is marked by the end of the sentence and which adds special emphasis to the intrusion of the owlet's cry.

When you study a poem, ask yourself the following questions:

Checklist for Analyzing Poetry
- What words have strong connotations?
- What words have multiple meanings?
- What images convey sensation?
- What figures of speech does the poet use?
- How does the poet use sound, rhythm, and rhyme?
- What does the poem mean?
- How do the various elements of the poem combine to convey meaning?

An essay about poetry need not necessarily explore all of these questions, but considering them helps you understand what the poet has accomplished—important preparation for whatever the focus of your essay will be.

Sample student paper about poetry

The following student essay, which begins on page 664, is about "Remember," a poem by Christina Rossetti. The assignment was as follows:

> Choose one of the poets we have discussed this term; then go to the library and locate at least three articles about this poet. Write an essay of six to eight pages in which you analyze one of this poet's works and determine how your response fits within critical views of the poet's work. Use MLA-style documentation.

Jane Wattam
Professor W. D. Shaw
ENG300Y
8.Oct.2002

Death as Dying in Rossetti's "Remember"

1   Scholars have noted how elegiac symbols
changed during the Victorian period. Typically
this change is attributed to the growing
disillusionment with religion and with the
intense philosophical questioning of this
period. Feminist scholars, such as Melissa
Zeiger, suggest women's use of the elegy has
resulted in a modification of its form (62).
This change has been attributed to the fact
that the elegy has typically been a site for
male bonding; thus, women have had to change
the elegy in order to make a space for their
own suffering. The elegy "Remember" by
Christina Rossetti provides an excellent
example of how the elegiac form has altered
because of distinctly female perspectives.
Examining Rossetti's "Remember" will reveal
how this poet distorts and begins to redefine
the genre, resulting in a uniquely female way
of mourning.

2   In Rossetti's "Remember," the female
speaker addresses her lover. She imagines a
time when she is dead and her lover is left to
live without her. On first reading this elegy,
it appears to be a wonderful lover's lyric.
However, when readers examine it more closely,
it becomes evident that there is a potentially
more ominous aspect to it. The title,
"Remember," is a command to remember the

speaker of the poem, but the remainder of the
poem illustrates the improbability that her
lover will abide by her request. The lines
"When you can no more hold me by the hand, /
Nor I half turn to go yet turning stay"
contribute to the poem's ambiguity because of
the complicated syntax of the phrase "half
turn to go yet turning stay" (1.3-4). The more
conventional way to read this phrase assumes
that the lovers resist parting but cannot bear
to leave each other. However, it is also
possible that the speaker imagines a time when
the lovers argued and the speaker "turn[ed] to
go yet . . . stay[ed]" reluctantly to hear
what her lover had to say in his defence. The
lovers' relationship is perhaps more
tumultuous than the reader first imagined. The
phrase "When you can no more hold me by the
hand" certainly alludes to the speaker's death
but can also suggest that there might be a
time when the lover will not be able to hold
the speaker's hand because of the couple's
dissolution.

There is an indication in this poem that 3
the lover controls the speaker. This is
evident in the line, "You tell me of our
future that you planned" (1.6). It is not a
life that they planned together; it is one the
lover planned for the speaker. Is it possible
that the future the lover plans is not one of
which the speaker dreams?

Rossetti disjoins the lines, "Only 4
remember me; you understand / It will be late
to counsel then or pray," which adds to the

Wattam 3

ambivalence of our reading. The punctuation of the sentence makes it clear that the words "you understand" belong to the phrase "it will be late to counsel then or pray." This results in a line that when read continuously says, "you understand it will be late to counsel then or pray." But if we read the sentence according to the line break the meaning changes. The words "you understand" now belong to the phrase "only remember me." The speaker commands the lover to remember her and only her: "Only remember me; you understand . . ." (1.7). The assertion that she must be the only one remembered questions the speaker's trust in the lover and subsequently the lover's sincerity. Perhaps there are other women in her lover's life.

5   The meaning of the word "remember" alters during the progression of the poem. The commands to remember the speaker in the octave "Remember me when I am gone away / Remember me when no more day to day" gradually devolve by the end of the poem (1.1, 1.5). In the sestet the speaker realizes the futility of commanding her lover to remember her and understands that in all probability she will be forgotten. Her final command is to ask him to "forget and smile" rather than "remember and be sad" (1.13-14). These last lines display her self-sacrifice, for she considers the happiness of her lover to be more important than her own desire to be remembered. However, the very fact that the speaker brings up the possibility that she

might be forgotten suggests uncertainty as to whether or not she will be remembered at all. Indeed, Rossetti's use of the verb "forget" is equivocal. It is a "darkness and a corruption" but it also ensures one will "smile" (1.11, 1.13). Conversely, remembering is attributed to sadness in the last line of the poem (1.14). The speaker inverts our expectations in the sestet: she actively encourages her lover to forget her when she has insisted throughout the poem that he should remember her.

Although Rossetti's use of the sonnet 6 form is conventional, the elegiac theme she employs in this poem is not. She is certainly effective at eliciting sympathy from the reader, but it is not for someone she knows who has died; rather, it is for the poet herself, in anticipation of her own death. Rossetti probes to the very heart of the elegy in "Remember" because she realizes that when we mourn it is both for the one who has died and for our own impending death.

Typically, elegies are cathartic for the 7 reader because they enable us to project our own suffering onto the poem. But by having as its focus the death of the speaker, this poem affects the way we respond to the elegy. This so-called elegy for the self represents a new kind of trope for this genre, one that discards the perfunctory consolation at the end of the poem. By broadening the scope of elegiac conventions, Rossetti creates a space, not only for universal loss, but also for

questioning of our own assumptions regarding
death. If, as Claudia Ottlinger points out,
"death is what man knows least through
experience," then Rossetti, through her
interrogation of it, ensures that it remains
enigmatic (36).

8   In contrast to some of the major elegies
of the nineteenth century (Tennyson's In
Memoriam or Shelley's "Adonais"), the elegies
of Rossetti do not memorialize a particular
individual. They portray death in a different
light, for she is keenly aware of its finality:
for her, death is dying. She challenges us to
confront the void, the nothingness that may
lie waiting at the end of life, and it is this
awareness that makes the sense of loss
associated with death all the more poignant.
Perhaps this perspective, combined with the
changes in the genre, can be viewed as a
uniquely female way of mourning.

Wattam 6

Bibliography

Anderson, Charles, R. Emily Dickinson's
    Poetry: Stairway of Surprise. New York:
    Holt, Rinehart and Winston, 1960.

Armstrong, Isobel. Victorian Poetry: Poetry,
    Poetics and Politics. New York:
    Routledge, 1993.

Cosslett, Tess, ed. Victorian Women Poets. New
    York: Longman, 1996.

Harris, Antony. "Intertextuality: Dante,
    Petrarch and Christina Rossetti."

Victorian Women Poets. Tess Cosslett, ed. New York: Longman, 1996.

Ottlinger, Claudia. The Death-Motif in the Poetry of Emily Dickinson and Christina Rossetti. Frankfurt: Peter Lang, 1995.

Richards, Bernard. English Poetry of the Victorian Period: 1830-1890. New York: Longman, 1988.

Sacks, Peter M. The English Elegy: Studies in the Genre from Spenser to Yeats. Baltimore: Johns Hopkins UP, 1985.

Shaw, W. David. Elegy and Paradox: Testing the Conventions. Baltimore: Johns Hopkins UP, 1994.

Shaw, W. David. Elegy and Silence: The Romantic Legacy. Lethbridge: University of Lethbridge Press, 1992.

Zeiger, Melissa F. Beyond Consolation: Death, Sexuality, and the Changing Shapes of Elegy. New York: Cornell UP, 1997.

Exercise 4

Write a short explication of the following poem. Then locate two different discussions of it in the library or on the World Wide Web. Summarize these discussions and show how they relate to your own interpretation of the poem.

XLIII

How do I love thee? Let me count the ways.
I love thee to the depth and breadth and height
My soul can reach, when feeling out of sight
For the ends of Being and ideal Grace.
I love thee to the level of everyday's
Most quiet need, by sun and candlelight.

I love thee freely, as men strive for Right;
I love thee purely, as they turn from Praise.
I love thee with the passion put to use
In my old griefs, and with my childhood's faith.
I love thee with a love I seemed to lose
With my lost saints,—I love thee with the breath,
Smiles, tears, of all my life!—and, if God choose,
I shall but love thee better after death.

—ELIZABETH BARRETT BROWNING

(5) Use proper form in writing about literature.

Writing about literature follows certain special conventions.

Tense   Use the present tense when discussing literature, since the author is communicating to a present reader at the present time. (See 7c.)

Sherwood Anderson lets the boy speak for himself.

Documentation   When writing about a work from a book used in the course, you usually do not need to give the source and publication information for the book. However, you should indicate if you are using another edition or anthology. One way of doing so is to use the MLA form for works cited, as explained in section 34a, although in this case your bibliography might consist of only a single work. (See the examples on pages 649 and 657.)

An alternative way of providing this information is by acknowledging the first quotation in an explanatory note and then giving all subsequent references to the work in the body of the paper.

¹Tillie Olsen, "I Stand Here Ironing,"
Literature: Reading, Reacting, Writing, ed.

Laurie Kirszner and Stephen Mandell, 3rd ed.
(Fort Worth: Harcourt, 1997) 154. All
subsequent references to this work will be by
page number within the text.

If you use this note form, you may not need a works cited list to repeat the bibliographical information. Check with your instructor about the reference format he or she prefers.

Whichever format you use for providing the publication data for your source, you must indicate specific references whenever you quote a line or passage. References to short stories and novels are by page number; references to poetry are by line number; and references to plays are usually by act, scene, and line number. This information should be placed in the text in parentheses directly after the quotation, and the period or comma should follow the parentheses. (See 20f and 34a.)

Poetry For **poems** and **verse plays**, type quotations of three lines or less within your text and insert a slash (21h) with a space on each side to separate the lines.

> "Does the road wind uphill all the way?" / "Yes, to the very end"—Christina Rossetti opens her poem "Uphill" with this two-line question and answer.

Quotations of more than three lines should be indented 2.5 cm from the left margin, with double-spacing between lines. (See pages 218–19.)

Author references Use the full name in your first reference to the author of a work and only the last name in all subsequent references. Treat male and female authors alike: Davies and Laurence, not Davies and Mrs. Laurence.

35b **Effective business communication is necessary in most professions.**

Effective business communication requires a strong sense of audience (28a), an ability to write clearly and efficiently (chapter 15), and an understanding of business conventions. These conventions are changing as technology redefines the workplace. Thanks to fax machines and e-mail, for example, many business people find themselves writing more than ever. They also have to take responsibility for their own writing. Although there are still some executives who dictate a letter for someone else to edit and type, many more business people are expected to write for themselves. The computers on their desks provide instant access to a wide range of written communication.

 (1) Use e-mail effectively in the workplace.

When first introduced, e-mail was perceived as a vehicle for fast communication that did not need to be as carefully written as a memo or a letter, and it is still perceived that way in academic and research environments where the use of the powerful but user-unfriendly UNIX and VAX systems can make editing difficult. The speed with which you can send an e-mail message continues to be one of its advantages, but businesses now generally use sophisticated messaging programs such as *Outlook* or *Eudora* that make correcting typographical errors in messages easier and, therefore, as important as it would be in any business communication.

E-mail is, however, a less formal medium than the traditional business letter or memo, so you will need to balance its implicit informality with a businesslike attention to detail. Since most businesses are hierarchical, the tone

(29a) of your e-mail should be suited to your own place in this hierarchy and the recipient's, that is, neither coldly formal nor overly familiar. Furthermore, in business, e-mail tends to be used for brief comments or requests and for social occasions (such as announcing a retirement party), whereas longer documents such as responses to reorganization plans and employee evaluations are generally still handled by letter or memo.

Be aware, also, that e-mail is not really private. Not only may your recipient keep your message in a file, print it out, or forward it to someone else, but it may remain on the company's main computer. Most businesses operate e-mail on their own networks, so the system administrator also has access to what you have written. Under these circumstances, you could be embarrassed or lose influence within your organization if your communication is poorly written. Present yourself well by reviewing every message to eliminate errors and inappropriate remarks.

Take care to spell your recipient's name correctly at the *To:* prompt, and be sure to enter an accurate and descriptive subject line. Busy people use the subject line to identify messages they need to respond to immediately, those they can safely postpone for a few hours, and those they can postpone indefinitely. Furthermore, many people find unnecessary e-mail inefficient and time-wasting. Send copies to anyone who is mentioned in your message or who has some other legitimate reason for being included, but do not send out copies of your messages indiscriminately. (See also **26c.**)

Checklist for Business E-mail
- Is my tone appropriate for my audience and occasion? Have I refrained from using sarcasm or irony? If I have used humour, can I be sure that it will be understood?

continued

continued from previous page

- Do I sound like the kind of person I want or need to be while at work? Am I signalling that I am competent and resourceful, helpful and accommodating?
- Is my content clear, concise, focussed, and accurate? Have I made any statements or errors that would embarrass me if copies of this message were distributed elsewhere?
- Does my subject line describe the content of my message?
- If I need a response, have I established the kind of response I need and when I need it?
- Have I sent copies to everyone who should receive one? To anyone who need not?
- Am I respecting the privacy of others or am I forwarding a personal message without permission?
- Have I respected copyright law by crediting any quotations, references, and sources?

(2) Write effective memos.

Like e-mail, memos are used to communicate a variety of information within an organization. Although e-mail is ideal for sending brief announcements and requests for information, many business writers prefer the more formal memo when communicating detailed information such as policy directives, activity reports, and monthly action reports. While the length of the memo varies according to its purpose, the basic format is relatively standardized. A memo begins with essentially the same information provided by the message header of an e-mail. The person or persons to whom the memo is addressed appear in the first line, the person who wrote it in the second, the date in the third, and the subject in the fourth.

If the memo is long, it sometimes begins with a statement of purpose and then gives a summary of the discussion. This summary helps a manager or executive decide which memos to read carefully and which to skim. The discussion is the main part of the memo and may benefit from the use of headings to highlight key parts. If appropriate, the memo closes with recommendations for action to be taken. You should clearly state in this part of the memo who is to do what and when. In the following example, excerpted from a longer memo, you can see how the writer opens with a statement of purpose.

An example of memo format

To: Regional Sales Managers
From: Alicia Carroll, National Sales Director
Date: January 26, 2003
Re: Performance review

Now that we have final sales figures for 2002, it is clear that sales are growing in the West, but declining in central Canada and the East. These results can be traced to numerous factors and should not be seen as a reflection of individual performance. Each of you will soon receive a confidential evaluation of your work. The purpose of this memo is to share information and to outline goals for the coming year.

(3) Write effective business letters.

Standard business stationery is $8\frac{1}{2} \times 11$ inches (21.6 cm $\times$ 27.9 cm) for paper and 4×10 inches (10.2 cm $\times$ 25.5 cm) for envelopes. In the workplace, you usually use company letterhead that can be fed right into the office printer. If you are writing a business letter from home and do not have letterhead, use only one side of white, unlined paper. On occasion, a business writer may handwrite a short note—either to provide a quick cover letter for forwarded material or to signal a personal relationship. In most cases, however, business letters should be word processed or typed.

Check to see if your company or organization has a policy about letter format. Most companies use a block format for regular correspondence (see page 678), though an indented format is sometimes used for personal business correspondence such as thank-you notes, congratulations, and the like.

A business letter has six parts: (a) heading; (b) inside address; (c) salutation; (d) body; (e) closing, which consists of the complimentary close and signature; and (f) added notations.

The **heading** gives the writer's full address and the date. Depending on your format, place the date flush left, flush right, or centred just below the letterhead. On plain stationery, place the date below your address. Arrange the letter so that it will be attractively centred on the page—flush with the left-hand margin, as in the letter on page 678. Notice that the heading has no ending punctuation.

The **inside address**, placed two to six lines below the heading, gives the name and full address of the recipient. Use the postal abbreviation for the province name. (For a list of these, see 25b.)

Place the **salutation** (or greeting) flush with the left margin, two spaces below the inside address, and follow it with a colon. When you know the surname of the addressee, use it in the salutation unless you are writing to someone who prefers to be addressed by first name. When writing to a woman, use Ms. unless this person has expressed a preference for Miss or Mrs. or can be addressed by her professional title.

Dear Ms. Samuelson: Dear Dr. Gillespie:

Dear Mayor Goulden: Dear Mr. Bourette:

In letters to organizations or to persons whose name and gender you do not know, current styles recommend omitting the salutation or using the office or company name:

Dear Petro-Canada:

Dear Registrar:

For the appropriate forms of salutations and addresses in letters to government officials, military personnel, and so on, check an etiquette book or the front or back of your dictionary.

In the **body** of the letter, single-space inside paragraphs and double-space between them. If you use a block format, do not indent the first line of each paragraph. If you use an indented format, indent first lines 1.25 cm to 2.5 cm (or 5 to 10 typewritten spaces).

Follow the principles of good writing. Organize information so the reader can grasp immediately what you want. Be clear and direct; do not use stilted or abbreviated phrasing:

~~The aforementioned letter~~ *Your letter*

Please send this to me ~~ASAP~~. *as soon as possible*

The **closing** is double spaced below the body. If your letter is in block style, type it flush with the left margin; if it is in indented style, align it with the heading. Use one of the complimentary closes common to business letters, such as the following:

Formal	Less Formal
Yours truly,	Sincerely,
Yours sincerely,	Cordially,

Place your full name four lines below the closing and, if you are writing on company or organization business, your title on the next line.

Notations, placed flush with the left margin two lines below your title, indicate any materials you have enclosed with or attached to the letter (*enclosure* or *enc.*, *attachment* or *att.*), who will receive copies of the letter (*cc: AAW, PTN* or *c: AAW, PTN*), and the initials of the sender and the typist (*DM/cll*).

Model business letter (block format)

Takuru, Poltuk, and Smith

---

529 Lake Side Boulevard　**Edmonton, AB T5J 2S1**
Telephone: (780) 863-8916　**Fax: (780) 863-7665**
Internet: mail@wds.com

LETTERHEAD
CONTAINING
RETURN
ADDRESS

January 7, 2003

Dr. Elizabeth Boroughs
Fairchild Clinic
1710 Sheridan Ave.
Leduc, AB T4H 5P3

INSIDE ADDRESS

Dear Dr. Boroughs:　}　**SALUTATION**

I have just given final approval to several organizational changes designed to ensure closer attention to the individual needs of our clients. Everyone here is excited about these changes, and I am writing to advise you of the one that will affect you most directly.

Effective the first of March, our certified public accountants will specialize in the areas in which they have the greatest expertise. Although we have always tried to direct clients to the accountant best suited to their needs, most staff members have had a diverse workload. This diversity worked well when the company was smaller, but it has become problematic during the past few years as we doubled the size of our staff in response to our growing list of clients.

BODY

As you probably know, tax laws have changed considerably in recent years. The new codes are complex, and interpretation continues to evolve. Given the complexity of the codes, the importance of guiding clients through effective tax planning, and the availability of highly trained personnel, accountants in our company will henceforth work within one of three divisions: corporate, small business, and individual.

Richard Henderson, who has prepared your taxes for the past three years, will now be working exclusively with individual clients. I have reviewed your tax records with him, and we agree that Grace Yee, one of our new associates, will give the Fairchild Clinic the best help we can offer. Although she is new to our staff, she comes to us with twelve years of experience working mostly with medical groups.

You can expect to hear separately from both Rick and Grace, but I wanted to let you know myself that Takuru, Poltuk, and Smith remains committed to serving you and your business.

Sincerely,   **Complimentary Close** ⎫

Ted Poltuk   **Signature** ⎬ **CLOSING**

Edward Poltuk   **Typed Name**

President   **Title** ⎭

EP/nfd } **NOTATION**

(4) Write effective application letters.

Writing a letter of application is an essential step in applying for a job. This letter usually accompanies a résumé (35b(5)), and it should do more than simply repeat information that can be found there. Your letter provides you with the chance to sound articulate, interesting, and professional. Make the most of the opportunity.

Address your letter to a specific person. If you are responding to an advertisement that mentions a department without giving a name, call the company and find out who will be doing the screening. A misspelled name creates a bad impression, so make sure you spell that person's name correctly when you write.

In your opening paragraph, you should state the position you are applying for, how you learned about it, and—in a single sentence—why you believe you are qualified to fill it. Devote the paragraphs that follow to describing the experience that qualifies you for the job. If your experience is extensive, you can establish that fact and then focus on how you excelled in one or two specific situations. Mention that you are enclosing a résumé, but do not summarize it. Your goal is to get a busy person to read the résumé. Few people enjoy reading the same information twice.

In addition to stating your qualifications, you might also indicate why you are interested in this particular company. Demonstrating that you already know something about it will help you appear to be a serious candidate. Extensive information on most companies is available directly from them in their annual reports. You can also find information by searching a good newspaper index or the World Wide Web. (See page 512.)

In your closing paragraph, offer additional information and make a specific request. Instead of settling for "I hope to hear from you soon," tell your reader how and where you can be reached and also mention any relevant information about your schedule during the next few weeks. Then try to arrange for an interview. At the very least, indicate that you are available for an interview and would enjoy the opportunity to exchange information. Some writers also indicate that they will telephone on a particular date to see how their application is doing.

Assume that your audience is busy and that there are many applications. These assumptions make it important for you to be concise (chapter 15). A good letter of application should run between one and two pages, depending on your experience. As you revise (29b), delete anything that is nonessential. To keep your letter to a single page, you may need to choose a smaller than usual font before you print it out—but make sure that the text is still easily readable.

Model application letter

431 Felton Ave.
Cambridge, ON N1Y 4C1
April 5, 2002

Mr. Thomas Flanagan
Journey Airlines
2546 Ashton Ave.
Kitchener, ON N2C 9P7

Dear Mr. Flanagan:

I am writing to apply for the position of
Assistant Director of Employee Benefits in the
Human Resources Department of Journey, as
advertised in this morning's <u>Times</u>. My
education and experience are well suited to
this position, and I'd welcome the chance to
be part of a company that has shown so much
growth during a period when other airlines
have been operating at a loss.

As you can see from my résumé, I majored in
Business Administration with an emphasis in
human resources. Whenever possible, I have
found campus activities and jobs that would
give me experience in working with people. As
an assistant in the Admissions Office at
Wilfrid Laurier University, I worked
successfully with students, parents, alumni,
and faculty. The position required both a
knowledge of university regulations and an
understanding of people with different needs.

I also benefited from working as an administrative intern last summer in the personnel division of Premier Bank, a department that handles the benefits for almost three thousand employees. Although banking may seem far removed from the airline industry, I learned procedures for monitoring benefits that are easily transferable. When I was working there, new computers were installed for the division, enabling us to use more powerful and comprehensive programs. Because I have extensive experience with computers, I was able to help other employees make the transition.

I am very much interested in putting my training to use at Journey and hope that we can schedule an interview sometime during the next few weeks. I will be here in Cambridge until May 7, when I leave to spend a week visiting my family in Winnipeg (204-283-1652). If I haven't heard from you by then, I will telephone to see if the position is still available.

Sincerely,

Marcia Baumeister

Marcia Baumeister

enc.

(5) Write effective résumés.

A résumé is a list of a person's qualifications for a job and is enclosed with a letter of application. It is made up of four categories of information:

1. Personal data: name, mailing address, telephone number
2. Educational background
3. Work experience
4. References

Most businesses appreciate résumés that highlight your experience and abilities.

Make your résumé look professional. Like the letter of application, the résumé is a form of persuasion designed to emphasize your qualifications for a job and get you an interview. Since there is usually more than one applicant for every job, your résumé should make the most of your qualifications. If you keep your résumé in a computer file, you can easily tailor it to each job you apply for so you can present your qualifications in the best light. After reading all the letters and résumés received, a potential employer usually decides to interview only the most qualified candidates.

Writing a résumé requires the same planning and attention to detail as writing a paper. First, make a list of the jobs you have had, the activities and clubs you have been part of, and the offices you have held. Amplify these items by adding dates, job titles and responsibilities, and a brief statement about what you learned from each of them. Delete any items that seem too weak or tangential to be persuasive.

Résumés can be organized in a number of ways. One is to list experience and activities in reverse chronological order, so that your most recent experience comes first. This is a good plan if you have a steady job history, without gaps that are hard to explain, and if your most recent experience is worth emphasizing. If older experience is more directly relevant to the job for which you are applying, you can emphasize it by giving your work history chronologically. An alternative way to organize a résumé is to list experience in terms of job skills rather than jobs held. This plan is especially useful when your work history is modest but you know you have the skills for the job in question.

However you choose to organize your résumé, remember that presentation is important (chapter 26). Your résumé is, in effect, going to someone's office for a kind of job interview, so make sure it is well dressed for the occasion. Use good-quality paper (preferably white or off-white) and a laser printer. Use boldface to mark divisions and experiment with different fonts. Although the design of your document should look professional, resist the impulse to create fancy letterhead or other design features that can make the overall effect too busy to be effective. When in doubt, choose simplicity. For sample résumés, see pages 687–89.

Checklist for Résumé Writing
- Make sure to include your name, address, and telephone number; unless relevant to the job, leave out personal data such as age and marital status.
- Identify your career objective simply, without elaborating on future goals. Reserve a detailed discussion of your plans until asked about them during an interview (and even then make sure they enhance your appeal as a candidate). Your interest should be to match your qualifications to the employer's needs.
- Mention your degree and pertinent areas of special training.

continued

continued from previous page

- Even if an advertisement asks you to state a salary requirement, any mention of salary should usually be deferred until the interview.
- Whenever possible, make the relationship between jobs you have had and the job you are seeking clear.
- To show that you are an efficient, well-organized, thoughtful person, use a clean, clear format and make sure the résumé is neat, orderly, and correct.

For further information on application letters, résumés, and interviews, you may find it helpful to consult one of the following books or a book published by your university or college career centre.

Arco and Ray Potter. *Resumes That Get Jobs*. 10th ed. New York: Arco, 2002.

Besson, Taunee. *Resumes*. 3rd ed. New York: Wiley, 1999.

Bolles, Richard N. *What Color Is Your Parachute? A Practical Manual for Job-Hunters and Career-Changers*. Berkeley: Ten Speed, annual.

Bolles, Richard N. *Job-Hunting on the Internet*. 3rd ed. Berkeley: Ten Speed, 2001.

Easto, Larry, and Reg Pirie. *From Learning to Earning: A Student's Guide to Landing the Right Job*. Toronto: Doubleday, 1996.

Eyler, David R. *Job Interviews That Mean Business*. 3rd ed. New York: Random, 1999.

Ferris, Donna MacDougall. *The Practical Job-Search Guide*. Berkeley: Ten Speed, 1996.

Petras, Kathryn, and Ross Petras. *The Only Job Hunting Guide You'll Ever Need*. Rev. ed. New York: Simon, 1995.

Schaffer, Karen. *Hire Power: The Ultimate Job Guide for Young Canadians*. Toronto: Prentice Hall, 1997.

Chronological résumé

Marcia Baumeister
431 Felton Ave.
Cambridge, ON N1Y 4C1
(519) 228-1927

Career Objective: A management position specializing in the administration of employee benefits.

Work Experience:

Intern, Premier Bank, June–August 2002.
Provided information to new employees, helped the personnel department get online with new information technology, and entered data for changes in medical benefits.

Student Assistant, Admissions Office, Wilfrid Laurier University, January 2000–May 2002.
Responded to queries from parents and prospective students, conducted campus tours, planned orientation meetings, and wrote reports on recruitment efforts.

Tutor, University Writing Centre, September 1999–May 2002.
Tutored students in business writing for six hours a week and worked as needed with other clients. Provided computer assistance, including ways to access information on the World Wide Web.

Education:

Wilfrid Laurier University, B.A. with honours, 2002.
Majored in Business Administration with an emphasis in
human resources. Minors in Economics and
Communications. Recipient of the 2002 Martin Award
for university service.

Active in Management Club, Yearbook, Business
Society

References available on request.

Emphatic résumé

MARCIA BAUMEISTER
431 Felton Ave.
Cambridge, ON N1Y 4C1
(519) 228-1927

CAREER OBJECTIVE
A management position specializing in the
administration of employee benefits

MANAGEMENT SKILLS
Familiarity with all contemporary models of effective
management; good writing and communication skills;
experience with planning and evaluating meetings;
experience with programming and tracking information
electronically; ability to teach computer skills.

PERSONNEL EXPERIENCE
Assisted in the transfer of data on medical benefits for
approximately three thousand employees at Premier

Bank in Cambridge; provided benefit information to employees; worked with students, parents, and faculty at Wilfrid Laurier University as an information specialist with an emphasis on student benefits.

ADDITIONAL EXPERIENCE

Tutored students in writing, helped edit the yearbook, gave campus tours, and served as a liaison between the Business Society and the university.

EDUCATION

Wilfrid Laurier University, B.A. with honours, 2002. Majored in Business Administration with an emphasis in human resources. Minors in Economics and Communication. Recipient of the 2002 Martin Award for university service.

EXTRACURRICULAR

Active in Management Club, Yearbook, Business Society

References available on request.

Exercise 5

Choose one of the following:

1. Write a letter to a former teacher to express appreciation for recommending you for a summer job.
2. In a letter, call the attention of your representative in city government to repairs needed on neighbourhood streets.
3. Write a letter to an automobile company complaining about the performance of a car it manufactured.
4. Write a memo to the members of an organization you belong to recommending a change in procedures.
5. Prepare a résumé, and then write a letter of application for a position you are qualified to fill.

Glossary of Usage

The following short glossary covers the most common usage problems. It also distinguishes between written and spoken English and formal and informal styles. An expression that may be acceptable in spoken English or in a letter to a friend is labelled **informal** and is usually not acceptable in academic or business writing. The following are labels used in this glossary.

Formal	Words or phrases listed in dictionaries without special usage labels; appropriate in college and university writing.
Informal	Words or phrases that dictionaries label *informal, slang,* or *colloquial;* although often acceptable in spoken language, not generally appropriate in college and university writing.
Unacceptable	Words or phrases labelled in dictionaries as *archaic, illiterate, non-standard, obsolete, substandard;* generally not accepted in formal or informal writing.

You may also wish to consult **22b** for a list of words that sound alike but have different meanings.

a, an   Use *a* before the sound of a consonant: **a** yard, **a** U-turn, **a** one-term government. Use *an* before a vowel sound: **an** empty can, **an** M.D., **an** axe, **an** X-ray.

accept, except   *Accept* means "to receive"; *except* means "to exclude": I **accept** your apology. All **except** Joe will go.

accidently   A misspelling of *accidentally.*

adapt, adopt   *Adapt* means "to change for a purpose"; *adopt* means "to take possession": You must **adapt** to extreme cold. The company will **adopt** a new policy.

adverse, averse *Adverse* means "antagonistic" or "unfavourable"; *averse* means "opposed to": We would have gone had it not been for **adverse** weather conditions. After seeing the weather report, I was **averse** to going on the trip.

advice, advise *Advice* is a noun, and *advise* is a verb: I accept your **advice**. Please **advise** me of the situation.

affect, effect The verb *affect* means "to influence" or "to touch the emotions." The noun *effect* means "result of an action or antecedent": Smoking **affects** the heart. His tears **affected** her deeply. Drugs have side **effects**. The **effect** on sales was good. When used as a verb, *effect* means "to produce an effect": The medicine **effected** a complete cure.

aggravate Widely used for *annoy* or *irritate*. Many writers, however, restrict the meaning of *aggravate* to "intensify, make worse": Noises **aggravate** a headache.

ain't Unacceptable in writing unless used in dialogue or for humorous effect.

allusion, illusion An *allusion* is a casual or indirect reference. An *illusion* is a false idea or an unreal image: The **allusion** was to Shakespeare. His idea of university is an **illusion**.

alot A misspelling of the overused and non-specific phrase *a lot*.

already, all ready *Already* means "before or by the time specified." *All ready* means "completely prepared."

alright Not yet a generally accepted spelling of *all right*, although it is becoming more common in journalistic and business writing.

altogether, all together *Altogether* means "wholly, thoroughly." *All together* means "in a group": That book is **altogether** too difficult, unless the class reads it **all together**.

a.m., p.m. (OR A.M., P.M.) Use only with figures: The show will begin at 7:00 **p.m.** OR at seven in the evening [NOT at seven in the *p.m.*]

among, between Prepositions with plural objects (including collective nouns). As a rule, use *among* with objects denoting three or more (a group), and use *between* with those denoting only two (or twos): danced **among** the flowers, whispering **among** themselves; reading **between** the lines, just **between** you and me.

amount of, number of Use *amount of* with a singular non-count noun: The **amount of** rain varies. Use *number of* with a plural count noun: The **number of** errors was excessive. See **number** and **1c(2)**.

and etc. *Etc.* is an abbreviation of the Latin *et* ("and") *cetera* ("other things"). Omit the redundant *and*. See also **etc.**

another, other *Another* is followed by a singular noun: **another** book. *Other* has no plural and is followed by a plural noun: **other** books.

ante, anti *Ante* is a prefix meaning "before," "in front of": **anteroom.** *Anti* is a prefix meaning "opposed to," "hostile": **antiwar.**

anxious Not to be used as a synonym for "eager."

anyone, any one; everyone, every one Distinguish between each one-word and two-word compound. *Anyone* means "any person at all"; *any one* refers to one of a group. Similarly, *everyone* means "all," and *every one* refers to each one in a group.

Was **anyone** hurt?   Was **any one** of you hurt?

Everyone should attend.   **Every one** of them should attend.

anyways, anywheres Unacceptable for *anyway, anywhere*.

apt, liable, likely *Apt* is generally accepted and now used interchangeably with *liable* and *likely* before an infinitive. *Liable* is generally limited to situations that have an undesirable outcome: He is not **likely** to get sick. He is **liable** to get sick. (See **liable, likely.**)

as 1. As a conjunction, use *as* to express sameness of degree, quantity, or manner: Do **as** I do. As a preposition, use *as* to express equivalence: I think of Tom **as** my brother [Tom = brother]. Use *like* to express similarity: Tom is **like** a brother.

2. Use *if, that,* or *whether* instead of *as* after such verbs as *feel, know, say,* or *see:* I do not know **whether** [NOT as] my adviser is right.

3. In subordinate clauses, use *because* to introduce a causal relationship or *while* to introduce a time relationship: **Because** [NOT as] it was raining, we watched TV. **While** [NOT as] it was raining, we watched TV.

assure, ensure, insure   *Assure* means "to state with confidence." *Ensure* and *insure* are sometimes used interchangeably to mean "make certain." *Insure* has the further meaning of "to protect against loss": Marlon **assured** me that he would vote for me. I **ensured** (or **insured**) that Vincent had his tickets before I left home. Min **insured** her car against theft.

as to   Imprecise; use the clearer *about:* He wasn't certain **about** [NOT as to] the time.

awful   Unacceptable for the often overused adverb *awfully:* She is **awfully** [NOT awful] intelligent.

awhile, a while   *Awhile,* an adverb, is not used as the object of a preposition: We rested **awhile.** [COMPARE We rested for **a while.**]

bad   Unacceptable as an adverb: Bill danced **badly** [NOT bad]. Acceptable as a subject complement after sense verbs such as *feel, look, smell.* See **4b.**

because   Unacceptable in the expression *is because,* since the *to be* form signifies equality between the subject and what follows. See **8e(1).**

being as, being that   Wordy and imprecise; use *since, because.*

beside, besides   Always a preposition, *beside* usually means "next to," sometimes "apart from": The chair was **beside** the table. As a preposition, *besides* means "in addition to" or "other than": She has many books **besides** those on the table. As an adverb, *besides* means "also" or "moreover": The library has a fine collection of books; **besides,** it has a number of valuable manuscripts.

better   Unacceptable for *had better:* We **had better** [NOT better] run the spell check. See **had better.**

between   See **among, between.**

biannual, biennial   *Biannual* means twice in one year, while *biennial* means every two years.

bring, take Both words describe the same action but from different standpoints. Someone *brings* something *to* the speaker's location, while someone else *takes* something *away* from the speaker's location: **Bring** your book when you come here. I **take** my notes home with my book.

busted Unacceptable as the past tense of *burst*.

but what, but that Informal after expressions of doubt such as "no doubt" or "did not know." Use *that:* I do not doubt **that** [NOT but what] they are correct.

can, may *Can* refers to ability and *may* refers to permission: I **can** [am able to] drive over 100 kilometres per hour, but I **may** not [am not permitted to] exceed the speed limit. Contemporary usage allows *can* and *may* denoting possibility or permission to be used interchangeably.

can't hardly, can't scarcely Unacceptable for *can hardly, can scarcely.*

capital, capitol A *capital* is a governing city; it also means "funds." As a modifier, *capital* means "chicf" or "principal." A *capitol* is an American statehouse; the *Capitol* is the U.S. congressional building in Washington, D.C.

censor, censure *Censor* (verb) means "to remove or suppress because of moral or otherwise objectionable ideas"; a *censor* (noun) is a person who suppresses those ideas. *Censure* (verb) means "to blame or criticize"; a *censure* (noun) is an expression of disapproval or blame.

centre around Informal for *to be focussed on* or for *to centre on.*

chairman, chairperson, chair *Chairman* is misused as a generic term. *Chairperson* or *chair* is generally preferred as the generic term.

cite, site, sight *Cite* means "to mention." *Site* is a locale. *Sight* is a view or the ability to see: Be sure to **cite** your sources in your paper. The prime minister visited the disaster **site**. What a tragic **sight**!

compare to, compare with *Compare to* means "regard as similar" and *compare with* means "examine to discover similarities or differences": The instructor **compared** the diagram **to** [NOT with] the finished product. The student **compared** the first draft **with** [NOT to] the second.

complement, compliment   *Complement* means "to complete" or "to supply needs." *Compliment* means "to express praise." *Complimentary* means "given free," as in "**complimentary** tickets": Their personalities **complement** each other. Betsy **complimented** Piotr on his performance.

continual, continuous   *Continual* means recurring at regular intervals: He coughed **continually.** *Continuous* means recurring without interruption: He talked **continuously.**

different than, different from   Both are widely used, although *different from* is generally preferred in formal writing.

disinterested, uninterested   *Disinterested* means "impartial" or "lacking prejudice": a **disinterested** referee. *Uninterested* means "indifferent, lacking interest."

don't   Not used in formal English for "doesn't": My father **doesn't** [NOT don't] dance.

drug   Unacceptable as the past tense of *dragged*.

due to   Usually avoided in formal writing when used as a preposition in place of *because* or *on account of:* **Because of** [NOT due to] holiday traffic, we arrived an hour late.

effect   See **affect, effect.**

e.g.   Abbreviation from Latin *exempli gratia* meaning "for example." Replace with the English equivalent *for example* or *for instance.* Do not confuse with **i.e.**

elicit, illicit   *Elicit* means "to draw forth." *Illicit* means "unlawful": It is **illicit** to **elicit** public funds for your private use.

emigrate from, immigrate to   The prefix *e-* (a variant of *ex-*) means "out of." To *emigrate* is to go out of one's own country to settle in another. The prefix *im-* (a variant of *in-*) means *"into."* To *immigrate* is to come into a different country to settle. The corresponding adjective or noun forms are *emigrant* and *immigrant:* The Katbas **emigrated from** Romania to Italy and then **immigrated to** Manitoba. (COMPARE **export, import.**)

eminent, imminent *Eminent* means "distinguished"; *imminent* means "about to happen": Linda Hughes is an **eminent** scholar. The storm is **imminent**.

ensure See **assure, ensure, insure.**

enthused Informal usage, not accepted in formal writing. Use *enthusiastic.*

especially, specially *Especially* means "outstandingly"; *specially* means "for a particular purpose, specifically": This is an **especially** nice party. I bought this tape **specially** for the occasion.

-ess A female suffix now considered sexist, therefore unacceptable. Use *poet, author, actor,* and *waiter* or *server* instead of *poetess, authoress, actress,* and *waitress.*

etc. From the Latin *et cetera* meaning "and other things." In formal writing substitute *and so on* or *and so forth.* Since *etc.* means "and other things," *and etc.* is redundant.

everyone, every one See **anyone, any one.**

except See **accept, except.**

explicit, implicit *Explicit* means "expressed directly or precisely." *Implicit* means "implied or expressed indirectly": The instructions were **explicit.** There was an **implicit** suggestion in her lecture.

farther, further Generally, *farther* refers to geographic distance: six kilometres **farther.** *Further* is used as a synonym for *additional* in more abstract references: **further** delay, **further** proof.

fewer, less *Fewer* refers to people or objects that can be counted; *less* refers to amounts that can be observed or to abstract nouns: **fewer** pencils, **less** milk, **less** support.

figure Informal for *believe, think, conclude,* or *predict,* all of which are more precise.

folks Informal for *parents.*

former, latter *Former* refers to the first of two; *latter* to the second of two. If three or more items are mentioned, use *first* and *last:* Sean and Ian are both British; the **former** is from Northern Ireland, and the **latter** is from Scotland.

genus Singular form for *genera*. Takes a singular verb: The genus **is** . . .

go, goes Inappropriate in written language for *say, says:* I **say** [NOT go], "Hello there!" Then he **says** [NOT goes], "Glad to see you!"

good, well *Good* is an adjective frequently misused as an adverb; *well* is an adverb: He dances **well** [NOT good]. He had a **good** time. *Well* in the sense of "in good health" may be used as a subject complement interchangeably with *good* in such expressions as "Amir doesn't feel **well** (or **good**)."

great Overworked for more precise words such as *skilful, good, clever, enthusiastic,* or *very well.*

had better (meaning *ought to*) Do not omit the verb *had:* We **had better** go home.

had ought (meaning *ought to*) Omit the verb *had:* We **ought to** go home.

half a, a half, a half a Use *half of a, half a,* or *a half.*

hanged, hung *Hanged* refers specifically to "put to death by hanging": She was **hanged** at dawn. *Hung* is the usual past participle: He had **hung** the picture.

he Used inappropriately as a generic term that possibly could refer to a woman. See **13c(2)**.

heighth Unacceptable for *height.*

hisself Use *himself.*

hopefully Means "with hope." Used inappropriately for *I hope* or *it is hoped.*

i.e. Abbreviation for the Latin *id est,* meaning "that is." Use *that is* instead. Do not confuse *i.e.* with **e.g.**

if, whether Use *if* to mean *in the event that; whether* suggests alternatives. I can't go **if** you drive; **whether** I go depends on who is driving.

illusion See **allusion, illusion.**

imminent See **eminent, imminent.**

implicit See **explicit, implicit.**

imply, infer   *Imply* means "suggest without actually stating," and *infer* means "draw a conclusion based on evidence": He **implied** that he was angry, but I **inferred** that he was satisfied.

incidently   A misspelling of *incidentally.*

ingenious, ingenuous   *Ingenious* means "creative or shrewd." *Ingenuous* means "innocent or unworldly": Terry's **ingenious** plan worked without complication. The criminal's **ingenuous** smile was misleading.

in regards to   Unacceptable for *in regard to.*

irregardless   Use *regardless.*

its, it's   *Its* is a possessive pronoun, as in "The dog buried **its** bone." *It's* is a contraction of *it is,* as in "**It's** a beautiful day."

kind, sort   Used interchangeably. Singular forms are modified by *this* or *that,* plural forms by *these* or *those:* **This kind** (**sort**) of argument is unacceptable. **These kinds** (**sorts**) of arguments are unacceptable.

kind of a, sort of a   Use *kind of* and *sort of:* This **kind of** [NOT kind of a] book . . .

lay, lie   Use *lay (laid, laying)* in the sense of "put" or "place." Use *lie (lay, lain, lying)* in the sense of "rest" or "recline." *Lay* takes an object (to **lay** something), while *lie* does not. See also **13c(3).**

Lay   He had **lain** [NOT laid] down to take a nap.
       The woman was **lying** [NOT laying] on the bed.

Lie   He had **laid** [NOT lain] the book on the table.
       The man was **laying** [NOT lying] the carpet.

learn   Not used in formal English for *teach, instruct, inform:* He **taught** me [NOT learned me] bowling.

leave   Unacceptable for *let* in the sense of allowing: **Let** [NOT leave] him have the hammer.

less   See **fewer, less.**

liable, likely   *Liable* usually means "exposed" or "responsible" in an undesirable sense. *Likely* means "probably," "destined," or "susceptible": If you wreck the car, you are **liable** for damages. With her brains, she is **likely** to succeed.

like   Although widely used as a conjunction in spoken English, *as, as if,* and *as though* are preferred for written English.

lose, loose   *Lose* is a verb: did **lose**, will **lose**. *Loose* is chiefly an adjective: a **loose** belt.

lots   Informal for *many, much.*

mankind   Considered offensive because it excludes women. Use *humanity, human race.*

many, much   *Many,* used with plural nouns, refers to numbers: **many** stores, too **many** cats; *much,* used with singular nouns, refers to amount: **much** courage.

may be, maybe   *May be* is a verb phrase; *maybe* is an adverb: The rumour **may be** true. **Maybe** the rumour is true.

may, can   See **can, may.**

media, medium   *Media* is plural; *medium* is singular.

moral, morale   *Moral* (an adjective) refers to correct conduct or ethical character: a **moral** decision. *Moral* (as a noun) refers to the lesson of a story: the **moral** of the story. *Morale* (a noun) refers to a mood or spirit: **Morale** was high.

most   Use *almost* in expressions such as "almost everyone," "almost all." Use *most* only as a superlative: **most** writers.

much   See **many, much.**

myself   Use only when preceded by an antecedent in the same sentence: Chin and **I** [NOT myself] went swimming. BUT I made **myself** go swimming.

nauseous, nauseated   Frequently confused. *Nauseous* means "producing nausea"; *nauseated* means "enduring nausea": I felt **nauseated** when I smelled the **nauseous** spoiled meat.

nowhere near   Informal. Use *not nearly:* I had **not nearly** [NOT nowhere near] enough money.

nowheres   Unacceptable for *nowhere.*

number   As subjects, *a number* is generally plural and *the number* is singular. Make sure that the verb agrees with the subject: **A number** of possibilities **are** open. **The number** of possibilities **is** limited. See also **amount of, number of.**

of Often mistaken for the sound of the unstressed *have:* "They must **have** [OR would **have**, could **have**, might **have**, ought to **have**, may **have**—NOT must of] gone home.

off of Use *off* in phrases such as "walked **off** [NOT off of] the field."

OK, O.K., okay Informal usage. All three are acceptable spellings. It is often better to replace *OK* with a more specific word.

on account of Use the less wordy *because:* I went home **because** [NOT on account of] I was tired.

ought See **had ought.**

plus Acceptable as a preposition. Weak when used instead of the co-ordinating conjunction *and.* I telephoned and [NOT plus] I sent flowers.

p.m. See **a.m., p.m.**

precede, proceed To *precede* is to "go ahead of"; to *proceed* is to "go forward": His song will **precede** the fight scene. He will **proceed** with the song.

principal, principle The adjective or noun *principal* means "chief" or "chief official." The noun may also mean "capital." The noun *principle* means "fundamental truth": The **principal** factor in the salary decision was his belief in the **principle** of sexual equality.

raise, rise *Raise (raised, raising)* means "to lift or cause to move upward, to bring up or increase." *Rise (rose, risen, rising)* means "to get up, to move or extend upward, ascend." *Raise* (a transitive verb) takes an object; *rise* (an intransitive verb) does not: Retailers **raised** prices. Retail prices **rose** sharply. See 13c(3).

rarely ever Use either *rarely* alone or *hardly ever:* He **rarely** (or **hardly ever**) [NOT rarely ever] goes to the library.

real, really Use *real* as an adjective, *really* as an adverb. *Real* is often misused in the following expression where it is an adverb modifying the adjective *beautiful:* It is a **really** [NOT real] beautiful day.

reason why Redundant. Use *reason:* The **reason** I went home was that I was ill.

regard, regarding, regards   Use *in regard to, with regard to,* or *regarding.*

sensuous, sensual   *Sensuous* refers to gratification of the senses in response to art, music, nature, and so on; *sensual* refers to gratification of the physical senses.

shall, will   *Shall* is now used mainly with the first person, for polite questions.

sit, set   Use *sit* in the sense of "be seated" and *set* in the sense of "to place something": Jonathon **sat** under the tree. Maria **set** the cookies on the table. See **13c(3)**.

so   Overused as an intensifier; use a more precise modifier: She was **intensely** [NOT so] focussed.

some   Informal and vague when used as a substitute for such words as *remarkable, memorable:* She was a **remarkable** [NOT some] athlete.

someone, some one   Distinguish between each one-word and two-word compound. See **anyone, any one; everyone, every one.**

sometime, sometimes, some time   *Sometime* is an adverb meaning "at an unspecified time"; *sometimes* is an adverb meaning "at times"; *some time* is an adjective-noun pair meaning "a span of time": Let's go to the movie **sometime. Sometimes** we go to the movies. They agreed to allow **some time** to pass before going to the movies together again.

somewheres   Unacceptable for *somewhere.*

sort, sort of   See **kind, sort** and **kind of a, sort of a.**

specially   See **especially, specially.**

stationary, stationery   *Stationary* means "in a fixed position"; *stationery* means "writing paper and envelopes."

sure   Informal when used as an adverb, as in "I **sure** like your new hat." Use *certainly* or *undoubtedly.*

take   See **bring, take.**

thataway, thisaway   Unacceptable for *that way* and *this way.*

that, which   Use *that* with a restrictive clause: The cup **that** is on the table is full (distinguishes a specific cup that is full). Use *which* with a nonrestrictive clause: The cup, **which** is on the table, is full. ("which is on the table" gives nonessential information). Read the two example sentences aloud to notice the different intonation patterns. Some writers, however, prefer to use *which* for restrictive clauses if it does not cause confusion. See 17d.

their, there, they're, there're *Their* is the possessive form of *they; there* is ordinarily an adverb or an expletive; *they're* is a contraction of *they are; there're* is a contraction of *there are:* **There** is no explanation for **their** behaviour. **They're** making trouble **there** on the ball field. **There're** no tickets left.

theirself, theirselves Use *themselves.*

them Unacceptable when used as an adjective: **those** apples OR **these** apples [NOT them apples].

then Sometimes incorrectly used for *than.* Unlike *then, than* does not relate to time. He's better than [NOT then] he knows.

this here, that there, these here, them there Redundant; use *this, that, these, those.*

thusly Use *thus.*

to, too Distinguish the preposition *to* from the adverb *too:* When the weather is **too** hot to play ball, they go **to** the movies.

toward, towards Both acceptable. *Toward* is preferred in North American usage.

try and Informal for *try to:* I will **try to** [NOT try and] see him today.

type See **kind.**

unique Because it means "one of a kind," it is illogical to use *unique* with a comparative, as in *very unique.* Do not confuse with *unusual.*

utilize Often pretentious; *use* is preferred.

wait on Unacceptable as a substitute for *wait for.*

ways Unacceptable for *way* when referring to distance: It's a long **way** [NOT ways] from home.

where   Informal as a substitute for *that:* I saw on TV **that** [NOT where] she had been elected.

where . . . at, where . . . to   Omit the superfluous *at, to:* **Where** is the library [OMIT at]? **Where** are you moving [OMIT to]?

which   When referring to persons, use *who* or *that*. See **that, which.**

who's, whose   *Who's* is the contraction of *who is:* **Who's** going to the movie? *Whose* indicates possession: **Whose** book is this?

with regards to   See **regard, regarding, regards.**

your, you're   *Your* is the possessive of *you:* in **your** house. *You're* is a contraction of *you are:* **You're** gaining strength. See also **its, it's.**

Glossary of Terms

This glossary presents brief explanations of frequently used terms. Consult the index for references to further discussion of most of the terms and for a number of terms not listed.

absolute phrase   A grammatically unconnected part of a sentence—generally a noun or pronoun followed by a participle (and sometimes modifiers): We will have a cookout, **weather permitting** [noun + present participle]; **The national anthem sung for the last time,** the old stadium was closed [noun + past participle with modifier]. Some absolute phrases have the meaning (but not the structure) of an adverb clause. See **1d(3), 9a,** and **12b(4).** See also **phrase** and **sentence modifier.**

abstract   A summary of the main points of a piece of writing, usually placed at the very beginning of the work.

abstract noun   A noun that expresses qualities, concepts, and emotions that cannot be perceived through the senses: truth, justice, fear, future. See **14a(4).**

accusative case   See **case.**

acronym   A word formed by combining the initial letters of a series of words: laser—light amplification by stimulated emission of radiation.

active voice   The form of a transitive verb indicating that its subject performs the action the verb denotes: Emily *sliced* the ham. See **7** and **11d(1).** See also **passive voice, verb,** and **voice.**

adjective   The part of speech modifying a noun or a pronoun. *Limiting adjectives* restrict the meaning of the words they modify: *that* pie, *its* leaves. *Descriptive adjectives* name a quality of a noun, including degrees of comparison: *red* shirt, *bigger* planes. *Proper adjectives* are derived from proper nouns: *Spanish* rice. See **23a.** Two or more adjectives separated by a comma, instead of by co-ordinating conjunctions, are referred to as *co-ordinate* *adjectives:* A *brisk, cold* walk. See **17c(2)**. *Interrogative adjectives* are used to ask questions: *Whose* book is it? See also **degree** and **predicate adjective**.

adjective clause A subordinate clause used as an adjective: people *who bite their fingernails.* An adjective clause may be restrictive. See **1e(2)**, **17d(1)**, and **5a**. See also **clause**.

adjective phrase A phrase used as an adjective: The woman *carrying the large notebook* is my sister. See **1d(3)**. See also **phrase**.

adverb The part of speech modifying a verb, an adjective, or another adverb: *rapidly* approached, *too* bitter, *very graciously* accepted. An adverb may also modify a verbal, a phrase or clause, or the rest of the sentence: *Usually,* an artist does her best work when she is focussing *entirely* on the task at hand.

adverb clause A subordinate clause used as an adverb. An adverb clause may indicate time, place, cause, condition, concession, comparison, purpose, or result: *Although he is usually quiet* [concession], everyone listens to him *when he speaks* [time], *because he makes good suggestions* [cause]. See **1e(2)**, **17b(1)**, and **12b(1)**. See also **clause** and **conditional clause**.

adverbial conjunction See **conjunctive adverb**.

adverb phrase A phrase used as an adverb. An adverb phrase may indicate time, place, cause, condition, concession, comparison, purpose, or result. See **1d(3)** and **9a(2)**. See also **adverb clause**.

agreement The correspondence in number and person of a subject and verb (*the dog barks, dogs bark*) or in number and gender of a pronoun and its antecedent (the *team* boarded *its* bus, the *members* carrying *their* bags). See **6a** and **7a**.

allusion A brief, unexplained reference to a work or to a person, place, event, or thing that the writer expects the reader to be familiar with. See also **35a(4)**.

ambiguity The capability of being understood in two or more different ways: "Reading alone comforts me" could mean "*Reading by myself* comforts me" or "*Only reading* comforts me."

analogy A rhetorical device using the features of something familiar (and often concrete) to explain something unfamiliar (and often abstract), or similarities between things that are not usually associated.

analysis A separation of a whole into its constituent parts.

analytical reading A reader's active engagement by the writer's ideas and how the ideas are expressed; paying attention to content and form.

antecedent A word or group of words that a pronoun refers to. The antecedent may follow (but usually precedes) the pronoun: *Pets* can be polite or rude, like *their* trainers. See **6b**.

antonym A word that means the opposite of another: *follow* is the antonym for *lead*.

APA American Psychological Association. See **34d–e**.

appeal The means of persuasion in argumentative writing; relies on reason, authority, and/or emotion.

appositive A noun or noun phrase placed next to or very near another noun or noun phrase to identify, explain, or supplement its meaning. Appositives may be restrictive. See **17d(2)**, **9a(3)**, **12b(4)**, and **12c(3)**.

appropriate Writing suitable for the audience, purpose, and occasion.

argument A kind of writing that uses various rhetorical strategies and appeals to convince the reader of the truth or falsity of a given proposition or thesis. See **appeal** and **thesis**.

article *The, a,* or *an* used as adjectives before nouns: *the* cups, *a* cup, *an* extra cup. *The* is a definite article. *A* (used before consonant sounds) and *an* (used before vowel sounds) are indefinite articles. See **16a**.

audience The person or persons for whom the writing is intended. See **28a**. A specific audience has considerable knowledge of the subject. A non-specialized audience does not have expertise on the subject but is willing to read about it.

auxiliary A form of *be, have,* or *will* that combines with a verb to indicate voice, tense, or mood: *was* going, *had* gone, *will* go.

Modals such as *will, would,* and *may* are also considered auxiliaries. See **7** and **16b**.

balanced sentence   A sentence with grammatically equal structures. See **11g**.

bibliography   A list of books, articles, essays, or other material, usually on a particular subject.

binary   See **file**.

Boolean operator(s)   Words used to broaden or narrow computer database searches. These include *or, and, not,* and *near.* See page 507.

brainstorming   A method of generating ideas about a subject; involves listing ideas as they occur in a session of intensive thinking about the subject. See **28c**.

browser   Software that finds and displays web pages. Most browsers can display images as well as text.

cardinal number   See **number**.

case   The form or position of a noun or pronoun that shows its use or relationship to other words in a sentence. The three cases in English are the *subjective* (or nominative), which is usually the subject of a finite verb; the *possessive* (or genitive), which indicates ownership; and the *objective* (or accusative), which functions as the object of a verb or preposition. See **6** and **19a**.

cause and effect   A rhetorical strategy by which a writer seeks to explain why something happened or what the results of a particular event or condition were or will be. See **27d(4)**.

CD-ROM   Acronym for Compact Disk—Read Only Memory. CD-ROMs store large amounts of information—as much as 300 000 pages.

chronological order   The arrangement of events in a time sequence (usually the order in which they occurred).

citation   Notation (usually parenthetical) in a paper that refers to a source. See **34a(1)** and **34d(1)**.

claim   A conclusion that a writer expects readers to accept. Should be supported by accurate and representative source material. See chapter **31**.

classification and division A rhetorical strategy in which a writer sorts elements into categories (*classification*) or breaks a topic down into its constituent parts to show how they are related (*division*). See 27d(6).

clause A sequence of related words within a sentence. A clause has both a subject and a predicate and functions either as an independent unit (*independent clause*) or as a dependent unit (*subordinate clause*, used as an adverb, an adjective, or a noun). See 1e and 9. See also **sentence.**

I saw the moon. It was glowing brightly [sentences].

I saw the moon, for **it was glowing brightly** [independent clauses connected by a co-ordinating conjunction].

I saw the moon, **which was glowing brightly** [adjective clause].

I saw the moon **because it was glowing brightly** [adverb clause].

I saw **that the moon was glowing brightly** [noun clause— direct object].

cliché An expression that may once have been fresh and effective but that has become trite and worn out with overuse. See 14c.

coherence The principle that all the parts of a piece of writing should stick together, one sentence leading to the next, each idea evolving from the previous one. See 5 and 27b.

collaborative writing A method of writing involving a cooperative effort between two or more persons.

collective noun A noun singular in form that denotes a group: *flock, jury, band, public, committee.* See 7a(8).

colloquialism A word or phrase characteristic of informal speech. "He's *grumpy*" is a colloquial expression describing an irritable person. See chapter 13.

comma splice, comma fault A punctuation error in which two independent clauses are joined by a comma with no co-ordinating conjunction. See chapter 3.

Comma Splice Patricia went to the game, her brother stayed home.

Revised   Patricia went to the game, and her brother stayed home.

common gender   A term applied to words that can refer to either sex (*parent, instructor, salesperson, people, anyone*). See **13c(2)**.

common noun   A noun referring to any or all members of a class or group (*woman, city, apple, holiday*) rather than to a specific member (*Emily Stowe, Kamloops, Winesap, New Year's Day*). See **noun**.

comparative degree.   See **degree**.

comparison and contrast   A rhetorical strategy in which the writer examines similarities and/or differences between two ideas or objects. See **27d(5)**.

complement   A word or words used to complete the sense of a verb. Although the term may refer to a direct or indirect object, it usually refers to a subject complement, an object complement, or the complement of a verb like *be*. See **1b**.

complete predicate   A simple predicate (a verb or verb phrase) with any objects, complements, or modifiers: We *ate the fresh homemade pie before the salad*. See **predicate**.

complete subject   A simple subject (a noun or noun clause) with any modifiers: *Everyone at the picnic* liked the pie. See **1b**. See also **subject**.

complex sentence   A sentence containing one independent clause and at least one subordinate clause: *My neighbour noticed a stranger* [independent clause] *who looked suspicious* [subordinate clause]. See **1f**, **9**, and **12c(1)**. See also **clause**.

compound-complex sentence   A sentence containing at least two main clauses and one or more subordinate clauses: *When the lights went out* [subordinate clause], *there was no flashlight at hand* [independent clause] *so we sat outside and gazed at the stars* [independent clause]. See **1f**. See also **clause**.

compound predicate   Two or more predicates having the same subject: Agnes Macphail *became the first female elected to Parliament* and *later founded the Elizabeth Fry Society*. See **2a** and **12c(2)**. See also **predicate**.

compound sentence A sentence containing at least two independent clauses and no subordinate clause: *The water supply was dwindling* [independent clause], so *rationing became mandatory* [independent clause]. See 1f, 17a, and 18a. See also **clause.**

compound subject Two or more subjects of the same verb: *Women, men,* and *children* call the crisis centre.

concession Agreeing with a point made by your opponent in response to your own argument. Doing so increases a writer's credibility, making the opposition more likely to agree with his or her argument.

conclusion A sentence, paragraph, or group of paragraphs that brings a piece of writing to a satisfying close, usually by summarizing, restating, evaluating, asking a question, or encouraging the reader to continue thinking about the topic. See 28f(2).

concrete, concrete noun Concrete nouns refer to things that can be experienced through the senses: *cologne, sunset, onions, thorns.* Concrete nouns make writing clear, vivid, and lively. COMPARE abstract noun. See **noun.**

conditional clause An adverb clause (beginning with such conjunctions as *if, unless, whether, provided*) expressing a real, imagined, or non-factual condition: *If she does a good job,* I will pay her. See 7d. See also **clause.**

conjugation A set or table of the inflected forms of a verb that indicates tense, person, number, voice, and mood. See chapter 7.

conjunction A part of speech (such as *and* or *although*) used to connect words, phrases, clauses, or sentences. *Co-ordinating conjunctions (and, but, or, nor, for, so, yet)* connect and relate words and word groups of equal grammatical rank: Colour-blind people can usually see blue, *but* they may confuse red with green *or* with yellow. See 1c(7) and 10. See also **correlatives.**

Subordinating conjunctions (such as *although, if, when*—see list on page 25) mark a dependent clause and connect it with a main clause: When Frank sulks, he acts *as if* he were deaf. See chapter 9.

conjunctive adverb A word (*however, therefore, nevertheless*) that serves not only as an adverb but also as a connective. See 3b, 18a, and 27b(3).

connective A word or phrase that links and relates words, phrases, clauses, or sentences (*and, although, otherwise, finally, on the contrary, which, not only . . . but also*). Conjunctions, conjunctive adverbs, transitional expressions, relative pronouns, and correlatives function as connectives. See **27b(3)**.

connotation The suggested or implied meaning of a word through the associations it evokes in the reader's mind. See **14a(3)**. See also **denotation**.

consonant A class of speech sounds represented in English by any letter other than *a, e, i, o,* or *u*.

context The surrounding information that helps give a particular word, sentence, or paragraph its meaning: *cabinet* means "a group of leaders" in a political context and "a place for storage" in a building context. Context also refers to circumstances surrounding the composition of a piece of writing—the occasion, the purpose, the audience, and what the writer and reader already understand about the topic. See **28a**.

contraction Condensing two words into one by adding an apostrophe to replace the omitted letter or letters: *aren't, don't.* Contractions are used primarily in spoken or informal written language.

contrast See **comparison and contrast**.

controlling idea The central idea of a paragraph or essay, often expressed in the paragraph's **topic sentence** or the essay's **thesis** statement. See **27a** and **28d**.

conventional Language that complies with the accepted rules of formal written English, generally termed *correct*.

co-ordinate adjective See **adjective**.

co-ordinating conjunction One of seven connectives: *and, but, for, or, nor, so, yet.* See **1c(7)**, **17a**, **9**, and **10**. See also **conjunction**.

co-ordination The use of grammatically equivalent constructions to link ideas, usually (but not always) those of equal weight. See **17c(2)**, **9b**, and **10**.

correlatives One of five pairs of linked connectives: *both . . . and; either . . . or; neither . . . nor; not only . . . but also;*

whether . . . or. Correlatives link equivalent constructions: *both* Jane *and* Fred; *not only* in Peru *but also* in Mexico. See **10c.**

count, non-count nouns Count nouns are individual, countable entities and cannot be viewed as a mass (*word, finger, remark*). Non-count nouns are a mass or a continuum (*humour*). See chapter **1.**

credibility The reliability of a person or evidence. See **31d.**

critical thinking/reading/writing The ability to analyze and synthesize ideas: to distinguish between fact and opinion, to recognize the importance of evidence and logic, to evaluate for credibility, and to avoid common fallacies. See chapter **31.**

cumulative sentence A sentence in which the subject and predicate come first, followed by modifiers. (Also called a loose sentence.) See **11b.**

dangling modifier A word or phrase that does not clearly refer to another word or word group in the sentence. See **5b.**

data Accepted fact or evidence. In computer language, information stored in computer-readable form.

database A kind of electronic filing system. Computer databases are usually organized hierarchically so that computers can find information more quickly. An *electronic database system* is a group of databases such as Dialog or ingenta. Most such systems are *retrieval* databases—users can get information from them but cannot add to them.

declension A set or table of inflected forms of nouns or pronouns. See the examples on page 60.

deduction A form of logical reasoning that begins with a generalization (*premise*), relates a specific fact to that generalization, and forms a *conclusion* that fits both. See **31f.** COMPARE **induction.**

definition A brief explanation of the meaning of a word, as in a dictionary. Also, an extended piece of writing, employing a variety of rhetorical strategies, to explain what something is or means. See **27d(7).**

degree The form of an adverb or adjective that indicates relative quality, quantity, or manner. The three degrees are as follows: *positive,* a quality of a single element; *comparative,* between two elements; and *superlative,* among three or more elements. Examples of sets of degree include *good, better, best* and *fast, faster, fastest.* See **4c.**

demonstratives   Four words that point out (*this, that, these, those*): **Those** are as good as **these** [pronouns]. **Those** curtains have never been cleaned [adjective].

denotation   The literal meaning of a word as commonly defined. See **14a(1).** See also **connotation.**

dependent clause   A subordinate clause. See **clause.**

description   A rhetorical strategy using details perceivable by the senses to portray a scene, object, performance, and so on. See **27d(2).**

details   Specific information, such as facts, sensory data, or examples, that clarifies and explains.

determiner   A word (such as *a, an, the, my, their*) that signals the approach of a noun: *the* newly mown *hay.*

development   The elaboration of an idea through organized discussion filled with examples, details, and other information. See **27c.**

dialect   A variety of language characteristic of a region or culture. Dialects are distinguished by vocabulary, pronunciation, and/or syntax: British English, Low German, and Cantonese. See chapter **13.**

dialogue   A reproduction in writing of conversation by two or more people, real or fictional. See **23e, 20a,** and **13b.**

dial-up access   Refers to using a modem and a telephone line to connect a computer to a network.

diction   The writer's choice of exact, idiomatic, and fresh words, as well as appropriate levels of usage. See chapters **13** and **14.**

direct address   A name or descriptive term (set off by commas) designating the one or ones spoken to: Out here, *Bruce.*

direct object   A noun (or noun clause) naming *whom* or *what* after a transitive active verb: Emily sliced the *ham.* See **1b(2).** See also **object.**

direct quotation A repetition of the exact spoken or written words of others: "Where an opinion is general," writes Jane Austen, "it is usually correct." See 20a and 33g.

discussion list See listserv.

documentation The citing of sources in a researched paper to conform to a given style, such as MLA or APA. See chapter 34.

double negative The non-standard combination of two negatives, which has a negative meaning: We ca*n't* do *nothing* about the weather. See 4e.

draft, drafting A working version of a piece of writing. The process of putting ideas in writing so they can be revised and edited. See 28f–g.

editing Reworking sentences for clarity, sense, and conformity to conventional rules of spelling, punctuation, mechanics, grammar, and sentence structure.

electronic mail See e-mail.

electronic resources Online research tools that enable the computer user to access publicly available information. These may include CD-ROM, databases, and Internet access. See e-mail, database, CD-ROM, and World Wide Web.

electronic sites Publicly available files on a computer that can be accessed through the Internet.

ellipsis Three or four spaced periods that indicate material omitted from a quotation. See 21i.

elliptical construction The omission of words while retaining the meaning: Cats are cleaner than pigs [are].

e-mail Electronic mail, used to transfer messages over a communications network. E-mail may be limited to a single network, but most often refers to messages sent via the Internet.

emoticon A small icon made up of punctuation characters. It shows how a sender wants a message to be interpreted; e.g., a smiling emoticon (for example, :-), often called a smiley) indicates a joke.

emphasis Special weight or importance given to a word, sentence, or paragraph by any of a variety of techniques. It may also mean stress applied to one or more syllables in a word. See chapter **11**.

essay A brief piece of nonfiction writing on a single topic in which a writer typically states the thesis in the introduction, develops several points in support of that thesis, and concludes.

ethos Can be translated as "arguing honourably" and is employed when you tell others the truth and treat them with respect. Many writing theories have suggested that effective arguments use not only ethos, but also **logos** (the logical use of language) and **pathos** (the use of language to stir the feelings of an audience). See page 456.

etymology The origin and historical development of a word, its derivation.

euphemism An indirect or "nice" expression used instead of a more direct one: *Correctional facility* instead of *jail*. See chapter **14**.

evaluation The process of finding and judging useful passages from source material. See **33f**.

evidence Facts, statistics, examples, testimony, sensory details, and so on that support generalizations.

example Any fact, anecdote, reference, or the like used to illustrate an idea. See **27c**.

expletive A signal of a transformation in the structure of a sentence that occurs without changing the meaning. The expletive *there* shifts the order of subject and verb in a sentence: *There were over 4000 runners in the marathon.* [COMPARE Over 4000 runners were in the marathon.] The expletive *it* transforms the main clause into a subordinate clause: It is apparent that the plane is late. [COMPARE Apparently, the plane is late.] See **7a(5)**.

expository writing See **referential writing**.

expressive writing Writing that emphasizes the writer's own feelings and reactions to a topic. See **28a**.

fact A reliable piece of information that can be verified through independent sources or procedures. A **fact** differs from an **opinion**. See **opinion**.

fallacy   A false argument or incorrect reasoning. See **31h.**

faulty predication   The use of a predicate that does not logically belong with a given subject: One superstition is a black cat. [The verb should be *involves*.]

figurative language   The use of words in an imaginative rather than a literal sense. See **14a(5).**

file   A collection of computer-readable information. *Binary* files contain information readable only by computers unless the file is decoded. People can read *text* files (often called ASCII files) without having to decode them.

finite verb   A verb form that can function as the only verb in the predicate of a sentence: They *ate* a can of pork and beans. Verb forms classified as gerunds, infinitives, or participles cannot do so. See **predicate;** contrast **verbal.**

first person   See **person.**

flaming   Engaging in heated, confrontational exchanges on e-mail.

focus   The narrowing of a subject to a manageable size; also the sharpening of the writer's view of the subject. See **28c** and **28d.**

formal/informal writing style   Considering the rhetorical situation (your audience, purpose, and occasion) to determine whether you need to use a formal or informal style. You should master a formal style for most university, college, and business writing, but you should also master an informal style for writing that highlights personal perspective and voice. See **13** and **28a** and the **Glossary of Usage.**

fragment   A group of words that begins with a capital letter and ends with a period but forms only part of a sentence. See chapter **2.**

freeware   Software available free of charge. Freeware programs are often available for downloading from the Internet; however, the computer user should be aware of the potential transmission of a computer virus. See **virus.**

freewriting   A method of finding a writing topic by composing for a specified length of time without stopping to reflect, re-read, or correct errors.

FTP   Abbreviation for File Transfer Protocol. People use FTP for transferring files on the Internet. See page 512.

function words   Words (such as prepositions, conjunctions, auxiliaries, and articles) that indicate the functions of other words in a sentence and the grammatical relationships between them.

fused sentence   Two or more sentences run together, with no punctuation or conjunctions to separate them. Also called a run-on sentence. Unacceptable in formal writing. See chapter 3.

gender   The grammatical distinction that labels nouns or pronouns as masculine, feminine, or neuter. In English, grammatical gender usually corresponds with natural gender.

general/specific, generalization   *General* words are all-embracing, indefinite, sweeping in scope: *food. Specific* words are precise, explicit, limited in scope: *spaghetti carbonara.* The same is true of *general* and *specific* ideas. A *generalization* is vague and may be untrue.

genitive case   See case.

gerund   A verbal (non-finite verb) that ends in *-ing* and functions as a noun. Gerunds may take objects, complements, or modifiers: *Riding* a bike is good exercise. [The gerund phrase—*riding* and its object, *bike*—serves as the subject of the sentence.] A noun or pronoun serving as the subject of the gerund takes the possessive case: *His* [or *Jim's*] *bicycle riding* is good exercise.

Gopher   A menu-based program for finding files on the Internet. See page 512.

grammar   The system of rules by which words are arranged into the structures meaningful in a language.

graphics   Images or pictures that can be displayed on a computer screen.

hardware   In computer terminology, the tangible components of the computer system such as the keyboard, the monitor, and the components inside the system box.

helping verb   A verb that combines with another verb to indicate voice, tense, or mood. See **auxiliary** and **modal**.

historical present A tense used to describe events in literature or history that are permanently preserved in the present: The tragedy *is* that Iago *deceives* Othello. See 7c and 35a.

homonyms, homophones Words that have the same sound and sometimes the same spelling but differ in meaning (*their, there,* and *they're* or *capital* meaning funds and *capital* meaning government city). See 22b.

hyperbole An intentional overstatement made for rhetorical effect. See 35a(4). COMPARE **understatement.**

idiom A fixed expression (within a language) whose meaning cannot be deduced from its elements: *put up a fight; to mean well.* See 14b.

illustration In writing, the use of specific details to give substance and interest to a subject. See 27c.

imperative mood See **mood.**

indefinites The article *a* or *an* (*a* banana, *an* insect), as well as pronouns (*anyone, everybody*) and adjectives (*any* car, *few* problems, *several* questions) that do not specify distinct limits.

independent clause See **clause.**

indicative mood See **mood.**

indirect object A word (or words) naming the one (or ones) indirectly affected by the action of the verb: Emily sliced *me* some ham. See **object.**

indirect question A question phrased as a statement, usually a subordinate clause: We can ask *whether Milton's blindness was the result of glaucoma,* but we cannot be sure. See 8e.

indirect quotation A report of the written or spoken words of another without using the exact words of the speaker or writer: The registrar said *that the bank returned my tuition cheque.* COMPARE **direct quotation.**

induction A form of logical reasoning that begins with evidence and interprets it to form a conclusion. See 31e. COMPARE **deduction.**

infinitive A verbal (non-finite verb) used chiefly as a noun, less frequently as an adjective or adverb. The infinitive is usually made up of the word *to* plus the present form of a verb (called the *stem* of the infinitive). Infinitives may have subjects, objects, complements, or modifiers: Kristine wanted *to continue* the debate. [*Debate* is the object of the infinitive *to continue; to continue the debate* is the object of the verb *wanted*.]

infinitive phrase   A phrase that employs the infinitive form of the verb: *to go to the store, to run the race.* See **phrase.**

inflection   A change in the form of a word to show a specific meaning or grammatical function:

Verb	*talk, talks, talked*
Nòun	*dog, dogs, dog's, dogs'*
Pronoun	*he, him, his; they, them, their, theirs*
Adjective	*thin, thinner, thinnest*
Adverb	*rapidly, more rapidly, most rapidly*

informal   Although often acceptable in spoken language, words or phrases that dictionaries label **informal**, colloquial (see **colloquialism**), or **slang** are not generally appropriate in university or college writing. See chapter 13 and **formal/informal writing style.**

informative writing   See **referential writing.**

intensifier   A modifier used for emphasis: *very* excited, *certainly* pleased. See **qualifier.**

intensive/reflexive pronoun   The -*self* pronouns (such as *myself, himself, themselves*). The *intensive* is used for emphasis: The teenagers *themselves* had the best idea. The *reflexive* is used as an object of a verb, verbal, or preposition: He blames *himself;* she bought a present for *herself.* An intensive or reflexive pronoun always refers to another noun or pronoun in the same sentence that denotes the same individual or individuals.

interjection   A word (one of the eight parts of speech) expressing a simple exclamation: *Hey! Oops!* When used in sentences, mild interjections are set off by commas. See 21c.

Internet   An international network of computers linked through telephone, cable, and fibre-optic lines.

interpretation   Use of inductive reasoning to help understand facts in order to reach probable and believable conclusions and avoid sweeping conclusions that can be easily challenged. See **31e**.

interrogative   A word like *which, whose,* or *why* used to ask a question: *Which* is the more expensive? [pronoun] *Whose* lights are on? [adjective] *Why* are treasury bills a good investment? [adverb]

interrogative adjective   See **adjective.**

intransitive verb   A verb (such as *appear* or *belong*) that does not take an object. See chapter **7**. See also **verb** and **transitive verb.**

introduction   The beginning of an essay, often a single paragraph, that engages the reader's interest and indicates, usually by stating the thesis, what the essay is about. See **28f(1)**.

invention   The process of using strategies to generate ideas for writing. See **27d** and **28b–c.**

inversion   A change in the usual word order of a sentence: "Into the valley of Death/Rode the six hundred." —TENNYSON. See **11f.**

irony   A deliberate inconsistency between what is stated and what is meant. Irony may be verbal or situational. See **14a(5)**.

irregular verb   A verb that is not inflected in the usual way— that is, by the addition of -*d* or -*ed* to the present form to form the past tense and past participle. Examples include *begin, began, begun* and *lend, lent, lent.*

jargon   Technical slang, appropriate as a shortcut to communication when the audience is knowledgeable about the topic and the terms; it should be avoided, curtailed, or accompanied by brief explanations in writing intended for a non-specialized audience. See **13c(1)**.

journal   A special-interest periodical (*Arctic, Canadian Journal of History*). Also a notebook in which a writer records personal thoughts and experiences.

journalling   Keeping a **journal.**

justification   Inserts spaces between words so that every line is the same length and makes the right or left margin, or both margins, straight.

linking verb   A verb that relates the subject complement to the subject. Words commonly used as linking verbs are *become, seen, appear, feel, look, taste, smell, sound,* and forms of the verb *be:* She *is* a writer. The bread *looks* burned. See **1a**, **4b**, and **6g**.

listing   An informal way of gathering ideas about a writing topic in which a writer lists any ideas that he or she has about the subject. See page 348.

listserv   A list of e-mail addresses to which messages can be automatically broadcast as if they were sent to a single user: a *discussion list* or a *mailing list.*

logic   The presentation of ideas that shows a clear, predictable, and structured relationship among those ideas. See chapters **8** and **31**.

logical operator(s)   See **Boolean operator(s)**.

log on   The process by which a user provides a username and a password in order to be recognized by a computer system and allowed to use its programs.

logos   See **ethos**.

loose sentence   See **cumulative sentence**.

main clause   See **clause**.

main idea   The part of the paragraph or paper to which all the other ideas relate. See **topic sentence** and **thesis**.

mechanics   The form of words and letters, such as capitals, italics, abbreviations, acronyms, and numbers.

memory   The way a computer stores information. Simply put, the main memory of the computer resides on chips and refers to the amount of information the computer can process at one time. Computers also store information by writing it to a storage device such as a fixed hard disk or a removable floppy disk. *RAM,* an acronym for Random Access Memory, is used to mean the main memory of a computer. *ROM,* for Read Only Memory, generally refers to the basic memory the computer needs to use its operating system.

metaphor   An imaginative comparison between dissimilar things without using *like* or *as.* See **14a(5)** and **35a(4)**.

misplaced modifier A modifier placed in an awkward position, usually far away from what it modifies: I read that there was a big fire *in yesterday's newspaper.* I read in yesterday's newspaper that there was a big fire. [Place the modifier after the verb *read.*] Sometimes a misplaced modifier confuses the reader because it could qualify either of two words: To do one's best *sometimes* is not enough. *Sometimes* to do one's best is not enough. To do one's best is *sometimes* not enough. [Place the adverb closer to the verb.] See **5a.**

mixed construction A garbled sentence that is the result of an unintentional shift from one grammatical pattern to another. See **8c(2).**

mixed metaphor A metaphor that confuses two or more metaphors: Playing with fire will drown you. See **8c(1).**

MLA Modern Language Association. See **34a–b.**

modal A helping verb (not conjugated) that shows ability (*can, could*); permission or possibility (*may, might*); determination, promise, or intention (*shall, should; will, would*); obligation (*ought*); or necessity (*must*).

modem Acronym for *mo*dulator-*dem*odulator. A modem is a device that allows a computer to transmit data over telephone or cable lines.

modifier A word or word group that describes, limits, or qualifies another: a *true* statement, walked *slowly,* yards *filled with rocks,* the horse *that jumped the fence.* See chapters **4** and **5.**

mood The way a speaker or writer regards an assertion—that is, as a declarative statement or a question (*indicative* mood); as a command or request (*imperative*); or as a supposition, hypothesis, recommendation, or condition contrary to fact (*subjunctive*). Verb forms indicate mood. See **1f** and **7e.**

mouse See **pointing device.**

narration A rhetorical strategy that recounts a sequence of events, usually in chronological order. See **27d(1).**

netiquette Internet etiquette.

network A group of two or more linked computer systems.

nominalization   The practice of using nouns instead of active verbs: She *made a list* of the schedule changes. [COMPARE She *listed* the schedule changes.] Excessive nominalization produces a wordy style.

nominative case   See **case.**

non-finite verb   A verb form (verbal) used as a noun, adjective, or adverb. A non-finite verb cannot stand as the only verb in a sentence. See 1c and 2a. See also **verbal.**

nonrestrictive   Nonessential to the identification of the word or words referred to. Set off by commas. A word or word group is nonrestrictive (parenthetical) when it is not necessary to the meaning of the sentence and can be omitted: My best friend, *Pauline,* understands me. See 17d.

non-standard   Speech forms that are common in informal writing but that should be avoided in formal writing. See chapter 13.

noun   A part of speech that names a person, place, thing, idea, animal, quality, or action: *Marie, Canada, apples, justice, goose, strength, departure.* A noun usually changes form to indicate the plural and the possessive case, as in *man, men; man's, men's.* See 1c(2).

TYPES OF NOUNS

Common	a **woman,** the **street,** some **dogs** [general classes]
Proper	**Ms. Garneau,** in **Ottawa,** the **Peace Tower** [capitalized, specific names—23a]
Collective	a **team,** the **committee,** my **class** [groups]
Concrete	a **truck,** the **cup,** my **foot,** two **fish** [tangibles]
Abstract	**love, justice, fear** [ideas, qualities]
Count	two **cents,** 16 **bytes,** an **assignment,** many **revisions** [singular or plural—often preceded by adjectivals telling how many]
Non-count	much **concern,** more **consideration,** less **revenue** [singular in meaning—often preceded by adjectivals telling how much]

noun clause A subordinate clause used as a noun. See 1e. See also **clause.**

number The inflectional form of a word that identifies it as singular (one) or plural (more than one): *river–rivers, this–those, he sees–they see.* See 7a and 22d(5). *Cardinal numbers* express quantity: *two (2), thirty-five (35). Ordinal numbers* indicate order or rank: *second (2nd), thirty-fifth (35th).*

object A noun or noun substitute governed by a transitive active verb, by a non-finite verb, or by a preposition. See 1b(2–3) and 1c(6).

A *direct object,* or the *object of a finite verb,* is any noun or noun substitute that answers the question *what?* or *whom?* after a transitive active verb. A direct object frequently receives, or is in some way affected by, the action of the verb: Bill hit the *ball. What* did he hit? A direct object may be converted into a subject with a passive verb. See **voice.**

An *object of a non-finite verb* is any noun or its equivalent that follows and completes the meaning of a participle, a gerund, or an infinitive: Building a *house* takes time. She likes to grow *flowers.*

An *indirect object* is any noun or noun substitute that states *to whom* or *for whom* (or *to what* or *for what*) something is done. An indirect object ordinarily precedes a direct object: She gave *him* the keys. I gave the *floor* a good mopping. It is usually possible to substitute a prepositional phrase beginning with *to* or *for* for the indirect object: She gave the keys *to* him.

An object of a preposition is any noun or noun substitute that a preposition relates to another word or word group: They play ball in the *park.* [*Park* is the object of the preposition *in.*]

object complement A word that helps complete the meaning of such verbs as *make, paint, elect, name.* An object complement refers to or modifies the direct object: They painted the cellar door *blue.* See 1b(3) and 4b. See also **complement.**

objective case See **case.**

online server A server available for remote access. A server is a machine that houses software for delivering information on a *network.* See **network.**

opinion   Ideas that may or may not be based on fact. See 31b.

ordinal number   See **number.**

over-generalization   Lacking specificity. See **general/specific, generalization.**

paradox   A seemingly contradictory statement that actually may be true. See 35a(4).

paragraph   Usually a group of related sentences unified by a single idea or purpose but occasionally as brief as a single sentence (or even a single word or phrase). The central, or controlling, idea of a paragraph is often explicitly stated in a **topic sentence.** A paragraph is marked by the indention of its first line or some other defining device.

parallelism   The use of corresponding grammatically equal elements in sentences and paragraphs. It aids the flow of a sentence, making it read smoothly, and also emphasizes the relationship of the ideas in the parallel elements. See chapter 10.

paraphrase   A sentence-by-sentence restatement of the ideas in a passage, using different words. See 33h(4).

parenthetical documentation   See **documentation.**

parenthetical element   A nonessential word, phrase, clause, or sentence (such as an aside or interpolation) usually set off by commas but often by dashes or parentheses to mark pauses and intonation: *In fact,* the class, *a hardworking group of students,* finished the test quickly. See 17d, 21e(2), and 21f.

participle   A verb form that may function as part of a verb phrase (was *thinking,* had *determined*) or as a modifier (a *determined* effort; the couple, *thinking* about their past).

The *present participle* ends in *-ing* (the form also used for verbal nouns: see **gerund**). The past participle of regular verbs ends in *-d* or *-ed;* for past participles of irregular verbs, see 7b. See also **irregular verb.**

Functioning as modifiers in *participial phrases,* participles may take objects, complements, and modifiers: The bellhop *carrying the largest suitcase* fell over the threshold. [The participle *carrying* takes the object *suitcase;* the whole participial phrase modifies *bellhop.*] See 5b(1).

particle A word like *across, away, down, for, in, off, out, up, with* combined with a verb to form idiomatic usages in which the combination has the force of a single-word verb: The authorities refused to *put up* with him.

parts of speech The classes into which words may be grouped according to their form changes and their grammatical relationships. The traditional parts of speech are *verbs, nouns, pronouns, adjectives, adverbs, prepositions, conjunctions,* and *interjections.* Each of these is discussed separately in this glossary. See also **1c.**

passive voice The form of the verb showing that its subject is not the agent performing the action of the verb but rather receives that action: The ham *was sliced* by Emily. See **7** and **11d(1).** See also **active voice.**

pathos See **ethos.**

pentad A method of exploring a subject. The pentad considers the five dramatic aspects: the act, the actor, the scene, the agency, and the purpose.

perfect tenses The tenses formed by the addition of a form of *have* and showing complex time relationships in completing the action of the verb (the present perfect—*have/has eaten;* the past perfect—*had eaten;* and the future perfect—*will/shall have eaten*).

periodic sentence A sentence in which the main idea comes last. See **11b.** COMPARE **cumulative sentence.**

person The form of pronouns and verbs denoting or indicating whether one is speaking (*I am*—first person), is spoken to (*you are*—second person), or is spoken about (*he is*—third person). In the present tense, a verb changes its form to agree grammatically with a third-person singular subject (*I watch, she watches*). See **7a** and **8e.**

personal pronoun Any one of a group of pronouns—*I, you, he, she, it,* and their inflected forms—referring to the one (or ones) speaking, spoken to, or spoken about. See chapter **6.**

personification The attributing of human characteristics to non-human things (animals, objects, ideas): "That night wind

was breathing across me through the spokes of the wheel."
—WALLACE STEGNER. See **35a(4)**.

perspective   A manner of considering a subject. A perspective
can be static, dynamic, or relative. See page 350.

persuasive writing   A form of writing intended chiefly to
change the reader's opinions or attitudes or to arouse the reader
to action. See **28a**.

phrasal verb   A unit consisting of a verb plus one or two unin-
flected words like *after, in, up, off,* or *out* (see **particle**) and having the force of a single-word verb: We *ran out* on them.

phrase   A sequence of grammatically related words without a
subject and/or a predicate. See **1d** and **2a**. See **verbal**.

plagiarism   The use of another writer's words or ideas without
acknowledging the source. Akin to theft, plagiarism has serious
consequences and should always be avoided. See **33g**.

plural   More than one. COMPARE **singular**.

pointing device   A device used to control the cursor (or
pointer) on the display screen. To control the cursor with a
mouse, the user rolls a small box-like device across a hard surface.
The user turns a ball resting in a stationary holder to operate a
trackball and moves a finger across a sensitive pad to use a
touchpad.

point of view   The vantage point from which the subject is
viewed. See **8e(6)**. It also refers to the stance a writer takes—
objective or impartial (third person), directive (second person),
or personal (first person).

positive   See **degree**.

possessive case   See **case**.

predicate   A basic grammatical division of a sentence. A predicate is the part of the sentence comprising what is said about the
subject. The *complete predicate* consists of the main verb and its
auxiliaries (the *simple predicate*) and any complements and modifiers: We *chased the dog all around our grandmother's farm.*
[*Chased* is the simple predicate; *chased* and all the words that
follow make up the complete predicate.]

predicate adjective The adjective used as a subject complement: The bread tastes *sweet*. See 1c(4) and 4b. See also **linking verb.**

predicate noun A noun used as a subject complement: Bromides are *sedatives*. See 1c(2) and 6g. See also **linking verb.**

predication The act of stating or expressing something about the subject. See **faulty predication.**

prefix An added syllable or group of syllables (such as *in-, dis-, un-, pro-*) placed before a word to form a new word: *adequate–inadequate*. A prefix ordinarily changes the meaning.

premise An assumption or a proposition on which an argument or explanation is based. In logic, premises are either major (general) or minor (specific); when combined correctly, they lead to a conclusion. See 31f. See also **syllogism.**

preposition A part of speech that links and relates a noun or noun substitute to another word in the sentence: The dancers leapt *across* the stage. [The preposition *across* connects and relates *stage* (its object) to the verb *leapt*.] See page 17 for a list of phrasal prepositions.

prepositional phrase A preposition with its object and any modifiers: *in the hall, between you and me, for the new van.*

present and past participle See **participle.**

prewriting The initial stage of the writing process, concerned primarily with planning.

primary source In research or bibliographies, the source that provides unedited, first-hand facts.

principal parts The forms of a verb that indicate the various tenses: the present (*give, jump*); the past (*gave, jumped*); and the past participle (*given, jumped*). See 7b.

process, process writing See **writing process.**

process analysis A rhetorical strategy either to instruct the reader how to perform a procedure or to explain how something occurs. See 27d(3).

progressive verb   A verb phrase consisting of a present participle (ending in *-ing*) used with a form of *be* and denoting continuous action: *is attacking, will be eating.*

pronoun   A part of speech that takes the position of nouns and functions as nouns do. See **1c(3), 6, 7a**. See also **noun** and the separate entries for the types of pronouns listed below.

> **Personal Pronoun**   She and I will drive to Carbonear.
>
> **Relative Pronoun**   Jack is a person **who** enjoys life.
>
> **Indefinite Pronoun**   **Each** of us played against **somebody**.
>
> **Intensive Pronoun**   I **myself** am an agronomist.
>
> **Reflexive Pronoun**   Jane enjoyed **herself** at the fair.
>
> **Demonstrative Pronoun**   **This** is closer than **that**.
>
> **Interrogative Pronoun**   **What** is it? **Who** said that?

proofreading   Checking the final draft of a paper to eliminate typographical, spelling, punctuation, and documentation errors. See **26d** and **29d**.

proper adjective   See **adjective**.

proper noun   See **noun**.

purpose   A writer's reason for writing. The purpose for nonfiction writing may be predominantly expressive, persuasive, or expository, though all three aims are likely to be present in some measure. See **28a**. See also **expressive writing, persuasive writing,** and **referential writing**.

qualifier   Any modifier that describes or limits: *Sometimes* movies are *too* gory to watch. Frequently, however, the term refers only to those modifiers that restrict or intensify the meaning of other words. See **intensifier**.

quotation   Repeated or copied words of another, real or fictional. See **20a** and **33g**.

RAM   See **memory**.

reading preview   To scan a piece of writing for the main ideas. Critical readers use this method to scan a reading assignment quickly to determine an assignment's main purpose, thereby allowing them to think about it critically.

reciprocal pronoun   One of two compound pronouns expressing an interchangeable or mutual action or relationship: *each other* or *one another*.

record   A set of related information usable by a computer.

redundant   Needlessly repetitious, unnecessary.

referential writing   Writing whose chief aim is to clarify, explain, or evaluate a subject in order to inform or instruct the reader. Also called expository or informative writing. See 28a.

reflexive pronoun   See **intensive/reflexive pronoun**.

refutation   A writer's introduction of reasons why others may believe differently followed by an explanation showing why these reasons are not convincing. See page 454.

regular verb   A verb that forms its past tense and past participle by adding -*d* or -*ed* to the present form (or the stem of the infinitive): *love, loved; laugh, laughed*. See chapter 7.

relative clause   An adjective clause introduced by a relative pronoun: the programs *that provide services.*

relative pronoun   A noun substitute (*who, whom, whose, that, which, what, whoever, whomever, whichever, whatever*) used to introduce subordinate clauses: He has an aunt **who** *is a principal* [adjective clause introduced by the relative pronoun *who*]. OR **Whoever** *becomes treasurer* must be honest [noun clause introduced by the relative pronoun *whoever*]. See chapter 6.

restrictive   A word, phrase, or clause that limits the word referred to by imposing conditions or by confining the word to a particular group or to a specific item or individual: Every student *who cheats* will be removed from the class. [The restrictive clause *who cheats* imposes conditions on—restricts—the meaning of *every student*. Only those students *who cheat* will be removed.] See 17d. See also **nonrestrictive**.

retrieval database   A database system that allows users to search by keyword, author, or title and that may often provide the full text of a document.

revision   Part of the writing process. Writers revise by rereading and rethinking a piece of writing to see where they need to add, delete, move, replace, re-shape, and even completely recast ideas.

rhetoric   The art of using language effectively. Rhetoric involves the writer's **purpose** (28a), the **audience** (28a), the discovery and exploration of a subject (28b and 28c), its arrangement and organization (28e), the style and tone in which it is expressed (28a), and the form in which it is delivered (26 and 28a).

rhetorical question   A question posed for effect without expectation of a reply: Who can tell what will happen?

rhetorical situation   The relationship between the writer, the audience, and the context that determines the appropriate approach for a particular situation.

run-on sentence   See **fused sentence**.

scroll bar   A bar on the side or bottom of a computer window that allows the user to control what part of the displayed file is visible.

search engine   A program that searches documents for a specific word (keyword) and returns a list of all documents containing that word.

secondary source   A source that analyzes or interprets **primary source** material.

sentence   A grammatically independent unit of expression. A simple sentence contains a subject and a predicate. Sentences are classified according to structure (simple, complex, compound, and compound-complex) and purpose (declaratory, interrogatory, imperative, exclamatory). See chapter 1.

sentence modifier   An adverb or adverb substitute that modifies the rest of the sentence, not a specific word or word group in it: *All things considered,* Yellowknife is a good place to live. OR *Yes,* the plane arrived on time.

server   A computer that manages network resources; for example, a Web server, a network server, or a mail server.

sexist language   Language that arbitrarily excludes one sex or the other or that arbitrarily assigns stereotypical roles to one or the other sex: A secretary should keep *her* desk tidy. [COMPARE Secreta*ries* should keep *their* desks tidy.] See **6b** and **13c(2)**.

simile   The comparison of two dissimilar things using *like* or *as*. See **14a(5)** and **35a(4)**.

simple tenses   The tenses that refer to present, past, and future time.

singular   One. See **number**. COMPARE **plural**.

slang   The casual vocabulary of specific groups or cultures, usually considered inappropriate for formal writing. Occasionally, slang can be effective if the writer carefully considers purpose and audience. See chapter **13**.

software   Computer programs that enable the user to perform specific tasks.

space order   A concept often used to organize descriptive passages. Details are arranged according to how they are encountered as the observer's eye moves vertically, horizontally, from far to near, and so forth. See **27b(2)**.

split infinitive   The often awkward separation of an infinitive by at least one adverb: *to* quietly *go*. See **infinitive**.

squinting modifier   An ambiguous modifier that can refer to either a preceding or a following word: Eating *often* makes her sick. See **5a(4)**.

stipulative definition   A definition that specifies how a certain term will be used within a certain context. See **14a(2)**.

style   An author's choice and arrangement of words, sentence structures, and ideas as well as less definable characteristics such as rhythm and euphony. See **8e(5)**.

subject   A basic grammatical division of a sentence. The subject is a noun or noun substitute about which something is asserted or asked in the predicate. It usually precedes the predicate. (In imperative sentences subjects are implied, not stated.) The *complete subject* consists of the *simple subject* and the words associated with it: *The woman in the grey trench coat* asked for information [simple subject—*woman*; complete subject—*the woman in the grey trench coat*]. COMPARE **predicate**. May also refer to the main idea of a piece of writing.

subject complement   A word or words that complete the meaning of a linking verb and that modify or refer to the subject: The old car looked *shabby* [predicate adjective]. *The old car was an eyesore.* [predicate noun] See **1b**, **4b**, and **6g**. See also **linking verb**.

subjective case   See **case**.

subjunctive mood   See **mood**.

subordinate clause   See **clause**.

subordinating conjunction   See **conjunction**.

subordination   The use of dependent structures (phrases, subordinate clauses) that are lower in grammatical rank than independent ones (simple sentences, main clauses). See chapter **9**.

suffix   An added sound, syllable, or group of syllables placed after a word to form a new word, to change the meaning of a word, or to indicate grammatical function: *light, lighted, lighter, lightest, lightness, lightly.*

summary   A concise restatement briefer than the original. See **33h(5)**.

superlative degree   See **degree**.

syllogism   A three-part form of deductive reasoning. See **31f**.

synonym   A word that has a meaning similar to that of another word.

syntax   Sentence structure; the grammatical arrangement of words, phrases, and clauses.

synthesis   **Inductive reasoning** whereby a writer begins with a number of instances (facts or observations) and uses them to draw a general conclusion. See **31e**.

tag question   A question attached to the end of a related statement set off by a comma: She's coming, *isn't she?* See **3a**.

Telnet   A program that connects a computer to a network server. The user then has access to programs and functions as if he or she were in the same physical location as the server. See page 512.

template   A pattern that serves as a model. Some writers create computer templates (like a fill-in form) if they often use the same standard layout.

tense The form of the verb that denotes time. Inflection of single-word verbs (*pay, paid*) and the use of auxiliaries (*am paid, was paid, will pay*) indicate tense. See chapter 7.

thesis The central point or main idea of an essay. It is one of the main ways an essay is unified (see **unity**). A specific, clearly focussed thesis statement helps the writer make all the other elements of the essay work together to accomplish his or her purpose. See also **28d**.

tone The writer's attitude toward the subject and the audience, usually conveyed through diction and sentence structure. Tone affects the reader's response.

topic The specific, narrowed idea of a paper. See **subject**.

topic sentence A statement of the central thought of a paragraph, which, though often at the beginning, may appear anywhere in it. Some paragraphs may not have a topic sentence, although the main idea is clearly suggested.

touchpad See **pointing device**.

trackball See **pointing device**.

transitions Words, phrases, sentences, or paragraphs that relate ideas and provide coherence by linking sentences, paragraphs, and larger units of writing. Transitions may be expressions (words or phrases such as *moreover, first, nevertheless, for example,* and so on) or structural features a writer uses, such as parallelism or repetition of key words and phrases. When they link larger units of writing, transitions may take the form of sentences or even brief paragraphs. See **27b**.

transitive verb A type of verb that takes an object. Some verbs may be either transitive or intransitive depending on the context: They *danced* [transitive] the polka. They *danced* [intransitive] all night. See **verb** and **intransitive verb.**

truth In deductive reasoning, the veracity of the premises. If the premises are true, the conclusion is true. An argument may be true but invalid if the relation between the premises is invalid. See **31f**. See also **validity**.

unacceptable Words or phrases labelled in dictionaries as *archaic, illiterate,* or *substandard;* generally not accepted in formal or informal writing.

understatement Intentional underemphasis for effect, usually ironic. See 35a(4). See also **hyperbole.**

Uniform Resource Locator See URL.

unity All the elements in an essay contributing to developing a single idea or thesis. A paragraph is unified when each sentence contributes to developing a central thought. See 27a and 28d.

URL Acronym for Uniform Resource Locator, which allows the computer user to locate resources on the Internet. A URL consists of several parts: the protocol to be used (e.g., http://; ftp://; gopher://), the Internet address and domain name, and the path to the file. Here is the URL for the National Library of Canada: <http://www.nlc-bnc.ca/ehome.htm>. In this example, *http://* indicates that the World Wide Web protocol is to be used, *www.nlc-bnc.ca* indicates the domain name for the National Library of Canada, and */ehome.htm* indicates the particular file—the English home page.

Usenet A worldwide bulletin board system that is available on the Internet. It contains over 80 000 *newsgroups* on a wide variety of topics. People interested in a topic can subscribe to a newsgroup, where they can discuss the topic with like-minded people.

validity The structural coherence of a deductive argument. An argument is valid when the premises of a syllogism are correctly related to form a conclusion. Validity does not, however, actually refer to the truthfulness of an argument's premises. See 31f. COMPARE **truth.**

verb A part of speech denoting action, occurrence, or existence (state of being). Inflections indicate tense (and sometimes person and number) and mood of a verb. Verbs may be either transitive or intransitive. See 1a and 7. See also **inflection, mood, voice, transitive verb,** and **intransitive verb.**

verbal A non-finite verb used as a noun, an adjective, or an adverb. Infinitives, participles, and gerunds are verbals. Verbals (like finite verbs) may take objects, complements, modifiers, and sometimes subjects: Sarah went *to see a movie.* [*To see,* an infinitive, functions as an adverb modifying the verb *went.* The object of the infinitive is *movie.*] See **gerund, infinitive, non-finite verb,** and **participle.** See also 1d.

verb phrase See **phrase**. See also **1d**.

virus A tiny, often destructive program that can replicate itself. Usually an executable program, a virus is generally transferred by infected disks, e-mail attachments, and bulletin board files. Some viruses can be transferred across networks.

voice The form of a transitive verb that indicates whether or not the subject performs the action denoted by the verb. A verb with a direct object is in the *active voice*. When the direct object is converted into a subject, the verb is in the *passive voice*. A passive verb is always a verb phrase consisting of a form of the verb *be* (or sometimes *get*) followed by a past participle. See **7** and **11d(1)**.

Active Voice	The batter **hit** the ball. [The subject (*batter*) acts.]
Passive Voice	The ball **was hit** by the batter. [The subject (*ball*) does not act.]

Speakers and writers often omit the *by* phrase after a passive verb, especially when the performer of the action is not known or is not the focus of attention: Those flowers *were picked* yesterday. We just heard that a new secretary *was hired*.

vowel A speech sound represented in written English by *a, e, i, o, u,* and sometimes *y.*

website See **World Wide Web**.

word order The arrangement of words in sentences. Because of lost inflections, modern English depends heavily on word order to convey meaning.

Nancy gave Henry $14 000.	Henry gave Nancy $14 000.
Tony had built a garage.	Tony had a garage built.

word processing An electronic method of producing text. The writer performs a number of computer operations, such as inputting, inserting, deleting, moving, blocking, and so forth, to facilitate writing.

World Wide Web (WWW) A system of Internet servers that store documents formatted in a special computer language (HTML). These documents are called *web pages*, and a location containing several such pages is called a *website*. Web pages can provide links to other sites as well as to graphics, audio, and video files. Users can jump to the linked sites by clicking on designated spots in the document. See page 512.

writing process   The various activities of planning (gathering, shaping, and organizing information), drafting (setting down ideas in sentences and paragraphs to form a composition), revising (rethinking, re-shaping, and reordering ideas), editing (checking for clear, effective, grammatically correct sentences), and proofreading (checking for correct spelling, mechanics, and manuscript form). The writing process sets no particular sequence for these activities but allows writers to return to any activity as necessary.

WWW   See **World Wide Web**.

Credits

Page 107: GUY VANDERHAEGHE. Excerpt from *The Englishman's Boy,* by Guy Vanderhaeghe. Used by permission, McClelland & Stewart Ltd. *The Canadian Publishers.*

Page 125: JOANNE FLEET and DENISE REAUME. Excerpt from *Power over Time: Student Success with Time Management,* by Joanne Fleet and Denise Reaume. © 1994. Reprinted with permission of Nelson, a division of Thomson Learning: www.thomsonrights.com. Fax 800 730-2215.

Page 134: PHILIP MARCHAND. Excerpt from "What I Really Think," *Saturday Night*, October 1997, p. 52. Reprinted by permission of the author.

Page 149: GAGE CANADIAN DICTIONARY. Entry for "admit." © 2003, 2000, 1998, 1997. Reprinted with permission of Gage Learning Corporation.

Page 165: GABRIELLE ROY. Excerpt from "My Manitoba Heritage," from *The Fragile Lights of Earth,* by Gabrielle Roy. McClelland & Stewart *The Canadian Publishers.*

Page 173: M. G. VASSANJI. Excerpt from *The Book of Secrets,* by M. G. Vassanji. Used by permission, McClelland & Stewart Ltd. *The Canadian Publishers.*

Page 197: LEWIS THOMAS. Excerpt from "Notes on Punctuation," copyright © 1979 by Lewis Thomas, from *The Medusa and the Snail,* by Lewis Thomas. Used by permission of Viking Penguin, a division of Penguin Putnam Inc.

Page 205: PICO IYER. Excerpt from "In Praise of the Humble Comma," *Time,* 13 June 1988, p. 80. © Time Inc. Reprinted by permission.

Page 235: ARTHUR J. RAY. Excerpt from *I Have Lived Here since the World Began: An Illustrated History of Canada's Native People* (Toronto: Key Porter, 1996), p. 191.

Copyright © 1996 by Arthur J. Ray. Reprinted with permission.

Page 237: ALDEN NOWLAN. Excerpt from "The Bull Moose," in *An Exchange of Gifts* (Toronto: Irwin, 1985). Reprinted by permission.

Page 295: JOANNE FLEET and DENISE REAUME. From *Power over Time: Student Success with Time Management*, by Joanne Fleet and Denise Reaume. © 1994. Reprinted with permission of Nelson, a division of Thomson Learning: www.thomsonrights.com. Fax 800 730-2215.

Page 295: HENRY MARTEY CODJOE. Excerpt from "Can Blacks Be Racist? Reflections of Being 'Too Black and African,'" from *Talking about Identity: Encounters in Race, Ethnicity and Language* (Toronto: Between the Lines, 2001). Reprinted with permission.

Pages 296–297: MARGARET LAURENCE. From *Heart of a Stranger*, by Margaret Laurence. Used by permission, McClelland & Stewart Ltd. *The Canadian Publishers.*

Page 298: MAKEDA SILVERA. Excerpt from "Her Head a Village," in *Her Head a Village & Other Stories*, by Makeda Silvera (Vancouver: Press Gang Publishers, 1994), p. 11. Copyright © 1994 by Makeda Silvera.

Page 298: BILL RICHARDSON. Excerpt from "Dog-eared Days," *Maclean's*, 23 June 1997, p. 50. Reprinted with permission.

Page 301: DENISE CHONG. Excerpt from *The Concubine's Children: Portrait of a Family Divided*, by Denise Chong. Copyright © Denise Chong, 1994. Reprinted by permission of Penguin Books Canada Limited.

Pages 302–303: GAIL ANDERSON-DARGATZ. Extracted from *The Cure for Death by Lightning*, by Gail Anderson-Dargatz. Copyright © 1996 by Gail Anderson-Dargatz. Reprinted by permission of Alfred A. Knopf Canada, a division of Random House of Canada Limited.

Page 303: DENISE CHONG. From *The Concubine's Children: Portrait of a Family Divided*, by Denise Chong. Copyright ©

University Press, 1969), pp. 103–112. Reprinted with permission.

Page 352: KEM LUTHER. Excerpt from "I Have Seen the Wind," *Saturday Night*, November 1997, pp. 75 and 96. Reprinted with permission of the author.

Page 353: MAUDE BARLOW. Excerpt from "*Maquiladoras* of the North: Free Trade Zones Come to Canada," *Canadian Forum*, October 1997, p. 9. Reprinted with permission of the author.

Page 355: ADRIENNE SHADD. Excerpt from "Institutionalized Racism and Canadian History: Notes of a Black Canadian," in *Seeing Ourselves: Exploring Race, Ethnicity and Culture* (Toronto: Thompson Educational, 1995), p. 129. Reprinted with permission.

Page 357: PETER C. NEWMAN. From *The Canadian Revolution, 1985–1995: From Deference to Defiance,* by Peter C. Newman. Copyright © Peter C. Newman, 1995. Reprinted by permission of Penguin Books Canada Limited.

Page 358: SASENARINE PERSAUD. Excerpt from "When Men Speak That Way," in *The Whistling Thorn: South Asian Canadian Fiction* (Oakville, ON: Mosaic Press, 1994), p. 20. Reprinted with permission.

Pages 358–359: PAT SMART. Excerpt from "The 'Pure Laine' Debate," *Canadian Forum*, November 1997, p. 15. Reprinted with permission.

Page 367: GEORGE ELLIOTT CLARKE. Excerpt from "The Complex Face of Black Canada," *McGill News: Alumni Quarterly*, winter 1997, p. 26. Reprinted with permission.

Pages 367–368: CHARLOTTE GRAY. Excerpt from "Crazy Like a Fox," *Saturday Night*, October 1997, p. 42. Reprinted with permission.

Page 368: JAYSON MYERS. Excerpt from "They're Okay; You're Not," *Canadian Business*, 27 February 1998, p. 27. Reprinted with permission.

Implications for Social Policy," in *Youth in Transition: Perspectives on Research and Policy* (Toronto: Thompson Educational, 1996), p. 63. Reprinted with permission.

Page 660: DAVE MARGOSHES. Excerpt from "The Persistent Suitor," in *Purity of Absence*, Beach Home Publishing, 2001, p. 22. Reprinted with permission.

Page 660: MARGARET ATWOOD. Excerpt from "You Fit into Me," in *Power Politics* (Toronto: House of Anansi, 1971, 1996). Reprinted with permission.

Page 660: AUDRE LORDE. "Walking Our Boundaries," from *The Black Unicorn*, by Audre Lorde. Copyright © 1978 by Audre Lorde. Used by permission of W.W. Norton & Company, Inc.

Page 661: W. H. AUDEN. Excerpt from "Musée des Beaux Arts," in *Collected Shorter Poems 1927–1957* (London: Faber and Faber Ltd., 1966) Reprinted with permission.

Page 662: GWENDOLYN MacEWEN. Excerpt from "Poem Improvised around a First Line," from *Afterworlds*, 1987. Reprinted with permission of the author's family.

Index

Numbers and letters in colour refer to rules; other numbers refer to pages.

ESL Index

Entries in this index identify topics basic to ESL usage. Numbers and letters in colour refer to rules; other numbers refer to pages.

MLA Index

This index refers to items in the parenthetical citations, the words-cited list, and the student papers in chapters 34 and 35. The italics indicate the page on which a given form is illustrated in a paper.

APA Index

This index refers to items in the parenthetical citations, the reference list, and the student paper in chapter 34. The italics indicate the page on which a given form is illustrated in a paper.

continued